THE SACRED BOOKS OF THE EAST

F. MAX MULLER (ED.)

LIST OF THE 50 VOLUMES

1. Upanishads.
2. Sacred Laws of Aryas.
3. Texts of Confucianism.
4. Zend-Avesta.
5. Pahlavi Texts.
6. Qur'an.
7. Institutes of Vishnu.
8. Bhagavadgita, & c.
9. Qur'an.
10. (i) Dhammapada.
10. (ii) Sutta-Nipata.
11. Buddhist Suttas.
12. Satapatha-Brahmana.
13. Vinaya Texts.
14. Sacred Laws of Aryas.
15. Upanishads.
16. Texts of Confucianism.
17. Vinaya Texts.
18. Pahlavi Texts.
19. Fo-sho-hing-tsanking.
20. Vinaya Texts.
21. Saddharma Pundarika.
22. Gaina-Sutras.
23. Zend-Avesta.
24. Pahlavi Texts.
25. Laws of Manu.
26. Satapatha-Brahmana.
27. Texts of Confucianism (Li Ki).
28. Texts of Confucianism (Li Ki).
29. Grihya-Sutras.
30 Grihya-Sutras.
31. Zend-Avesta.
32. Vedic Hymns.
33. Minor Law-Books.
34. Vedanta-Sutras.
35. Milinda.
36. Milinda.
37. Pahlavi Texts.
38. Vedanta-Sutras.
39. Texts of Taoism
40. Texts of Taoism
41. Satapatha-Brahmana
42. Atharva-veda.
43. Satapatha-Brahmana.
44. Satapatha-Brahmana.
45. Gaina-Sutras.
46. Vedic Hymns.
47. Pahlavi Texts.
48. Vedanta-Sutras.
49. (i) Buddhakarita.
49. (ii) Mahayana Texts.
50. A General Index

The Sacred Books of the East, Vol. 31

THE ZEND-AVESTA

PART-III

THE YASNA, VISPARAD, AFRINAGAN, GAHS, AND MISCELLANEOUS FRAGMENTS

Edited by

F. MAX MULLER

Translated by

L. H. MILLS

GYAN

Published by

GYAN

Gyan Publishing House
5, Ansari Road
Daryaganj, New Delhi-110002
Phone: 011-47034999, 9811692060
E-mail: books@gyanbooks.com

Distribution Network
gyanbooks.com
India, USA, Canada, UK, Australia, France

ISBN : 978-81-212-2937-1 (Set)
ISBN : 978-81-212-2816-9 (PB)
First Published, 1887

2nd Impression 2021

Printed at: Gyan Press, Delhi.

The Sacred Books of the East, Vol. 31

The Zend-Avesta, Part-III
Edited by: F. Max Muller, Translated by: L. H. Mills

THE

SACRED BOOKS OF THE EAST

TRANSLATED

BY VARIOUS ORIENTAL SCHOLARS

AND EDITED BY

F. MAX MÜLLER

VOL. XXXI

Oxford

AT THE CLARENDON PRESS

1887

THE ZEND-AVESTA

PART III

THE YASNA, VISPARAD, ÂFRÎNAGÂN, GÂHS, AND MISCELLANEOUS FRAGMENTS

TRANSLATED BY

L. H. MILLS

Oxford

AT THE CLARENDON PRESS

1887

CONTENTS.

TRANSLATIONS.

PREFACE.

It would savour of affectation for me to say very much by way of meeting the necessary disadvantages under which I labour as in any sense a successor of Professor Darmesteter. It is sufficient to state that I believe myself to be fully aware of them, and that I trust that those who study my work will accord me the more sympathy under the circumstances. Professor Darmesteter, having extended his labours in his University, found his entire time so occupied that he was obliged to decline further labour on this Series for the present. My work on the Gâthas had been for some time in his hands[1], and he requested me, as a friend, to write the still needed volume of the translation of the Avesta. Although deeply appreciating the undesirableness of following one whose scholarship is only surpassed by his genius, I found myself unable to refuse.

As to my general treatment, experts will not need to be informed that I have laboured under no common difficulties. On the one hand, it would be extremely imprudent for any scholar not placed arbitrarily beyond the reach of criticism, to venture to produce a translation of the Yasna, Visparad, Âfrînagân, and Gâhs, without defensive notes. The smallest freedom would be hypercriticised by interested parties, and after them condemned by their followers. On the other hand, even with the imperfect commentary which accompanies the Gâthas here, the generous courtesy of the Delegates of the Clarendon Press has been too abundantly drawn upon. One does not expect detailed commentaries in this Series. My efforts have therefore been chiefly confined to forestalling the possible assaults of unfair or forgetful critics, and so to spare myself, in so far as it may be possible, the necessity for painful rejoinder.

[1] See the Revue Critique, Nov. 26, 1883.

To print a commentary on the Yasna, &c., which would be clear to non-specialists, and at the same time interesting, would occupy many times more space than could be here allowed. In treating the Gâthas however, even at the risk of too great extension, I have endeavoured to atone for the necessary obscurity of notes by ample summaries, and a translation supported by paraphrase, as such matter has more prospect of being generally instructive than a commentary which must necessarily have remained obscure. These summaries should also be read with the more indulgence, as they are the first of their kind yet attempted, Haug's having been different in their scope. With regard to all matters of mere form, I expect from all sides a similar concession. It will, I trust, be regarded as a sufficient result if a translation, which has been built up upon the strictest critical principles, can be made at all readable. For while any student may transcribe from the works of others what might be called a translation of the Yasna, to render that part of it, termed the Gâthas, has been declared by a respected authority, 'the severest task in Aryan philology[1].' And certainly, if the extent of preparatory studies alone is to be the gauge, the statement cited would not seem to be an exaggeration. On mathematical estimates the amount of labour which will have to be gone through to become an independent investigator, seems to be much greater than that which presents itself before specialists in more favoured departments. No one should think of writing with originality on the Gâthas, or the rest of the Avesta, who had not long studied the Vedic Sanskrit, and no one should think of pronouncing ultimate opinions on the Gâthas, who has not to a respectable degree mastered the Pahlavi commentaries. But while the Vedic, thanks to the labours of editor and lexicographers, has long been open to

[1] 'Es bilden diese fünf Gâthâs, die insgesammt metrisch abgefasst sind, den sprachlich wichtigsten, aber auch den weitaus schwierigsten teil des ganzen Avesta, ja man kann sagen, ohne dass man fürchten muss der übertreibung geziehen zu werden, sie bilden den schwierigsten teil der ganzen indogermanischen philologie.' Altiranisches Verbum; von C. Bartholomae; Einleitung, s. 3.

hopeful study, the Pahlavi commentaries have never been thoroughly made out, and writer after writer advances with an open avowal to that effect; while the explanation, if attempted, involves questions of actual decipherment, and Persian studies in addition to those of the Sanskrit and Zend; and the language of the Gâthas requires also the study of a severe comparative philology, and that to an unusual, if not unequalled, extent.

The keen observer will at once see that a department of science so circumstanced may cause especial embarrassment. On the one hand, it is exposed to the impositions of dilettanti, and the hard working specialist must be content to see those who have advanced with studies one half, or less than one half completed, consulted as masters by a public which is only ignorant as regards the innermost laws of the science; and, on the other hand, the deficiencies of even the most laborious of specialists must leave chasms of imperfection out of which the war of the methods must continually re-arise. In handling the Gâthas especially, I have resorted to the plan of giving a translation which is inclusively literal[1], but filled out and rounded as to form by the free use of additions. As the serious student should read with a strong negative criticism, he may notice that I strive occasionally after a more pleasing effect; but, as we lose the metrical flow of the original entirely, such an effort to put the rendering somewhat on a level with the original in this respect, becomes a real necessity. I have, however, in order to guard against misleading the reader, generally, but not always, indicated the added words by parenthetical curves. That these will be considered unsightly and awkward, I am well aware. I consider them such myself, but I have not felt at liberty to refrain from using them. As the Gâthas are disputed word for word, I could not venture to resort to free omissions; and what a translation would be without either additions or omissions, may be

[1] That is approximately so; absolute literalness, even when treated as I propose, would be unmanageably awkward. In another work, I give a word for word rendering of the Gâthas.

seen from the occasional word for word renderings given. Beyond the Gâthas, I have omitted the curves oftener. I have in the Gâthas, as elsewhere, also endeavoured to impart a rhythmical character to the translation, for the reason above given, and foreign readers should especially note the fact, as well as my effort to preserve the colour of original expressions, otherwise they will inevitably inquire why I do not spare words. To preserve the colour and warmth, and at the same time to include a literal rendering, it is impossible to spare words and syllables, and it is unwise to attempt it. Non-specialists may dislike the frequency of alternative renderings as leaving the impression of indecision, while, at the same time, a decision is always expressed by the adoption of a preferred rendering. The alternatives were added with the object of showing how nearly balanced probabilities may be, and also how unimportant to the general sense the questions among specialists often are.

In transliterating, I have followed the plan used in the preceding volumes to avoid confusion, but since the first volume was published, great progress has been made in this particular, and in a separate work I should have adopted a different arrangement[1]. As to other unimportant variations from the preceding volumes in matters of usage and fashion, I trust that no one will dwell on them for a moment[2]. As regards the usual and inevitable differences of opinion on more serious questions, see the remarks in the Introduction[3]. I would also state that I have often avoided rendering identical passages in identical language, as irksome both to reader and writer. I have also not invariably cited the obviously preferable variations of text which have been adopted, and which are so familiar to the

[1] Chiefly as to [illegible]; but I write ص ṣ, ظ ẓ.

[2] As in Âramaiti, Vohu Manah, &c. I also write Neryosangh, and in a few places Gâtha(â), Ahunavaiti(î), &c. I regret not to have written Mazdâh everywhere.

[3] Where I differ from Professor Darmesteter, I desire to be considered as merely proposing alternative renderings. I have therefore omitted a mass of references to the previous volumes as unnecessary.

eye in Westergaard, Spiegel, and Geldner. The texts of Westergaard have been followed necessarily as to extent of matter, as this work is printed before the completion of Geldner's text. The oft-recurring formulas and prayers at the ends of chapters and sections have been left unrendered, and finally for the most part unnoticed, by striking out the useless notes. Citations of the Pahlavi and Sanskrit translations have been given occasionally in full, in order to meet the extraordinary statements which sometimes appear to the effect that they have not been vital to the interpretation of the Gâthas. But by giving these extracts and by frequently citing the Pahlavi, Neryosangh, and the Persian, I have perhaps exposed myself to the misconception that I am an extreme advocate of the so-called tradition[1], whereas all conscientious critics will acknowledge that I follow the indications of these works with more reserve than any writer who professes to have studied them; in fact I may well apprehend censure from 'traditionalists' in this particular. These Asiatic renderings are cited by me the more fully when those who neglect them agree with their indications; and they are therefore cited to show that, whereas those most opposed to them are nevertheless forgetfully indebted to them in nearly every line, therefore in all cases of great difficulty they should be studied as an absolute necessity before rash conjectures are adopted. For it is exactly where we are all most in doubt, that their indications become of most worth, when rationally considered. These translations should be examined for the relics of the truth, the hints, and traces of original explanations, which may most abound where they are themselves most faulty as translations. I therefore never search them for exact reproductions. But the citations which I give

[1] The relics of a 'tradition' direct from the fountain-head are present in the Asiatic commentaries, and also the relics of a tradition from later, and, as it were, modern scholarship; and, lastly, there are also present the direct results of an ancient scholarship; but to speak of the Pahlavi translations as 'tradition,' is merely to use a convenient phrase. I know of no scholar who supposes these commentaries to be in a simple sense 'tradition' from the earliest Zend writers.

here constitute only a very small fraction of those needed. An argument should be built up on the fullest statements of the circumstances, elucidated with scientific completeness. This alone would have any prospect of obliging investigators to acknowledge the truth; for not only inertia and prejudice are arrayed on the other side, but even interest. This much is said of the Pahlavi translations; for Ner. is properly cited only as a translation of a translation, and, as such, of the highest authority[1]; so of the Persian.

Zendists will observe that I by no means abandon explanations merely because they are old, a practice which seems almost the fashion. I, however, fully approve of testing and assailing again and again all suggestions whether old or new. I would simply assert that, while the tasks before us remain still so very extensive, it would be better for scholars to exercise their sagacity upon passages which call loudly for wise conjecture, leaving those which are clear as they stand, for later assaults. It will be seen that I myself by no means approve of refraining from conjecture[2], but I would only in all humility insist that we should not abandon ourselves to unprepared conjecture. As is known[3], I have attempted the present rendering after more than ten years of close labour, and after a full trans-

[1] It is to be hoped that our occupations are sufficiently serious to allow us to pass over the imperfections of Neryosangh's Sanskrit style. He was especially cramped in his mode of expressing himself by a supposed necessity to attempt to follow his original (which was not the Gâthic but the Pahlavi) word for word. His services were most eminently scholarly, and, considering his disadvantages, some of the greatest which have been rendered. Prof. R. v. Roth and Dr. Aurel Stein have kindly transcribed for me valuable variations.

[2] It will be regarded, however, as especially desirable that, in a report from a specialist to the learned public in general, the texts should on no account be violated by conjectural improvements where they are at all translatable; alternatives are therefore added. As has been remarked by a recent reviewer on the new version of the Scriptures, there is scarcely a line of very ancient writings which scholars are not tempted to amend; but such emendations are seldom agreed to among specialists. A first translation should always be attempted with the texts as they stand.

[3] See the Athenæum, April 12, 1884; and the Academy, Sept. 13, 1884. On the entire subject in its connection with the Gnostic and modern philosophies, my special labours have included a much longer period of time than that mentioned.

lation of the Pahlavi and Sanskrit translations, together with an edition of the Zend, Pahlavi, Sanskrit, and Persian texts of the Gâthas. It is proper to add that for the purpose of keeping the judgment free from prejudice, and open to honest conviction from the influence of the *Rig*-veda, I have followed the practice for a number of years of transcribing the Hymns of the Veda into English in word for word written studies, having already so treated by far the greater part of them; some of these are in curtailed statement, others needlessly full. I have also, on the other hand, turned a large portion of the Gâthas into Vedic Sanskrit. (This, however, is practically a universal custom, as all words are compared with the Vedic, so far as analogies exist between the Gâthas and the *Riks*.) If therefore the opposed schools regard me as erring in too implicit a reliance on the hints of the Asiatics on the one side, or in too decided a tendency to read the Gâthic as Vedic on the other, they may be assured that I have not erred from interest or prejudice. That my results will please both parties it is folly to expect, in fact perfection in the rendering of the Gâthas (as of some other ancient works) is for ever unattainable, and not to be looked for; moreover, it would not be recognised, if attained; for no writer, whosoever he may be, can produce a rendering of the Gâthas without meeting the assaults of ignorance or design. However imperfect my results may be supposed to be, it is to be hoped that they will contribute some little toward establishing a convention among scholars as to what the Gâthic and Zend writings mean; meanwhile it is confidently expected that they will fulfil the requirements of the science of comparative theology. Whatever may be the ultimate truth as to questions of close detail, the Yasna, as well as the rest of the Avesta, is clear as to its creed.

My list of obligations is a long one, in fact so long that I fear I can express but little compliment in naming advisers, as I have made it a practice to consult all available persons, as well as books. Making one exception, I will therefore reserve to myself the pleasure of recalling them to a future occasion.

It is sufficient to say here that while I follow a new departure in the treatment of the Asiatic commentaries, yet the most prominent writers of the opposing schools have courteously favoured me with their advice. Availing myself of the exception named, I would take the liberty to express my gratitude, here especially, to Dr. E. W. West, our first authority on Pahlavi, for placing at my disposal various readings of the Pahlavi text of the Yasna, of which we have hitherto only possessed a single MS. in the Pahlavi character, that contained in the oldest Zend writing, the Codex numbered five, in the Library of Copenhagen. The variations referred to were transcribed by Dr. West from the venerable MS., the hereditary property of Dastur Dr. *G*âmâspgi Mino*k*iharg*i* Asana of Bombay, and written only nineteen (or twenty-two) days later than that numbered five in the Library of Copenhagen. By this generous loan I have been enabled to print elsewhere the first text of the Pahlavi of the Gâthas yet edited with comparison of MSS., likewise also for the first time translated, in its entirety, into a European language. For this Dr. West, during an extended correspondence, has furnished me with information on the Pahlavi not obtainable elsewhere, together with corrections and revisions. There is another eminent friend whose sacrifices of time and labour on my behalf have been exceptional, but I will defer the mention of Zend scholars.

I take this opportunity to express my acknowledgments to Professor Dr. von Halm of the Hof- und Staatsbibliothek, in Munich, for allowing me the free use of Codex 12[b], of Haug's Collection, both at Stuttgart and Hanover; also to Professor Dr. Wilmanns of Göttingen; Geheimrath Dr. Förstemann of Leipsic; and Herr Rath Bodemann of Hanover, for the loan of a large number of valuable works from their respective public libraries, often, with great liberality, renewed.

L. H. MILLS.

HANOVER, February, 1886.

INTRODUCTION.

MANY readers, for whom the Zend-Avesta possesses only collateral interest, may not understand why any introductory remarks are called for to those portions of it which are treated in this volume. The extent of the matter does not appear at first sight a sufficient reason for adding a word to the masterly work which introduces the first two volumes, and, in fact, save as regards questions which bear upon the Gâthas, I avoid for the most part, for the present, all discussion of details which chiefly concern either the sections treated in the first two volumes, or the extended parts of the later Avesta treated here. But the Gâthas are of such a nature, and differ so widely from other parts of the Avesta, that some words of separate discussion seem quite indispensable, and such a discussion was recommended by the author of the other volumes. A second reason why a word of introduction is necessary, when the translation of the successive parts of the Avesta passes from one hand to another, is a reason which bears upon the subject with exceptional force.

It is this: the Avesta, while clearly made out, so far as the requirements of comparative theology are concerned, yet presents difficulties as to minute detail so great, that as yet no two independent scholars can entirely agree as to their solution. Master and pupil, friend and friend, must differ, and sometimes on questions of no trivial moment.

The preliminary studies requisite to the formation of ultimate opinions are so varied, and of such a nature, involving the rendering of matter as yet totally unrendered with any scientific exactness in either India or Europe, that no person can claim to have satisfied himself in these respects. Scholars are therefore obliged to advance biassed by the fact that they are preponderatingly Iranists, or preponderatingly Vedists, and therefore certain at the outset that they must differ to a certain degree from each other, and to a certain degree also from the truth. It was also, as might well be understood without statement, with a full knowledge of the fact that I was inclined to allow especial weight to a comparison with the Veda, and that I modified the evidence of tradition somewhat more than he did, that Professor Darmesteter urged me to accept this task. But while I am constrained to say something by way of a preparatory treatise here, a sense of the fitness of things induces me to be as brief as possible, and I must therefore ask indulgence of the reader if my mode of expressing myself seems either rough or abrupt.

As to what the Gâthas are in their detail, enough has been said in the summaries and notes. From those representations, necessarily somewhat scattered, it appears that they comprise seventeen sections of poetical matter, equal in extent to about twenty-five to thirty hymns of the *Ri*g-veda, composed in ancient Aryan metres, ascribing supreme (beneficent) power to the Deity Ahura Mazda, who is yet opposed co-ordinately by an evil Deity called Aka Manah, or Angra Mainyu. In all respects, save in the one particular that He is not the Creator of this evil Deity, and does not possess the power to destroy him or his realm, this Ahura Mazda is one of the purest conceptions which had yet been produced. He has six personified attributes (so one might state it), later, but not in the Gâthas, described as Archangels, while in the Gâthas they are at once the abstract attributes of God, or of God's faithful adherents upon earth, and at the same time conceived of as persons, all efforts to separate the instances in which they are spoken of as the mere dispositions of the divine or saintly mind, and those in which they are spoken of as personal beings, having been in vain.

We have therefore a profound scheme, perhaps not consciously invented, but being a growth through centuries; and this system is the unity of God in His faithful creatures. It is not a polytheism properly so-called, as Ahura forms with his Immortals a Heptade, reminding one of the Sabellian Trinity. It is not a Pantheism, for it is especially arrested by the domain of the evil Deity. It might be called, if we stretch the indications, a Hagio-theism, a delineation of God in the holy creation. Outside of the Heptade is Sraosha, the personified Obedience (and possibly Vayu, as once mentioned); and, as the emblem of the pious, is the Kine's soul, while the Fire is a poetically personified symbol of the divine purity and power. As opposed to the good God, we have the Evil Mind, or the Angry (?) Spirit, not yet provided with full personified attributes to correspond to the Bountiful Immortals. He has, however, a servant, Aêshma, the impersonation of invasion and rapine, the chief scourge of the Zarathu*s*trians; and an evil angel, the Dru*g*, personified deceit, while the Daêvas (Devas) of their more southern neighbours (some of whose tribes had remained, as servile castes, among the Zarathu*s*trians) constitute perhaps the general representatives of Aka Manah, Aêshma, the Dru*g*, &c. The two original spirits unite in the creation of the good and evil in existence both actually in the present, and in principles which have their issue in the future in rewards and punishments. The importance of this creed, so far stated, as the dualistical creation, and, as an attempted solution, of the hardest problem of speculation, should be obvious to every enlightened eye. If there existed a supreme God whose power could undo the very laws of life, no evil could have been known; but the doctrine denies that there is any such being. The good and the evil in existence limit each other. There can be no happiness undefined by sorrow, and no goodness which does not resist sin. Accordingly the evil principle is recognised as so necessary that it is represented by an evil God. His very name, however, is a thought, or a passion; while the good Deity is not responsible for the wickedness and grief which prevail. His power itself could not have prevented their occurrence. And He alone has an especially objective name, and one which could only be applied to a person. These suggestions, whether true or false, are certainly some of the most serious that have ever been made[1], and we find them originally here.

[1] Haug long since called attention to the likeness of Hegelianism to the

As to the nature of religious rewards and punishments, we have suggestions scarcely less important in the eye of scientific theology, and, as a matter of fact, very much more extensively spread. To say that the future rewards held out in the Gâthas were largely, if not chiefly, spiritual, and in the man himself, would be almost a slur upon the truth. The truth is, that the mental heaven and hell with which we are now familiar as the only future states recognised by intelligent people, and thoughts which, in spite of their familiarity, can never lose their importance, are not only used and expressed in the Gâthas, but expressed there, so far as we are aware, for the first time. While mankind were delivered up to the childish terrors of a future replete with horrors visited upon them from without, the early Iranian sage announced the eternal truth that the rewards of Heaven, and the punishments of Hell, can only be from within. He gave us, we may fairly say, through the systems which he has influenced, that great doctrine of subjective recompense, which must work an essential change in the mental habits of every one who receives it. After the creation of souls, and the establishment of the laws which should govern them, Âramaiti gives a body, and men and angels begin their careers. A Mãthra is inspired for the guidance of the well-disposed. The faithful learn the vows of the holy system under the teaching of the Immortals, while the infidel and reprobate portion of mankind accept the seductions of the Worst Mind, and unite with the Daêvas in the capital sin of warfare from wanton cruelty, or for dishonest acquisition. The consequence of this latter alliance is soon apparent. The Kine, as the representative of the holy people, laments under the miseries which make Iranian life a load. The efforts to draw a livelihood from honest labour are opposed, but not frustrated, by the Daêva-worshipping tribes who still struggle with the Zarathustrians for the control of the territory. The Kine therefore lifts

chief ideas in the Zarathustrian philosophy as centring in its dualism. And I think that it is quite evident, and I believe conceded by experts, that the Hegelian sublated dualism is a descendant from the Zarathustrian through the Gnostics and Jacob Boehme.

her wail to Ahura, and His Righteous Order, Asha, who respond by the appointment of Zarathustra, as the individual entrusted with her redemption; and he, accepting his commission, begins his prophetic labours. From this on we have a series of lamentations, prayers, praises, and exhortations, addressed by Zarathustra and his immediate associates to Ahura and the people, which delineate the public and personal sorrows in detail, utter individual supplications and thanksgivings, and exhort the masses assembled in special or periodical meetings.

Here, it must be noted, that the population among whom these hymns were composed were chiefly agriculturists and herdsmen. Circumstances which affected their interests as such were of course paramount with them, and as their land and cattle represented their most valuable property, whatever threatened them was the most of all things to be dreaded. Accordingly rapine, and the raid, whether coming from Turanians or Daêva-worshippers, were regarded as the most terrible of visitations. But their moral earnestness in their determination to avoid rapine on their part, even when tempted by a desire for retaliation, is especially to be noted[1]. It was as awful when regarded as a sin as it was when suffered as an affliction; and their animus in this particular was most exceptional. While the above facts explain to us, on the one hand, the principal deities, and the peculiar hopes and fears which inspired their worship, they lead us also, on the other hand, to wonder the more that so subtle a theology as we have found expressed in the documents, should have arisen amid so simple a community.

In the course of the recitations we have also special intimations of an organised struggle of the Daêva-party to overwhelm the Zarathustrians. At times they seem very nearly to have accomplished their object. A distinct reference to a battle in the lines occurs, while sanguinary violence is alluded to more than once as in

[1] They pray against Aêshma without qualification. They might practise desolating havoc in time of war; but the raid, as in times of nominal peace, seems to have been foreign to them.

the line, or in skirmish. We conclude from the prevalence of a thankful tone that the Zarathustrians gained the upper hand during the Gâthic period, but although the result may have been assured, the struggle at the time of the last Gâtha was by no means over. In the latest Gâtha, as in the earliest, we have signs of fierce and bloody conflict. The same type of existence prevailed greatly later, in the time of the Yasts, but the scene seems very different, and Zarathustra's human characteristics are wholly lost in the mythical attributes with which time and superstition had abundantly provided him. By way, then, of summarising the chief characteristics of his original system, we may say that he and his companions were struggling to establish a kingdom under the Sovereign Power of God, whose first care was to relieve suffering, and shelter the honest and industrious poor[1]. This kingdom was to be conducted according to His holy Order, or plan of salvation, to be permeated by living Piety, and with the ultimate object of bestowing both Weal and Immortality. This high ideal was also not left as an abstract principle to work its way. Society was far too rudimental, then as ever, for the efficient survival of unsupported principles. A compact hierarchical system seems to have existed, the sacramental object being the fire, before which a priesthood officiated with unwavering zeal; but the traces of this are very restricted in the Gâthas, and, according to all probability, it was greatly less elaborated at their period than later.

Such, in very brief outline, is the system which meets us as Zarathustrianism in that period of Mazda-worship when Zarathustra lived and composed the Gâthic hymns.

As to the further question, 'Who was Zarathustra, and when and where did he live?' diversity of opinion still pre-

[1] The practical operation of this prime principle seems to have been at times beneficial to a remarkable, if not unparalleled, extent. Under the Sasanids the lower classes enjoyed great protection. See the remarks of Professor Rawlinson, The Seventh Oriental Monarchy, page 410 ff. Also recall the extraordinary treatment of the poor during the drought and famine under Perozes. The account is, however, exaggerated. See Tabari II, p. 130, cited by Professor Rawlinson, p. 314.

vails, so much so that as regards it I differ slightly even from my eminent friend and predecessor. As such differences on the subject of the Avesta are however matters of course, I freely state my impressions. Who was then the person, if any person, corresponding to the name Zarathustra in the Gâthas? Did he exist, and was he really the author of these ancient hymns? That he existed as an historical person I have already affirmed; and as to the hymns ascribed to him and his immediate associates, I have also no hesitation. Parts of these productions may have been interpolated, but the Gâthas, as a whole, show great unity, and the interpolations are made in the spirit of the original. And that Zarathustra was the name of the individual in which this unity centres, we have no sufficient reason to dispute. The name is mentioned in the most sacred connections, as well as in those which depict the reality of the prophet's sufferings; and there is no reason at all why it should have come down endeared to humanity, unless it belonged to one, who, in the presence of a Sovereign and a kingdom, could impress his personality with greatly more defined distinctness upon his contemporaries than either that Sovereign or any of his adherents [1]. That any forgery is present in the Gâthas, any desire to palm off doctrines upon the sacred community in the name of the great prophet, as in the Vendîdâd and later Yasna, is quite out of the question. The Gâthas are genuine in their mass, as I believe no scholar anywhere now questions.

For the characteristics of this great teacher, I refer to the hymns themselves, which stand alone, of their kind, in literature. Nowhere, at their period, had there been a human voice, so far as we have any evidence, which uttered thoughts like these. They are now, some of them, the great commonplaces of philosophical religion; but till then they were unheard (agustâ).

And yet we must say of Zarathustra, as of all our first announcers, that while he antedates all whose records have come down to us, he was probably only the last visible link

[1] See especially the remarks preceding Y. L.

in a far extended chain. His system, like those of his predecessors and successors, was a growth. His main conceptions had been surmised, although not spoken before. His world was ripe for them, and when he appeared, he had only to utter and develop them. I would not call him a reformer; he does not repudiate his predecessors. The old Aryan Gods retire before the spiritual Ahura; but I do not think that he especially intended to discredit them. One of the inferior ones is mentioned for a moment, but the great Benevolence, Order, and Power, together with their results in the human subject, Ahura's Piety incarnate in men, and their Weal and Immortality as a consequence, crowd out all other thoughts. His mental insight is as evident from his system as his deep moral inspiration. As to his secondary characteristics, his manner of thought and expression, we find them peculiar to the last degree. He has given us writings in which every syllable seems loaded with thought, sometimes much repeated, and to us of the present day, very familiar; but then, when he wrote, one would suppose that he intended to 'utter his dark speech.' Succinctness is carried to an unexampled extreme[1], while the wonderful idea that God's attributes are His messengers sent out into the human soul to ennoble and redeem, makes him at times so subtle that the latest scholars cannot tell whether he means Asha and Vohu Manah personified as Archangels, or as the thoughts and beneficent intentions of the Deity reproduced in men. I can recall no passage whatsoever in which Vohu Manah, Asha, Khshathra, &c., are not strongly felt to mean exactly what they signify as words, while at the same time they are prayed to, and besought to come, as Gods or angels. Either the personification is purely poetical, which would make it, as found in the Gâthas, considering their age and place, a very remarkable phenomenon, or else, having dogmatically personified the divine attributes, Zarathustra never forgets to express a respect which is higher than 'a respect for persons,' that is,

[1] I regard it as most unfortunate that Zendists should search for easy and natural expression in the Gâthas, and the expression of commonplace detail. It is only in passionate utterance that their style becomes simple.

a respect for the principles which they represent. In making every laudatory statement, however, I take for granted, what I fear is nevertheless far from uniformly granted, and that is, that the reader will weigh well what makes all the difference, namely, the very remote period at which we are obliged to place the Gâthas, and the comparatively rude civilisation amid which we must suppose them to have been composed. We must set the ideas which lie before us in this framework of time and place. If we fail to do so, as a matter of course the thoughts and their expression will contain for us nothing whatever new; but as viewed in the light of relation, after long weighing the matter, I cannot refer to them in any other terms than those which I use, without becoming aware that I am recoiling through fear of exaggeration from stating what I believe to be the truth.

As to the personal sentiment of Zarathustra, we can only say that it was devoted. His word zarazdâiti gives the keynote to his purposes. We are certain that he was a man of courage; but that he was not scrupulous at shedding blood is also evident. He was not reticent under misfortune, while yet endowed with rare persistence to overcome it.

His sphere was not restricted. The objects which concern him are provinces as well as villages, armies as well as individuals. His circle was the reigning prince and prominent chieftains, a few gifted men deeply embued with religious veneration for the sacred compositions which had come down to them from primeval antiquity in ancient metres; and these, together with a priesthood exceptionally pure, leading on a sobered population, were also his public. But three orders appear in it, the king, the people, and the peers. That the times were disturbed is involved in what has already been said. One feature alone needs mention, it is that the agitations involved the tenure of the throne. Vîstâspa had no easy seat, and the prospect of revolution in the sense of supersedure was continually before him. As to the family life of Zarathustra, we can only say that he commanded respect; nothing whatever is further known.

It will be seen from the above sketch that I make the widest distinction between the Gâthic period and that of the later Avesta. I do so, not influenced very greatly by the fact that the Gâthas are cited in the later Avesta. Most of these citations are indeed genuine and valid as proofs of priority, while others are mere displacements of the Gâthas made for liturgical purposes, as Genesis is read in churches sometimes after portions of later matter. But a book may be cited by another when it is merely prior to it, and not much older. Nor do I lay too much stress upon the difference between the Gâthic dialect and the so-called Zend; but I do lay very great stress upon the totally dissimilar atmospheres of the two portions. In the Gâthas all is sober and real. The Kine's soul is indeed poetically described as wailing aloud, and the Deity with His Immortals is reported as speaking, hearing, and seeing; but with these rhetorical exceptions, everything which occupies the attention is practical in the extreme. G*re*hma and B*en*dva, the Karpans, the Kavis, and the Usi*g*s(-ks), are no mythical monsters. No dragon threatens the settlements, and no fabulous beings defend them. Zarathu*s*tra, *G*âmâspa, Frashao*s*tra, and Maidhyômâh; the Spitâmas, Hvôgvas, the Haê*ĉ*a*t*-aspas, are as real, and are alluded to with a simplicity as unconscious, as any characters in history. Except inspiration, there are also no miracles. All the action is made up of the exertions and passions of living and suffering men. Let the Zendist study the Gâthas well, and then let him turn to the Ya*s*ts or the Vendîdâd; he will go from the land of reality to the land of fable. He leaves in the one a toiling prophet, to meet in the other a phantastic demi-god. However ancient the fundamental ideas in the myths of the Ya*s*ts and Vendîdâd may be (and some of them were certainly older than the Gâthas or the oldest *Ri*ks) in the forms in which they now stand, they are greatly later.

As we enter into further and necessary detail, this seems to be the place for a word as to the relative ages of the several sections which make up these hymns. We see struggle and suffering, fear and anger in some of them, and we naturally group these together as having been composed at a particular stage in Zarathu*s*tra's career. We read expressions of happy confidence, and we refer them to a period of repose, as we do those sections where meditation, speculation, or dogmatic statement, are prominent; but nothing is certain except that Y. LIII must have been written after Zarathustra had attained to a sufficient age to have a marriageable daughter. An ancient leader may have reached a position of influence from doctrinal productions, and afterwards expressed the vicissitudes of an active political career. One circumstance must, however, be held in view; and that is, that neither the Gâthas, nor any other ancient pieces, which were hardly at first committed to writing, have been preserved in the form in which they were delivered for the first time. The poet himself would file them into better (?) order at each subsequent delivery, and verses which referred originally to one period of time would, if especially striking, be reproduced in subsequent effusions. And pieces which the composer may have left in one shape, his early successors would be likely to modify by interpolations, excerptions, or inversions. I believe that the Gâthas show the presence of less foreign matter than is usual, and that the interpolations which are present in them, are themselves of great antiquity, or even practically synchronous with the original. Certainly few of them show anything like an ingenious attempt at imitation. If there exist any interpolations, and we may say à priori that all existing compositions of their antiquity are, and must have been, interpolated, the additions were the work of the author's earliest disciples who composed fully in his spirit, while the position of sections in this or that Gâtha has little or nothing to do with the question of their relative age, the metres being all ancient, and the Ustavaiti, Spenta-mainyu, &c., showing as decided evidence of originality as any parts of the Ahunavaiti. (See remarks on the Gâtha Ustavaiti, p. 91 ff.)

As we proceed from the question of the relative age of the particular sections as compared with each other to that of their age considered as a whole, we are first met by the question as to place. Were the Gâthas first sung in the East or the West of Iran? I would here say that I regard this point as especially open, as I am even inclined to differ in one particular from my eminent friend

Professor Darmesteter, but let it be understood, only or chiefly, as to the place of origin of the Gâthas. I think that the scene of the Gâthic and original Zarathustrianism was the North-east of Iran, and that the later Avesta was composed during the hundreds of years during which the Zarathustrian tribes were migrating westward in Media.

One certain fact is the occurrence of geographical names in Vendîdâd I, which are obviously intended to describe the earliest homes of the Iranian races whose lore was the Avesta. The present forms of those names, as they appear in the Avesta, are indeed not the most ancient, but they occur in passages which plainly repeat very ancient myths. These names describe a region from the middle of the North of Iran to the East of it, including ancient Bactria, but extending as far West as Ragha; and, as the Gâthas are unanimously acknowledged to be the oldest portion of the Avesta, dealing as they do with Zarathustra as an historical person, we naturally look for the scene of his life in the oldest seats. The Zarathustrian Ragha, much further West than the other places mentioned, seems to have a special claim to be regarded as his birthplace, as it possesses so firm a hold upon his name, but the epithet Zarathustrian, together with the special eminence of the governor of Ragha as needing no 'Zarathustra' over him, that is, no imperial chief (see Y. XIX, 19), may both be attributed to successors of Zarathustra. From some reason, probably the migration of Zarathustrian influence toward the West, Ragha became a stronghold of his descendants; or his name, entirely apart from all family connection, may have become a title for leading politico-ecclesiastical officials (compare the Zarathustrôtema). There is no mention of a foreign origin of Zarathustra in the Gâthas, nor is there any expression from which we might infer it. His family seems as settled as himself. The Spitâmas are mentioned with the same familiarity as the Hvôgvas, and the persons named are, some of them, related to him. He was no isolated figure among the people whom he influenced. Unless then we can place Vîstâspa and *G*âmâspa, Frashaostra, and Maidhyômâh, in Ragha, we cannot well place Zarathustra there, for he is to be placed beside them. Tradition of a late and dubious character places Vîstâspa in Bactria; but it is better to leave the exact region undecided, as certainty can never be reached.

The other circumstances which are imperative with many for a decision for the East as the region where Zarathustra laboured, have been stated with perhaps the greatest power and beauty by Darmesteter [1], who still inclines to the West. These are the strong analogies existing between the Zend language and the Vedic Sanskrit on the one side, and between the gods, heroes, and myths of the Avesta, and those of Veda, on the other.

As bearing, however, in favour of a western origin of the Gâthic, as well as of the later Avesta, we must confess that the West Iranian of the Cuneiform Inscriptions possesses the same analogies with the Vedic which the language of the Avesta possesses with it; and no reader should need to be reminded that the West Iranian as well as the East Iranian was in no sense derived from the Vedic. The old Aryan from which all descended was once spread without distinction over both West and East, while, on the other hand, the mythological features of the Avesta, kindred as they are to those of the Eastern Veda, are yet reproduced for us, some of them, in the poetry of the mediæval West as drawn from the Avesta; and the name of Mazda, unknown (?) to the *Riks* [2], appears cut in the rocks of Persepolis and Behistun, while all the sacred books of the Zarathustrians, including the Gâthas as well as the later Avesta, together with their interpretations, have come down to us from the West, where the Greeks also found their system from the time of Herodotus down.

Added to which we must acknowledge that the differences in dialect between the Avesta and Veda make a wide separation as to place far from startling, while myths as well as religions migrate as by a law.

We must therefore consider well before we venture to differ from those who decide for the West as the scene of Zarathustra's life.

[1] See the Introduction to the first two volumes, and also Ormuzd and Ahriman.

[2] But cp. *Rv.* VIII, 20, 17, divó—ásurasya vedhásah (medhasah (?)).

But as we mention the Inscriptions, we must make a very careful distinction. Is their theology that of Zarathustra? If it is, this would certainly constitute a point in conjunction with the descriptions of the Greeks, in favour of a still more extensive prevalence of Zarathustrianism in the West at the dates which the Inscriptions cover.

As to this disputed point, I would answer that their theology may be the Zarathustrian in a sense as yet too little applied to the term, for it may be Gâthic Zarathustrianism, or at least a Mazda-worship at a stage of development corresponding to the stage of Mazda-worship in which it stood when Zarathustra left it; but that it was the later and fully developed Zarathustrianism, provided with all the regulations of the Vendidâd, seems out of the question.

In the first place there is no certain mention of Angra Mainyu, or of the Amesha Spenta, in the Inscriptions; and this silence must be accounted for[1] in any case[2].

The ready and just suggestion is made that the documents are exceedingly limited; that many deities would not be named on so narrow a space, while the statements of Herodotus and his successors make it probable that the entire system of Zarathustra was known in the near neighbourhood, and must have been very familiar to the persons who ordered the Inscriptions to be cut. To this the necessary rejoinder might be made, that the familiarity of Darius with the later, or indeed with the original, Zarathustrianism, if he was familiar with it, renders the absence of the name of Angra Mainyu at least all the more striking.

What more imperative call could there be for the use of that name than in denouncing the opponents whose overthrow forms the theme of the mighty writings?

As the 'grace of Auramazda' is mentioned on the one

[1] Some relief is given by a mention of the Draogha, but the bagâhya are probably Mithra and Anâhita (see the Inscription of Artaxerxes Mnemon, 4) rather than the Amesha Spenta. As we notice the name of Mithra, however, we must remark that, as the Mithra worship undoubtedly existed previously to the Gâthic period, and fell into neglect at the Gâthic period, it might be said that the greatly later Inscriptions represent Mazda-worship as it existed among the ancestors of the Zarathustrians in a pre-Gâthic age or even Vedic age.

[2] Angra Mainyu and the Amesha are also prominent in the Gâthas.

side, one naturally expects to see some reference to the 'opposition' of His chief adversary on the other, and one also expects to trace some certain recognition of the Bountiful Immortals. I think that both were omitted because their names retained less weight, as we cannot suppose that they were unknown, or, if once known, then forgotten. But allowing that it is not quite fair to reason from such scanty texts, we are met by the positive fact that an important Inscription is written on a tomb[1]; and, as the burial of the dead was one of the most flagrant violations of the Zarathustrian ceremonial law, it is not conceivable that Darius could have been a Zarathustrian according to the later Faith. He was either a heretical schismatic departing from a sacred precept, or he was following the creed of his fathers, a Mazda-worshipper, but not 'of Zarathustra's order,' or, if a Zarathustrian, then a partial inheritor of Zarathustra's religion at an undeveloped stage, while burial was not as yet forbidden by it; and at the same time he neglected also prominent doctrines of the Gâthas.

It is not possible that he could have been an isolated schismatic as to such a particular. If he composed the Inscriptions as a monarch of another religion than that of the later Avesta, it would seem to prove either that he was an adherent to a cruder, or half effaced, form of Gâthic Zarathustrianism, which had found its way during the long periods of its existence westward before the later Zarathustrianism arose in the western settlements, or else that it, the religion of the Inscriptions, simply originated where we find it, from an original and wide-spread Mazda-worship which had not yet forbidden the burial of the dead[2].

---

[1] And all are the Inscriptions of buried men. See also the statements of Professor de Harlez on the subject.

[2] And perhaps it had also not forbidden cremation. Geiger (see 'The Civilisation of the Eastern Iranians in Ancient Times;' English translation by Dârâb Dastur Peshotan Sañgânâ, B.A., p. 90) conjectures that the dakhma were originally places for cremation. If this is a correct surmise, both burial and cremation may have been permitted at the Gâthic period, being forbidden long after. At least the original Mazda-worship did not recoil from cremation, otherwise the story of the attempt to burn the Lydian Crœsus could not have arisen. The earlier Persians had no abhorrence of either burial or burning. Only the developed Zarathustrian Magism of the Medes obeyed the Vendîdâd.

That such a Mazda-worship once existed in primeval Iran seems certain, and that it was greatly earlier than Zarathustrianism[1]. It is also very probable that some form of it survived unadulterated by Zarathustrianism. And this is as probable à priori when we reflect on what might have happened, as it is when we seek for an explanation of the burial of a Mazda-worshipper in a tomb.

As the Asura (Ahura) worship extended into India with the Indians as they migrated from Iran, a form of Asura worship arose in Iran which added the name of Mazda to the original term for God. In the East it began to acquire additional peculiarities out of which, when Zarathustra arose, he developed his original system, while in other parts of Iran, and with great probability in Persia, it retained its original simplicity. At subsequent periods only, the Zarathustrian form spread, first at the Gâthic stage, and later a second time, and from a centre further West, as the Zarathustrianism of the later Avesta which is reported by the Greeks. Either then Darius was a Mazda-worshipper, like his fathers, following an original and independent type of Mazda-worship, or he was following a mutilated Gâthic Zarathustrianism, which may not yet have forbidden burial[2], he and his chieftains adhering to this ancient form, while the masses yielded to the novelties, as the patrician Jews held to Sadduceeism after the masses had become Pharisees, and as the patrician Romans clung to Paganism after Rome had become Catholic. In either case it seems to me that the Mazda-worship of the Inscriptions might be severed from the later Zarathustrianism; and that it must be so severed on some theory or other, all with one voice seem to agree.

In deciding for the North-east[3] as the scene of Zarathustra's personal labours, and for the Gâthic dialect as its more particular form of speech, I am not, I trust, solely

[1] Compare even the Scythic name Thamimasadas, cited by Professor Rawlinson (Herod. 3rd edit. iii, p. 195). Were branches of the Scyths themselves in a sense Mazda-worshippers, or could the name have been borrowed?

[2] And which insisted less upon the personality of Satan.

[3] The name Bactrian cannot be considered as more than a convenient expression.

or unduly influenced by the occurrence of the eastern names in the first chapter of the Vendîdâd, for those names may indicate primeval homes from which the ancestors of Zarathustra migrated toward the west centuries before his appearance. I merely say that the occurrence of the names shows that the ancestors of the Zarathustrian Mazda-worshippers once lived in East Iran; and if that is the case, their descendants may have still lived there when Zarathustra developed his system, and it is also possible that masses of Zarathustrians may long have remained behind in the East Iranian mountains after the Zarathustrians of the later Avesta had gone west. The descendant may have arisen in the home of his ancestors, and in fact, other things being equal, there is a stronger probability that he arose there. I do not think that the appearance of a later Zarathustrianism in the west, is a sufficient reason for doubting that the founder of the system laboured nearer the land of the Vedas, where a Vîstâspa once ruled (?), where a Daêva-worship long lingered, and where the common names of the Irano-indian gods were heard as household words, and which, we may add, was precisely the place where we should suppose the Indo-aryans to have left the Irano-aryans, as they descended into the Puńgâb.

Having formed an opinion as to the place where Zarathustra laboured, and proceeding to the question as to when he lived and wrote the Gâthas, we find ourselves under the necessity to form our estimate first as to the age of the later parts of the Avesta. While interpolated passages, or indeed whole Yasts, may be very late, I cannot place the later Avesta in its bulk later than the Cuneiform Inscriptions of Darius, for the fact that the Inscriptions preserve either a pre-Zarathustrian Mazdaism, or the Zarathustrianism of the Gâthas long previous as it was in its origin to that of the Vendîdâd, has nothing whatever to do with the relative age of the Inscriptions themselves. The later Avesta, with its forbiddal of burial and cremation, must have existed for a long time side by side with that religion which has left sepulchral monuments, and whose adherents could contemplate the burning of captives; and analogous facts are universal.

But aside from the seeming difference in the type of Mazda-worship, which simply severs the religion of the Inscriptions from that of the more developed Zarathustrianism, and which has, as we have seen, nothing whatever to do with the question of the relative ages of the Inscriptions and the later Avesta, I think that we have some signs of a later age in the language of the Inscriptions apart from their contents. As, however, Darmesteter is inclined to regard the West Iranian, or Cuneiform, as better preserved than the Zend of the later Avesta, I make my few remarks only with great hesitation.

The termination [Zend]-, which would otherwise be justly considered as an evidence of degeneration in the Zend, I regard as merely a wrong writing for -ahya = Gâthic ahyâ. The letter [Zend] is a relic of the time when the Avesta stood in the Pahlavi character; I think that it is here merely a lengthened [Zend] = ya[1]. Terminations also seem much mutilated in the Cuneiform, and the name Auramazda written as one word, does not seem to me so original.

We must indeed remember that a later generation, owing to an isolated position, often preserves an older dialect, as it may an older form of religion, whereas an earlier generation, if its predecessors have lived in a compact society in smaller districts, varies the ancient forms, as the old Indian developed into Sanskrit and Prâkrit. Still we have little reason to be certain that the civilisation of Media and

[1] Also [Zend] is simply ayam, and should be so transliterated; so also in a throng of other words. Salemann has noticed the origin of [Zend] = ê, but gives no other indication in the present sense. I think that [Zend] and also [Zend], where they equal Aryan ya, should be corrected everywhere, like all other instances of miswriting. Unless indeed we can regard the [Zend], for which [Zend] [Zend] were often clearly miswritten, as itself of double significance, as in Pahlavi. [Zend] might then regularly and properly equal both ê and ya; so [Zend] may equal long ê or yâ (ayâ). Other instances of miswriting in Zend would be dat. dual -bya. The Aryan -âm was first written as the nasal vowel -ã, and still further carelessly reduced to -a, but never so spoken. On the contrary, in the acc. fem. &c., the nasalisation was over-written, too much expressed. The final nasal caused the scribes to write the preceding letter as if nasalised, 'ã,' but it was never nasalised in speech

Persia was either more or less condensed and social than that of Bactria and the East. But beside a priority to the Inscriptions, we are obliged to consider the time needed for developments. The Greeks of the time of Herodotus probably, and those later certainly, found a form of Zarathustrianism in full development in Media; but if the contemporaries of Herodotus heard familiarly of a Zarathustrianism there, a long period of time must be allowed for its development if it originated in Media, and a still longer period if it found its way there from the East. If, then, the bulk of the later Avesta existed at the time of Herodotus and at that of Darius, how long previously must it have been composed; for such systems do not bloom in a day?

We have the evidence of historical tradition that the Magi[1] were influential even at the time of Cyrus, not dwelling upon the possibility of their existence at the earliest mention of Medes as the conquerors and rulers of Babylon.

Can we then, considering the recognised stagnation of ancient Eastern intelligence, ascribe to the development of the Median Zarathustrianism a shorter period than from one to three centuries? If, then, the bulk of the later Avesta must be placed so long before the Inscriptions of Darius, where shall we place the earlier Avesta with its most important remaining fragments, the Gâthas[2]?

After studying the Gâthas carefully in detail, and becoming also familiar with them as a whole by frequent perusal, we must measure the time needed for the change from their tone to that of the later Avesta. Could it have been less than a century, or centuries? Was not as much time needed for the Zarathustra of the Gâthas to become the Zarathustra of the later Avesta, as was afterwards consumed by the migration of the creed from the North-east, if it really originated there? As there is undoubtedly a

[1] I regard the Magi as representing the Zarathustrianism of the Vendîdâd. This the false Bardiya endeavoured to introduce, demolishing the temples which the old Mazda-worship permitted in Persia. See the Cuneiform Inscription of Behistun II; Darius 61.

[2] All in the Gâthic dialect is old.

difference of several centuries between the dates of the newest and oldest parts of the later Avesta, so we must think of a considerable interval between the oldest parts of the later Avesta and the latest parts of the older Avesta, for there is the other consideration which imperatively constrains us to avoid concluding for short periods in the stages of development. The Vedic Hymns, sung in metres closely similar to those in both the Gâthas and the later Avesta, and naming gods, demons, and heroes so closely related, not to speak of myths, challenge us to say whether they are, the oldest of them, older or later than the oldest parts of the Avesta, and, if there exists any difference as to the ages of these ancient productions, how great that difference is. The oldest *Ri*ks have now an established antiquity of about 4000; were the hymns sung on the other side of the mountains as old? The metres of these latter are as old as those of the *Ri*g-veda, if not older, and their grammatical forms and word structure are often positively nearer the original Aryan from which both proceeded. If it were not for two circumstances, we should be forced to ask very seriously which were the older, and to abandon altogether our mention of later dates. Those circumstances are the absence of the Aryan gods from the Gâthas; and, secondly, their abstract conceptions. These latter are so little offset with expected puerilities that it is often hard to believe that the Gâthas are old at all. Their antiquity is placed beyond dispute by the historic mention of Zarathustra. But, if Zarathustra were not indisputably a living man in the Gâthas, their depth and refinement, together with the absence of Mithra, Haoma, &c., would, in themselves considered, force us to place them rather late. As it is, the absence of Mithra and his colleagues, who reappear in the later Avesta, permits us to place the Gâthas considerably later than the oldest *Ri*ks. For no sudden and intentional dismissal of the ancient gods is to be accepted with Haug, nor any religious schism as the cause (!) of the migration of the Indians toward the south. The process was of course the reverse.

The migrating tribes, in consequence of their separation

from their brethren in Iran, soon became estranged from them, and their most favoured Gods fell slowly into neglect, if not disfavour.

We need time to account for this change, and no short interval of time. We can therefore place the Gâthas long after the oldest *Ri*ks. While, therefore, in view of the established age of the *Rig*-veda, the Gâthas may possibly have been composed as early as about 1500 B.C., it is also possible to place them as late as (say) 900–1200 B.C., while the fragments in the Gâthic dialect must be considered somewhat later. The dates of the composition of the several parts of the later Avesta, on the other hand, must be supposed to extend over many centuries, as the various sections in the Zend dialect are so much more numerous than those in the Gâthic, the Gâthas themselves representing practically but one date. Placing then the oldest portions of the later Avesta somewhat earlier than Darius, we are obliged to extend the period during which its several parts were composed so far as perhaps to the third or fourth century before Christ, the half-spurious matter contained in them being regarded as indefinitely later.

It seems necessary to state here for the information of non-specialists, and as bearing very seriously upon all the questions involved, that a very unusually severe controversy prevails upon the exegesis of the Avesta, and that it centres in the question as to the value of the Asiatic translations of it. A similar debate was once held on the *Rig*-veda, but that is now silenced, all agreeing that the traditional renderings are neither to be slavishly followed, nor blindly ignored. Very different has been the fate of Zend philology, and in one important particular the studies are poles apart; for whereas the commentaries on the *Ri*ks are written in Sanskrit, which is clear to experts, those on the Zend-Avesta are written in a language upon which the lexicography is most incomplete, and the elucidation of these explanations themselves remains by far the most difficult task now before us. Professor von Spiegel has accomplished much toward breaking the rough road of science in this direction, and scholars of the first order have followed his leading, while all with one accord express to him their acknowledgments. But Professor von Spiegel has not intended his editions and citations to represent full translations. He has, as a matter of course, taken it for granted that those who oppose him, as well as those who follow him, have studied his Pahlavi editions, not paying him the undesired compliment of making his commentaries the sole source of their knowledge of tradition. Moreover in no branch of science does scholarship make more rapid strides than in Pahlavi, several important works having appeared since Spiegel's commentaries.

In the attempt to master the Pahlavi translations of the Avesta we must consider many and difficult problems.

In the first place, and as a matter of course, they cannot be at all reasonably attempted without a full knowledge of the Gâthic and Avesta texts so far as they have been as yet otherwise and approximately elucidated. The two problems hang together like the arches of a circular building, and they should be studied together word for word; for the Pahlavi used is not fully that of the books. It is often turned quite out of its course, as Pahlavi, by an effort to follow the more highly inflected Zend literally. Then, again, a question of the utmost importance meets us in estimating the glosses, which are often, but not always, from a later hand. A translation of the Pahlavi must of course first be considered as in the light of the glosses, for the language is so indefinite as to many of its grammatical forms, that such an indication as a gloss, if it be proved to have been written by the same person who composed the text, would be decisive in determining the rendering; but a final translation should be made more strictly in the light of the Gâthic, so far as it affords on its side positive indications, and the glosses, where they do not correspond, should be set apart as from a later hand. Then, once more, and on the contrary, where the gloss is obviously right, and the text erroneous, the former should be appropriated unencumbered by the latter [1]. We must recognise the traces of former accurate scholarship whether we see them in text or gloss, and, from the accumulation of the correct surmises, we should construct an argument for the probability of the correctness of the hints of the Pahlavi in cases of great difficulty. In rendering the Pahlavi as a necessary prelude to rendering the Avesta, all possible help should of course be sought from the Asiatic translations of the Pahlavi, from those of Neryosangh in Sanskrit, and from the still later ones in Parsi and Persian. Here, again, those who read the Pahlavi only as rendered by Neryosangh need great caution. If Neryosangh is simply read like the classical Sanskrit, great errors will be committed. He needs a glossary of his own, and should be read solely in the light of the Pahlavi which was chiefly his original. So of the Parsi Persian translations, they must be read with especial attention to their originals. After these original translations have been fully mastered, and compared with an improved rendering of the Gâthic, likewise also studied in the full light of the Veda, the patient scholar will be surprised at the result. He will find that to a certain extensive degree, the two sources of information coincide when reasonably estimated, and, moreover, that where the Pahlavi gives us an indication differing from that derived from the Vedic, the surmise of the Pahlavi is the more often correct. I say 'reasonably estimated,' for not only is the Pahlavi, as a less highly inflected language, incapable of rendering the Avesta literally, but its authors do not uniformly make the attempt to do so; nor do they always follow the order of the Gâthic or Zend. Their translations generally run word for word as to their outward forms, for the ancient interpreters probably regarded such a following as essential to a complete rendering, but they found them-

[1] I would here state to the distinguished scholars who have done me the honour to study my work on the Gâthas, that the Pahlavi translations contained in it are those made in the light of the glosses. Here and there final ones will be added in a later volume, as from the Pahlavi texts sometimes considered apart from the Pahlavi glosses, and in consequence often much nearer the Gâthic than those from both text and gloss.

selves compelled to resort to the most important exceptions. And, lastly, the rejection, or total neglect of the Pahlavi translations and their successors, on the ground that they contain errors, is a policy which seems to me defective, and to the last degree. What absurdities can Sâya*n*a be capable of, and yet who would utter final opinions upon the *Ri*g-veda without either the ability, or the attempt, to read Sâya*n*a[1]?

It is hardly necessary to mention that the restoration of texts goes hand in hand with translation. For how are we to interpret a passage before we know that it exists? And of what inestimable worth are the Pahlavi translations as evidence to texts! Who does not see that where the ancient scribe is most free or erroneous as to form, or root, his rendering often shows plainly which of two words stood before him in his manuscripts. Our oldest MS. (that of Copenhagen, numbered 5) dates from the year 1323 A.D.; and what were the dates of the ancient documents before the eyes of the Pahlavi translator who writes in it?

We must now ask whether our present Pahlavi translations are improvements upon their predecessors, or the reverse. That they are improvements in some few instances is undeniable, for, as we have seen, some of the glosses to them from later hands give the truth where the text is wide. But the glosses which show a later origin are, for the most part, inferior in richness to the texts. Here and there a talented, or fortunate, Parsi threw new light on the subject, but the general tendency was one of deterioration; that is, before the revival of Parsi-learning under Neryosangh (400–500 years ago). This deterioration would naturally decrease as we approach successive periods in going back to the time when MSS. of the Gâthas existed according to positive evidence, that is, to the time when, according to the Ar*d*â Vîrâf, Alexander's servants found skins at Persepolis on which the Avesta had been traced in

[1] Well has Geldner mentioned the 'epoch-making' Études Iraniennes of Darmesteter (KZ. vol. xxviii, p. 186). It is to be hoped that these brilliant pieces will stimulate the study of the relation between the Zend and the New Persian through the Ancient Persian and the Pahlavi.

gilded letters (for it is not positively proved that the informants of Herodotus heard the Magian priests singing their 'theogonies' from written books). At each of these periods scholarship is proved to have been competent by the results which it accomplished. The first of them we must place in the sixth century when, on Spiegel's estimate[1], the Zend characters were modified into their present lucid form from the Pahlavi, and distinct short vowels took the place of the unknown signs which existed previously. Then all MSS. which were to be found must have been collected and copied, and, so to speak, re-edited; and here we must accordingly place a period when the Pahlavi translations were more valuable than those of any later date. As we go further back we come upon another period, when, under Shapur II, Âdarbad Mahraspend brought the surviving portions of the Zend-Avesta together (about A.D. 330). Still earlier the servants of Artaxerxes, the Sasanian, collected yet more abundant writings, when Zarathustrianism was instituted as the state religion. Then, under the Arsacids (possibly under Vologeses the first), those most competent in the realm were directed to gather the then extant documents.

While, if we hold that the entire Avesta was written originally in some character different from the Pahlavi, we must finally infer the existence of an early epoch, when the entire Avesta was brought over in its bulk from the earlier East (or West?) Iranian character in which it was first inscribed. If this character differed radically from the Pahlavi, this transliteration must be regarded as one of the most remarkable of literary events. Notwithstanding all the now rapidly corrected errors, the texts have been handed down with the minutest distinctions of dialect preserved[2], and this proves the existence of competent interpreters at a period practically contemporaneous with the composition of the later portions of the later Avesta. What commentaries must then have existed, not free from

[1] Eranisches Alterthumskunde III, s. 767.
[2] See Hübschmann, KZ. bd. 24, s. 326.

error, as we see from the Zand of the Avesta, but, as to language and general sense, how close! Even if the degree of linguistic knowledge increases only gradually or steadily in going back, without any epochs from the time of Neryosangh to the inferable date of the latest Zend writings, and if the character in which the Avesta was first recorded (after a lengthy life as an orally extended lore) differed only as to mode and fashion, and not radically, from the Pahlavi (which, so far as the later Avesta is concerned, is most probable), we have yet the transliteration of the Gâthas to account for, which perhaps were brought over (after long oral life) from the so-called Aryan character, while the existence of a gradual tradition of a scholarship does not refute the fact that this scholarship must have been at times of the highest character; it makes high scholarship more probable.

What translations, we again remark, may have existed among these early sages! And, if they could once make translations fresh from the exegesis of the latest Zend writers themselves, is it not practically certain, considering the tenacity of life manifested by Zoroastrianism, that their explanations still lurk in the commentaries which have come down to us. And if these inferences be at all correct, how should we labour to discover from our present translations what these predecessors were; and what scholar cannot perceive that gems of evidence as to texts and sense may yet linger in those of our present Pahlavi translations which may yet be otherwise most filled with phantastic error? And shall we not therefore conclude that their expected inaccuracies, whether small or great, cannot destroy their inherent value? What, then, are we to think of it, when the New Persian, a quasi-daughter of the Pahlavi, is superficially referred to for linguistic analogies, when even the Armenian is also scanned, while the Pahlavi is left unmastered? Is a quasi-mother language of the New Persian any the less likely to afford linguistic analogies because an actual translation of the Avesta has been attempted in it, and because the Avesta once stood in its characters, while it may also present claims to be considered to a certain limit a daughter language to both the Gâthic and Zend?

And should the acknowledged difficulty of the character continue to be a reason for avoiding all efforts to make it out[1]?

In the endeavour to divide our Avesta texts into originals and gloss, we are greatly aided by the metre. Interpolated words and phrases are often obvious at a glance, and we should never suspend our efforts to discover all the traces of metre which exist in the Avesta, as a necessary step to the restoration of the documents to their first form; but we should avoid exaggeration, and a carelessly dogmatic procedure in insisting upon reducing lines to an exact, or to a supposed exact, number of syllables[2]. I regard it as unwise to suppose that the metrical lines of the Avesta, or indeed of any very ancient poetical matter, have been composed with every line filed into exact proportions. The ancient poets would have brought out the measures in many a place by accent and a sandhi which are no longer known to us. The Vedic Hymns may, to a great extent, form an exception, but who would not say that where uniform evenness is at hand, an effort to improve the metre has often corrupted the text. Priests or reciters of intelligence would here and there round off an awkward strophe, as year after year they felt the unevenness of numbers. Metre must inevitably bring a perfecting corruption at times, as a deficiency in the metre must also prove a marring corruption. Cases should be carefully discriminated. The expression of passionate feeling, for instance, would be likely to cause

---

[1] One of the most powerful tributes ever paid to the Pahlavi translators was Haug's conversion to them. Before studying them he lost no opportunity to stigmatise their deficiencies; later, however, he followed them in many an important place, and sometimes with little reserve.

As writers of the opposed extremes seem honestly convinced of the radical error of each other's views, it is obvious that association and interest have much to do with decisions. A scholar should put himself fully under the influence first of one school and then of the other. The necessity for well-balanced studies is extremely great.

[2] It is only lately that the variation from eleven to twelve syllables in the lines of Trish*t*up has been applied to the Gâthic metres, nor has the possibility of a shifting caesura been acceded to till lately.

unevenness in lines. The language would be vigorous and idiomatic, and of unusual value as a fragment of ancient phrase, but the metre would have suffered.

Then as to conjectured texts; after texts have been improved from all available relics of ancient tradition, or scholarship, as afforded by the Pahlavi translations, and from the evidence of metre, we are at times still left with readings before us which could not have been original. The composers have indeed here and there constructed sentences which they either could not, or would not, make easy, but as a general thing we may say, that where the text, as it stands, gives no satisfactory sense to us, after we have exhausted the resources of previous Asiatic scholarship, or direct analogy, in our efforts to explain it, it is in that case not the text as the composer delivered it. We are then reduced to conjecture, for how are we to translate a text before we are certain that it is integral? Our first efforts should be directed to the detection of losses; for a text may still be of great value when considered as a mass of broken sentences, for, if we are certain that such is its character, we can often fill out the missing members with much probability. But whether we insert supplementary conjectures, or merely bracket later interpolations, we must by all means in cases of real necessity make the effort to amend the text (as also in the Veda).

Even if we fail in our attempted improvements, we are often little worse off than before, for whereas it is possible, or even probable, that the composers wrote what we suggest, it is sometimes not possible that they wrote exactly what stands in our texts. We should even suggest alternative readings where our present ones are only less probable (for the suggestion of an alternative is not the wholesale destruction of a sentence), while even when we declare their outcoming meaning totally unsatisfactory, the MSS. still remain to other writers to begin on afresh. And in estimating what would be reasonable meanings, we should guard carefully against both extremes, and we should especially exercise a strong negative criticism against the recognition of too much meaning, or too subtle a meaning. Profound and subtle conceptions placed where we are obliged to place the Gâthas, and other ancient portions of the Avesta, are indeed precious relics, as such conceptions at any age show a higher mental power, but we must doubt them only so much the more, and doubt, if we would be scientific and conscientious, till doubt becomes no longer possible. Beyond that we should turn our suspicions against our doubts themselves, which is the proper course if we would exhaust the meanings of the Gâthas. Unless these are a fortuitous concourse of syllables, religiously profound modes of thought are manifest throughout. It is therefore strictly unscientific to force parts of them to express shallow details. and it is above all deplorable to change the text itself in order to produce out of it less enlarged meanings[1]. I say to force parts of them, for the great mass of them confessedly defies all attempts to reduce them to the statements of simple commonplace.

They can never possess the rich colour of the *Rik*s; it is therefore the more to be deplored if we fail to see their deep, but awkwardly expressed, and oft-repeated thought. I must express my regret that until lately, when the enclitics have been more carefully considered, the form of sentences in the Gâthas does not seem to have been noticed, writers conjecturing infinitives and simple accusatives at the ends of sentences. Both may, of course, fall there, but when we wish to reconstruct a word, we should not change it to a form which is not placed according to prevailing analogies. Infinitives and accusatives generally, both in the Gâthas and the *Rig*-veda, avoid the end of the sentence. The accusative, when it falls there, is generally preceded by qualifying words often in apposition or agreement with it. Also in the conception of translations, authors seem to sup-

[1] Non-specialists must not suppose that our texts are more apparently uncertain than (say) many portions of the Old Testament. Large portions of them are also as clear, at least, as the *Rig*-veda; and the emendations referred to need very seldom affect the doctrines. Let the learned public, however, insist on scholars making honest attempts to render the texts as they stand before their emendations, and greater harmony would result.

pose it impossible that the lines can contain anything but lengthened prosaic sentences (too often with an accusative, or infinitive, pushed awkwardly out to the end). To me the Gâthic sentence is often very short, and so better adapted to poetic expression.

It has been already implied, and it has been taken for granted throughout[1], that the Avesta should be closely compared with the Veda, but let it never be forgotten, in the name of science, that the force and meaning of analogous words in the Gâthic and the Vedic cannot be expected to be uniformly identical, considering the extent of territory, and the length of time, by which those who spoke the two languages were separated. The meanings of the Vedic words could not hold their own even in India, developing into the Sanskrit and Prâkrit which differ widely, how truly misguided is it therefore to attribute necessarily the same shades of meaning to the terms of the two sister tongues. If even the Gâthic hymns stood in the Indian forms, and had been discovered in India, having also reference to Indian history, no thoughtful writer would have rendered them in complete analogy with the *Rig*-veda. The Gâthic usages would have been added in our dictionaries to those of the Vedic, just as the Sanskrit definitions are added.

An additional word seems called for as to the results of Zarathustrian theology. Besides its connection with the modern philosophy through Gnosticism which has been already noticed[2], a relation between it and the Jewish theology since the Captivity has long been mentioned. The hagiology, the demonology, the temptation, the parables, the eschatology, have all been supposed to show traces of the time when Persian power was dominant in Jerusalem, and with it, Persian literature; but the discussion of such questions requires separate treatises.

As to the general benefit which has resulted from Zarathustrianism in the past, few reflections need to be added. If the mental illumination and spiritual elevation of many millions of mankind, throughout long periods of time, are of

[1] See remarks in the Preface, p. xv.

[2] See note on p. xix.

any importance, it would require strong proof to deny that Zarathustrianism has had an influence of very positive power in determining the gravest results. That men should be taught to look within rather than without, to believe that suffering and sin do not originate from the capricious power of a Deity still called 'good,' that the 'good thought, word, and deed' should be recognised as essential to all sanctity, even in the presence of a superstitious ceremonial, that a judgment should have been expected according to the deeds done in the body, and the soul consigned to a Heaven of virtue or to a Hell of vice, its recompense being pronounced by the happy or stricken conscience, these can never be regarded by serious historians as matters of little moment, and if, on the contrary, they are allowed to be matters of great moment, the Zend-Avesta should be revered and studied by all who value the records of the human race.

ABBREVIATIONS.

Barth. = Bartholomae.

B.V. S. = Vendidad Sade, von Dr. Hermann Brockhaus. Leipzig, 1850.

D. = dastur.

De inf. = De infinitivi linguarum sanskritae bactricae persicae graecae oscae umbricae latinae gotticae forma et usu, scripsit Eugenius Wilhelmus, phil. doctor. 1872.

G. = *G*âmâspgi.

H. = Hübschmann.

Inf. = Geschichte des Infinitivs im Indogermanischen, von Dr. Julius Jolly. 1873.

K. = Kopenhagen MSS.

K. Z. = Kuhnische Zeitschrift für vergleichende Sprachforschung.

M. î K. = Mainyô-î Khard. Ed. West. 1871.

Ner. = Neryosangh.

P. = Paris MSS.

*R*v. = *Ri*g-veda.

Sp. = Spiegel.

Trlr. = translator.

V. S. = Ein Kapitel vergleichender Syntax, von Dr. Julius Jolly. 1872.

Wg. = Westergaard.

Z. D. M. G. = Zeitschrift der deutschen morgenländischen Gesellschaft.

An asterisk denotes irregularities.

THE GÂTHAS.

THE five Gâthas of Zarathustra and his immediate followers are placed here before the other parts of the Yasna on account of their higher antiquity. There existed no other Yasna for years or centuries beside them.

The more remarkable circumstances connected with them have been already discussed in the Introduction.

If it is necessary to recall any of them here, the most prominent would be that they are undoubtedly the productions of a small group of influential men who are referred to in them for the most part by name; that Zarathustra, everywhere else nearly or quite a demi-god, is here a struggling and suffering man. He is a prophet, or a divinely appointed instructor, but thoroughly human and real, so far as his situations become apparent.

Secondly, their historical tone may be emphasised. Their doctrines and exhortations concern an actual religious movement taking place contemporaneously with their composition; and that movement was exceptionally pure and most earnest. Their tone is therefore everywhere serious. Nearly all myths are dropped, and likewise, as perhaps their most striking peculiarity, even the old Aryan gods, who reappear in the later Yasna, Vendîdâd, and Yasts, are, save one, wholly absent.

The movement in its reformatory character seems to have thrown them out, not perhaps with definite intention, but because the minds of the devout enthusiasts excluded them as having inferior interest, in view of the results immediately before them.

So far as a claim to a high position among the curiosities of ancient moral lore is concerned, the reader may trust himself freely to the impression that he has before him an anthology which was probably composed with as fervent a desire to benefit the spiritual and moral natures of those to whom it was addressed as any which the world had yet seen. Nay, he may provisionally accept the opinion that nowhere else are such traces of intelligent religious earnestness to be found as existing at the period of the Gâthas or before them, save in the Semitic scriptures.

As to their speculative depth; wherever theosophical speculation is put into words, the evidence of their grasp and subjectivity becomes positive. As the extent of documents necessarily produces a certain impression upon the mind of an investigator, it must not be forgotten that the Gâthas were in all probability many times more voluminous than the fragments which now remain to us. The historian may argue from what has survived to what once existed, and the inevitable conclusion is imposing.

For additional details see the Introduction, and the summaries at the head of each Gâtha and chapter.

THE GÂTHA(Â) AHUNAVAITI(Î).

This Gâtha, consisting of seven chapters of the Yasna (XXVIII–XXXIV), takes its name from the similarity of its metre to that of the Ahuna-vairya formula which also occurs before it in the Yasna. It is composed of homogeneous material, but as its material is also homogeneous with that of the other Gâthas, it probably owes its existence as a group of sections to its metrical form. Its lines were intended to number sixteen syllables, and they are put together in stanzas of three. It is all very ancient and probably nearly all original with Zarathustra himself, though parts seem to be put into the mouths of his immediate associates and disciples. Whether any persons existed in the immediate circle of the sage capable of composing hymns like these unaided, is of course a question; but that some were able to put poetical matter together under his guidance or inspiration seems certain.

An analysis and general summary is placed before each chapter as more convenient than massing them all together. The reader is reminded that the rhythm of the original, so far as it could be reasonably conjectured, is somewhat imitated in parts of the translations.

THE GÂTHAS.

YASNA XXIX.

THE WAIL OF THE KINE. THE CALL OF ZARATHUSTRA. HIS PRAYER FOR AID.

This chapter, the second in the manuscripts of the Gâtha Ahunavaiti, is placed here as in a more natural order. It may be regarded as containing the terminus a quo of the divine revelation. The Soul of the Kine, as representing the herds of the holy Iranian people, their only means of honourable livelihood, raises its voice, and expressing the profoundest needs of an afflicted people, addresses Ahura and His Divine Order, Asha, in bitterness.

1. Recalling another and a later 'groan of the creation,' she demands wherefore and for whom she was made, since afflictions encompass her; and as her comfort, if not her existence, was threatened as much by the unsettled habits induced by constant alarms as by the actual incursions of her predatory neighbours, she beseeches the Bountiful Immortals to instruct her as to the benefits of civilised agriculture, and confirm her protectors in its practice, as her only remedy against the evils of which she complains.

2. Ahura answers by a question to Asha, the personified Righteous Order, as to what guardian he had appointed in order to smite back the fury which assails her, intimating that some chief ought to have been set over her originally who would have averted her miseries, training her people in steady tillage and bucolic skill, and repelling the destructive raids.

3. Asha answers that her sufferings were inevitable, that no chief could be appointed who could prevent them since none was himself without his share of injustice and of passionate resentment. He could not answer why this was the case. The question, involving the insolvable problem of the origin of evil, lay at the foundation of those influences which move the stars of destiny; that the religious revelation afforded by the Ratu (as in

chapter XXX) was intended to meet these problems so far as they could be answered[1], and that therefore all who were entering upon active enterprises were in the act of approaching, not him Asha, the subordinate archangel, but Mazda himself, who was the greatest of beings, and alone able to answer their prayers and questions.

4. Zarathustra[2], poetically conceived to be present, here intervenes to reaffirm the homage just paid by Asha. He declares Ahura Mazda to be himself the most mindful of all the previously revealed assertions and directions uttered by himself, and fulfilled in the actions of both the Demon-gods of their enemies, and of good or evil men. He is also said to be fully cognisant of what they will do in the future, and to discriminate between what is good and evil as an infallible judge, allotting to us all our destiny in future sufferings or rewards. 5. Addressing Ahura and Asha, and uniting with the Kine's Soul in her supplication, he questions Mazda in his doubt, not in peaceful confidence, as later in the impressive hymn, each verse of which begins with the words, 'This ask I Thee, aright, Ahura! tell me!' but deprecating from himself, and constructively from the Kine, the impending destruction which he sees will justly fall upon the wicked as visited by the discriminating vengeance acknowledged to be Ahura's attribute (see verse 4). 6. At last Ahura, showing the intention of His questions, answers them himself; no regulating lord in full sympathy with the Righteous Order had as yet been discovered or discoverable, but He himself will make a selection. He therefore declares himself as solemnly appointing Zarathustra to that office.

And Zarathustra, inspired by His Good Mind, and guided by His righteousness, will accomplish more than has as yet been done to rally the thrifty community, and settle their virtuous polity upon its desired basis of training and defence. 7. As Zarathustra is a listener in the colloquy between the Deity, the Kine's Soul, and Asha, the Righteous Order, so the other Immortals beside Asha[3], here join in, as if the appointment just made had not been heard, or was incredible (see below). Mazda is indeed declared to have revealed the sacred Word-of-reason in harmony with the consenting Righteousness, and to have provided food for the Kine and

[1] Something like this is implied.

[2] If verses 4, 5, 6, were originally connected.

[3] Or possibly a company of the religious chiefs poetically conceived to be present.

the needy consumers, but who was there adequately endowed with the Good Mind, who could promulgate that Māthra with its revealed directions as to sustenance of both body and mind?

8. Ahura repeats his announcement of Zarathustra, as if to silence the objections.

As Zarathustra alone had heard the doctrines from the voice of inspiration, so he desired to declare them, and had authority to do so, together with a settled position of such a character as to make his statements felt.

9. But an unexpected difficulty arises. The Kine's Soul is by no means impressed by the personality of the individual selected as her guardian. So far from being the demi-god of the other parts of the Avesta, Zarathustra's declarations are characterised by her as 'the voice of a pusillanimous man,' while she, on the contrary, expected one truly kingly in his rank and characteristics, and able to bring his desires to effect, while the Bountiful Immortals (or the attending chieftains), as if they had meant their question in verse 7 to be a question uttered in mere perplexity or contempt, join in with chorus, asking when indeed an effective helper will be provided.

10. Zarathustra, undismayed by the coldness of his reception, enters at once upon his office as priest and prophet, praying Ahura for the people; and recognising the names of the 'Immortals,' Khshathra, Asha, and Vohu Manah, in their original sense, asks Ahura to grant to the people in their straits, a Sovereign Authority established in the Divine Order, and bestowing the needed quiet and happiness for which the suffering provinces, as represented by the Kine's Soul in her wail, had expressed their desire.

And as he prays, he avows his own steadfast confidence in Ahura rather than in the Daêvas, as the prime possessor and bestower of blessings.

11. Then, as if eager to receive full equipment upon the spot, he not only beseeches for the Righteous Order, the Kingly Power of God, and His Good Mind for the masses as represented by the Kine, but asks when they are coming to him, and hastening; and he entreats Ahura to bestow His help at once for the great cause, and to a very abundant degree, upon himself and his associates. (It is singular that the name of Âramaiti does not occur in this section.)

Translation.

(Homage to you, O Sacred Gâthas!)

1. Unto you (O Ahura and Asha!) the Soul of the Kine (our sacred herds and folk) cried aloud: For whom did ye create me, and by[1] whom did ye fashion me? On me comes the assault of wrath, and of violent power, the blow[2] of desolation, audacious insolence, and (thievish)[3] might. None other pasture-giver[4] have I than you, therefore do ye teach me good (tillage) for the fields (my only hope of welfare[5])!

Ahura speaks.

2. Upon this the Creator[6] of the Kine (the holy

[1] K*e* mâ tasha*t* can only mean this here. The Pahlavi translator probably read kahmâi. He has val mûn li tukhshî*d* (?) hômanam.

[2] One might think of 'inertia' as a rendering for remô, (if read), but the afflictions complained of seem rather to imply active violence.

[3] Or read tâyus*k*â (robbery?) with the Pahlavi translation; 'yu' and 'vi' would be written much alike in a manuscript.

[4] Vastâ has been found, as I understand, in some manuscripts. The Persian manuscript of Haug has a curious vâstîrî*d*âr (vâstarî*d*âr?) in the Pahlavi text, which seems to confirm vastâ in the sense given.

[5] As there are very many non-specialists to whom it is important to weigh this present subject as closely as it may be possible, and as everything here is a matter of the keenest questioning among experts, I add occasionally a word-for-word rendering, although necessarily very uncouth: To you the Kine's soul cried-complaining: For whom me did ye fashion? Who me made? Against me assaulting-rapine, violence-and, desolations-[blow], daring-insolence-and, (thievish) might-and (possibly change the text). Not for me a pasture-giver than-you other; therefore to-me teach-ye good (things) for-the-pasture (adj. acc. pl. neut.).

[6] I fear that I cannot follow Haug in his later view, where he follows tradition in rather an extreme manner, rendering 'the cutter (wounder) of the Ox.' Neither Spiegel nor Justi would confide to a later myth to this degree (see Y. XXXI, 9 and XLVI, 9). This is

herds) asked of Righteousness[1]: How (was) thy guardian for the Kine (appointed) by thee when, as having power (over all her fate), ye made her? (In what manner did ye secure) for her, together with pasture, a cattle-chief who was both skilled and likewise energetic? Whom did ye select[2] as her (life's) master who might hurl back the fury of the wicked[3]?

Asha answers.

3. To Him the (Divine Righteousness) answered with[4] his sanctity. (Great was our perplexity); a chieftain who was capable of smiting[5] back (their fury), and who was himself without hate (was not to be obtained by us); among such things as these, those things are not to be known (by beings such as we) which are the influences which approach[6] (and move) the lofty fires[7] (revealing the favour and the will of God[8]).

Of beings He is the mightiest to whom those[9]

mentioned, however, not as complaining of an error, but solely to guard the reader against the mistake of an eminent authority. (See also Roth, Z. D. M. G., Bd. 25, s. 9.)

[1] Observe the personification of righteousness.

[2] Or, 'what salvation-lord,' governed by dâtâ from the preceding line; so also the Pahlavi translator mûn avŏ pavan nadûkîh khû*d*âî. U*s*tâ occurs only here as a verbal form. Supply angha*t* in b.

[3] The Pahlavi aêshmŏ anâêr zani*s*nŏ.

[4] Or read ashem. The Pahlavi has ashavahi*s*tŏ pasukhvŏ gûft. I am not at all inclined to accept vocatives for nominatives in the Gâthas.

[5] Sar-*g*an, compare Verethra*g*an. The Pahlavi indicates this by tanû sardârîh.

[6] Possibly, 'by which he approaches.'

[7] The Pahlavi rôshanŏ î râstŏ.

[8] Cp. Y. XXX, 1: *y*â rao*k*ebî*s* daresatâ urvâzâ.

[9] The Pahlavi indicates a third person; and keredushâ is far the most simply explained as a nom. pl. Recall mâ mashâ and man (?) mathâ. Otherwise, 'to whom I will come with activity and invoking.'

who have performed their actions approach with invocations. (He has no need to ask!)

Zarathustra intervenes [1].

4. The Great Creator [2] (is himself) most mindful of the uttered indications which have been fulfilled beforehand hitherto in the deeds of [3] demon-gods [4] and (good or evil) men, and of those which shall be fulfilled by them [5] hereafter. He Ahura is the discerning arbiter; so shall it be to us [6] as He shall will [7]!

5. Therefore it is that we both, my soul [8] and (the soul) of the mother [9] Kine, (are) making our supplica-

---

[1] A verse or verses may here have fallen out.

[2] I cannot persuade myself to accept the nearly universally accepted comparison of Mazdau and medhâ. See note on p. 104.

[3] Or, 'He has done by Daêvas?' If thus, absolute and not qualified sovereignty would be indicated. See the last line.

[4] Observe that while 'by Daêva-worshippers' would be an admirable rendering for Daêvâis, because more commonplace and therefore safer, it is here impossible on account of mashyâiskâ. We are closely confined to the acceptance of a large idea. Ahura was mindful of what transpired in the deeds of Daêva-gods, and not in those of Daêva-worshippers alone. The inst. must be modified.

[5] As varshaitê is elsewhere used in an active sense, it is possible, but not probable, that a special predestination may be indicated. 'He shall do by means of Daêvas and men.'

[6] 'To us men,' not to us Ameshôspends, of course!

[7] Verbatim. Mazda the-words most-mindful which for have-been-fulfilled before by-means-of- (the actions of) Daêvas-and men-and what-and (shall)-be-done after, He the discriminating lord; so to-us shall-it-be as He shall-choose.

[8] This seems to prove positively that a human being speaks here and in the previous verse; 'the soul of Righteousness' is of course impossible.

[9] Some have referred the word to the root zan obscurely present in it; otherwise a drivable cow; one mature and fit for use. The term used in the Vendîdâd in a common meaning as merely

tions for the two worlds to Ahura, and with hands stretched out in entreaty, when (we pray to the Great Creator[1] with questions in our doubt[2]; (and He will answer).

Not for the righteous liver, not for the thrifty (tiller of the earth), shall there be destruction[3] together with the wicked!

Ahura.

6. Upon this the Lord, the Great Creator, He who understands the mysterious grace[4] by His insight[5], spake thus: Not in this manner[6] is a spiritual master found for us, nor a chieftain moved by Righteousness and appointed (in its spirit); therefore Thee[7] have I named[8] (as such a head) to the diligent tiller of the ground[9]!

---

designating a cow at a certain age, may be the familiar use of an adjective here applied in the ancient Gâtha in a sacred sense.

[1] This passage is one of the strongest for the comparison of Mazdau and medhấ. The sense 'asking wisdom in our doubt,' is admirable. I cannot however accept the comparison.

[2] Pavan gûmânîkîh hampûrsânî; root dî.

[3] The Pahlavi awasînisnîh*, but in other connections fragyâitis might well mean 'continued life;' 'life long endured with the wicked.'

[4] The Pahlavi has vishûpisnŏ, which here affords a better meaning; see however Y. XLVIII, 9. We might read as alternative here, 'knowing the calamity to be averted.'

[5] Uncertain. The Pahlavi however indicates 'discernment.'

[6] One is strongly tempted to read aêvô, 'not a single chief,' but the ancient writing read by the Pahlavi translator had aêvâ ahû.

[7] This indicates that Zarathustra had been the speaker in the previous verses.

[8] Appointed.

[9] Verbatim. Thereupon spake Ahura Mazda knowing the-wonderful (thing) through-insight (?) not thus a master found, nor a ruler righteous-order-from-even from, therefore for thee to-the-thrifty-and to-the-husbandman-and (I) as-a-creator I-have-made.

The Ameshôspends[1].

7. Mazda has created the inspired Word-of-reason which is a Mãthra of fatness (for the offering), the (Divine) Righteousness consenting with Him in his deed. Food he has prepared for the Kine and for the eaters[2], He the one bountiful with his (saving) doctrine; but whom hast Thou, endowed with the Good Mind, who may give forth those (doctrines) by word of mouth to mortals[3]?

Ahura.

8. This man is found for me here who alone[4] has

---

[1] Or a company of the saints conceived to be present.

[2] So some writers, accepting an irregular reading *hv*arushaêibyô after the indication of the Pahlavi translation. Otherwise compare 'rush' (?), uru=ru, and render 'to the estranged.' We have often to stretch the meaning more than this. Converting instructions are elsewhere suggested for 'all mankind.'

[3] The translation of Neryosangh is added here not merely because it is of interest, but because it is, together with the Pahlavi translation, of the last importance in forming correct conclusions. It may be rendered as follows; and the reader may regard it as a specimen, but by no means a particularly favourable one. At the words âzûtôi*s* and maretaêibyô different texts were before him and the Pahlavi translator as well. Those words are elsewhere rendered by the latter *k*arpîh and an*s*ûtââ*n*: This greatest magnitude (sic) of the Mãthra, the Lord produced together with righteousness as his fellow-worker [ ]. The Great Wise One discloses the herds to the eaters; and he discloses also the great matter to the well-taught scholars. Who is thine, who endowed with the best mind, gives the two things, with the mouth to those who are prosecuting studies (sic)? To expect an ancient rendering to be closer would be unreasonable. The errors (as to root) are not errors, but the certain signs of differing MSS. This constantly occurs; and it is hardly necessary to add that sometimes from such supposed mistakes we get the only possible means of recovering the original text.

[4] Repeating the announcement in verse 6. The aêvâ in 6 would incline one to read aêvâ (*ye ne* aêvâ), but the manuscript before the Pahlavi translator read aêvô=khadûk. It is quite out of the question to suppose his aêtûnŏ and khadûk to be accidental. A sharp distinction is made.

hearkened to our enunciations, Zarathustra Spitama! Our mighty and completed acts of grace he desires to enounce for us, for (Me), the Great Creator and for Righteousness; wherefore I will give him the good abode[1] (and authoritative place) of such an one as speaks[2]!

The Geus Urvan.

9. Upon this the Soul of the Kine lamented (: Woe is unto me) since (I have obtained for myself) in my wounding a lord who is powerless to effect (his) wish, the (mere) voice of a feeble and pusillanimous man, whereas I desire one who is lord over his will (and able as one of royal state to bring what he desires to effect[3]).

The Ameshôspends[4].

((Aye,) when shall he ever appear who may bring to her[4] help strong-handed[5]?)

---

[1] So the Pahlavi translator, giving the only critical etymology in his hûdemûnîh, the gloss aside.

[2] The Pahlavi text corrected by the Persian MS. may be rendered as follows: This gift I obtained [ ]. For this one is he who was listening to that which is our teaching, Zartûsht, the Spitâmân. For us, Aûharmazd, and for Aharâyîh is his desire, [that is, that perfectly performed duty, and good works are desired by him]. He recites also a remedy-making (free or erroneous), [that is, he declares a remedy-making against the Drûg who is in the world]; on account of which saying for his word of piety which he utters, they give him a good abode [ ]. (The glosses are often from a later hand and erroneous. Sometimes, however, they contain the truth while the text is futile. I drop them in the present citations when they are of no importance.)

[3] Observe that Zarathustra, like other prophets, met at times little honour from his fellow-countrymen who are here well represented by the voice of the Kine's Soul. (See Y. XLVI, 1.)

[4] Or could not hôi be taken in a reflective sense, and referred to the first person like the possessive sve; see the connection.

[5] Verbatim. Thereupon-and the Kine's Soul wept: (I) who

Zarathustra [1].

10. Do ye, O Ahura and thou, O Righteousness! grant gladness unto these (our disciples), and the sovereign Kingdom (of the Deity) such as (is established) in (His) Good Mind by which one bestows upon them the peaceful amenities of home and quiet happiness (as against the fearful ravages which they suffer [2]), for of these, O Great Creator! I ever thought Thee first possessor [3]!

11. And when shall the (Divine) Righteousness, the Good Mind (of the Lord, and His) Sovereign Power (come) hastening [4] to me (to give me strength for my task and mission), O Great Creator, the Living Lord! (For without his I cannot advance

---

(lament) one-not-able-to-effect-his-wish in-wounding as-a-master (or, I established?) [ ], whom as-against I-wish one wish-controlling-and-effecting-as-a-sovereign. When ever he may-(shall)-be who to her (possibly to-me-myself?) shall-give effected-by-the-hand help.

[1] Zarathustra, having accepted his call to be the Ratu or his substitute, at once interposes with a prayer for his suffering charge.

[2] See verse 1, to which reference is continually made as the chief expression of the sufferings to be remedied.

[3] The Pahlavi without glosses may be rendered as follows: Give ye assistance to these, O Aûharmazd, Ashavahist and Khshatraver! So also Vohûman, who gives him a pleasing habitation, and also joy. I also think that the first gain and obtaining of this is from thee. (With the gloss slightly different; but valman should be rendered according to ahyâ.)

The text literally is as follows: (Do) ye to these, O Ahura! happiness (? possibly strength; see the Pahlavi) grant, O Asha! Khshathra-and (=the Kingdom) such (kingdom as) by Vohu Manah by-which amenities peaceful-joy-and (one) may give-or-establish; I-even of this, O Mazda! Thee I thought foremost possessor.

[4] So the Pahlavi translation indicates; compare gimâ and frâ man (?) mathâ; otherwise mâmashâ = I hasten (to fulfil my mission).

or undertake my toil.) Do ye now therefore assign unto us your aid and in abundance[1] for our great cause. May we be (partakers) of the bountiful grace of these your equals[2] (your counsellors and servants)[3]!

---

[1] The Pahlavi has kabed. For the fundamental idea compare p*ri*ksh + suffix.

[2] The Ameshôspends just mentioned, together with whom Ahura governs and blesses His people. Ahmâ (so conjecturing with Barth.), is also quite sufficiently indicated by the lanman of the Pahlavi. Whether an instrumental *e*hmâ can be accepted is doubtful. The form should be altered.

If *e*hmâ stands, i*s*tem must be understood, or the instrumental taken in a possessive sense.

Ahmâ has no authority from MSS., but is better than anghâmâ, as being nearer the MSS.

[3] As an impartial specimen I render Ner. thus: Whence will that gift come to me, (the gift which is) A*s*avahista, Gvahmana, and Saharevara, [that is, sanctity, the highest (best) mind, and the sovereignty, where is the place of the reward which will thus come to me?]. (Here the translation falls into confusion from an error which is most interesting and instructive, because it is corrected by Ner. in an alternative rendering in the gloss. As has been seldom noticed his original was the Pahlavi word pâ*d*adahi*s*nînê*d*, rather than the Gâthic paitî-zânatâ. This Pahlavi form he could not at first believe to be a second plural. Indeed the Pahlavi glossist may have taken it as a third sg. Neryosangh therefore abortively renders word-for-word as follows: You, O Great Wise One! it offers or presents more excellently through the 'greatest exaltation' (the holy cause). But he recovers himself in the gloss by reading the Pahlavi pâ*d*âdahi*s*nŏ vâdûnyên as an imperative: [Provide a reward through that spotless exaltation (the irreproachable cause)] continuing: Here, O Lord! is the gift (which is) ours, and (which comes) to us from Thee.)

YASNA XXVIII.

PRAYERS CHIEFLY FOR GRACE AND FOR THE WORDS OF REVELATION.

2. Zarathustra, having entered upon the duties of his office (XXIX, 11), composes a liturgy for the use of some of his more eminent colleagues, possibly, but not at all probably, for the original mover in the entire religious effort (see the expressions 'to Zarathustra and to us,' 'to Vîstâspâ and to me,' 'to Frashaostra and to me'). This reciter, whoever he may have been intended to be, is represented as standing in the appropriate place as a priest, with hands stretched toward Ahura, or His Fire, and praying for the possession of spiritual graces from an unselfish motive, and in order that he might appease the grief of the Kine's Soul, for whose relief Zarathustra had just been appointed (see XXIX, 1, 6, 8).

3. He approaches Ahura Mazda, spiritually inspired by the Good Mind as he declares, and asking for attainments and boons for both the bodily and spiritual lives, derived from Righteousness, whereby that personified Righteousness might establish the elect in a beatified state.

4. The personality of the Ameshôspends comes again strongly forward, as it does so often in worship, in addresses in which Righteousness (Asha), the Good Mind (Vohu Manah), Khshathra (the active Power of the Divine Sovereignty), and Âramaiti (practical piety in the souls of believers), are besought to come, as the Vedic Gods so often are, to the appeals of the supplicant, and to his help in the act of worship itself, which is recognised to be the one efficient means for furthering the cause of redemption which is ever held in view.

5. As one who offered his soul to heaven, and would know by actual experience the blessed rewards bestowed by the holy ceremonial and moral actions prescribed by Ahura Mazda, the reciter declares that he will teach on in the effort to propagate the holy Religious Order, and possessed by the one desire for its increase, while power shall last.

6. With a piety as fervent as it is profound, and speaking with great earnestness, he asks Righteousness, as a person, when he shall see him, becoming fully acquainted with the Good Mind of God, the way which leads to Him, and above all with Obedience. But although he addresses these lofty abstractions as persons, it is utterly

out of the question to suppose that he did not speak in the deepest meaning of the words as expressing states of mind, and qualities of character: O thou Divine Righteous Order! (Thus he seems to have meant), O thou divine Righteous Order! when shall I see Thee as if present in my own soul and in those of the people whom Ahura has committed to my charge? When shall I know the Divine Benevolence as made one with the disposition of my congregation? When shall I possess by knowledge that only way to our most bountiful Ahura which is, not a mythical angel Sraosha only, but that angel interpreted 'Obedience to Ahura' (observe the dative). One cannot well exaggerate the religious depth or subjectivity. Then, with a bathos which shows how then as ever superstition could hold its own side by side with the truest piety, he exclaims (if the third line was really so composed by him as it has come down to us); 'By such a prayer as a Māthra spell we can with the greatest vigour repel the unclean beasts and creatures which defile our sanctity, or endanger our lives.'

7. Alluding immediately to this revelation, he beseeches Ahura once more to 'come with His Good Mind,' and to grant, not booty, nor even wealth, but 'Asha-gifts,' and (as a bestower of righteousness) long life and powerful spiritual grace to the leading agent Zarathustra (in all probability the composer of the section), and to himself, the officiating priest with his helpers, in order that, not with carnal weapons, but by his 'lofty' and holy 'words,' they all combined may overcome the torments of the ravagers who had made havoc of the settlements, and who were still liable to overwhelm the faithful with their raids and rapine (see XLIV, 20).

8. With an intentional and interesting alliteration he prays to Asha for an ashi; that is, a blessing, even the strenuously attained-to gifts of the great Benevolence. Âramaiti likewise becomes the object of his petition together with Ahura; and this time for the benefit of Vistâspa the monarch, and for himself that they might hear the gracious Māthras, which is indeed the burden of the entire piece.

9. Once more he affords an early (or the earliest (?)) instance of the rhetorical trick, and fills one line with three 'vahistas,' praying Ahura, as being of one mind with Asha (here, for the first time in the Avesta, called 'the best'), to grant the same blessing; and this time again with an intentional change, 'to himself and to Frashaostra;' and not for this world, but for 'all the duration of the Good Mind,' using the expression in its concrete sense as heaven; for heaven to him consisted in an inward state. (So also elsewhere in the Avesta,

even where the palate and the olfactory nerve are the media of felicity or of torture, there also conciliating language on the one side, or 'vile speech' pointed with finest irony on the other, is equally prominent. It is the mind which chiefly enjoys or suffers.)

10. Deeply sensible of the spiritual benefits for which he is asking, he seems touched with gratitude. Accordingly he adds one more petition, which is, that he and his coadjutors, the three just mentioned, may never anger the indulgent mercy which had granted them their request; and that they may persevere, as they have begun, in the strenuous service of Ahura, Asha, and Vohu Manah. For they are, as he declares, easy to be entreated, and beings who desire to bestow spiritual blessings upon mortals, rather than to exercise merely capricious favour or cruelty, and who also possess the power to bring their benevolence to effect.

11. As if unwilling to trust his own perception as to his real spiritual needs, he prays Ahura 'to fill up his desire,' not with what he, the reciter, may in particular request, but with what He, Ahura, knows to be the gifts of Righteousness and the divine Benevolence. And these gifts are again mainly the holy revelation, for he knows, so he earnestly declares, the words of those mighty three to be never void, and to be a sustenance able indeed to fill up his wishes, giving him more than he has of himself either the intelligence or the grace to ask.

12. Having added, in verse after verse, some particular to heighten the fervour of his request, he sums up all in a final expression, as remarkable for its earnestness as for its depth, and begs Ahura, as one set for ever for the defence of the Righteous Order and the Good Mind (whose hallowed influences he accurately foresaw were destined to endure for ages), to tell him, with His very 'voice of spirit,' in order that he may declare them to the waiting masses, the laws which pervade the moral universe, and according to which it arose. For according to these holy principles and so alone, could he promulgate a system which might reclaim society from its imperfections and the Iranian saint from his sufferings. Ahura who, be it remarked, is alone addressed in this culminating verse, hears and answers by a revelation of these eternal principles, and this answer is contained in chapter XXX. By a thorough comprehension of that most important document, I hold that we may see how it met its purpose as indicated by the capacities and needs of those to whom it was addressed, and how by discriminating truth from falsehood it helped on the defence of Asha, and the founding of the true Benevolence.

Translation.

1. (A strengthening blessing[1] is the thought, a blessing is the word, a blessing is the deed of the righteous Zarathustra. May the Bountiful Immortals[2] accept and help on[3] the chants. Homage to you, O sacred Gâthas[4]!)

2. With venerating (desire) for this (gift) of gracious help, O Mazda[5], and stretching forth my hands (to Thee) I pray for the first (blessing) of (Thy) bountiful Spirit; (that is, I beseech of Thee that my) actions

---

[1] Yânîm cannot well mean 'revealed,' except by the most far-fetched conception. The Indian yâna, as in devayấna, should give the fundamental idea, easily reconcileable as it is with the ancient rendering of the Pahlavi translator.

[2] Notice that the Ameshôspends are mentioned in this early heading. In the Gâthas themselves the name, 'Bountiful Immortals,' does not occur.

[3] Possibly, 'take up and continue on the Gâthas.' Literally, 'seize forth.'

[4] It is hardly necessary to say that this is no part of the Gâthas. It is, however, in the Gâthic dialect, and as it needs not, or perhaps cannot, be considered an intentional imitation, it must be very old.

[5] Vocative with the Vendîdâd Sâdah, otherwise the accumulation of genitives would be suspicious. Ahura is, however, beyond any question elsewhere spoken of as 'the most bounteous Spirit.' The usage is like that of the Semitic scriptures; the Holy Spirit is both God and 'of God.' As to the rendering 'bounteous,' I fear that 'holiest' (so many) is too bold. Ashavan occurs side by side with spe*n*ta as applied to Ahura, and ashavan cannot mean 'righteous' there, but must mean 'holy.' The Pahlavi renders etymologically afzûnîk. Comp. *s*vânta. The sole etymological bases for the meaning 'holy' are presented by the Lithuanian and Ecclesiastical Sclavonic; but, as Justi has well remarked, in the conceptions of the Avesta that which increases the kingdom of Ahura is equivalent to what is holy. 'Bountiful' must therefore be understood in a particular sense, only to be rendered by the words, 'gracious, sacred, and august.'

(toward) all (may be performed) in (the Divine) Righteousness; and with this I implore from Thee the understanding of Thy Benevolent Mind, in order that I may propitiate the Soul of the Kine[1] (our herds and folk, which cries so bitterly to Thee).

3. And therefore, O Great Creator, the Living Lord! (inspired) by Thy Benevolent Mind, I approach You[2], (and beseech of Thee[3]) to grant me (as a bountiful gift) for both the worlds, the corporeal and (for that) of mind, those attainments which are to be derived from the (Divine) Righteousness, and by means of which (that personified Righteousness[4] within us) may introduce those who are its recipients into beatitude and glory[5]!

4. O (thou Divine) Righteousness, and thou Be-

[1] See Y. XXIX, 1.

[2] The plural of majesty, or the literal plural, referring to the Bountiful Immortals as together.

[3] Plural and singular interchange throughout.

[4] Possibly, 'one may introduce.'

[5] See Y. L, 5. *Hvâthrâ* and its allied forms are so often associated with rao*k*ah and the like, that I do not hesitate to accept an Iranian *hv*an=to shine (with Justi). As there is an Indian svar which means 'to roar,' and another 'to shine,' and again a svan=to sound, so in Iranian there is a *hv*an=to sound, and another=to shine, as in asmanem *hv*anva*n*tem. The 'comfortable stone heaven' is difficult. Comfortable, or even 'delectable mountains' (so we should have to say elsewhere), are not very likely to have been recognised or appreciated in the Avesta. 'Glorious beatitude' is a better rendering here. If *hv*âthrâ always means 'comfort,' how comes it that *hv*arenô is said to be *hv*âthrava*t*? 'Comfortable glory' is hardly probable. Compare also the ancient *s*ubha. When it is the fashion to accept a separate Iranian root at every difficulty, small and great, I see no reason for stopping here, where the pressure is considerable. The Pahlavi also may be read to favour my view. (Comp. *hv*eng=*hv*an.)

nevolent Mind (of Deity)! I will worship you, and Ahura Mazda the first[1], for all of whom the Pious ready mind (within us) is[2] causing the imperishable Kingdom to advance. (And while I thus utter my supplications to You), come Ye to my calls to help[3]!

5. (Yea, I will approach You with my supplications, I) who am delivering up (my)[4] mind and soul to that (heavenly) Mount (whither all the redeemed at last must pass[5]), knowing (full well) the holy characteristics and rewards[6] of the (ceremonial and moral) actions (prescribed) by Ahura Mazda. (And)

---

[1] Or, 'having no first' (Roth, reading apourvim).

[2] I am very far from a positive rejection of the forms suggested by the Pahlavi translator, although he should never be pressed on such a point, being often free. As alternative read 'may Piety who bestows increase (fem. participle) come to my calls to give grace.'

[3] The Pahlavi translator, unable to credit '*ye* as=I who' (so also modern authority sometimes with regard to other occurrences of *ye* in this chapter), renders as follows: When I shall be your own (thus for 'worship,' and possibly deceived by the form of the words, ufyânî and nafsman being nearly alike in the Pahlavi character), O Ashavahist and Vohûman! the first [ ], Aûharmazd's also [his own I shall be], through whose unweakened acquisition his rule over them exists [ ], and [hers also I shall be], Spendarmad's, the giver of increase. She comes to me with joy when I invoke her [when I shall call upon you, come ye on toward me with joy]. (A plain and noticeable instance of an alternative rendering in the gloss. The verb was first thought of as a 3rd sing. middle subjunctive, afterwards as an imperative 2nd plural.)

[4] Me*n̄* = m + the nasal vowel, and may represent man, or I think also mām, adverbially for m*e*nâ; or 'mân'='demânê.'

[5] Mount Alborg, where the *K*inva*t* Bridge extends; so also important authority; but we might read m*en*gairê=mângairê (Garô*d*man).

[6] Ashi, a blessing given in reward; so elsewhere.

so long as I am able and may have the power, so long will I teach [1] (Your people concerning these holy deeds to be done by them with faith toward God, and) in the desire (for the coming) of the (Divine) Righteousness (within their souls) [2].

6. And, thou Righteousness! when shall I see [3] thee, knowing the Good Mind (of God), and (above all the personified) Obedience [4] (of our lives which constitutes) the way [5] to the most beneficent Ahura Mazda. (Asking this, I thus beseech thee, for) with this holy word of supplication we most hold off [6] with tongue the flesh-devouring fiends, (the very sign and power of all spiritual foulness) [7]!

---

[1] I think it is better to hold by the parallel passage and the sense of 'teach' here. The Pahlavi has an irregular form which probably means 'I teach,' but might be intended for 'I am taught.'

After the words 'so long as I have the power,' 'I will teach' is rather more natural than 'I will learn.' Haug's rendering of this word has never been accepted. Those most opposed to tradition follow it here. Perhaps, 'I will teach to desire R.'

[2] The Pahlavi translation corrected by MSS. may be rendered thus: He who gives up his soul within Garô*d*mân does so by the aid of Vohûman [ ], and is also intelligent concerning the veneration which belongs to the doers of good works [ ] in that which is Aûharmazd's [religion]; as long as I am a suppliant and have the power, so long do I inculcate the desire of Righteousness [which is, duty and good works].

[3] Kadấ m*ri̥l*ikấ*m* sumánâ abhí khyam (Rv. VII, 86, 2).

[4] Obedience, throughout the Avesta and Parsi literature, guides the soul to heaven.

[5] Or, 'knowing the throne of Ahura' (so the Pahlavi, most scholars following); but the construction would be awkward. 'Finding the way' occurs in the *Ri*ks, and gâtu need not always mean 'place' in the Gâthic, because it has that sense most frequently in the Zend.

[6] Possibly, 'we may teach the foul polluted men.' Or, 'confess the greatest One with Khrafstra(-slaying) tongue.' Perhaps the text is to be amended; yet see XXXIV, 5, 9.

[7] The Pahlavi translation may be rendered thus: O Ashavahist! when do (shall) I see thee? I know this one by means

7. And do Thou, O Lord, the Great Creator! come to me with Thy Good Mind; and do Thou, who bestowest gifts through Thy Righteousness, bestow alike long-lasting life on us. And (that this life may be spent aright, do) Thou by means of Thy lofty words (bestow) the (needed) powerful spiritual help upon Zarathustra and upon us[1], whereby we may overcome[2] the torments of the tormentor.

8. (And) do thou, O (Divine) Righteousness, bestow (upon me) that sacred blessing which is constituted by the attainments of the Good Mind (within my soul)[3]; and do thou also, O Piety! grant unto

---

of a good mind's instruction [that is, I see thee in that time when every man is intelligent because he is pious; but when shall it be?]. And the place of Aûharmazd, when do (shall) I see it, I who am a suppliant for a benefit? That place is known through Srôsh [ ], that greatest of Māthras is to be taught, given forth with tongue to him whose understanding is confused.

[1] It certainly involves a question how the words 'to Zarathustra and to us' can be compatible with Zarathustra's authorship. Vîstâspa and Frashaostra (verses 8, 9) are equally excluded. Who is then the individual who thus refers to himself with others? And is this verse an interpolation, and with it 8 and 9? This last seems to me a very feeble suggestion. Was this piece, together with the rest (for they all are connected), the work of some unnamed man of influence, the true author of Zarathustrianism? I think that there is also little gained by this supposition. There is no particular reason why Zarathustra's name should have come down to us as the chief figure, while that of the prime mover failed to reach us. I should say that the piece was composed by Zarathustra and put into the mouth of a leading priest, or that it was composed with many others under his inspiration. Or, can there have been a school, or family, of Zarathustrians, religious poets, similar to the Vedic seers? (See chap. LIII, 2 Zarathustris Spitâmô.)

[2] This mention of 'overcoming an enemy,' strengthens the probability of my view of vâvarôimaidî (vâurôimaidî).

[3] The Good Mind is now, as we should say, 'the Spirit of God' in the mind of God, and again His Spirit in the human soul.

Vîstâspa and to me our wish; (yea) may'st Thou grant (us), O Mazda, ruler[1] (as Thou art! that grace) whereby we may hear[2] (with understanding) Thy benignant words.

9. That best (of gifts therefore) do I beseech (of Thee), O Thou best (of beings) Ahura! who art one in will with (Thy Divine) Righteousness (within us, likewise), the best[3] (of spirits), desiring it (as I now do) for the (heroic) man Frashaostra, and for me[4], upon whom also may'st Thou bestow it (not for time alone), but for all the ages of Thy Good Mind (that reign of Thy Benevolence which shall be to us as Heaven[5])!

---

[1] The Pahlavi correctly renders pâdakhshâ.

[2] Probably originally heard, inspired words. Compare Manyeus hakâ Thwâ aunghâ, verse 12. So often. Oral communications are figuratively alluded to everywhere. No literal articulation or sound (!) is of course intended. (Or 'sravayaêmâ=proclaim.')

Neryosangh may be rendered as follows: Grant, O Sanctity! this devotion which (results) from the priority (an error from misreading the characters of the Pahlavi, chiefly his original) of the Good Mind [that is, make me so religious that prosperity may result to me from my good conduct]. Grant thou to the perfect mind [in, or to, the earth (so the Parsis understood Âramaiti)] the wish that proceeds from Gustâspa and from my people [ ]. Grant praisers, O great wise One! kings, who may be announcers of your word, and bestowers of arrangements (for the service); [that is, who may teach thy word, and render it progressive].

[3] The earliest occurrence of Asha Vahista. The Pahlavi: 'Since the best thing that Thou hast [Thy Religion] is better than all other things, the best through Righteousness.'

[4] See verses 7 and 8.

[5] In the millennial (sic) renovation as well as in heaven. See chap. XXX, 4, where Vahista Manah is equivalent to heaven. The Pahlavi gloss has: Aîgh Frashôstar va hâvistân î Frashôstar, vad tanû î pasînŏ hamâî nadûkîh padas vâdûn; that is, for Frashôstar and the disciples of Frashôstar for ever, until the final body provide a benefit thereby.

10. And (impressed and moved) by these gifts of strengthening grace[1] (which Thou may'st give in answer to these prayers) may we never anger You, O Ahura Mazda! (nor Thy) Righteousness (within us), nor yet Thy Kindly Mind (toward us), since we have most earnestly made effort (helping to advance Your cause) in the (chanted)[2] offering of Your praisers, for most easy to be invoked (are Ye). (Yours are verily both) the desire for (spiritual) blessings (for us), and the (Divine) Possession (of their power)[3].

11. And therefore do Thou, O Lord, the Great Creator! fill up and satisfy (my[4]) desire with these attainments (of the grace) of Thy Good Mind, which Thou dost know to be derived from Righteousness, (and) which (are verily) sublime[5], for I have known[6]

[1] Possibly, 'may we not anger you with our prayers for these blessings.' Kím me havyám áh*r*i*n*âno gusheta.

[2] That dasemê may now better be referred to a similar root with dasvare, I regard the more probable because the Pahlavi also freely renders as if it so understood. Its author knew the meaning of dasema=da*s*ama. One is reminded of course of the dá*s*a-gva.

[3] The Pahlavi with its peculiar view of anâi*s* (not to be rejected too confidently; see note at another occurrence of it) is interesting (as corrected by the Persian MS.): On account of a not-coming to you, O Aûharmazd! This I would not do [ ]. Ashavahi*s*t also I will not pain for the sake of a blessing; [that is, I do not desire a single blessing which appears displeasing to Ashavahi*s*t (this turn of the sense is followed by some who have hitherto opposed tradition, but I cannot follow it, although I value every hint of the ancient writers). Also Vohûman, the excellent [I do not harass him].

[4] Or, 'to those whom thou seest as creatures (?) of V. fill up the desire with attainments.'

[5] Possibly, 'the righteous,' erethw*e*ng; cp. *ri*tâvânas (?). Pahl. trans. 'î frârûnŏ.'

[6] Possibly, 'I obtain.'

Thine instructions to be never void[1] of their effect (in the struggles) for our (daily) food[2], and therefore worthy objects of desire[3].

12. (Yea, I approach Thee with my prayers, I) who by these (great gifts of grace) will[4] protect (Thy) Divine Righteousness, and (Thy) Good Mind (within us) for ever. And do Thou therefore, O Ahura Mazda! teach me from Thyself, yea, from Thine own mouth of spirit, that I may declare it forth to (these Thy waiting people) by what (powers and according to what laws[5]) the primeval world arose[6]!

---

[1] Ner. has analaso(-a*h*) for asûnâ more correctly than the Pahlavi asû*d*ak.

[2] Or, 'well reaching their aim;' but the Pahlavi translator gives his evidence for the meaning 'food'=khûri*s*nô. Recall the constant prayers for nourishment in the *Ri*ks. And as favouring the ancient translation, see XXIX, 7, where 'food for the eaters' is declared to be the gift of God, who is at the same time 'bounteous with his doctrine.'

[3] Neryosangh: Eva*m* ye dharmasya vettâra*h* * uttamasya*k*a dâter manasa*h* [ ] ekahelayâ * Mahâ*g*ñânin Svâmin! tebhya*h* * pûr*n*a*m* pari*k*inohi * kâma*m*; [kila, [ ] *s*ubha*m* tebhya*h* kuru]. Eva*mk*a igisne*h* * analaso labhatâ*m* khâdyâni vastrâ*n*i*k*a vadanena.

[4] One is tempted to read nip*a*unghê as an infinitive, but the Pahlavi translation anticipates us all with its more critical barâ netrûnam.

[5] This question is answered in Y. XXX.

[6] Ner. improving upon the Pahlavi has as follows: Yadi sunirîksha*n*atayâ dharma*m* pâlayâmi mana*sk*a * uttama*m* sadâpravr*i*ttaye; [kila, *k*et satyasya sadvyâpârasya*k*a rakshâ*m* karomi]. Tvam tat * Mahâ*g*ñânin Svâmin! prakr*i*sh*t*am me *s*ikshâpaya * [ ] vâ*k*i. Ad*ris*ya Tvatto mukhena [sphu*t*aya] antar bhuvane pûrva*m* babhûva [tâm s*ri*sh*t*im me brûhi].

A translation truly remarkable considering the circumstances under which it was made.

YASNA XXX.

THE DOCTRINE OF DUALISM.

1. Accustomed to instruct the masses who throng him on public occasions seeking light, the composer constructs this hymn for similar opportunities. He may be regarded as continuing the thoughts in the close of Y. XXVIII, where he besought Ahura to inform him concerning the origin of the world. He says that he will declare the counsels of God, by which, as we see, he means the great doctrines concerning the origin of good and evil. With these he will declare also the praises, the laudatory portions of the Māthra, and the sacrifices. And he prays that propitious results may be discerned in the heavenly bodies.

2. He further introduces what he has to say by telling the throngs before him that a decisive moment is upon them. They are to choose their religion, and not by acclamation with the foolish decision of a mob, but man by man, each individually for himself. They should therefore arouse themselves and hear with all attention, and gaze at the holy Fire with a good and receptive disposition of mind.

3. He then delivers the earliest statement of dualism which has come down to us. There were two original spirits, and they are called, be it well noted, not two persons, or at least not only two persons, but a better thing, or principle, and a worse one. (The qualifying words are all in the neuter [1].)

At the next sentence they are personified as a pair, each independent in his thoughts, declarations, and actions. Such is the short Theodicy, followed at once by an admonition to those before him to choose the better.

4. These two spirits came together as by natural combination, to make the opposing phenomena of life and its absence, of Heaven and of Hell.

And Hell is described not as a scene of cruelty inflicted on the innocent and the ignorant, but as 'the worst life,' and Heaven as equally remote from a superstitious paradise; that is, as the 'best mental state.'

---

[1] It is also noticeable that the name Angra Mainyu does not occur in this section.

This is the proper Zarathustrian creation. It is undeniably 'abstract,' very, and just in proportion as it lacks colour and myth are its depths visible. The account of it is also very limited. But it must never be forgotten that its existence is the probable proof that very much more of the kind existed beside it. Instead of there being one hymn sung like this, Y. XXX, there were probably many. The two original forces or beings, although separate clearly, come together; but they do not lose their distinction. Their difference remains as clear as their union. 5. They do not blend unrecognisably; for having created the two principles, they choose each his own particular realm. Ahura chooses the righteous order of religion, and with it the pious of all ages. The evil spirit chooses the wicked.

The point and meaning of the entire doctrine is that a good God cannot be responsible for permanent evil; that imperfection and suffering are original, and inherent in the nature of things, and permanently so. The swallowing up of sin and sorrow in ultimate happiness belongs to a later period. It is not Gâthic Zarathustrianism. Evil was the work of an independent being.

The great thinker saw his point; and it was that the Deity Himself could not prevent the evolution of base and revolting moral qualities with their consequent miseries in both victim and aggressor. An evil God was therefore their author.

6. But the blood-feuds of War, not to speak of the theological animosity, were too much for his philosophy. The sage could not regard all men and their circumstances with broad and equable impartiality.

The hated Daêva-worshippers, who were doubtless equally conscientious with the Zarathustrians, are said to have failed of correct discernment.

As they were deliberating, so he recalls, the Worst Mind, a very real although 'abstract' Satan, came upon them, to induce them to choose him and his evil realm. They acceded, becoming furious in their intention to injure human life. This may be regarded as a dramatic, but at the same time, in a moral sense, a philosophical statement of a temptation and fall. (For a later one, with more colour and less truth, see the temptation proper of Zarathustra himself[1], recalling as it does so vividly the temptation in the Gospels.)

7. If we can accept the words ahmâikâ to mean merely 'upon

[1] Comp. Vd. XIX, 1–10. Consider how much time would be required for the name of Zarathrustra to become so involved in myth.

this,' we may hold that the statements proceed without a break. Even a gap of lost verses does not interrupt the sense. The clothing of souls with bodies seems indicated. If so, the doctrine of the Fravashis, otherwise foreign to the Gâthas, may have its origin by inference here, and directly in verse 4. After the creation and first activity of the souls of the Archangels on the one hand, and of the Daêvas on the other, together with their respective human adherents, the one choosing good and the other evil, the remaining Ameshôspends unite with Âramaiti in bestowing a body upon the newly created soul. (So we must conclude from the language.) And the prophet breaks in with the prayer that in the future, and possibly at the Frashakar*d*, the completion of progress, these created souls might possess such advantages as they had when Ahura came at first with his acts of creation; that is, that they might be restored again to a state of sinless happiness, provided with bodies by Âramaiti as at the first. (See Yast XIX, 89.)

8. But, as he implies, and perhaps expresses in a lost verse, vengeance shall come upon the wretched beings who choose the Evil Mind as their master. And it shall come, not in the abstract merely by any means, but as executed by a numerous, if not once predominant party, 'the offspring of the Evil Mind.' And when this shall have been completed (and XXXI, 18 shows us that the weapons to be used to bring it about were not to be those of verbal argument alone) then, as he declares with enthusiasm, 'to God shall be the Kingdom,' a Kingdom established in the Divine Benevolence, which will pervade its organic life, and which will likewise, as the personified 'Immortal,' utter encouragements and commands to its loyal citizens. And these citizens will then not only defeat the Lie-demon, who is the life of the Daêva-party, but they will deliver her up as a captive to the great Genius of Truth, the personified Righteousness. 9. And, as he ardently hoped for the coming of the Kingdom into the hands of Ahura, he as ardently beseeches that he and his coadjutors, the princes already named, may be honoured as the immediate agents in bringing on this 'millennial' completion; nay, he even prays that they may be as Ahuras[1] in merciful services, declaring that all their thoughts were centred in that scene where religious light dwelt as personified in her home.

10. Once more he announces the certain defeat and chastisement of the incarnate falsehood and her adherents, which enables

[1] As the Ahuras of Mazda, the Ameshôspends.

him only the more impressively to describe the rapid reunion of the righteous amid the home-happiness of Heaven.

11. Having delivered his brief but weighty communication, he commends his hearers for learning the holy vows of the Religion on account of the duration of the announced rewards and punishments. They shall be long indeed; and upon their complete inauguration full salvation shall be realised for those who shall have learned and heeded the invaluable truths.

Translation.

1. And now I will proclaim, O ye who are drawing near and seeking[1] to be taught! those animadversions[2] which appertain to Him who knows (all things) whatsoever; the praises which are for Ahura, and the sacrifices (which spring) from the Good Mind, and likewise the benignant meditations inspired by Righteousness. And I pray[3] that propitious results may be seen in the lights.

---

[1] As 'ish' means approaching with desire, the Pahlavi translator has, freely, khvahîsnŏ.

[2] Read mãzdathâ.

[3] So with long ê; but *yaêkâ* (P[11] supported by the Pahl.) may be the lost dual neuter of the pronoun, referring to the two principles discussed below. Yê**kâ* = I pray for, although the most natural rendering grammatically, does not seem so well adapted here, as a prayer for the success of his communication does not harmonise with the otherwise dogmatic statements of the composer. The urvâtâ (vrata) founded upon the doctrine of dualism bring about salvation. They may therefore be touched upon in this introductory verse. And that the heavenly bodies contained indications bearing directly or indirectly upon human destiny seems to have been early an accepted doctrine. (Compare also chap. XXIX, 3, where 'the lofty fires' seem alluded to as moved by the Deity, and this in immediate connection with the discussion of the most important problems concerning the fate of the holy community.) It is, however, not impossible that the lights of the altar may have been meant. (See sû*kâ* in the second verse.) The Pahlavi translation

2. Hear ye then with your ears; see ye the bright flames[1] with the (eyes of the) Better Mind. It is for a decision as to religions, man and man, each individually for himself. Before the great effort of the cause, awake ye[2] (all) to our[3] teaching!

3. Thus are the primeval spirits who as a pair[4] (combining their opposite strivings), and (yet each) independent in his action, have been famed (of old). (They are) a better thing, they two, and a worse[5], as to thought, as to word, and as to deed. And between these two let the wisely acting choose aright. (Choose ye[6]) not (as) the evil-doers[7]!

---

has dên rôshanŏ pavan vênisnŏ hû-ravâkh-manîh. As to yê*kâ or yaêkâ, the Pahlavi does not favour a verbal form. But if the pronoun is accepted, even then change is needed; yaêkâ yâ = yéka yéna is hardly possible. We should be obliged to render: And which two things (were those?) whereby (adverbially) propitious results have been seen in the stars. Others have experienced difficulty, and even ashayaêkâ(?) has been conjecturally suggested for this place and chap. LI, 2. Neither Sp. nor Westg. report a long ê.

[1] Gôshânŏ srûd nyôkhshisnîh [aîghas gôsh barâ vasammûnd]—Zak î rôshanŏ. Otherwise 'with the eye;' but see yâ raokebîs daresatâ urvâzâ. The altar-flame would not unnaturally be mentioned after the heavenly lights.

[2] Literally, '(be ye) wakeful.'

[3] Hardly, 'to teach us.' Possibly, 'to teach this, each one.'

[4] Pahl. transcribes. Notice that paouruyê (pourviyê) is neut.* as are vahyô and akemkâ, which is not lightly to be passed over.

[5] The Pahlavi freely: Benafsman—[aîghsânŏ vinâs va kirfak benafsman barâ yemalelûnd]. They announced themselves as sin and good works. Ner. yau punyam pâpamka svayam avokatâm.

[6] Barâ vigîd. Ner. vibhaktavân*. If a third plural subjunctive, still the force is as if imperative. Possibly it is preterit.

[7] On this important verse I cite Neryosangh. He may be rendered as follows: Thus the two spirits [Hormigda and Âharmana] who uttered first in the world each his own (principle); [that is, who each uttered, one his own good (deed), and the other his own sin], these were a pair, in thought, word, and deed, a highest

* Adverb (?).

4. (Yea) when the two spirits came together at the first to make[1] life, and life's absence[2], and to determine how the world at the last shall be (ordered), for the wicked (Hell) the worst life, for the holy (Heaven) the Best Mental State[3],

5. (Then when they had finished each his part in the deeds of creation, they chose distinctly each his separate realm.) He who was the evil of them both (chose the evil), thereby working[4] the worst of possible results, but the more bounteous spirit[5] chose the

and a degraded one. And of these two, the one endowed with good intelligence [ ] was the distinguisher of the true, and not the one endowed with evil intelligence [ ]. (Both he and the Pahlavi fail to credit a plural form in ere*s* vîshyâtâ with Spiegel and Hübschmann.)

The Gâthic verbatim. Yea (=thereupon) the-two the-two-spirits the-two-first-things which-two two-twins two-self-acting-ones were-heard-of in-thought in-word-and in-deed these-two a-better an-evil-and. Of-which-two-and the wisely-acting (ones) aright may discern, not the evil-acting ones.

[1] The Pahlavi read as an infinitive, dazdê=avŏ zak dahi*s*nŏ. (So also an important authority recently.) Otherwise it has the place of a third dual perfect; 'they two made.' The place of an infinitive is not generally at the end of a sentence in Gâthic. Can it be simply a third singular? '(Each) makes' (*k*amasá karóti).

[2] Pavan zendakîh—va mûni*k* azendakîh. Ner. *g*îvitena*k*a a*g*îvitena*k*a. Observe the singular abstract a*gy*âitî*mk*â, which is not lightly to be passed over. Why not a more ordinary expression? Have we not here an unusual antithesis? The danger is great that by aiming to reduce all to commonplace for the sake of safety, we may demolish many an interesting conception of antiquity.

[3] Observe the subjectivity. These verses settle the question as to the depth of the Zarathu*s*trian hymns. Grammar forces us to see that the composer had large ideas. The entire cast of reflection in the Gâthas tends to be abstract as well as subjective. Not so their invective and partisan exhortations.

[4] Verezyô is a nom. sing. masc., as would seem natural from its position in the sentence. Compare mãthrâi*s* verezyâi*s*.

[5] Observe that Ahura is undoubtedly called speni*s*ta mainyu. Elsewhere we must sometimes render, 'His bountiful spirit.'

(Divine) Righteousness; (yea, He so chose) who clothes upon Himself the firm[1] stones of heaven (as His robe). And He chose likewise them who content Ahura with actions, which (are performed) really in accordance with the faith[2].

6. And between these two spirits the Demon-gods (and they who give them worship) can make no righteous choice[3], since we have beguiled[4] them. As they were questioning and debating in their council[5] the (personified[6]) Worst Mind approached them that he might be chosen. (They made their

---

[1] Zak î sakht sag nihûftŏ âsmâni*k*. Ner. Gâ*dh*ataram* âkâ*s*a*m* dadau.

[2] 'Who with actions really good piously content Ahura.' Let it be noticed that fraore*t* is not independently translated by the Pahlavi. It is freely included in avŏ Aûharmazd; and yet this is supposed by some to be a word-for-word rendering! Ner. praka*t*âi*sk*a karmabhi*h*.

Verbatim. Of-these-two spirits he-chose-to-himself (he)-who (was) the evil (the one) the worst (deeds) working*. The-Righteous-Order (accusative) (chose) the spirit most-bountiful (he-)who the most-firm stones clothes-on-himself, (those) who-and will-content Ahura with real actions believingly Mazda.

(Properly a verbatim rendering is only possible in an inflected language.)

[3] Lâ râstŏ vigînênd. They suffer judicial blindness; a common idea in the Gâthas; compare, 'who holds them from the sight of the truth,' &c.

[4] The root is indicated by va mûni*k* valman*s*ân frîft. I can see no escape from the above rather adventurous rendering. See also dafshnyâ he*n*tû in chap. LIII, 8. Perhaps the idea of injury here preponderates over that of deceit; 'since we have impaired their power.' The choice between a preterit or an improper subjunctive is also difficult. Possibly, 'so that we may fatally deceive them.' Poss. nom. 'deception came upon them, even A. M.'

[5] This recalls Vendîdâd XIX, 45, where the demons assemble in council to consider the advent of Zarathu*s*tra.

[6] Compare verse 4, where Vahi*s*tem Manô equals heaven. The

fatal decision.) And thereupon they rushed together unto the Demon of Fury, that they might pollute[1] the lives of mortals[2].

7. Upon this[3] Âramaiti (the personified Piety of the saints) approached, and with her came the Sovereign Power, the Good Mind, and the Righteous Order. And (to the spiritual creations of good and of evil) Âramaiti gave a body, she the abiding and ever strenuous[4]. And for these (Thy people) so let[5] (that

word is the subject of '*gasat*,' and has the proper place of a nominative in the sentence; cp. Vedic usage.

[1] That they might disease (so literally) the lives of those who had not yet been tempted or fallen.

The Pahlavi: Vîmârînidŏ ahvân î mar*d*ûmân [aîgh, levatman aêshm an*s*ûtâân ahûkînên*d*].

Ner.: Ye nigaghnur bhuvana*m* manushyânâ*m*.

Hübschmann: 'um durch ihn Plagen über das Leben des Menschen zu bringen.'

[2] Verbatim. Of these two spirits not aright may choose the Daêvas, since these we have beguiled (or have injured). To the-questioning ones upon came-he in-order-that he might-be-chosen (subjunctive middle) he-the worst mind. Thereupon to-furious-rapine they rushed-together in-order-that (yena) they might disease (or ruin) the-life of-man.

[3] Or, 'to him;' some unnamed benefactor; hardly 'to us.' The Pahlavi has, avŏ valman, but Ner. has only tatra*k*a. Observe ahmâi in chap. XLIII, 1, and in chap. XLVII.

[4] Root ăn = in. The Pahlavi freely, pavan astûbîh. He seems to have thought of nam + a priv.

Kehrpem is feminine. Ănmâ may be a neuter in apposition.

Otherwise we must accept -mâ as a suffix. Or can kehrpem (corpus) be a neuter here? The clothing of the spirits with corporeal natures enabled them to advance in the development of moral qualities by self-restraint and pursuit. As has been observed in the summary, no Fravashis appear in the Gâthas. Have we here possibly an indication of the pre-existence of souls? If Âramaiti gave a body, it may be inferred that a period elapsed between the acts of the two spirits and this.

[5] That bodies are to be given to the saints as at the first is to

body) be (at the last), O Mazda! as it was when Thou camest first with creations[1]!

8. And (when the great struggle shall have been fought out which began when the Daêvas first seized the Demon of Wrath as their ally[2]), and when the (just) vengeance shall have come upon these wretches, then, O Mazda! the Kingdom shall have been gained for Thee by (Thy) Good Mind (within Thy folk). For to those, O living Lord! does (that Good Mind[3]) utter his command, who will deliver the Demon of the Lie into the two hands[4] of the Righteous Order (as a captive to a destroyer).

9. And may we be such as those who bring on

---

be inferred from Yast XIX, 89. (Which see in part ii of the translations of the Zend-Avesta.)

[1] Verbatim. To-this (to us?)-and with-Khshathra came, with-Manah Vohu, with Asha-and (Âramaiti) thereupon a-body the-continuing gave Âr(a)maiti the strenuous (Âramaiti, or the body, a vigorous and strenuous thing).

Of these thine (or to thee) to let-it (the body)-be as thou-camest in-creations the-first.

[2] See verse 6.

[3] What else can be the subject of sastî?

[4] Observe the pronounced personification of Righteousness. As a matter of course the ultimate sense is more commonplace, as is the case with all poetical matter. 'Into the hands of Asha,' is the same as to say, 'into the power of the servant of God.'

But would this be a proper mode of rendering a line of real though rudely primitive poetry? Such renderings are commentary rather than translation. The Pahlavi may be rendered as follows: Thus also in that creation [in the final body] hatred comes to these haters and sinners; [that is, the avengers shall execute chastisement upon them]. And, therefore, O Aûharmazd! what to thee is the sovereignty, by that (so possibly) shall Vohûman give a reward. Through these, O Aûharmazd! [through the religion of Aûharmazd], when one is instructed in Righteousness, [that is, as to the interests of the pious] then the Drûg is given into one's hand, [the Drûg who is Aharmôk].

this great renovation, and make this world progressive, (till its perfection shall have been reached). (As) the Ahuras of Mazda[1] (even) may we be; (yea, like Thyself), in helpful readiness to meet[2] (Thy people), presenting (benefits[3]) in union with the Righteous Order. For there[4] will our thoughts be (tending) where true wisdom shall abide in her home[5].

10. (And when perfection shall have been attained) then shall the blow of destruction fall upon the Demon of Falsehood, (and her adherents shall perish with her), but swiftest in the happy abode of the Good Mind and of Ahura the righteous saints

---

[1] Otherwise, 'the Ahura-Mazdas,' or, 'O Mazda and the Ahuras!' I think that the most natural rendering according to the grammar should first be given, notwithstanding something uncommon about it. 'All the Ahura-Mazdas,' has been seen by Roth in chapter XXXI, 4.

[2] The Pahlavi has the gloss [aîghsân hamîshakŏ hangaman madam tanû î pasînŏ kûnisnŏ], needlessly enlarged of course, but showing the proper root, which is mit; (so Spiegel.)

[3] Or possibly sustaining (the feeble). The Pahlavi reads simply dedrûnisnŏ.

[4] The Pahlavi renders hathrâ in the Indian sense as asâr*, endlessly; so others elsewhere. Hathrâ and yathrâ are of course distinctly in antithesis.

[5] The Pahlavi mihânŏ, Persian makân. That maêthâ is an adverbial instrumental meaning, 'in one's home,' seems the more probable from the two hathrâ, yathrâ, adverbs of place. Compare, for instance, athrâ-yathrâ in XLVI, 16, where shaêitî follows. Hübschmann, 'Dort mögen (unsre) Sinne sein, wo die Weisheit throut;' see also husitôis in the next verse.

The Parsi-persian MS. has—Aedûnŏ (sic) ham mâ kih ân i tû hastam (sic); [kû ân i tû 'hwês hastam] în—rastâ'hiz kardan andar gihân.

(c) Kih—minisn bêd [kû minisn pah—dârad] as ângâ dânâî hast [kû, â'hir i kîz pah nêkî bih dânad] andar makân.

shall gather, they who proceed in their walk (on earth) in good repute[1] (and honour)[2].

11. Wherefore, O ye men! ye are learning[3] (thus) these religious incitations which Ahura gave in (our) happiness[4] and (our) sorrow[5]. (And ye are also learning) what is the long wounding for the wicked, and the blessings which are in store for the righteous. And when these (shall have begun their course), salvation shall be (your portion[6])!

[1] Pahlavi, 'mûn vâdûnd zak î *s*apîr nâmîkîh=they are creating a good repute,' as if zaze*n*tê were understood in the sense of produce. See the sense 'bear' as given for hâ, Rig-veda 843, 2 (X, 17). The analogy is, however, not strong.

[2] The Pahlavi translation may here be rendered as follows: Thus in that dispensation [in the later body] the Drû*g* [who is Ganrâk Mînavad] will be overthrown [ ] when (his) host is scattered. Thus they move keenly on [to seize the reward], which is attained through the good citizenship of Vohûman [when they shall have dwelt in piety]. They who are creating a good renown are thus moving on toward Aûharmazd and Ashavahi*s*t [that is, the person who is of good repute goes forward to seize the reward].

[3] Once more the anomalous form âmûkhti*s*nŏ meets us in the Pahlavi. May this not be intended to express 'learning,' whereas âmûzi*s*nŏ would express 'teaching?' I hardly think so.

[4] The Pahlavi translation is only remotely if at all responsible for *hv*îti*k*â as=sua sponte. This would require *hv*îti as=**hv*âti with difficulty comparing 'yim' and 'y*e*m'(?). It is generally considered now as=hu+iti; but the letter ﻳﻮ='ﻉ seems doubtful.

[5] Read anitî='with impeded progress.' 'In prosperity or adversity.' But these are conjectures.

[6] The Pahlavi: Aêtûnŏ akhar valman*s*ân aîtŏ nadûkîh. I do not think that we ought to regard the words of the original as expressing universal restoration. But they may well have given the first indication toward this later view. Literally, they state it, but not when correctly understood.

(SUPPLEMENTARY NOTE. The Pahlavi word yômâî which transcribes y*e*snâ in verse 4 cannot mean 'by day.' Its imperfect form induced the translators to translate rûzhâ and bhûmandale, but these scholars, as in many other instances, hinted at a correction.)

YASNA XXXI.

THE PROGRESS AND STRUGGLES OF THE CAUSE.

This composition differs from that in XXX as descending from the more general to the particular, and from the doctrinal to the practical. One might even trace an immediate connection, urvâtâ occurring in the last verse of the one and in the first of the other. It is, of course, very possible that the verses before us are only a remnant of those which originally constituted the piece, and here and there one may have been interpolated from other scriptures.

Some writers prefer to assume a loss of the original text or an addition to it at the smallest change of tone, and to assume also a change of subject with it. I do not regard it as very useful to lay too much stress upon these occurrences.

Whether caused by gaps or interpolations, they do not at all affect the fact that the subject-matter is homogeneous and contemporaneous; and, probably, like many more modern compositions, the verses gain in rhetorical effect by being weeded of repetitions.

We might divide as follows 1, 2, an address to the congregation to be connected with XXX as its concluding words; 3–5, an address to Ahura; 6, an address to the faithful; 7–17, to Ahura; 18, to the congregation; 19, to Ahura; 20, 21, to the congregation; 22, an addition.

Treating the section then as containing homogeneous matter which combines well into a unit, I proceed as follows. The sage chants his hymn in the presence of the multitude as before.

1. He declares that while he is reciting things unwillingly heard by the hostile party, those same truths are valued as the best of existing things by those who are sincerely devoted to Mazda, their good disposition quickening their perception.

2. He then declares that if the truths of the holy Religion are not yet clearly seen by the instrumentalities provided, he will approach them still more effectively in accordance with the especial regulation of the spiritual chieftainship, which Ahura Mazda had prepared in response to the lament of the soul of the Kine; i. e. of the Iranian herds and people possibly as representing the entire holy, or clean, creation upon earth. And he further asserts that this regulation concerns the struggle of the two parties, and will bring the cause of the Righteous Order to a successful issue.

3. Changing his address to Ahura, he proceeds to pray at once

for that satisfying decision which would be the natural result of the regulation just promised, and which could be given by the instrumentality of the Sacred Fire and holy ritual, affording mental keenness to the two contending parties. And he declares that this is the doctrine which should be proclaimed for the conversion of mankind. Here we observe that the Zarathustrian Mazda-worship was aggressive and missionary in its spirit, and in a proselyting sense by no means indifferent to the final destiny of the Gentile world. (The later and traditional system announced indeed the restoration and so the conversion of all men, and that not as an object proposed to the efforts of charity, but as a necessary result (so by inference; see Bundahis (West), pp. 126, 129). I can find no trace of this in the Gâthas.

Here we have only the effort to convert.)

4. Addressing all the Bountiful Immortals, and with the striking title of the Ahuras of Mazda, he prays for the establishment of the 'mighty kingdom' by means of which he might overcome the personified and aggressive falsehood of the opposing and persecuting Daêva-worshippers.

5. In order to enable himself to fulfil his mission, he asks for prophetic and judicial knowledge as to what ought to be done, or as to what is about to happen in the immediate future.

6. He lauds the Mãthra which we may suppose him to recognise as delivered to him afresh in answer to his prayer for prophetic light, and he praises co-ordinately with the Word of God that Sovereign Authority of Ahura, which was to be established in a kingdom where goodness would increase, and be prosperous, if not predominant.

7. He takes the heavenly bodies as evidence of the wisdom of Him who created the Sacred Order personified as the 'Immortal' Asha, and also the Good Mind, his equal. And he ascribes the support and extension of their hallowing influence to Ahura, because He never changes.

8. He reiterates, in expressions which form the basis for another hymn, his conception of Mazda as the supreme object of devotion, as the father of the Good Mind personified as His child, as the creator of the Righteous Order, and as both the controller and the judge of human actions. Therefore the Good Mind and Righteousness are to be worshipped as standing in the closest possible relation to him.

9. He ascribes the 'Immortal' Piety to Him as well. She is His own, and elsewhere His own daughter. He is declared, as in

chapter XXIX, to be the Creator of the Kine, and of Understanding, (His own intelligence), to guide Him in the disposition of the destiny of the holy Iranian people. And according to it He makes the path for the Kine, which as a matter of course has no meaning as applied to bucolics, but is full of meaning when read in view of the wail of the Kine's Soul in chapter XXIX, and of the intervention of the Deity in her behalf, for He actually appointed Zarathustra to meet her necessities. He adds, however, that her free choice is not abolished by the construction 'of this path.' It is elsewhere called the 'religion of the Saviour-prophets,' and she is free to proceed in it, guided by the first prophet, the ideal husbandman, or she can follow the profaner nomad.

10. But he thankfully exclaims that she does not pause in indecision, nor does she choose perversely. She selects the guardian appointed by Ahura, the diligent and pious husbandman, elsewhere identified with Zarathustra himself. He is rich with the spiritual wealth of the Good Mind; and she rejects in his favour the idle and free-booting nomad, excluding him from all share in the sacred religious system.

11. The composer then delineates the struggle which inevitably follows this establishment of the needed means of deliverance. When Mazda has completed the inspiration of doctrines, teaching whither the one endowed with free volition (like the Kine [verse 9]) should direct his choice in action (12), there upon the spot, as it were, the ignorant Daêva-worshipper makes himself heard beside God's spokesman. But the prophet is consoled by the reflection that the pious mind will not question the evil Spirit, or the good Spirit superficially. It searches both the Spirits, questioning them, as it were, in their very home. (Hence it is that Ahura speaks so fully concerning Angra Mainyu, delineating his opposition to Him in extended detail. See XLV, 2.)

13. The composer is still more reanimated by the certainty that Ahura is gazing into the depths of all questions, trivial and profound; which is to say that he observes most closely the men who are discussing them. And he declares that he also sees the cruel injustice of the punishments which the tyrants visit upon the smallest offences, as well as the more flagrant wickedness of those who persecute his adherents without even a pretence of justice.

14. As he recalls the divine forecasting omniscience, he asks Ahura once more concerning the future which was close at hand with its portentous events. And he inquires as to the nature of the veritable and not iniquitous confessions, which were properly due to

be made by the righteous believer in order to avert the impending calamities, and secure the upper hand in the struggle for the throne. And he inquires also as to the proper expiatory prayers which were to be offered by the believer. He does not however fail to inquire analogously concerning the wicked, nor to ask how they, as well as the righteous, shall be situated in the final consummation.

15. Particularising as to the latter, he asks what shall be the punishment for those who succeed in installing an evil monarch, one of the Daêva-party, a prince who cannot exist without the ruthless persecution of the pious husbandman, who repudiates the Lie-demon presiding over the counsels and efforts of the opposing religion.

16. He further asks how and by what actions the wise man may become like Ahura, or his faithful adherent, the expressions used implying deep religious feeling.

17. Striving to arouse the perceptions of his hearers, he inquires as to which one of the two parties holds to the greater or more important religion, the disciple of Asha, the personified Righteous Order Ahura's immediate creature (see above), or the opponent. And he prays that no blind guide may deceive him, or those who belong to him, 'but that the enlightened, yea, even Ahura Himself, may speak to him, and become the indicator and demonstrator of the truth.'

18. Closing this address to the Deity, he turns to the congregation, vehemently forbidding them to listen to the doctrines of his opponents, warning them against the ruin and death which would ensue, and fiercely appealing to the sword.

19. Once more addressing Ahura, he prays that they may on the contrary listen to Him who has power to vindicate the conscientious Zarathustrian, inculcating veracity upon him, and encouraging him in its practice; and this by means of the holy sacrifice, or ordeal of the Fire.

20. He solemnly warns those who would seduce the righteous of their ultimate fate, and adds that their sorrows will be self-induced, if they persevere in their hostility. Their own consciences (as we see from Yast XXII) would not only bring on their ruin, but would form a part of their punishment.

21. On the other hand, happiness and immortality will be the lot of the faithful. And these 'eternal two' will be given to them, accompanied by the fulness of Righteousness, and the exuberant vigour of the Good and Kindly Mind within them and bestowing its blessings upon them.

22. In conclusion he apostrophises the manifest certainty of the truths which he declares, and, addressing Ahura, animates the faithful not merely with the hope of the objective recompense, but with the prospect of being efficient as servants of God.

Translation.

1. These doctrines (therefore) we are earnestly declaring to You as we recite them forth from memory, words (till now) unheard[1] (with faith) by those who by means of the doctrinal vows[2] of the harmful Lie are delivering the settlements of Righteousness to death, but words which are of the best unto those who are heartily devoted to Ahura[3].

2. And if by this means the indubitable truths[4] are not seen in the soul[5], then as better (than these words) I will come to you all (in my person) with

[1] Roth, 'wollen wir Worte künden—ungern gehört von denen, welche nach des Unholds Geboten,' &c. Hübschmann preferring 'wir sprechen Worte nicht anhörbar für diejenigen' (Casuslehre, s. 223). A dative of the pronoun is certainly more natural than the ablative as inst. But on the whole agushtâ seems better in its ordinary sense, although in so rendering we are obliged to supply a word.

[2] Valmansân mûn pavan âfrîngânîh î Drûg zak î Aharâyîh gêhân barâ marenkînênd.

[3] The Pahlavi may be rendered as follows: Both these benedictions, which I (we) recite as yours [the Avesta and Zand], we are teaching by word to him who is no hearer, [to the destroyer of sanctity (the heretical persecutor) [ ]]. Those who utterly slay the world of righteousness through the benedictions of the Drûg [ ], even those might be an excellent thing, if they would cause progress in what belongs to Aûharmazd.

[4] Read perhaps advayâo; see the Pahlavi. Otherwise 'the way' advâo as panthâs; but the participle * does not agree. Compare for meaning kavím ádvayantam, sákhâ ádvayâs.*

[5] The Pahlavi renders 'in the soul' freely by 'believes:' Pavan nikîrisnô lâ hêmnunêdô as pavan zak î agûmânîkîh. The general indications are to be observed.

* Is it a loc.?

that power, and in that way according to which Ahura Mazda knows and appoints His ruler[1], that ruler over both the two (struggling) bands[2], in order that we (in obedience to him), may live according to Righteousness[3].

3. And that keenness, that deciding satisfaction, which Thou hast given by (Thy) Spirit[4], and (Thy) Fire, and by Thy Righteousness (itself) to the two battling[5] (sides), do Thou declare unto us, O Ahura! that vow which is for the seeing[6] (as those endowed with mental light). Yea, do Thou declare this that we may know it, O Mazda! With the tongue of Thy mouth do Thou speak it (that as I preach its mighty truths[7]) I may make all the living believers[8]!

---

[1] Comp. chap. XXIX, 2, where the Ratu is discussed; here the word might be the abstract.

[2] Roth, 'dieser beiden Parteien (Yasna XXXI).'

[3] He repels and condemns the evil, and he hallows and helps the good.

[4] Most striking is the use of mainyu. It is 'the Spirit'=God. It is 'His Spirit.' It is also used of man's spirit.

[5] Or, 'from the two ara*n*i;' but see äsayâo in verse 2. The Pahlavi translator has avŏ patkâr*d*ârânŏ shnâkhtârîh; so uniformly. In Y. XLIII, 12, K5 and most MSS., except K4, and likewise excepting the printed B.V.S., read ranôibyô which excludes the dual form; also the fire is not mentioned there. It is however far from impossible that the present Pahlavi translation may be a growth beyond an earlier one more in accordance with ara*n*i. The strivers, or fighters, might describe the two rubbing-sticks (?).

[6] Aîmar (sic), vigâr*d*âr. This meaning suits the connection admirably. The word is otherwise difficult, and this general sense is followed by some who do not so often cite the Pahlavi translator.

[7] See verse 1.

[8] Roth, 'wie ich alle lebenden bekehren soll.' So also the general indication of the Pahlavi translator. Pavan hûzvânŏ î Lak—zîvandakân harvist-gûn hêmnund. Observe that the religious system contemplated universal proselytism.

4. And when the Divine Righteousness shall be inclined to my appeal[1], and with him all those (remaining ones who are as) Mazda's[2] (own) Ahuras then with the blessedness (of the reward), with (my) Piety and with Thy Best Mind (active within me), I will pray[3] for that mighty Kingdom by whose force[4] we may smite the Lie-demon[5].

5. Aye, do Thou tell me that I may discern it, since through (Thy) Righteous Order the better (lot) is[6] given; tell me this that I may know it with (Thy) Good Mind (as it speaks within me), and that I may ponder[7] that to which these my truths[8] belong (and

[1] The general indications karîtûntâr and bavîhûnam point to the proper sense.

[2] Or, with Roth, 'wenn wirklich sich rufen lassen die Ahura-Mazdas.' Otherwise, 'O Mazda and the Ahuras.' Hübschmann also maintained that Mazd*a*u was here a plural; (see his Y. XXX, 10.)

[3] Roth, rendering ishasâ in accordance with the Pahlavi, 'erbitte ich.'

[4] Mûn pavan zak î valman gûrdîh—khûshî*d*ŏ Drû*g*ŏ aê sufficiently indicates the proper sense. Roth, 'kraft deren wir den Unhold bemeistern mögen.'

[5] The Pahlavi may be rendered thus: Since in that dispensation [in the final body], I shall be an invoker of Ashavahist, and of Aûharmazd also [ ]; and of her who is veneration 'Spendarmad' [ ], I desire [that best of things which is the reward] of Vohûman. Let also that authority which belongs to my people [ ] be from the strong one [ ] by whose fortitude [ ] the Drû*g* is overcome [ ].

[6] Literally, 'Ye gave.'

[7] I am far from sure that the indication of the Pahlavi is not correct here. According to it, when properly understood, we have here an accusative with the infinitive; 'that I should establish.' Its own translation is however avŏ li yehabûnâi. M*en*=man or mãm; *en*(g)=ã the nasal vowel. The Pahl. translator recognises m*en* elsewhere as=mînisnŏ. It was from no ignorance (!) of the particular word that he wrote 'li' here.

[8] Or 'my prophet;' comp. *ri*shi; that is, 'that with which my prophet is concerned.'

of which my prophet speaks; yea), tell me those things, O Mazda Ahura! which may not be, and which may be[1].

6[2]. And that verily shall be the best of all words to Him which the All-(wise one) will[3] declare to me in very deed, that word which is the Mãthra of Welfare and of Immortality (for it proclaims His beneficent power). And to the Great Creator (shall there be) a Realm such as that (whose strength I asked for victory[4]), and which (at the last) shall flourish[5] in its holiness to His (glory[6])!

7. (For He has sovereign control.) He who conceived of these (truths of the Mãthra) as their first (inspirer), (and as He thought their existence they

---

[1] Or, possibly, 'which shall not be, or which shall be.' Is the subjunctive here used to express obligation? Roth has 'was nicht sein soll oder was sein soll.' Ner. may be rendered as follows: Tell it to me distinctly [ ], that which is the highest gift, and which is given to me through sanctity; [that is, because duty and righteousness are fulfilled by me, the best gift of thy reward (is gained) by this means; but how is it possible to make it (actually) one's own?]. Grant me the knowledge through the best mind; [that is, declare that intelligence to me which comes through good conduct], and by which also safety is (secured) to me [ ]. And declare either that which is not, or that which is, O Great Wise One, the Lord! [ ].

[2] An interval of silence seems here to intervene, or lost verses leave an unexplained transition. The sage turns again to the people.

[3] Vao*k*â*t* K4 (Barth.).

[4] See verse 4.

[5] The Pahlavi has Aûharmazd având (sic) khû*d*âyîh *k*and dên valman vakhshê*d* Vohûmanô.

[6] The Parsi-persian MS. is as follows: Û hast buland, kih ân man âgahîhâ (sic) gû-î â*s*kârah [ ] mânsar *i* tamâm raftanî; [kû, tamâm pêdâi*s*n pah râh *i* mânsar bâz ân 'hwê*s*î *i* Hôrmuzd rasêd], kih pah Ṣawâb dârad—bî-marg raftanî aza*s* [ ]. Hôrmuzd —'hudâî *k*and andar û afzayêd Bahman [Kû*s* pâdi*s*âhî pah tan *i* mard—*k*andî (?) Hôrmuzd pah tan mihmân].

(all) as (His) glorious[1] (conceptions first) clothed themselves in the stars[2]), He is through His understanding the Creator[3] of the Righteous Order. And thus likewise He supports His Beneficent Mind (in His saints). And these (holy creatures) may'st Thou cause to prosper by Thy Spirit (since they are Thine own), O Ahura Mazda! Thou who art for every hour the same[4]!

8. Therefore[5], as the first[6] did I conceive of Thee, O Ahura Mazda! as the one to be adored with the mind in the creation, as the Father of the Good Mind within us, when I beheld Thee[7] with my (enlightened) eyes as the veritable maker of our Righteousness, as the Lord of the actions of life[8]!

9. Thine, O Ahura! was Piety; yea, Thine, O Creator of the Kine! was understanding and the

---

[1] Mûnas avŏ rôshanîh gûmîkhtŏ khvârîh. *Hv*âthrâ and khvârîh can hardly mean 'comfortable' here. 'Ease' is the later sense.

[2] Rao*k*ebîs certainly means, with illuminating objects, stars or shining lights.

[3] Hübschmann, 'der Schöpfer des Asha.'—Casuslehre, s. 190.

[4] Pavan mînavadîkîh vakhshînê*d* [ ] mûn kevani*k* ham khû*d*âî.

[5] Compare the frequent expression 'spe*n*tem a*t* Thwâ menhî,' in chap. XLIII.

[6] Roth, 'vornehmsten.'

[7] When I seized Thee (took Thee in) with my eye. The Pahlavi: Amatam [ ] pavan ham*k*ashmîh avŏ ham vakhdûn*d* hômanih.

[8] Dên ahvânŏ pavan kûnisnŏ khû*d*âî hômanih.

Ner. may be rendered as follows: Thus thou wert thought at the first by me, O Great Wise One, the Lord! when thou wert engaged in the production of Gvahmana [ ]. In which (production) they apprehend the father of the Best Mind when they observe him with a full-faced look [ ]. (And thou art the father) of that creation which is manifestly righteous; [that is, thou makest the purer creation good in conduct]. Thou art a King in the world as to action; [that is, where it is fitting to confer a benefit, and also where it is fitting to inflict a punishment, in each of these thou art capable].

Spirit[1], when Thou didst order a path for her (guiding). From the earth's tiller (aided[2]) she goeth[3] (in that allotted way), or from him who was never tiller. (Thy path hath given her choice[4].)

10. (But she did not pause in temptation.) Of the two she chose[5] the husbandman, the thrifty toiler in the fields[6], as a holy master endowed with the Good Mind's wealth[7]. Never, Mazda! shall

---

[1] His spe*n*ta mainyu; otherwise 'spiritual (understanding),' but mainyu is used elsewhere (verse 3 and 7) alone, and certainly not as an adjective even with a substantive understood. The rendering 'spirit' as 'Thy spirit' is suspiciously significant; but what is the help? We are forced by grammar so to translate.

[2] The ablative has this force as in Ashâ*t* ha*k*â.

[3] I can hardly accede to an infinitive here: -tê is a rare infinitive termination in Gâthic. Also the infinitive seldom falls to the end of the sentence. The Pahlavi has yâtûnê*d*, a present; but the Pahlavi should never be positively cited for the forms, as it is free.

[4] Observe that we are forced by every dictate of logic and common sense to avoid the commonplace rendering here. Cattle do not have 'paths' made for them, nor do they cry aloud for an overseer, or complain at the appointment of one who does not appear to them promising; nor is it one main effort of religion 'to content the soul of cattle.' Cattle, as the chief article of wealth, are taken to signify all civic life. The 'path' is the path for the people to walk in, securing safety for soul and life and herds. The adhvan is 'the way' which 'is the religious characteristics and teachings of the prophets' (XXXIV, 13).

[5] Observe that this cow (some would say 'ox') chooses her master, unlike other cattle. But observe also, what is more interesting, that she seems reconciled to the guardian appointed by Ahura. In Y. XXIX, 9, she actually 'wept' at the naming of the pusillanimous Zarathu*s*tra, desiring a kingly potentate. Now, however, we see that she must have dried her tears, as she is satisfied with the simple workman whom he represents notwithstanding high rank.

[6] In the later Avesta this first vâstrya f*s*uya*n*t is declared to be Zarathu*s*tra.

[7] Mûn f*s*uîh pavan Vohûmanô.

the thieving[1] nomad share the good creed[2]. (For the Kine's choice would bestow it[3]!)

11. (And this doctrine was the first of rules to regulate our actions. Yet the opposer speaks beside Thee.) For when first, O Ahura Mazda! Thou didst create the (holy) settlements, and didst reveal the religious laws[4]; and when Thou gavest (us) understanding from Thine own mind, and madest our (full) bodily life[5], and (didst thus determine) actions (by Thy power), and didst moreover deliver to us (nearer) injunctions whereby (as by a rule) the wisher may place his choices[6],

12. (There strife at once arose, and still is raging.) There (beside Thy prophet) the truthful or liar, the enlightened or unenlightened, lifts his voice (to utter

---

[1] Pahlavi davāsahak; Ner. pratârayitre.

[2] Khûpŏ-hôshmûrisnîh. 'Judicial blindness' is everywhere indicated. (The wicked are kept from the sight of the truth.) Hübschm., Casuslehre, 'der frohen Botschaft.'

[3] This seems implied.

[4] Or, 'madest the worlds and the souls (?).'

[5] Geldner admirably 'flesh.' The Pahlavi: tanû-hômandânŏ gân yehabûnd. Notice that 'bodily life or flesh' is mentioned after 'understanding.' Compare Y. XXX, 7, where Âramaiti gives 'a body' after previous creations.

[6] The Pahlavi has the following interesting gloss: [That is, even the actions and teachings of the pious are given forth by thee; and this was also given in this wisdom of thy mind]. And when there is a person in whom there is a desire for the other world, that desire is granted to him by thee; [that is, what is necessary when he is arriving in the other world, this which is thus required (or desired) by him at that time, is given by thee—through that which is thy mind and wisdom]. Although not able to follow the indications of the Pahlavi fully, I think that there is no question but that we have an important statement in the last line. It does not seem to me possible to render less profoundly than 'where the wisher may place his choices,' his religious preferences and beliefs, including all moral volition.

his faith), and with devoted mind and heart[1]. (But without hindrance from this striving, or pausing with feeble search[2], our) Piety steadily[3] questions the two spirits[4] (not here on earth) but (there in the spirit-world) where (they dwell as) in their home[5].

13. (Yea, my Piety questions searchingly, for Thou, O Maker! hast Thy view on all; we cannot question lightly.) What questions are asked which are open[6] (permitted to our thoughts), or what questions (are asked) which are furtive[7] (hiding themselves from the light), or (what decision soever we may make, and the man) who for the smallest sin binds on the heaviest penance, on all[8] with Thy glittering eye(s) as a righteous guard Thou art gazing[9]!

---

[1] Avŏ zak libbemman.

[2] See verse 13.

[3] Pavan hagismŏ î: the Persian MS. (Haug XII, b) transliterates khêzismŏ: Ner. has mano-utthânena (sic). Or, 'immediately.'

[4] The evil as well as the good spirit is questioned. The two spirits of Y. XXX, 3–6 were here inspiring the conflict.

[5] The Pahlavi unvaryingly in the sense of mihânŏ [-as gâs tamman yehevûnêdŏ]; Ner. paralokanivâsân. See Y. XXX, 9; XXXIII, 9; XXXIV, 6. A questioning which was lightly made would indicate a willingness to tamper with error. The Persian MS. following the Pahlavi has: Ânga bâng *i* buland ân *i* durûgh guftâr [Ganâ Mînû] wa ân ham *i* râst guftâr [Hôrmuzd], &c. But Neryosangh is more accurate or literal: Atra bumbâm* karoti [antar gagati], mithyâvaktâ vâ satyavaktâ vâ, &c.

[6] Pavan zak î âshkârakŏ.

[7] Nîhânîk.

[8] Thou seest even the questions and decisions of our thoughts as to matters which are simple or difficult, permitted or occult.

[9] I have not followed what may yet possibly be a valuable and correct hint of tradition. I render Neryosangh: He who asks through what is open [through righteousness], or he who asks through what is secret [through sin]; or he (also) who through, or on account of, a little sin which has been committed, commits the great one to secure a purification; [that is, who for the sake of purification necessary on account of a little sin which has been committed, commits a greater one, in order that the first may not

14. This then I will ask Thee, O Ahura Mazda! (as I seek Thy counsel once again[1]). What events are coming now, and what events shall come in the future[2]; and what prayers with debt-confessions[3] are offered with[4] the offerings of the holy? And what (are the awards) for the wicked? And how shall they be in the (final) state[5] of completion[6]?

15. And I would ask Thee this, O Mazda! (concerning the coadjutor of the wicked): What is the award[7] for him who prepares the throne[8] for the evil, for the evil-doer[9], O Ahura! for him who cannot else reclaim[10] his life, not else save[11] with lawless

become known], upon these two, each of them, look with thy two eyes. [Over sins and righteous actions thou art in one way, everywhere and again, the Lord.] The concretes here may give the right indication.

[1] See verse 5.

[2] Mûn ma*d*ô, mûni*k* yâmtûnê*d*ô, 'What has come? And what is coming?'

[3] Mûn âvâm.

[4] Ha*k*â in the Indian sense.

[5] Angar*d*îkîh, the judgment; but Ner. vipâkatâ, consummation.

[6] Neryosangh has as follows: Tad dvitaya*m* tvatta*h** p*rikkh*âmi, Svâmin! yad âgata*m*, âyâti*k*a, yo* *rinam* dadate dânebhya*h* *pu*n*yâtmane [Hormigdâya yathâ yugyate dâtu*m*], ye*k*a, Mahâg*ñ*ânin! durgatimadbhya*h*; katha*m* teshâ*m* asti vipâkatâ* eva*m* [kila, ya*h* tat kurute, tasmai nidâne prasâdadâna*m* ki*m* bhavati, ya*sk*a tat kurute, tasmai*k*a ki*m* bhavatî 'ti; me brûhi!] This seems to me very close, far more so than we have any right to expect as a general rule from a Parsi living in India, and only five or six centuries ago, too late for 'tradition,' and too early for close criticism.

[7] Roth, 'Ich frage—was die Strafe ist?'

[8] The head of a party seems to have been plotting to introduce a hostile sovereign.

[9] Î dû*s*-kûni*s*nô.

[10] The Pahlavi translator, nîvîdînê*d*ô, (otherwise nivêkînê*d*, which I much suspect has become confused with nîvîdînê*d*ô through a clerical blunder); Ner. labhate. They both refer vînastî to vid (so Justi) followed by most. Roth (Yasna XXXI, p. 11), 'der sein Brot nicht findet ohne Gewalthat an der Heerde.'

[11] The Pahlavi translator sees the root han in the sense of

harm to the tiller's herd, to the pious husbandman's flock, who speaks no word with lying, (who abjures the Lie-demon's faith[1])?

16. Yea, I would ask Thee such a thing as this: How such an one as he who, with wise action, has striven to promote (Thy holy) Rule[2] over house, and region, and province, in the Righteous Order and in truth, how he may become like Thee[3], O Great Creator, Living Lord? And when he may so become, (this also I would ask), and in what actions living he may so be[4]?

17. And which of the (religions) is the greater (and the more prevailing[5] as to these questions which thus concern the soul?) Is it that which the

---

acquisition, and not from ignorance of the sense given above. In another place, he renders vigîd min; (see XLVII, 5.)

[1] Neryosangh may be rendered as follows: Thus I ask thee: What is for him who seizes upon destruction, and who provides the sovereignty for the wicked [ ], and commits that evil action, O Lord! from which he does not acquire life even through a bribe* (so meaning), [ ] and who is a calamity to the man who acts for herds and men removing calamities from them [ ]?

[2] Roth, 'der die Herrschaft über Hof Gau und Land um das rechte zu fördern hat.'

[3] Pahlavi, Lak hâvand; Neryosangh, tvattulyo; Roth, 'deiner werth.'

[4] I render the Sanskrit of Neryosangh thus (it improves on the Pahlavi): I ask (thee) thus: How [dost thou bestow] the sovereignty upon one when he is beneficently wise? [ ] (in the body) of him who, through the increase of sanctity, is no opposer (of prosperity) in provinces or villages; [that is, with him who is discharging his duty and performing acts of sanctity. He is this teacher's teacher, he does not contend]. Thine equal, O Great Wise One, the Lord! thus is he verily, who (is such) in action, [who is thus Thine equal through activity].

[5] Possibly mazyô has the sense of mazista in chap. L, 1. There 'the most prevailing' seems to be the proper rendering.

righteous believes, or the wicked[1]? (Let then our questionings cease.) Let the enlightened (alone) speak to the enlightened. Let not the ignorant (further) deceive us, (high though he may lift his voice[2]). Do Thou thyself, O Ahura Mazda! declare[3] to us (the truth) as Thy Good Mind's full revealer.

18. (And you, ye assembled throngs!) let not a man of you lend a hearing to Māthra, or to command of that sinner[4] (ignorant[5] as he is), for home, village, region, and province he would deliver to ruin[6] and death. But (fly ye to arms without hearing), and hew ye them all with the halberd[7]!

---

[1] Literally, 'Which of the two (creeds as) the greater does the righteous (the believing saint) or the wicked (opponent) believe?'

[2] See verse 12.

[3] Or with others 'be Thou'; but the gloss of the Pahlavi translation contains an explanation which may well afford the true solution as in so many instances in which he is both consciously and inadvertently followed. It reads [aîghmânŏ barâ khavîtûnînŏ—]. May we not see an az=ah in the form, or at least a separate Iranian root, as also in azdâ (L, 1), where the Pahlavi translator gives the same explanation admirably suited to the context.

Neryosangh: Which is it, the pure of soul, or the wicked who teaches as the great one? [ ] The intelligent speaks to the intelligent [ ]. Be not thou ignorant after this; because (ignorance is) from the deceiver. Instruct us, O Great Wise One, the Lord! [ ] Furnish us with a sign through the Best Mind; [that is, make me steadfast in good conduct through the recognition of the dîn]. Such renderings may suffice to show that an examination of these ancient translations in our search for hints is imperative. Yet the practice prevails of omitting a knowledge of the Pahlavi language, on which not only the oldest translation of the Avesta, but also the irregular Sanskrit of Neryosangh, closely depends.

[4] Jolly, 'Keiner von euch höre auf die Lieder und Gebote des Lügners.' Roth, 'Rath und Befehle.'

[5] Compare evîdvâo in verse 17.

[6] Dûs-rûbisnîh.

[7] Sazê*d* sanêh, 'prepare the sabre.' It was however a two-handed weapon; see Y. LVI, 12, (4 Sp.).

The Parsi-persian MS.: Wa ma kas aêdûn az sumâ kih û

19. Let them hear Him who conceived of the Righteous Order for the worlds, the (all)-wise One, O Ahura! For truthful speech He rules with absolute sway over words, and ever free of tongue (to guide us in our way[1]). By Thy shining flame[2] (He doth guide us[3], Thine altar's flame with its signs of decision and of grace) sent forth for the good of the strivers[4].

20. (But, O ye listening men!) he who renders

---

darwand mânsar *s*unawad wa âmû'btis*n* (sic); [kû az Âs*m*ôkân (?) Awestâ wa Zand ma *s*unawad], *k*ih andar—ma*h*all *s*ahar wa deh dehad bad-raftis*n* wa marg ân *i* Âs*m*ô*gh*; aêdûn (sic) ôs*â*n Âs*m*ô*gh*ân râ sâzad silâ*h*. (Again very close.)

[1] So conjecturally.

[2] Compare chap. XXX, 2. 'Behold ye the flames with the better mind;' possibly, also chap. XXX, 1, 'the signs in the lights seen friendly.'

[3] According to the grammatical forms the agent here must be a divine being, as *ye* ma*n*tâ ashem ahûbi*s* (see verse 7) is characteristic of the Deity. The vocative, strange as it may seem, does not necessarily exclude Ahura, as the subject referred to in *ye*. Several analogous cases occur. The Deity may here however represent His prophet, as the Daêvas do their worshippers in the later Avesta. Some writers force the language into a reference to the human subject for the sake of the greatly to be desired simplicity.

One places Ahurâ in the instrumental, a case in which the Almighty seldom appears. The above translation needs no alternative, as the language would be the same whoever *ye* refers to.

[4] See note on verse 3, and read as alternative 'from the two ara*n*i.' As an inferior rendering of tradition I cite Neryosangh here: The matter should be heard (taking gûshtâ as a third singular in a subjunctive sense); [that is, a study should be made of it by him] who is even (in any degree) acquainted with the righteous design of Hormigda for both the worlds. He is independent in the literal truth of his words, in his freedom of speech, [and his fear has no existence]. Thy brilliant fire gives the explanation to the contenders. [It makes purity and impurity evident.]

the saint deceived[1], for him shall be later destruction[2]. Long life shall be his lot in the darkness; foul shall be his food; his speech shall be of the lowest[3]. And this, which is such a life[4] as your own, O ye vile! your (perverted) conscience through your own deeds will bring[5] you[6]!

21. But Ahura Mazda will give both Universal Weal and Immortality[7] in the fulness of His Righteous Order, and from himself[8] as the head[9] of Dominion (within His saints). And He will likewise give the Good Mind's vigorous might[10] to him who in spirit and deeds is His friend[11], (and with faith fulfils his vows[12]).

---

[1] I follow the admirable lead of the Pahlavi here, as the previous verse mentions veracity. Its indication is pavan frîfisnŏ, freely.

[2] I differ with diffidence from the hint of the Pahlavi here (as elsewhere). It has shîvan=tears, which however is free for 'calamity' and 'sorrow.' Nom. sing.; see its position.

[3] Anâk rûbisnîh yemalelûnêdŏ. This, placed together with such passages as XLVI, 11, XLIX, 11, and LI, 13, formed the basis for the more complete Yast XXII.

[4] Others prefer 'place,' but see âyû in line b.

[5] 'Has led on'?

[6] I cite Ner.: He who betrays the pure through his fraud, may (deceit) be (also his portion) at the last; [that is, let it be so afterwards; it is in his soul]. Long is his journey, and his arrival is in darkness; and evil food and increasing lawlessness is his [ ]. Darkness is your world, O ye wicked! your in-bred deeds, and your dîn, are leading you on.

[7] That Ameretatâ*t* means more than long life is clear from amesha.

[8] Afas nafsman patîh. The Gâthic would be more literally perhaps 'from His own Dominion.'

[9] Sardârîh.

[10] Vazdvarîh; Ner. pîvaratvam.

[11] One naturally thinks of urvatha (vratha), as having something of the sense of vratyá. But usage compels also the sense of friendship. Hübschmann, Casuslehre, s. 259, 'der durch Gesinnung und Thaten sich ihm als freund erweist.'

[12] Ner.: Mahâg*ñ*ânî dadau Svâmî* avirdâdât* amirdâdât sa*m*pûr-

22. And to the wise are these things clear as to the one discerning with his mind (not blinded by the perverter[1]). With Thy Good Mind and Thy (holy) Kingdom he follows the Righteous Order both in his words and his actions. And to Thee, O Ahura Mazda! such a man shall be the most helpful and vigorous being[2] (for he serves with every power[3])!

---

*n*atva*m* pu*n*yâtmane [ ] ni*g*a*m* prabhutva*m* râ*g*ñe * âdhipatyena [ ] uttamena pîvaratva*m* manasâ [-tasmâi dadate], yo ni*g*asya adr*ís*-yamûrte*h* karma*n*â mitra*m*.

[1] So according to frequent indications.

[2] Tanû aîtŏ. Ner.: Sa te—mitram asti niveditatanu*h*.

[3] See chap. XXXIII, 14. The Pahlavi translator renders freely as follows: Manifest things (so possibly; otherwise 'manifestly') (are) these to (so a MS. not yet elsewhere compared) the wise when according to his understanding he disposes and reflects, [that is, he who meditates with thought upon that which his lord and dastur declares to him]. Good is the King for whom they would effect righteousness in word and deed, the man whose body is a bearer of Thee, O Aûharmazd!

YASNA XXXII.

THE STRUGGLE IS CONTINUED IN THE MIDST OF REVERSES.

1. The same author may well be supposed to continue. The first stanzas have been lost, but we observe that the subject of the section is still face to face with the Daêva party. He seems to see them arrayed and engaged in hostile devotions. But he is not intimidated. The friendship of Ahura is before his mind, and he expresses his desire that he and his colleagues may become, or continue, His apostles, notwithstanding the temporal sorrows which, according to XLIII, 11, we see that he clearly anticipated as the portion of those who would propagate the holy faith.

2. Mazda answers him, and through him his followers, as established in His spiritual sovereignty, accepting the devotion of their piety with commendations and implied encouragements. He whom they would serve is supreme; they need not fear.

3. After reporting this response of Ahura, the composer turns with vehemence toward the Daêvas, poetically conceived to be present as if before their adherents, who also, according to verse 1, are supposed to be in sight (or are dramatically so conceived) celebrating their profane devotions; and he addresses them as the 'very seed' of Satan. Their worshippers belong to the religious falsehood and perversity. And they have persistently propagated their evil creed, which is in consequence spreading.

4. They have, so he acknowledges with grief, perverted men's minds, making them spokesmen for themselves, and in consequence deserters from the great Kindly Disposition of Ahura Mazda, and outcasts, fallen from His understanding.

5. They have destroyed the hopes of mankind for a happy life upon earth, and for Immortality in heaven. And in this they are not only the seed of the Evil Mind personified, but his servants rallying at his word.

6. Their leader is striving energetically, so he mournfully bewails, to effect his evil ends; but it is time that he should recall the counteracting measures of Ahura. His holy doctrines are to be announced, and their authority established by the divine Khshathra, His Sovereign Power personified.

7. The composer then contemplates with religious irony the infatuated security of the wretched delinquents whom he is apostrophising. Not a man of them knows the destruction which awaits him, and which, as he intimates, is close at hand, but Ahura, he significantly exclaims, is aware of it. And it will be proportionably severe. The blindness of sinners to danger seems as definite a judgment upon them in his estimate as their blindness to the truth.

8. To point his anger with an instance he names the apostate Yima, whom he supposes to have erred in first introducing the consumption of the flesh of cattle. He disavows community with him as with them all, declaring himself separate from them in Ahura's sight.

9. He acknowledges that their leader has to a certain degree defeated his teachings, and impaired the just estimates of life which he had striven to form within the people, (or that he will do this if not checked), declaring also that he had made inroads upon his property, which was sacred to the holy cause. And he cries aloud to Ahura and to Asha with the words of his very soul.

10. He repeats that their leader threatens to invalidate his teachings, blaspheming the supreme object of nature, the Sun, together with the sacred Kine, injuring the productive land, and carrying murder among the saints.

11. He utters his bitter wail in view of attempted slaughter, and actual spiritual opposition. He points out the plots among the powerful and their illegal confiscation of inheritances, as well those of women as those of men. And he declares that his opponents are endeavouring to injure his adherents, as if repelled by the best spiritual qualities which an individual could possess.

12. He announces the solemn judgment of God upon it all, especially reprobating those who deal treacherously against the mystical Kine; that is, the holy herds and people, and apostrophising those who prefer the Gr*e*hma above the saving and sanctifying Asha, and the Kingdom of the Lie-demon above the Divine Khshathra.

13. He declares that Gr*e*hma, an opposing chief, desired that evil kingdom in the abode of the personified Hell. And he cannot refrain from adding that he also enviously desires to share in the holy apostleship. But, as he severely rejoins, the messenger of God will hold him afar from the sight of the (Divine) Righteousness. He can have no share in the Faith.

(Here it may be noticed that we have some data for presenting the main features of the struggle. In several instances, centring perhaps in the actual description of a battle in XLIV, 15, 16, we see traces of the closeness of the controversy. In XLIV, 15, the two hosts seem to be closing in regular lines for the 'holy vows themselves.' Here, on the other hand, we read of willing complaint or 'regretful desire,' while judicial blindness is referred to over and over again under various phrases. One might suppose that the Daêva-party were very near the Zarathustrians in many of their religious peculiarities, but that they could not accede to, or understand, the dualism. After the manner of Pagans they implicated the Gods in their sins. (Compare the drunken Indra.) At all events a bitter and violent war of doctrines was waging with both speech and weapons. I think it looks like the struggle 'of two parties' who each claimed to be the proper representative of some similar form of faith, similar, of course I mean, outwardly.)

14. Deploring the establishment of the Kavis who approach with stratagems and false teachings to aid the opposing party, the composer declares that they say that the Kine herself is to be injured instead of blessed by the very fire-priest who kindles[1] the altar-flame.

15. He supports himself however with the hope of ultimate success, and with the prospect of his reward, when he and his fellow-labourers should be gloriously borne to heaven by Weal and Immortality, the 'eternal two,' who not only, as we see, bear saints to bliss, but also constitute the beatitude of heaven itself.

16. He confides all at last to Ahura, who is able to control all events, and to solve all doubts, and who will support his servants in bringing the wicked to vengeance by means of verbal instructions and commands.

Translation.

(That rival-monarch (thus we may supply the sense of lost verses) for whom some are plotting to secure the sovereignty, and who, once in power, would deliver over home, village, town, and province to ruin and to death[2], is active in his efforts, and offer-

[1] See, however, the notes.

[2] Compare XXXI, 15, 18.

ing the devotions of his false religion to accomplish his ends.) 1. His[1] lord-kinsman will pray[2] (as I Zarathustra prayed), and his labouring villagers, with his (trusted) peers, and his (fellow) Daêva-worshippers[3]. But in my mind is the friendship[4] of Ahura Mazda, the Great Creator, the living Lord; and Thine heralds, O Ahura! may we be; may we hold back[5] those who hate and who offend You!

2. To these (for whom the prophet spake) Ahura Mazda answered, ruling[6] as He does through His Good Mind (within their souls), He replied from His Sovereign Power, our good friend (as he is) through His surpassing[7] Righteousness: We have accepted

---

[1] Some prominent teacher, representing the entire Daêva-party, is alluded to; see verses 6, 7, 9, 10.

[2] Compare yâsâ in XXVIII, 2.

[3] Or, 'his are the Daêvas;' but the verb yâsa*t* perhaps affords a sufficient expression for Daêvâ; yâsen or he*n*tî may be understood. We may also understand the Daêvas here, as the embodied Daêvas, in the manner in which the pious worshipper is called Vohu Manah. That Daêva should however be used quite simply for Daêva-worshipper in this early composition is not probable. In the later Avesta it is frequent usage.

[4] Or, 'the friend;' I recoil as much as possible from abstracts, but the Pahlavi has hû-ravâkh-manîh, and Geldner admirably proposed brahman.

[5] Aîgh*s*ân min Lekûm lakhvâr yakhsenunêm; so the Pahlavi translation, first venturing on the meaning 'holding back from;' dar in the sense of pâ, which latter in Iranian can mean hold back from advantages as well as from misfortunes. High modern authority coincides with the most ancient authority on this latter point. It is apt to be a subject of scepticism with some who neglect the evidence of tradition.

[6] 'Pavan sardârîh î Vohûman;' Ner. svâmitâyâm *. It seems difficult to apply the meaning 'being as a refuge' here; see the following 'from His Kingdom.'

[7] Lit. 'glorious.' This casts light upon the expression *hv*anvaitî*s* verezô.

your good and bountiful Piety, and we have chosen her; ours shall she be[1]!

3. But you, O ye Daêvas! are all a seed from the Evil Mind[2]. He who offers sacrifice[3] to You the most[4] is of the Lie-demon, and (he is a child) of perversion[5]. In advance[6] (are your) deceits whereby ye are famed in the sevenfold[7] earth!

4. For ye (are) confusing our thoughts[8], whereby men, giving forth the worst deeds, will speak[9], as of

---

[1] Aîgh Spendarma*d* Lekûm râî *s*apîr dôshêm [bûndak mînis*nî*h] zak î lanman aîtŏ [aîghmânŏ pavan tanû mâhmân yehevûnâ*d*].

Neryosangh: To these the Great Wise (One), the Lord, answered in the lordship of the highest (best) mind; [that is, if, or since, Gvahmana had arrived, as a guest, within (their) body]; from Saharevara he answered [ ] through (their) righteousness, from the well-inclined, and through good conduct, [if truly good conduct had arrived as a guest within (their) body]. And he said: I befriend your Earth (so Âramaiti was later understood), the perfect-minded one, and your highest one; she is mine [ ].

[2] Compare Yasna XXX, 6. Where the Daêvas are approached by the worst mind as they are consulting.

[3] As those who offer sacrifice to these Daêvas are mentioned separately, we are forced to concede a large idea to the composer. He addresses the Daêvas as poetically conceived to be present, and not merely their worshippers as in verse 1. And this must have its weight in the exegesis of other passages.

[4] The Pahlavi translator has kabed. Or ma*s* for mashyô (?).

[5] Or possibly arrogance, avarmînis*n*tar; Ner. apamanastaras*k*a.

[6] Sâtûnînê*d* freely, but indicating the root. The word is a locative.

[7] The seven karshvars, or quarters of the earth, were already known.

[8] I correct frô m*e* (=man) mathâ (adj. nom. pl.; compare yimâ keredushâ and mâ mashâ). I do so after the admirable reading of the Pahlavi translator, a*s* frâz mînis*n*ŏ var*d*înê*d* [aîgha*s* barâ frîfê*d*, afa*s* mînis*n*ŏ barâ avŏ vinâs kar*d*anŏ var*d*înê*d*]. Ner. prak*ri*sh*t*am mana*h*—mathnâti. Notice that a*k*is*t*â is awkward as a masc., although I have so rendered as more personal.

[9] Vakhshye*n*tê stood in the ancient writing used by the Pahlavi translator, as also now in some of our surviving MSS.; otherwise

the Demon-gods beloved, forsaken by the Good Mind[1], (far) astray from the understanding of the Great Creator, the Living Lord, and (far astray) from His Righteousness!

5. Therefore ye would[2] beguile mankind of happy life[3] (upon earth) and of Immortality (beyond it), since the Evil Spirit (has ruled) you with his evil mind. Yea, he has ruled[4] you, (ye) who are of the Demon-gods, and with an evil word unto action, as his ruler[5] (governs) the wicked[6]!

---

reading vakhshe*n*tê with Justi and most others, and mîmathâ with Bartholomae: 'Ye have caused that men who produce the worst results are flourishing, loved of the Daêvas (as they are).' But in the Casuslehre, Hübschmann preferred 'sie sprechen was den Devas angenehm ist,' also reading vakhshe*n*tê (?) (page 240).

[1] So the Pahlavi also indicates a*s*ân Vohûman sîzd; Ner. Gvahmana*h** dûre* âste.

[2] Improper subjunctive; otherwise ye (have) beguiled.

[3] The Pahlavi also freely frîfê*d* an*s*ûtâân pavan hû-zîvi*s*nîh.

[4] Fra*k*inas far from necessarily means 'gave'; 'assigned,' 'indicated' renders it more closely. The Pahlavi has here correctly, but freely, *k*âshê*d*.

[5] The Pahlavi has here *s*alîtâîh for khshayô, and in XXVIII, 8 it has pâ*d*akhshâ for khshayâ. I do not think that the word is an accusative there. A simple accusative does not so naturally fall to the end of the sentence in Gâthic; it is generally in apposition when so situated. The nominatives tend toward the end of the sentence.

[6] Ner.: It is through both of these that he is deceiving (sic, unable to follow the Pahlavi which probably renders as a second plural; see mûn lekûm) mankind in regard to prosperity and immortality, [(saying) if it is possible to live, immortality lies in our path]. Since he is yours, O ye base-minded! O ye base Devas! he is inculcating the lowest actions [ ] of the miscreants; he says that sovereignty [is from Âharmana; (that is, the sovereignty) of certain ones (meaning over every one)].

The Gâthic verbatim is as follows: Therefore ye beguiled (would beguile) man of-happy-life, of-immortality-and since you with-evil mind (you) who-(are)-and Daêvas' (worshippers) the evil-and spirit with an-evil (-word as concerning) action with-word (rules), by

6. Full of crime (your leader) has desired to destroy[1] us, wherefore he is famed, (and his doctrine is declared); but if this be so of these, then in the same manner, O Ahura! Thou possessest[2] (because Thou knowest) the true (teachings) in Thy memory[3]. And in Thy kingdom and Thy Righteous Order I will establish Thy precepts (in Thy name)[4].

7. Among these wretched beings[5] (this their leader[6]) knows not that those things[7] which are de-

---

which (same) means (has-)commanded the wicked (his) ruler (nom. sing. masc.; see Y. XXVIII, 8). The nom., as in Vedic, at the end.

[1] Or, Full of crime ye have striven to attain your ends (?) by those things which are reported. (If verse 5 originally preceded) *e*nakh*s*tâ would naturally be regarded as a singular as paouru-aênâo is an impossible plural masculine. It might, however, be a singular used collectively. In that case we could put the verb in the plural with verse 5 in view. As to concrete or abstract, the first is obviously correct, and is also so rendered by the Pahlavi translation.

[2] Vid (with the perf. vaêdâ) seems to occur in the Gâthas in this sense. Or, 'Thou knowest with the Best Mind.'

[3] Or 'in the memorised recital;' Ner. praka*t*a*m* kalayati.

[4] Parsi-persian MS.: Bisyâr kînah-varzandah kînah 'hwâhad, [kû*s* wanâh-kârân pâdafrâh kûnêd], kih, guft + srûd îstêd [kih guft îstêd]; kû, kih ô*s*ân bî-*s*umâr [kû, pâdafrâh pah ân zamân tamâm bih kunand, kih ruwân bâz ân tan dehad]. Ẓâhir *s*umâr-kunandah Hôrmuzd [kû pah wanâh wa kirfah *s*umâr-kunand]; wân *i* buland âgâh pah Bahman [muzd dânad; kû ân kih bâyad dâdan]. Pah ân *i* Tû *i* *S*umâ, Hôrmuzd! 'hudâ, ân *i* Ṣawâb âmû'htan bih dânêstuwân (sic vid); [kih *S*umâ padi*s*âhî tamâm bih bêd + ya'hnî + bâ*s*ad, har kas pah nêkî âgâh bih bâ*s*ad].

[5] The Pahlavi has kînîkânŏ.

[6] The *h*v*a*êtu of the first verse, the du*s*sasti of the ninth, &c.

[7] The Pahlavi curiously errs with his rôshanŏ = clear; Ner. parishphu*t*atara*h*. It would be straining a point to call him free in interpreting what is 'collected' and so 'obvious' as 'clear.' We must, however, never forget that the supposed error of the Pahlavi is sometimes the reflex of our own (often necessary) ignorance. Vîdv*a*u must refer back to the same subject as ahyâ in the first verse, or possibly to Aka Manah, going a step further back.

clared as victorious[1] (by his allies) are bound together for the smiting; yea, those things by which he was famed (as victorious) by his (blade of) glittering iron[2]. But the utter destruction[3] of those things Thou, O Ahura Mazda! knowest[4], most surely[5]!

8. Of these wretched beings[6] Yima Vîvanghusha was famed to be; he who, desiring to content[7] our men, was eating kine's flesh in its pieces. But from[8] (such as) these, O Ahura Mazda! in Thy discerning discrimination, am I (to be seen as distinct[9]).

---

[1] Possibly, 'which are by Thee announced as destined and proper to be smitten.' The Pahlavi has mûn zanisnŏ âmûkhtênd (sic). Jôyâ=jâyâ to jan, as âkâyia is to kan.

[2] Compare other allusions to weapons, snaithisâ, and possibly dakhshtem.

[3] So also the Pahlavi, ristak and pâdafrâs.

[4] Naêkît vîdvau and vaêdistô ahî are in antithesis and emphatic.

[5] A literal rendering of this difficult verse would be as follows: Of these wretches, nothing knowing (is he that) for the smiting (dat. jâ, jan; cp. form Sk. jâ, jan) (are) the-collected-things, which things (as) victorious (read jayâ) are declared forth, by which (things) he has been heard (of) through glittering iron, of which things Thou, O-Ahura! the ruin, O-Mazda! most knowing art. Others take senghaitê in the sense of 'cut' (?) and render very differently.

[6] The Pahlavi has shedâân; Ner. tân dveshinah.

[7] Or 'teaching,' so the Pahlavi; Ner. samâsvâdayati.

[8] The Pahlavi translator hits the true rendering here: 'from among these I am chosen out by Thee.' Otherwise we have a question: Am I of these? The allusion is to the fall of Yima. As to the first eating of the flesh of beasts, recall Genesis ix. 3. Some have rendered: With regard to these I am of Thine opinion, O Mazda (?).

[9] The Pahlavi may be rendered as follows: Among (of) these demons Yima of the Vîvanhânas is famed to have been a wicked scourge. It was he who taught men thus: Eat ye our flesh in pieces [wide as the breast, long as the arm—(or better with West, 'in lapfuls and armfuls')]. From among these [ ] I am chosen out by Thee, O Aûharmazd! hereafter; [that is, even by Thee I am considered as good].

9. An evil teacher (as that leader is), he will[1] destroy (our) doctrines, and by his teachings he will pervert the (true) understanding of life, seizing away[2] (from me) my riches[3], the choice and real wealth of (Thy) Good Mind. To You and to Asha, O Ahura Mazda! am I therefore crying with the voice of my spirit's[4] (need)!

10. Aye, this man will destroy my doctrines (indeed, for he blasphemes the highest of creatures that live or are made). He declares that the (sacred) Kine[5] and the Sun are the worst of things which eye can see; and he will offer the gifts of the wicked (as priest to their Demon-gods). And at the last he will parch[6] our meadows with drought, and will hurl his mace at Thy saint (who may fall before his arms[7]).

---

[1] An improper subjunctive. Otherwise: He (has) destroyed (not irretrievably, of course; the case was not decided, and finally issued favourably).

[2] Apô—ya*n*tâ; otherwise 'they would take'; Ner. apaharati.

[3] Zak î li îshtî avôrtô [—khvâstak î pavan dastôbar].

[4] Pavan valman*s*ân milayâ î mînavadîhâ; Ner. vâgbhi*h* mânasav*ri*ttyâ aham—âkrandaye (not following our present Pahlavi text, the gloss however). Observe that in reading Ner. we by no means ipso facto read the Pahlavi, either in correct translation, or as following our texts. Compare XLVI, 2.

[5] One thinks somewhat of the familiar foes of the Vedic kine; but there can be of course no connection. The Iranian sacred Cow did not represent the rain cloud, at least not at all directly.

[6] Read viyâpa*t* as a demon. without sign: 'v' was miswritten for 'y' as often 'y' for 'v.' The Pahlavi language, not to speak of the Pahlavi translation, suggests it. How are we to account for the word vîyâvânînê*d*? We should not arrest our philology at the Zend and Sanskrit. The long vowel is most awkward for a comparison with the Indian vap=shear. And I think that 'destroying the means of irrigation' gives as good a meaning as 'shearing the land.' Notice that elsewhere a more correct form appears, vîâpôtemem (Vd. III, 15, (51 Sp.))=viyâpôtemem.

[7] Literally, 'he will discharge his club at the righteous.'

11. Yea, these will destroy my life, for they consult with the great[1] of the wicked (enlightening themselves by their words[2]). And they are seizing away[3] the gifts of inherited treasures[4] from both household-lord and from house-wife[5]; (wretched men that they are), and those who will fiercely wound (my folk, repelled and in no way kindly moved) by the better mind of the holy[6].

12. (But Ahura will speak His rebuke, for) as to those doctrines which (such) men may be (basely) delivering[7] (repelled) by the holiest action, (and galled[8] by its sacred truth) God hath said: Evil (are they! Yea, unto these He hath said it) who have slain the Kine's life by a blessing (and have cursed her while they offered to help her[9]), men by whom Gr*e*hmas are loved above Righteousness, and the Karpans,

---

[1] The Pahlavi translator erroneous, or free, as to *k*ikôitere*s*, indicates the proper sense of mazibî*s* by pavan masâî [—pavan pêshpâyîh va pâspâyîh—]; but Neryosangh, mahattayâ-pura*h*-saratayâ.

[2] Comp. XXXI, 12, 'there high his voice lifts the truthful or liar.'

[3] Literally, 'he takes.'

[4] Riknah vindi*s*nŏ.

[5] Ka*d*ak-khû*d*âî gabrâ nê*s*man.

[6] Reshînênd; see V, 10. The ablative of the cause, comp. ashâ*t* ha*k*â; otherwise with Hübschm., 'Sie die Schaden nehmen mögen durch den besten heiligen Geist, O Mazda!' (Casuslehre, s. 241.)

[7] The Pahlavi translator had probably before him a text reading rashayen; he renders freely rêsh srâyênd. With such a text which is far preferable to the one afforded by the MSS. we may read: Whereby (yéna) men will be opposing and retarding (literally wounding) the doctrines which (are derived) from the best (moral and ceremonial) action; but to these men Mazda declared: Evil (are ye). See the previous verse.

[8] See the previous verse.

[9] The Pahlavi has hû-ravâkh-manîh yemalelûnd.

and the Throne of those who have wished[1] for the Demon of lies (as their deity and friend[2]).

13. And the Gr*e*hma will seek[3] for these things by means of his (evil) kingdom[4] in the abode of (Hell which is[5]) the Worst Mind (who both are together) the destroyers of life, and who, O Mazda! will bewail[6] with glad but (envious) wish the message of Thy prophet. (But he will not abate with his vengeance), he will hold them afar from the sight[7] of the truth!

14. His is Gr*e*hma[8]; aye, his! And to (oppose) Thee[9] he will establish the Kavis and (their) scheming

---

[1] So also indicated by the Pahlavi bavîhûnd.

[2] There is elsewhere evidence enough of a desire to encroach upon the truth.

[3] So also indicated by bavîhûnê*d*.

[4] Or, 'which kingdoms, sovereign power.'

[5] Comp. XXX 6.

[6] Or, 'they gladly complain;' so also the Pahlavi: Mûn—garzi*s*nŏ kâmak. The singular *g*îgereza*t* is difficult with yaê*k*â. Many would alter the text at once, and the temptation is great.

[7] Hübschm., '*ye* î*s* pâ*t* daresâ*t* ashahyâ der sie abhalte vom Schauen des Asha' (Casus. 241). So of XLVI, 4. So also indicated by pâ*d*ênd mîn nikêzi*s*nŏ î Aharâyîh; evidence of a struggle, or at least of a desire on the part of a rival party to possess themselves of some religious privilege or precedence. See the previous verse; also XXXI, 10: Never, O Mazda! never shall the thriftless and thieving one share the good doctrine. See still further XLIV, 15, where the two hosts meet in hostility 'on account of the doctrinal vows.'

[8] Gr*e*hma appertains to, but is not the particular evil teacher referred to throughout. The Pahlavi translator indicates bribery as the meaning of the word. Possibly some impious chieftain is meant whose procedure was of that nature. The word occurs in the plural.

[9] Â hôi; Thwôi is difficult. Or (see Y. XLIV, 14), 'Thine understanding has subdued the Kavis.' The Pahlavi translator renders masîh, as if he had read ahuthwôi, offering an important alternative.

plans. Their deeds[1] of power are but deceits since they have come as an aid to the wicked[2], and since he has been (falsely) said (to be set) to conquer the Kine[3], he who shall kindle that (very) help of grace which removes our death afar, (and lightens Thy saving flame).

15. And therefore will I drive from hence[4] the Karpans' and Kavis' disciples. And after these (have thus been driven hence and away) then these (my princely aiding saints) whom they (now) render no longer rulers at will over life, (and deprive of their absolute power), these shall be borne (at

---

Read: In his dominion he has established the Kavis and their intended plans. Reading hôithôi, 'his G. is to be bound.'

[1] The predecessors of the Pahlavi translator seem to have understood the word var(e)*k*au as conveying the idea of power rather than that of brilliancy. He renders freely pavan zak î varzânân avârûnŏ dânâkânŏ. Supposing the text to stand, and not supplying a formation from var(e)z, we may hold that there existed a var(e)*k* beside var(e)z, as there undoubtedly was a har(e)*k* (see hareke) beside har(e)z. This casts light on the Vedic vár*k*as.

[2] Amati*k* pa*d*îrênd valman darvandân aîyyârîh [ ] amati*k* avŏ Tôra zani*s*nŏ gûftŏ. The sufferings of the sacred Kine form the central thought of much that occurs.

[3] Can gâu*s* be a genitive here? But if a nominative, must not *ye* refer to it? How then could the Kine 'kindle' the aid of grace? A genitive looks difficult. It is, however, accepted by Spiegel, although he renders differently from my translation. The Pahlavi may give us invaluable relief here by restoring the text. The ancient translator read vao*k*aya*t*. Reading with him, we might render: When the Kine which (yâ?) caused a death-removing help to be declared, was said to be meet for subjection (or slaying, reading an infinitive from *g*an). This rendering is more probable than that from sao*k*aya*t*. The Kine distinctly caused this help to be declared. See XXIX. But I make it a matter of principle to follow the MSS. in a first translation, where that is at all possible.

[4] The Pahlavi translator differs greatly here, having taken anâi*s* with adverbial force, and as possessing the a priv. (they being

last) by the (immortal[1]) two to the home of (Thy) Good Mind (in Heaven)[2]!

16. (And) this entire[3] (reward of the righteous) is from that Best One who teaches[4] in the wide (mental) light of the pious[5], ruling (as supreme), O Mazda Ahura[6]! whose are my woes and my doubt-

---

not inclined). He also read somewhat as follows: anâis avaênî(?) as *ye*=from his non-inclination he was blind who (belongs to the Karpan and to the Kavi). Whether a truer text is indicated by him here is doubtful on account of XLIV, 13, and its nâshâmâ; but the unvarying explanation of the Kavis as blind probably derives its origin from some such reading here, or elsewhere in lost documents.

Certainly if âi*s* can be used as a particle, anâi*s* is not altogether impossible in some such sense. Moreover, the Pahlavi translation here and elsewhere has afforded us such a multitude of valuable concretes, that we shall do well to think twice before we reject its most startling suggestions. Lit. trl. 'what (things are) of the K.'

[1] The Pahlavi translation gives a fine suggestion in the concrete sense here; seeing the dual âbyâ, it explains it as referring to Haurvatâ*t* and Ameretatâ*t*, which is very probably correct. So Spiegel also renders. It is very difficult to decide in which sense *yeng* dai*n*tî nôi*t* jyâte*u*s khshayamane*ng* vasô is to be taken. If in an evil sense (as vas*e*-khshaya*n*t is sometimes elsewhere taken) one might think of such a rendering as this: I have driven the Karpans' and Kavis' disciples hence to those (evil rulers) whom they (my servants) render no longer wanton tyrants over life. But these (my champion saints) shall be borne by the two to the home of Thy Good Mind. But strict grammar demands of us that tôi should refer back to *yeng*. Accordingly I suggest as above first.

[2] Observe that Vohu Manah equals heaven. Recall XXX, 4, 'but for the holy Vahi*s*ta Manah; that is heaven.'

[3] The Pahlavi has ham; Neryosangh has sarvam.

[4] Reading sâ*k*(a)yăs*k*î*t* (P[11], s*k*yas*k*î*t*; Pahlavi, âmûkhti*s*nŏ (sic); Ner., *s*ikshâpa*n*am). Otherwise syas*k*î*t*, which may well mean 'lying, reposing' in the wide (mental) light of the pious (or of the offering). Geldner lately admirably suggests a 2nd sg.

[5] Pavan farâkhû hûshîh.

[6] If this 'best one' is the Ratu of XXXIII, 1, all is grammatically clear; but the expressions are rather strong in view of

ings[1] (yea, they lie in His power to heal), when I shall make (my prophets) men to be sought[2] for the harm of the wicked. And this I shall do by the word of my mouth (to defend and avenge my saints)!

XLVIII, 9, where similar language is certainly applied to Ahura. If Ahura is here meant, we have only one instance more to add to the many in which Ahura is spoken of in the third person, with an address to Him thrown in. See the differing views of XLV, 11. Possibly the 'Best One' was Ahura's Spe*n*ta Mainyu.

[1] Zak î pavan gûmânîkîh. As to âithi, âithiva*n*t seems to prove that its meaning must be calamity also in this place. Otherwise one is strongly tempted to heed the vigorous indication of the Pahlavi translator. Here and in XLVIII, 9, he renders 'manifest,' 'what is clear in the midst of my doubt.' The etymology would be far simpler. Alternatively dvaêthâ = terror (bî).

[2] Valman î pûmman khvâstâr. The Pahlavi sees 'to be desired' in ishy*eng*. Otherwise one might render: I will cause (verbal) missiles (comp. zastâ-i*s*tâi*s*) to be cast forth from the mouth for the harm of the wicked.

(SUPPLEMENTARY NOTE. 'Parch with drought' in verse 10 may be regarded as having figurative application. The destruction of the means of irrigation, so often resorted to in the same regions later, would point also to a literal sense, but 'waste our meadows like drought' is a safer expression. See further vîvâpa*t*, and vîvâpem = viyâpa*t*, viyâpem.)

YASNA XXXIII.

Prayers, Hopes, and Self-Consecration.

Brighter times seem to have arrived. The vengeance so confidently promised in the close of XXXII is described as near at hand. In fact the first three verses seem to belong as much to XXXII as to the present chapter. They remind one of the choruses of attending saints, or 'Immortals,' in XXIX, perfectly germane to the connection, but referring in the third person to a speaker who closes the last chapter with a first, and who begins again with a first in verse 4. The propriety of a division of chapters here rests upon the fact that the thought comes to a climax at XXXII, 16, beginning afresh at XXXIII, 4. Whether Zarathustra, or the chief composer, whatever his name may have been, composed these three verses relating, as they do, to himself, and put them into the mouth of another, or whether their grammatical form indicates another author, is difficult to determine. I doubt very greatly whether either the expressions 'I approach,' 'I offer,' &c., or the words 'he will act,' 'let him be in Asha's pastures,' are at all meant to express more than some modern hymns which use 'I' and 'he.' Both are in constant employment in anthology with no change in the person indicated. 'I' and 'Thy servant' are merely verbal variations. Here, however, the change is somewhat marked by the allusion to the chastisement of the wicked just previously mentioned in XXXII, 16. 1. It is to be noticed that the strictest canon with the original, as indeed with the later, Zarathustrians of the Avesta was the 'primeval law.' Unquestionably the precepts understood as following from the dualistic principle were intended; that is to say, no trifling with any form of evil, least of all with a foreign creed, was to be tolerated. Ahura has no share in the evolution of anything corrupt. We may even add that He had no power to prevent either sin or sorrow, although He possessed all conceivable power to oppose them. According to these fundamental laws, then, the Ratu is said to act, as sternly severe upon the evil as he is beneficent to the saint. 2. The fierce hostilities hitherto pursued are more than justified. The injury of the wicked by denouncing, planning, or by physical violence, is on a par with advising the good. They who pursue the enemies of Ahura are actually operating in love to God, and sacrificing to religion itself.

3. And accordingly the reciter is made to pray in this immediate connection for a sincere and useful friend (a vahista) to the believer, to whichever class he may belong, whether chief, allied peer, or villager, a friend spiritually enlightened (vîdâs), and, according to Ahura's prescript (XXIX, 2), keen, persevering, and brave in the cultivation of cattle (thwakhshanghâ gavôi). 'Let such an one as this, so asked for by the Lord himself, so needed by the Kine, let him,' he prays, 'be supported in his holy toil for us. Let him till and tend, not in the pastures of our valleys only, but in the spiritual pastures of the Divine Benevolence where the mystic kine is grazing.'

4. Taking up the peculiar 'I who' of XXVIII, the composer returns to the first person, continuing in that form with little exception until the last verse, which, naming Zarathustra in the third person, implies (if it is not an addition, which, however, it may be) that Zarathustra had been the speaker throughout. As it is highly probable that the author who uses this 'I who' is the same who uses it in XXVIII, and if we may take verse 14 as fair evidence that Zarathustra is the speaker here, we acquire some additional grounds for believing that the person who wrote (if we can apply such an expression to the author) the words 'to Zarathustra and to us,' as well as 'to Vîstâspa and to me,' and 'to Frashaostra and to me,' was universally recognised to be Zarathustra himself composing a piece to be recited by another. As if in response to the expression in verse 3, recalling that although a vahista (a best one) to some of each class (verse 1) he was no contenter of the wicked (XLIII, 15), he begins a prayer which is only completed by its izyâ in verse 6, and which gathers force by each preceding profession of fidelity. And true to a practical dualism, he first abjures the leading sin of disobedience to God, and of arrogance, discontent, and dishonesty toward man, accompanied (as it seems to have been) with neglect of the all-important duties to the cattle who shared the sanctity of 'the soul' of their representative. And perhaps it is this practical severity of dualism as opposed to the more facile 'lying' of the opposed religion, which was the cause of that high reputation of the Persians for veracity, which was grouped with avoiding debt by Herodotus among the virtues of the race.

5. I, he goes on to say, or to imply, I who not only abjure disobedience, insolence, complaint, and lying, but especially invoke the great genius who is Obedience himself, Obedience toward God, (Thee), endeavouring as I do by this abjuration and prayer to attain, not to a 'hundred autumns' of booty and glory, but to a long life in the kingdom which was established in the spirit of

the Divine Benevolence, and to paths not only for the war-cart, or for commerce, but to those rigidly straight paths of moral purity in which Ahura dwells, 6. I, he adds once more, who am thus Thine actually invoking (zbayâ) invoker, 'straight' like the paths (erezus), I am seeking with longing (kayâ) to know from that Best Spirit (Thy Spenta Mainyu?) animated once more by that best mind, to know-what? Shall we regard it as a bathos when we read that he thus with cumulative urgency prays to know what the Best Spirit thought should be done for the recovery and perfection of the fields? If we turn back to XXIX, 1, we shall see that the identical word (vâstryâ) describes the original want of the kine's soul. It was vohû vâstryâ which she implored as her salvation; and it was the sacred agriculturist who alone could afford it, and who as the 'diligent tiller of the earth' always remained the typical saint. And as his useful deeds in reclaiming, irrigating, and cultivating land, were justly ranked among the first services of a human being, and as the last preparation of the gathered grain was perhaps humorously, but yet pungently, said to make the Daêvas start, and shriek, and fly (see Vendîdâd III, 32, Sp. 165), and as further, a life from the fruits of the earth to this day constitutes the main difference between those who live by murderous theft and those who live honestly in nearly the same regions, I think we may not only see no bathos here, but on the contrary admire the robust sense of this early religion[1], and say that a knowledge as to a true policy in the department of agriculture was one of the wisest possible desires, and the most of all things worthy of a 'sight of Mazda and of consultation with Him.' How the fields had better be worked, and how the people could best be kept from bloody freebooting as aggressors or as victims, this involved Ahura's Righteous Order, Benevolence, Power, and Piety, the four energising Immortals all at once. And this only could secure the other two rewarding personifications, Welfare and Immortality.

7. Having prayed for that which is the first virtue of civilised existence, work (verezyêidyâi), he proceeds to further petitions. 'Come Ye,' he beseeches in Vedic fashion. Come Ye, O Ahura, Asha, and Vohu Manah! and behold the attentive monarch, the leading Magavan, as he listens to my instructions with the other

[1] In this particular. As to ceremonies it had at a later period more than its share of absurdities; but as to honest work as against 'foraging on the enemy' there is a great difference between the Gâthas, and some other ancient hymns, for instance the *Ri*ks of the Veda. In fact these latter may be regarded as representing the opposite extreme.

chiefs, and the thronging masses. And let too the sacrificial gifts pour in for offering and worship.

8. He rests at no bare morality for the simple multitude. He knows too well the human foible, therefore he asks with vigour for sacrifice and hymn.

9. Encouraging the two pious chiefs whose souls go hand in hand, he prays that an influence like that of the 'eternal two' might bear their 'spirit' (sic) to the shining home of Paradise, it having attained to perfection by the help of the Best Mind of God within it. (For mainyu in this sense compare XLIV, 11.)

10. Asking of Mazda to grant in His love (or 'by His will') all the happy phases of life which have been, or which shall ever be experienced, he prays that their bodies, that is, their persons, as separate accountable individuals (compare nar*e*m narem *hv*ahyâi tanuyê) might flourish in the graces of the Good Mind, the Holy Sovereignty, and the Sacred Order, till they were blessed with the us*t*â, the summum bonum.

11. He here prays all the grand abstractions, Piety, the Righteous Order (which alone can 'push on' the settlements), the Good Mind of God within His people, and His kingdom, to turn their mental ears and listen, and listening to pardon.

12. And specifying the one central object of desire, the Thrift-law, the Avesta of the Ratu, or Saoshya*n*t, he asks Ahura to arise to his help and give him spiritual strength by sustaining him through the inspiring Righteousness and the Good Mind, in an effective invocation.

13. With a spirituality still deeper than his Semitic colleague, he asks, not to see the person of God, but His nature, and especially to be able to comprehend and bring home to his mind what the Sovereignty of God implies with its 'blessed rewards.' And he asks of Piety as first acquired, practised, and then speaking within him, to reveal the Gnosis, the Insight, that is, the Religion.

14. After the fervent language of the previous verses we may accept verse 14 as a legitimate continuation. Its 'Zarathus*t*ra' may mean 'I' just as 'David' is used by the Psalmist for 'me.' And the language can mean nothing but a dedication of all that he is and has to God, his flesh, his body, his religious eminence, the obedience which he offers in word and deed, inspired by Righteousness, and the Kingdom which he has succeeded in saving and blessing. (I do not think that I have at all exaggerated the grasp and fervour of this section. Less could not be said, if the words are to be allowed their natural weight.)

Translation.

1. As by the laws of the primeval world, so will our spiritual chieftain act (that chief besought-for by the Kine[1], and named as Zarathustra[2] by the Lord). Deeds most just he will do toward the wicked, as toward the righteous, and toward him whose deeds of fraud[3] and righteous deeds combine (in equal measure).

2. Yea, (he will act with justice but with vengeance, for) he who does evil to the wicked by word, or with thought (and plan), and (who therein does not dally, but toils labouring as) with both the hands, or he (again) who admonishes one for his good[4], such as these are offering (a gift) to their religious[5] faith in the love (and with the approving view) of Ahura Mazda[6]; (they are offering to conscience.)

---

[1] See XXIX, 1.

[2] See XXIX, 6, 8.

[3] So the Pahl.; and so also Roth (Z. D. M. G., vol. xxxvii. 5, 223) taking mithahyâ as a nom. pl. (comp. va*k*ahya). But I am strongly inclined to a former view of my own. Yêhyâ-mithahyâ look irresistibly like two genitives. I would render as an emphatic alternative 'what fraud he may lay hold of (he*m*yâsaitê with the gen.), reach (of the one), and what (seem) to him the righteous deeds (of the other).' But if Roth and the Pahlavi are right, we have here the origin of the later hamêstagã, the souls in the intermediate place between Heaven and Hell, whose sins and good works have been equal (West, Gloss. to M. î K.). The Persian manuscript of Haug 12 b. has: Kih i*k* (pro ham) û *î* ân ham rasîd êstêd ân i durû*gh*, kih i*k* (ham) û ân *î* 'hâli*s* [kû, hamêstân].

[4] So the Pahlavi also indicates: Val valman î *s*apîr—*k*âshi*s*n. Ner. uttamasya vâ âsvâdayanti dehina*h*.

[5] Literally, 'they are offering a gift to their own choice' (var= varena; comp. yâvarenâ).

[6] They are holding fast by the holy cause, and their vehemence in vengeance does not negative the fact that they are toiling in the love of Ahura. Pahlavi: Pavan zak î lak dôshi*s*nô, Aûharmazd I

3. (And so may it be), O Ahura! Let the man who is the best toward the righteous saint, whether lord's kinsman[1], or as village labourer, with the allied[2] peer (of the master), having light, and endowed with energy for the cattle (a Ratu such as Ahura sought to satisfy their wail), let such an one be (for us)[3] in the work-field of the Righteous Order, in the pastures of Thy Good Mind[4].

4. (And I beseech for Thine instruction), I who will abjure[5] all disobedience (toward Thee, praying that others likewise may withhold it) from Thee; I who abjure the Evil Mind as well, the lordly kinsman's arrogance[6], and that lying sin which is (alas!) the next thing to the people[7] (their most familiar fault), and the blaming ally's falsehood, and from the Kine the worst care of her meadows[8] (the crime of stint in labour[9]),

---

[1] Literally, 'with, or as, the kinsman.'

[2] 'With the true ally.'

[3] See XXIX, 2: 'Let that pasture-giver whom ye would appoint for us, teaching by example and precept vohû vâstryâ, let him be on our sacred pastures, and on our side.'

[4] The Pahlavi may be rendered as follows: He who affords increase to the righteous on account of the relationship [that is, something is given to him?] does so also on account of the labourer's duty, or class [that is, the labourer is to be considered as his own]. Through the loyalty; that is, the loyal class, that which adheres to Aûharmazd, he has a thorough understanding as to what is (true) energy toward the herds. Thus Vohûman (a good mind) is a workman with him to whom Righteousness also belongs.

[5] Hübschm. Casuslehre, 'der ich von dir den Ungehorsam und schlechten Sinn durch Gebet abwenden will' (s. 180).

[6] Observe that *hv*aêtu certainly designates an upper class. Why else arrogance?

[7] Possibly this severity was the cause of the later high reputation of the Zarathustrians for veracity.

[8] Literally, 'from the pasture of the Kine.'

[9] The Pahlavi may be rendered: Him who will not listen to

5. I, who (abjuring these sins), call earnestly on Thine Obedience of all (assisting guardians) the greatest one for our help [1], gaining (thereby [2]) long life in the Realm of (Thy) Good Mind (incarnate in our tribes), and paths that are straight from their Righteous Order, wherein Ahura Mazda dwells [3],

6. (Yea), I who, as this Thy faithful priest, invoke Thee through (my) Righteousness, (now) seek [4] with longing from (Thy) Best Spirit, and with that [5] (best) intention of mind, (to know) what [6] he himself thought of the working of (our) fields [7]. Therefore (because I abjure the Evil Mind, and all disobedience,

---

Thee, O Aûharmazd! will I abjure, and Akôman also, for by him there is the despising of relations, and the deception of the labouring men who live close at hand [that is, of neighbours]. And he is ever bringing censure upon the clients. And he holds to the lowest measure of duty toward the Herd.

[1] Avanghâ *ne*, or avanghânê, an infinitive (see Wilhelm, de Infin. p. 16). The Pahlavi has avŏ aîyyârîh.

[2] Sraosha (= listening obedience) is the greatest for help, because by a Mãthra which appeals to him the way to Ahura is found out (XXVIII, 6) and the Demon defeated. If apânô is read, so strictly. The Pahlavi translator seems to have understood apâ *ne*; barâm ayâfînâi pavan dêr-zîvisnîh, zak î pavan khû*d*âyîh î Vohûman.

Ner.: Avâpaya dîrghe *g*îvitatve. This may well restore for us the proper text. Reading apâ *ne* we should render 'obtain for us.'

[3] Ahura Mazda dwells as in His abode amid the paths where His saints walk (see XLVI, 16).

[4] So also indicated by bavîhûnê*d*. Kayâ properly refers to *ye*.

[5] The Pahlavi translator seems to have seen an imperative in avâ, rendering it freely aîyyârînê*d*ŏ.

[6] Yâ may be an instr. sing. or an acc. pl. neut. 'I ask what he thought meet to be done;' yâ does not necessarily equal yéna in every instance.

[7] I need hardly remind the reader that agriculture was the great question of orderly and religious life with the Zarathustrians. Without it there was of course no resource but wandering and plunder for them.

arrogance, falsehood), O Mazda! would I beseech of Thee for a sight of Thee, and for consultation with Thee! (What is Thy will and mind?)

7. Come Ye, then, to my best (regulations. Come to my men, and my laws[1]), my very own, O Mazda! and let them see through the Righteous Order and (Thy) Good Mind (which Thou wilt bestow in Thy drawing near) how I am heard before the rich giver[2] (in the assembly of Thy worshippers). Yea, (come Ye); and let the manifold offerings of worship be manifest among us[3]. (Arouse Ye, and help our zeal[4]!)

---

[1] So I render from the context. Otherwise see tâ tôi izyâ in the previous verse.

[2] I was formerly inclined to understand Ahura here, Indian usage permitting. (Indra and other Gods are maghavan.) But modern authority, aided by the ancient Pahlavi translator, brings me to a better mind. The Pahlavi has pavan fravôn magîh. It is better to refer the word to the disciple. The more prominent members of the congregation are meant.

[3] Ner. renders the last line thus: And may these offerings be manifest in the midst of us, and accompanied with (sincerest) worship.

[4] There are certain cases where allowance for an ancient scholar working under great disadvantages becomes a critical necessity. Here the Pahlavi translator was clearly the victim of a manuscript. The word 'âidûm' (sic) stood, as similar words so often stand, in his MS. as 'âi. dûm.' Deeply imbued with a superstitious regard for every letter, and with a public equally scrupulous, he saw no course before him but to translate each as best he could. He chose to render 'âi' by an infinitive, preserving the root, and could only think of a form of 'dâ' for dûm (so also moderns in another case). Many writers, seeing such a step, cast away his paper, regarding themselves as absolved by such a 'blunder' from mastering his translations. But a little honest labour will always bring one back to sounder exegesis. In the next following verse we have identically the same form in another word, which he renders awkwardly but correctly, using dâ again, but as a proper auxiliary.

8. (Come Ye) and show me the worthy aims of our faith, so that I may approach and fulfil them with (Thy) Good Mind, the offering, O Mazda! of the One like You[1], or the words of praises offered with Righteousness. And give Ye as Your offering[2] (of grace to me) the abiding gifts of Your Immortality and Welfare!

9. And let (one like those[3]), O Mazda! bear on to Thee the spirit of the two leaders who cause the holy ritual Truth to flourish; let him[4] bear them to (Thy) brilliant home[5] with[6] preternatural insight, and with the Better Mind. Yea, let him bear that spirit on as a fellow-help[7] in (furthering) the readi-

[1] To approach the offering of a praiser seems certainly an unnatural expression. I think that we are obliged to regard khshmâvatô as another way of saying Yourself rather than 'of Yours'; and if it equals 'Yourself' here, it may elsewhere; see XXXIV, 2, khshmâvatô vahmê, also XLIV, 1, neme khshmâvatô. All acknowledge mavaitê to mean 'to me.' Hübschmann, Casuslehre, s. 200: 'dass ich mit frommem sinne an eure Verehrung, Mazda, gehen kann.'

[2] It is curious that draonô seems to be in apposition here. The word is used merely in the sense of offering in the later Avesta. It might possibly mean 'possessions' here.

[3] See XXXII, 15. There helping princes are spoken of 'as borne by the two (Haurvatât and Ameretatât).' Here in immediate connection with the same two it is said: Let one bear the spirit of the two united chiefs. By the term 'spirit,' which sounds so suspiciously modern, we must nevertheless understand very nearly what the word would mean in a modern phrase. By these two leaders we may understand either *G*âmâspa and Vîstâspa (XLIX, 9) or *G*âmâspa and Frashaostra. (Compare yâvarenâ Frashaostrâ *G*âmâspâ.)

[4] 'Let one bear them.'

[5] Khvârîh mânînisnŏ.

[6] The Pahlavi gives its evidence for an instrumental and for a less pronounced meaning than the one above.

[7] Hamkar*d*ârîh. If the second kar is the root, the sense is figurative.

ness[1] of those (in their holy work) whose souls go hand in hand[2].

10. (And not for these alone do I pray, but for us[3] as well.) All prosperous states[4] in being which have been enjoyed in the past, which men are now enjoying, and which shall be known in the future, do Thou grant (me) these in Thy love[5]. (Yea), cause (our) bodily and personal life to be blest with salvation[6] through (Thy) Good Mind, (Thy) Sovereign Power, and (Thy) Sanctity[7].

11. And, O Thou who art the most beneficent Ahura Mazda! and thou who art Âramaiti (our piety), and also the Righteous Order who dost further on the settlements; and Thou, the Good Mind, and the Sovereign Power! hear ye me all, and have mercy[8] for every deed which I do whatsoever[9]!

---

[1] Bûndakô. [2] Pavan akvînô rûbânô.

[3] So more probably. See the first person in verses 8 and 11.

[4] So the Pahlavi also, hû-zîvisnîh.

[5] So the Pahlavi also: Pavan banâ î lak dôshisnô. 'In Thy will' is here very weak.

[6] Nadûkîhi*k* î avô tanû [am yehabûn]; Ner. *s*ubha*m* tanau.

[7] Neryosangh: Let them continue to live well, and be prosperous in all things [ ] those females (yâ*h* most curiously) who are born thus [that is, come from elsewhere (and not from us)], and who are [gained over by myself]. Those, O Great Wise One! who shall exist [(or) come in the future], let them render these persons thine own through friendship to thee. Cause thou the Best Mind to increase within me, O Lord! [that is, make my mind ever the more piously zealous]. And in view of my righteousness grant me a benefit in my body, or person [ ].

[8] So the Pahlavi also: Am barâ âmûrzê*d*.

[9] Observe that all the Ameshôspends, except the two mentioned in verse 8, are here bidden as persons to listen and be merciful. These recurring instances (recall the two hands of Asha &c.) necessitate the view that the idea of personality is never lost in that

12. And Thou, O Ahura! do Thou (Thyself) arise[1] to me! Through Âramaiti give me power, O most bountiful Spirit Mazda! through (my) faithful appeals and offerings[2]; and for (my) Righteousness grant me mighty strength, and (Thy) thrift-law[3] through (Thy) Good Mind[4].

13. (Arise to give me power), and then for grace in a wide perception[5] (that I may view its depth and extent), do Thou reveal to me Thy[6] nature (?), O Ahura! (the power of Thine attributes), and those of Thy (holy) kingdom, and by these, the blessed gifts[7] of (Thy) Good Mind! And do Thou, O bountiful Piety[8] show forth the religious truths through (Thy) Righteous Order.

---

of the abstract quality; and vice versâ; (the latter especially in the Gâthas where the names always retain much, if not all of their original force). As to âdâi; see vanghuyâ (sic) zavô-âdâ in the next verse.

[1] We seem obliged to suppose that Ahura was poetically conceived of as sitting (like Vohûman in Vendîdâd XIX, 31 (Wg.)) upon an ornamented throne, or we may take the expression as pure metaphor equalling 'exert Thy power.' Âramaitî may be a voc.

[2] See âdâi in verse 11.

[3] Pavan zak î Vohûman sardârîh. The 'thrift-law' is the regulation established by the Ratu demanded in Y. XXIX for the redemption of the Kine. It expresses the entire polity and theology of the Zarathustrian people as summed up in the original Avesta.

[4] Neryosangh: Up! O Lord! purify me [that is, make me pure, or free, from the influence of that tormentor, the Evil Mind]; and grant me perfect spirituality and zeal. For we are recipients of Gvahmana, O more mighty spirit [that is, let him be as a guest, arrived within my body]! And let sanctity have power over the murderer (?) [ ], and through the lordship of the Best Mind.

[5] The Pahlavi has here pavan kâmak *k*âshis*n*ŏ, on which see Darmesteter, Études Iraniennes, vol. ii, as per index.

[6] Literally, 'Your.'

[7] Ashi has this meaning in the later Avesta. It also means 'sacred regularity,' 'exactness' in religious duties.

[8] So the Pahlavi also: A*s* pavan Aharâyîh dînô frâz dakh-

14. Thus, as an offering, Zarathustra gives the life[1] of his very body. And he offers, likewise, O Mazda! the priority of the Good Mind, (his eminence gained) by his holiness (with Thy folk); and he offers (above all his) Obedience (to Thee) in deed and in speech, and with these (Thine established) Sovereign Power[2]!

---

shakînŏ; Ner.: Puṇyena dînim prakihnaya. Possibly, 'give light to our consciences through Asha' would be better.

[1] The tissues; the word seems contrasted with bones elsewhere. The Pahlavi has khayâ, and Ner. *givam* (sic).

[2] The Pahlavi translation may be rendered as follows: Thus, as a gift of generosity, I who am Zartûst (so freely, and with no error from ignorance (!)) give the life of my own body, as the advance [as the chieftainship] to Vohûman and to Aûharmazd, and to Ashavahist, in actions [that is, I would do the deeds which Aharâyîh desires], and would give obedient attention to the word (literally the hearing of the word) to (i.e. of) Khshatraver.

YASNA XXXIV.

1. A tone of thankfulness continues. As if in gratitude for better fortunes, the prophet declares that he will bestow upon Ahura with the foremost, according to the measure of the gifts which he has received. Those gifts were the secured Immortality (not mere temporal 'deathlessness'), the Righteous Order, and the Sovereign Power established in holiness and bestowing the Universal Weal.

2. The kind of gifts which are proposed for offerings are not sacrificial beasts or fruits, but the actions of the truly pious citizen whose soul is intimately united with Righteousness, the homage of prayer, and the songs of praise. As no piety could exist without strict ecclesiastical regularity, so no ceremonial punctuality was conceived of apart from honour and charity (see verse 5 and Yast XXII).

3. Accordingly the meat-offering, the mention of which immediately follows, is spoken of as offered with homage to the Righteous Order and to the Divine Sovereignty for the benefit of all the sacred settlements, in order to equip the wise man fully, and as a helpful blessing among the Immortals themselves and their adherents.

4. And the Fire is likewise mentioned, which was worshipped not so much like Agni as the friendly god of the hearth and the altar, but more and chiefly like Agni as the priest of the church.

Not unlike Agni, it is called upon both for inward spiritual strength and for temporal blessings in various forms, together with vengeance hurled very much as if in the form of a thunderbolt (zastâ-istâis derestâ-aênanghem). 5. To explain what he means by his supplications for the coming of the Kingdom, and for holy actions (that is, to make it certain that he does not mean punctilious ritualism apart from the noblest charity), he rhetorically asks: 'And what is Your Kingdom, that which Zarathustra establishes and offers to You? (XXXIII, 14). What is the kind of prayer (comp. XLVIII, 8, and LIII, 1) which I must use, so that I may become Yours (Your property) in my actions, not to load Your priesthood with sacrifices, nor to fatten Your princes with booty (as too often in the *Ri*ks), nor yet to secure a heavy gift to the poet, but to 'nourish Your poor?' This was the essence of the desired Sanctity and the Sovereign Authority. The Kingdom of God, exalted and personified as a separate intelligence, is positively said to be something more than a gaudy pageant of material display, even Tavâ Khshathrem yâ erezigyôi dâhî drigavê vahyô (LIII, 9). (See also even Vendîdâd II [part i], where moral duties are lauded.)

And the composer himself seems to be so conscious of the sharply defined difference between such a kingdom and that of the rival religion, that he immediately adds an interdict: 'Such is Your Kingdom, caring for the righteous poor, and therefore we declare You irreconcilably distinct from the Daêvas and their polluted followers. Ye are beyond them and before in the spirit of Your Reign!'

6. He then utters an impressive doubt, which only deepens our admiration at his expressions of faith: 'If it be really true,' he continues (see XLIV, 6), 'that Ye are thus with the Righteous Order and the Good Mind, the God who looks upon the goodness of the heart and the activity of the hands, then give me a sign of it, that I may persevere and increase in the depth of my homage while life shall last.' 7. For the struggle, though not without signs of a favourable issue, was far from over yet. (Hence his misgivings.)

He then asks with some wistfulness after the 'ar(e)drâ,' the men that could help, who from the experience of the grace of God, could turn sorrow into blessing by establishing the holy religious system firmly, but with enlarged and not narrowed understanding. And, still a little dispirited, he declares, as so often: 'None have I other than You; therefore I can wait for the ar(e)drâ. Do ye save us alone by Your already offered means of grace.'

8. 'For Ye have given me already, as it were, a sign. The enemy are checked, and for the moment cowed, if they are not repelled. They among whom there was death for so many when they had the upper hand, and when their ruler persecuted the holy vows, are not only struck with terror by the action which we take, but their chief retribution is, as we hold it, spiritual, and therefore, in the eye of truth the more severe. They will not encourage righteous Order and righteous intentions, and accordingly, the personified Good Intention, grieved, will depart from them.'

9. 'Yea,' he reiterates, amplifying, 'the unfortunate sinners who depart from Thy kindly and sacred Piety in this ignorance of all experience of Thy Good Mind, will suffer an equal desertion. The characteristics of righteousness will, in their turn, avoid them as the unclean creatures flee from us.' 10. 'And this is,' thus he continues, 'a sign or result which the All-wise declares to me to steady my soul as I waver.' 'And these are indeed the cheering proofs of Thy favour,' he adds, addressing Ahura, 'which terrify our enemies

and advance us, giving us a righteous eminence (XXXIII, 14) in Thy Kingdom.'

11. 'Therefore that kindly Piety whom these desert in their judicial ignorance, will increase for us both the all-comprehensive blessings; spiritual Deathlessness begun in anticipation here, and its necessary condition, Welfare. And they shall be increased as food (sic) for Mazda's straitened people, or better, to His glory as their monarch. And by their means Ahura may defend Himself efficiently from the persecuting and idolatrous foe.' 12. Taking into consideration all that depends on a correct understanding as to religious and political duties, he fervently prays to be guided aright in the establishment of a ceremonial and of praises, beseeching Mazda to speak, declaring the kind of worship which may secure the ashis (which are the blessed rewards). And he asks to be taught those religious paths about which no error was possible, the paths which are the Good Mind's own.

13. After a fashion already known to us (as in XXIX), he answers his question himself. That way which Ahura had already revealed as the Good Mind's own, was made up of the revealed precepts of the Saoshya*n*ts. There, as in the paths where Ahura dwells (XXXIII, 5; XLVI, 16), the well-doer may prosper from his devotion to the religious truths, and gain a reward immediately from the hand of God. 14. As if never forgetting the original calamity, the woes of the Kine, he further declares that way to be the one of all to be chosen for this earthly life, as the vestibule to the heavenly one. And he asserts that they who toil for the Kine (who represents here, as generally, the holy settlements as well as their chief source of riches and support) are striving to further and demonstrate the wisdom of that way by every righteous contrivance.

Nay, he declares that the deeds of Piety are themselves the highest wisdom, just as the words and righteous actions of the Saoshya*n*ts not only declare and make, but constitute, 'the way.'

15. Again, concluding with a climacteric and synoptical prayer, he beseeches Ahura to speak and reveal to him all the most available statements, ceremonies, and praises. And never forgetting that all ceremonies, hymns, and sacrifices, sacred as they are, are only means to a greater end; he prays the Deity that He may exert that Sovereign Power which is alone supremely efficient in relieving actual distress (LIII, 9), for by its holy laws and spiritual arms it can alone bring on the Frashakar*d*, and produce that condition in society in which all human progress shall have become complete.

Translation.

1. As to those (three gifts of blessings), Immortality, the Righteous Order, and the (established) Kingdom of Welfare, which Thou, O Mazda! hast given through (holy) deeds, words, and the sacrifice unto these (Thy servants here in my sight[1]), gifts (shall) be offered[2] by us in return to Thee, O Ahura! and with the foremost of them all.

2. Yea, and all those gifts of the Good Spirit[3] have been given (back in gratitude) to Thee by the mind and the deed of the bountiful man, whose soul goes hand in hand[4] with the Righteous Order in the settlement, in homage toward the One like You[5],

[1] The hymns seem to be all composed for public declamation, as is evident from various passages. Similar indications often occur in the Veda. I formerly connected aêshãm with Ameretatâ*t*, &c., 'a thank-offering for these (gifts).'

[2] I am very sorry to oppose progress on such a subject as dastê, but I do not think that it is an infinitive, nor that âitê or mrûitê are such. -Tê, or what it represents, I regard as seldom or never a Gâthic suffix, and especially not, as here, where dastê falls to the end of the sentence. Too little attention has been paid to the Gâthic sentence. The infinitive seldom falls to the end of it; vîdvanôi vao*k*â; ta*t* môi vî*k*idyâi vao*k*â; vîduyê (vîdvê) vohû mananghâ; me*nk*â daidyâi yêhyâ mâ rishis; ashâ fradathâi asperezatâ; âgôi (?) hâdrôyâ; *ye* a*k*i*s*tem vaênanghê aogedâ; but zbayâ avanghânê (?) yâ verezyêidyâi ma*n*tâ vâstryâ; srûidyâi Mazdâ frâvao*k*â; kahmâi vîvîduyê (-vê) vashî; ta*t* verezyêidyâi hya*t* môi mraotâ vahi*s*tem; arethâ vôizhdyâi kâmahyâ t*e*m môi dâtâ; dazdyâi hâkerenâ; but vasmî anyâ*k*â vîduyê (-vê); *men*-dâidyâi yâ Tôi Mazdâ âdi*s*ti*s*, &c. The Pahlavi renders here with admirable freedom as a first person, yehabûnêm.

[3] Observe this expression. It is the spe*n*ta mainyu which, like the 'Holy Spirit of God,' is sometimes identical with Him.

[4] Souls are elsewhere said to go hand in hand; see Y. XXXIII, 9.

[5] I suppose that it is possible that khshmâvatô, here and elsewhere, may refer to the human subject, 'to the praise of your wor-

O Mazda! and with the chants of the (thankful) praisers[1].

3. And unto Thee, O Ahura! will we offer the (thankful) meat-offering with self-humbling praise, and to Thy Righteousness (like Thee a person), and for all the settlements in Thy kingdom which are guarded[2] by Thy Good Mind. For in the perfect preparation of the justly acting (has that offering its power), O Mazda! together with all (others of its kind). Among those like You and worthy of Yourselves, it is a blessing[3].

4. And we pray likewise for Thy Fire, O Ahura! strong through Righteousness (as it is), most swift, (most) powerful, to the house with joy receiving it, in many wonderful ways our help, but to the hater, O Mazda! it is a steadfast[4] harm as if with weapons hurled from the hands[5].

---

shipper,' but it does not sound at all natural. I think that khshmâvatô is merely another way of saying 'of you,' as mava*n*t=me. So the Pahlavi also seems to render here: Avô zak î lekûm va nîyâyi*s*nŏ. Ner. also: Samâga*kkh*âmi yushmâkam namask*ri*taye, Mahâ*g*ñânin.

[1] This recalls the dasemê-stûtãm of Y. XXVIII, 10.

The Pahlavi renders freely and not uncritically, regarding the spe*n*ta nar as Zarathu*s*tra himself: Aftânŏ dên Garô*d*mânŏ stâyem. Ner.: Garothmâne staumi te.

[2] So also the translations: Aîgha*s* parvari*s*n va min frarûnîh. Ner.: Uttamena pratipâlyâ manasâ. Compare Y. XXXII, 2: sâremanô khshathrâ*t*. The singular verb is difficult.

[3] Or, 'for as those justly acting, and in preparation will we offer it as a blessing together with all who are among "Your own."' Here khshmâva*n*t equals 'Your own'; rather than 'Yourselves.'

[4] Or 'visible' as fire, but this seems too feeble a conception for the place. The Pahlavi translator read dere*s*tâ as a participle from dar(e)z, which is quite as possible as that it should be from dar(e)s. He renders yakhsenunê*d* kînŏ; Ner., vidadhâti nigraham. That he so translated because he was not aware that dere*s*tâ could be also a participle from dar(e)s, is no longer tenable.

[5] As by no means a partially selected specimen, let the reader

5. What is[1] then Your Kingdom, O Mazda? What are Your riches? that I may become[2] Your own in my actions, with the Righteous Order, and (Thy) Good Mind, to care for Your poor (in their suffering[3]). Apart from all would we declare You, yea, apart from Daêvas[4], and Khrafstra-polluted mortals!

consider the following from the Pahlavi: Thus, O Aûharmazd! this which is Thy Fire, which is so powerful, is a satisfaction to him whose is Aharâyîh [-when my chieftain (the glossist seeming to have a text with a first pronoun; otherwise the first translator who never saw? us(e)mahî) becomes one by whom duty and charity are fulfilled], for it is quick and powerful [the Fire], and remains continually in friendship with him, and makes joy manifest to him. And therefore, O Aûharmazd! on him who is the tormentor it takes revenge as if with a mighty wish.

[1] Ka*t* is often a mere interrogative particle, so modern interrogatives are also often merely formal.

[2] Bartholomae admirably follows K4 here with its hakhmî; it gives a more common explanation of vâo, which I am obliged to take in a possessive sense beside n*e*. The manuscript used by the Pahlavi writer had, however, ahmî, as many others now extant.

[3] Note the recurrence of this care for the poor, showing what the frequent mention of righteousness, the good mind, &c. meant.

[4] Observe that daêvâi*s* must mean the Demon-gods and not their worshippers here; par*e* vâo indicates this, and also mashyâi*s* = men, who are separately mentioned. The Pahlavi translator is finely critical here, giving us our first hint as to the meaning: Pêsh Lekûm min harvisp-gûnŏ levînŏ gûft hômanê*d* [aîgh tûbânkar*d*ar hômanê*d*, &c.]. So with antare-mrûyê (-vê), he was the pioneer also. I render with impartiality: Which (of what kind) is your sovereignty? [that is, what thing can I do, whereby your sovereignty may be increased through my instrumentality?] And which is your wealth? [that is, what thing shall I do whereby riches may be kept in your possession by my means?] How thus in the actions of Aûharmazd shall I become yours? [That is, I (?) shall do that thing through which, by my means, your sovereignty is extended; and also wealth is kept in your possession by me.] For whenever I (?) shall do righteous deeds, [that is, when I (?) shall do duty and good works], Vohûman gives nourishment to our poor. Before all of every kind, even before them ye are

6. If thus Ye are in verity, O Mazda! with the Righteous Order and Thy Good Mind, then grant Ye me a sign[1] of this in this world's entire abiding[2] (while I live amid its scenes), how offering sacrifice and praising[3] You the more devoutly[4], I may approach You (in my worship)!

7. Where[5] are Thine offerers, O Mazda! Thy helpers, who as the enlightened of the Good Mind are producing the doctrines with wide mental light as inherited treasures, (delivering them as Thy word) in misfortune and in woe[6]? I know none other than You; then do Ye save us through Your righteousness!

8. Through these our deeds (of sacrifice and zeal[7]), they are terrified[8] among whom there was (once) destruction, and for many (at the time) when the

---

declared; [that is, ye are more capable] than the demons, for their (?) intellect is perverted, (and ye are also before) men.

[1] So also the Pahlavi dakh*s*ak.

[2] So indicated by ketrûnânî. I have no doubt whatever that maêthâ should have this sense. See also Y. XXX, 9.

[3] So also the Pahlavi: Pavan âfrînagânŏ dahi*s*nŏ va stâyi*s*nŏ sâtûnam madam.

[4] Urvâidyâo, if in its original form, looks like a comparative. One naturally thinks of a *vrâd (?) equivalent to 'v*ri*dh.'

[5] Rhetorically interrogative as often in English, or indeed a mere particle. (Compare XLVI, 9.)

[6] So also the Pahlavi indicates with its âmûkhti*s*nŏ (sic) î hûvari*s*nŏ [î avŏ kâr va kirfak], mûni*k* pavan âsânîh va mûni*k* pavan tangîh vâdûnyên frâkh-hushîh. Ner.: *S*ikshâm satyâya ya*h* samâdhânatve, sa*m*ka*t*atve* 'pi kurute vipula*k*aitanya*h* [kila, ya*h* kârya*m* pu*n*ya*m* yat sam*ri*ddhatayâ kurute] ta*kk*a yat sa*m*ka*t*atayâ 'pi kurute, tasya vig*ñ*âna*k*aitanya*m* tasmâd bhavati.

[7] Nâo being taken in a possessive sense.

[8] But the Pahlavi has: 'Min zak î valman*s*ân maman kûni*s*nŏ lanman bîm'; possibly 'by these actions they terrify us'; the middle in the sense of the active.

oppressor of Thy holy vows was as the stronger oppressing the weaker[1]. They who have not thought (in consonance) with Thy Righteous Order, from these Thy Good Mind[2] abideth afar.

9. Aye, they who desert Thy bountiful Piety, O Mazda! that one desired of Thee[3], O Thou omniscient! and who thus abandon her by reason of the evil-doer, and in their ignorance of (Thy) Good Mind, from such as these (Âramaiti) with her holiness utterly departs[4] as the red Khrafstras (who destroy and pollute all life, flee) from us[5] (Thy faithful servants).

10. Through the action of this (His) Good Mind (as he works his grace within us) the benevolently wise[6] One declared a result as its fruit, He knowing the bountiful Piety, the creatrix of righteous beings[7]. These all, O Mazda Ahura! in Thy Kingdom (are

---

[1] It is a mistake to suppose that the Pahlavi translator and his followers, Ner. and the Persian MS. (of Haug's Collection), refer nâidy*a*unghem and nade*n*tô to the same Sanskrit word. They translate them as if referring the first to nâdh, and the last to nid.

[2] Min valman*s*ân barâ rakhîk aîtŏ Vohûman. Asmanô seems an impossible reading, and cannot be reconciled with Vohû.

[3] The hint of the Pahlavi points, as usual, to the general sense, leaving us the task of discovering the grammatical structure.

Here I do not follow the indication of sedkûnyên; Ner. parikshipyanti. The voc. 'O Thou' is free.

[4] So also in general the Pahlavi: Min valman*s*ân kabed Aharâyîh segdak; Ner. tebhya*h** prabhuto dharma*h** prabhra*s*yati.

[5] So if ahma*t* is read, but the MS. before the Pahlavi translator read ahmât; Ner. etebhya*h* (freely). A simpler rendering results; 'as from him flee away.'

[6] Observe the evidence of the Zend to the prevalent meaning of 'khratu.'

[7] Or reading hithăm, and in the sense of 'bond,' we coincide with Ner. sukhanivâsam. Haithăm = the true; hâtăm ? = of beings. Lit. 'the true creatrix of Asha (the holy).'

'helps to our progress') for they smite (our tyrants) with fear[1].

11. And for Thee hath Âramaiti (who is Our Piety) increased both the Universal Weal and (its continuance in) Immortality, and (with them as ever united) the Righteous (ritual and moral) Order (established and made firm) in the Kingdom of (Thy Good Mind). Those powerful lasting two (hath she increased) to (give us the needful) food[2]. And through these, O Mazda! art Thou with Thy perfect expellers of hate[3]. (Thou removest Thy foes afar[4]!)

12. What then are Thy regulations[5]? And what wilt Thou? What of praise, or of (fuller) offering? Speak forth that we hear it, O Mazda! what will establish the blessed rewards of Thine ordinance[6]!

---

[1] The word voyathrâ is difficult to place; the Pahlavi translator divided, reading âvo-yathrâ (possibly âvoi athrâ), and rendered frô*d* kûshî-aît=is smitten down; the Persian better: Frôd zadar, is smiting down. We may well hesitate before rejecting this indication, which may point to a better text. Like vafu*s*, it may indicate the severity of the influences of the righteous system, in the midst of genial allusion. The tâ vîspâ might refer quite naturally to du*s*-*s*kayasthanâ in the previous verse. The form voyathrâ (corrected) may represent some derivative from the root bî=to fear. Compare bya*n*tê in verse 8.

[2] So likewise the Pahlavi with its khûri*s*nŏ; otherwise 'for glory;' *hv*ar=svar. Lit. 'To Thee (are) both Weal and Immortality.'

[3] *Gavîd* bêsh min lak hômanih; Ner. vîtakash*t*as tva*m* asi.

[4] Ner.: Thus both are (to be derived) from thee, Avirdâda's food, and that of Amirdâda also, [the (food) of the Lord-of-water, and of the Lord-of-wood* (so the later Avesta and Parsism)], and in the kingdom of the best mind, righteousness is making a revelation together with the perfect mind. Do thou also bestow zeal and power upon this one, O Great Wise One, the Lord! From torment art thou exempt.

[5] So also vîrâyi*s*nŏ.

[6] Pahlavi ârâyi*s*nŏ.

* Otherwise simply 'water and tree.'

Teach Thou us the paths through Righteousness, those verily trod by (Thy) Good Mind[1] as he lives within Thy saints[2].

13. (Do I ask what is that path?) That way which Thou declarest to me as the path of the Good Mind, O Ahura! (is made[3] in its parts by) the religious precepts and laws of the Saviours, wherein the well-doer thrives[4] from (his) Righteousness[5]. And it marks for the good a reward of which Thou art Thyself the bestower.

14. For that (reward), O Mazda! ye have given as the one to be chosen for (our) bodily[6] life through

---

[1] The Pahlavi has the gloss: Teach us the way of the original religion.

[2] Neryosangh: Kim te sammârganam [kila, kâryam, te kim mahânyâyitaram?] Kah kâmah? Kâka yushmâkam stutih? Kâka yushmâkam igisnih? Srinomi, Mahâgñânin! prakrishtam brûhi! yat ketsi* dharmasya sammârganam, [aho viseshena pasya! tasmât mahânyâyitarât kuru!] Sikshâpaya* asmâkam dharmasya mârgam uttamena svâdhînam manasâ. [Mârgam yam pûrvanyâyavantam asmabhyam brûhi.]

[3] Observe the certainty of a subtle meaning, 'the way *is* the consciences or laws.'

[4] Geldner has admirably suggested a comparison with vrag on account of the connection 'way.' But as this necessitates two urvâz=vrâz, and as Ahura is spoken of as 'dwelling' in 'paths,' I do not think that 'thriving in paths' is very difficult. The prominent thought is not the going, but the 'right going.' That path indicates a reward (so also the Pahlavi kâshîdô, Ner. âsvâdayah). But we must be thankful for the keen and vigorous discussion. Compare urvâkhshanguha gâya gighaêsa. The Pahlavi has hûravâkh-manîh and in Y. XLIV, 8. If vrag is compared, the idea must be happy progress; but varh (Justi) seems the more obvious correspondent.

[5] Asha, very often personified, is a stronger expression than 'correctly.'

[6] Of course our life on earth, merely in the bodily state. Comp. Y. XXVIII, 3. There astavataskâ evidently means 'of earth,' mananghô, 'of heaven' (—of corporeal—of mind, without body).

the deeds of Thy Good Mind (in us). They who work in the toil of the mother[1] Kine, these further[2] Your merciful care through the understanding's action[3], and (taught) by Thine Order's (word)[4].

15. Yea, (show me, O Mazda! that path and its reward); tell me the best (of truths); reveal the best words and best actions, and the confessing[5] prayer of the praiser through Thy Good Mind (living within us); and through the Righteous Order, O Ahura! And by Your Sovereign Power and grace may'st Thou make life really progressive[6] (till perfection shall have been reached)!

---

[1] Or the 'mature,' 'drivable' (?) cow. She 'goes on her path' of toil.

[2] So frâz yehabûn*d*.

[3] Observe that vereze*n*â cannot well mean 'stall' in this line. The Pahlavi likewise sees varzî-aît in it; Ner. vidhîyate, both free as to form.

[4] Neryosangh: Sa yato, Mahâ*g*ñânin! kâmo 'smâka*m* yat tanumate *g*îvamate dîyate [â*k*âryâya], uttamena karma*n*e manasâ [khshatriyâya], ya*sk*a gavâ* â*k*ârayitre* Aginâmnyâ, [ku*t*umbine], yo yushmâka*m* sunirvâ*n*ag*ñ*ânatayâ, Svâmin! buddhyâ*k*a, pu*n*yapradattayâ vidhîyate [dîni*h*].

[5] I concede this shade of meaning to the constant and unvarying evidence of the Pahlavi translator. He translates uniformly by avâm yehabûnê*d* or its equivalents.

[6] Bring on 'millennial' perfection when progress shall have been completed.

The Pahlavi translation is as follows: Pavan zak î lekûm khû*d*âyîh-Aûharmazd! frashakar*d*ŏ pavan kâmakŏ âshkârakŏ dên ahvânŏ yehabûnî-aît.

Ner.: Yushmâkam râ*g*yena, Svâmin! akhshayatvam sve*kkh*ayâ parisphu*t*a*m* dâsyate bhuvane.

THE GÂTHA(Â) U*S*TAVAITI(Î).

This Gâtha, consisting of Yasna XLIII–XLVI, is named from the word which begins it, like the three last collections. The fact that the word u*s*tâ possesses special significance may have influenced the minds of the Parsis of a later age, inducing them to associate this first chapter with happy anticipations, but it was of course not owing to any such circumstance that the name was given to the Gâtha. The Gâtha, like its fellows, has its existence as a unit from the nature of its metre.

It has lines generally of eleven syllables, arranged in stanzas of five. It seemed convenient to chant all the hymns of one particular metre together. This hymn, from some unknown reason, or from pure accident, having stood first in the collection in this metre, the Gâtha was named from its first word.

The question naturally arises at this place whether this Gâtha, in its parts or as a whole, is older than the Ahunavaiti and the others. For supplementary statements on this subject, see the Introduction, page xxvii, also elsewhere. It is sufficient to recall here that the procedure of the Ahunavaiti, and the sequence of the other Gâthas in the MSS. of the Yasna, have little importance in determining the question of relative age. If originally grouped in the order of their age, they might easily become transposed for the purpose of liturgical recitation. (See the inserted Haptanghâiti, and Y. LII.) As to the metres present, they afford no indications as to relative age. The metre of the U*s*tavaiti, approaching as it does the Trish*t*up, may be as old as, or older than, that of the Ahunavaiti. The oldest *R*ishis sang in Trish*t*up. The sole remaining test of the relative age of pieces, is their contents. Do those of the Ahunavaiti show a priority to those in the U*s*tavaiti as regards the particular circumstances of which they treat? So far as I am able to judge, no part of the Ahunavaiti is older than Y. XLVI. There we have the man before us at a period in his life before he had attained to his supreme position. He not only laments the unfavourable prospects of his cause, but he is full of vehement animosity, urging on his adherents to the overthrow of some powerful opposing leader, and anticipating an armed struggle so formidable that its partisans are elsewhere alluded to (in Y. XLIV) as 'hosts.' We see him also exhorting the various chiefs of his party as they are evidently standing before him in some large assembly, possibly as the army on the eve of an important encounter.

He refers intimately to the monarch, to his own family, the Spitâmas, and to the Hvôgvas, as represented by Frashaostra. He offers the rewards of Ahura, as he pronounces His threats and condemnations. Every feature bears the strongest evidence of originality. But have we not the same in the Gâthas Ahunavaiti, Spe*n*tâ-mainyu, and the others? Beyond a question. Those passages which express grief, fear, and passionate resentment, we should naturally refer to Zarathu*s*tra personally, and to the earlier portion of his career; and we can make no distinction between such passages when they occur in the Ahunavaiti, U*s*tavaiti, or elsewhere. As to chapter XXIX with its logical commencement, as expressing the sufferings to be remedied in the entire effort, together with the call of Zarathu*s*tra in immediate connection, and chapter XXX with its theosophical statements, we should say that they were composed later, during a period of success and reflection. But this would be a mere surmise. The time of the sage need not necessarily have been consumed in struggles even during the early years of his career.

Chapter LIII seems to belong to a period of mature age, but not necessarily to a period of advanced age. It celebrates the marriage of Zarathu*s*tra's daughter, but maidens were married early. With the exception of Y. LIII, I would say that the occurrence of a piece in this or that Gâtha has little, if anything, to do with determining the question of its relative age.

YASNA XLIII.

Salvation is announced as universal for believers. Reflections of Zarathustra upon the sublimity and bountifulness of Ahura.

As, in every instance, it is probable that verses have fallen out here and there in this important piece, and some may have been inserted, not necessarily from another composer, but from other compositions. After certain limits, however, marked signs of at least external connection are present. After the first three verses, which are quite apart, then from the fourth and fifth on, every alternate verse has the formula Spe*n*tem a*t* thwâ Mazdâ m*e*nhî Ahurâ. It would indeed present no difficulty for a successor to add these words to stanzas otherwise also imitated, but whether from the leading sage or not, whether from him in one strain, or from him as collected from different fragments, the course of thought does not so fail in logical sequence as that it is either impossible, or displeasing, as a whole in a poetical composition.

Verses 1–3 are admirable as preliminary. Verses 4–6, with their lofty descriptions of power and benevolence in the Deity, prepare the way well, with their allusions to the final judgment, for the closer reflections in verses 7–15 upon the prophet's call, uttered at the instigation of Sraosha (his obedient will). Verse 16 is a closing strophe looking much like an addition from another hand, not at all because Zarathu*s*tra is mentioned in the third person, but from its general cast. It possesses, however, very great interest from these circumstances. If a later addition, it enables us to see how the principal features of the system were viewed at a period not identical with the earliest, but closely following it.

1. If we can accept the deeply interesting suggestion of the Pahlavi translator, which is, 'Salvation to him to whom there is salvation for every man,' we need then suppose no necessary loss of verses. Otherwise we are obliged to consider the loss of some laudatory verse, or verses, containing such matter as perhaps Y. XXXIV, 14, 'This princely priest has devoted all to Thee, therefore, salvation to him, whosoever he may be.' Whatever may be the actual truth, the main stress of the thoughts is clear and appropriate. Using the word vas*e*-khshayãs in a good sense,

the composer beseeches Ahura to grant those two 'mighty and eternal ones,' which logically form the complement to each other, universal wholeness, welfare of soul and body, without which beatitude was inconceivable, and then the unlimited duration of that condition; for it is quite impossible that 'long life' alone was here meant by a term, the equivalent of which soon after designated the Bountiful Immortals. We have here again ample data for affirming the richness and depth of the religious conceptions.

The 'powerful and continuous two' are sought together with splendour as rewards, not for the gratification of any selfish sentiment, but in order to maintain Asha, the religious Order, on which the sacred polity, and the tribal, as well as the national wealth depended, but more than any general blessings, the individual sanctity of life. 2. And this is signalised as the highest good; and to this a prayer is added for the 'mâya,' which recalls the supernatural wisdom of the Indian Hercules, about which much phantastic and highly coloured myth is grouped; but here, with the ever-recurring contrast, the mâya is the mysterious wisdom of the Divine Benevolence, colourless and abstract indeed, but yet possessing how great religious depth!

3. The highest blessing, in another and more than once repeated phrase, is again besought, as 'the better than the good,' even the attainment of the one who guides to the 'straight paths,' which are the 'way, even the conceptions and revelations of the Saviours' (Y. XXXIV, 13; LIII, 2), in which the believer prospers, and Ahura dwells, as he dwells in his kingdom, and his 'chosen home' itself (Y. XLVI, 16). Whether 'this man who shows the paths' of 'the bodily and mental world' is the same as he who prays for the âyaptâ ahv*a*u astvatas*k*â hya*t*kâ mananghô (the boons of the two worlds) in Y. XXVIII, 3, here referred to in the third person, there speaking in the first, and whether he is Zarathu*s*tra himself, are questions. It is only necessary to say that, if any relief is gained by the supposition, then beyond a doubt Zarathu*s*tra may have been the composer of both pieces or fragments, here, as in Y. XXVIII, 7. referring to himself as in the third person, there, in Y. XXVIII, also further representing another who prays, referring by name to him as in the third.

But was Zarathu*s*tra the only sacred singer, or was he the centre of a group only, of which he was the life? (Compare Yathrâ v*e* afsmâinî (?) s*e*nghânî—*G*âmâspâ Hvôgvâ; Y. XLVI, 17; see also the Introduction.)

4. Proceeding as if the first three verses were absent from his

mind (as indeed they may have been only later brought together with what now follows), the composer begins his ascriptions of praise. He will regard Ahura as all-bountiful and mighty, since He has carefully nurtured, as with His very hand, the aids of grace which He will bestow, as gifts of forbearance on those now wicked, in the hope of penitence, and in the merciful threat of punishment, and to the devout disciple, whose piety is never ceremonial only. And these means of grace, although abounding in the inculcation of moral sanctity in thought, and word, and deed (see Vendîdâd VIII, 100 (Sp. 283)[1], where 'thought' clearly refers to intention in the strongest sense of the term), are yet profane, aside from the flame of that holy Fire which rallied the masses to a national worship, and which was strong for the holy order, as well as by means of it. For these reasons he adores their giver, but for still another. It was because the might of the Good Mind of Ahura approached him within them, and gave him strength for all that was before him. 5. Like the Semitic prophet, he poetically conceives himself as having beheld Ahura, as the chief of the two spirits, and as sovereign over all other powers when the world was born. And he regards Him as having also then established rewards and punishments by his holiness, so separate in its dualistic distinction from all complicity with evil either by infliction or permission. And these rewards and punishments were to have their issue not in time alone, but in 'the last turning of the creation' in its course.

6. And for Ahura's coming in this last changing he fervently beseeches, as well as for the appearance of the Sacred Kingdom, established and guarded by the divine Benevolence. And this consummation, he implies, will take place when the settlements shall be furthered in the Righteous Order, and by means of it, the end of progress having been attained; for then the piety of men's souls will itself be their instructor, delivering the regulations which shall silence the controversy of the two sides (Y. XXXI, 3). And these regulations are as the wisdom of Ahura's understanding (Y. XXVIII, 2), so penetrating that all thoughts lie bare to it (Y. XXXI, 13).

7. He now declares the principles on which he accepted the divine call. Sraosha (verse 12), he says, drew near to question him. As he is called by Ahura, Obedience, the same who constitutes the way to Ahura (or finds His throne (Y. XXVIII, 6)), now draws near

[1] Anaêshem manô, anaêshem va*k*ô, anaêshem *s*kyaothnem prove that the thought, word, and deed referred to were not limited to a ritual meaning.

him, (I say Sraosha (i. e. Obedience), for if he is not so described as drawing near in this verse, he assuredly is so described in a verse nearly following (the twelfth)). Beyond a question, the fine subjectivity here expressed was intended. As the seer cried: O Righteousness! when shall I see thee (in myself and within my people), so now he means that his obedient spirit listens to the call of God. 8. And as his personified conscience questions him as to his origin, and the principles on which he would proceed, it represents the obedient people, as well as the obedient sage (for the sense of Sraosha, while originally applied to the personal will, is not restricted to it). 'Loyalty' questions him, that 'loyalty' may report his answers. He therefore responds, speaking in his name as Zarathu*s*tra (or else one thoroughly in unison with him, here speaks in his name). And this is his statement as to the indications which shall determine his personality. His course will be without a compromise. The unbelieving opposers, as he declares, shall meet no favour at his hands, but detestation, while to the devout disciple he will be as powerful an aid. And this because his mind and thought are (as if blinded to the present) fixed upon the ideal Kingdom, while for the present he never ceases to toil on, making preparations for the Frashakar*d*, and constructing hymn after hymn to set up the needed machinery of lore.

9. Again, his conscience and obedient will, as the angel of the Deity, questions him; and this time offers him that chief of wished for objects to him, religious knowledge. He mentions the holy Fire, with its proper offering, as the theme of his first inquiry.

10. And he beseeches Ahura to answer and to favour him, since he invokes such a complete endowment, going hand in hand with true Piety, and with no selfish interest in his prayer. He then, with a depth which I confess seems suspicious, asks of Mazda to put his petitions for him, recalling Y. XXVIII, 11, where he beseeches Ahura to fill up his desire with what not he, the speaker, but with what He, Ahura, knows to be the Good Mind's gifts. Or, with a conjectural improvement (?) of the text, he asks of Ahura to question him that he may be questioned indeed, saying as it were, 'search me, and know me.' But the other reading being retained as having superior point, and needing no conjectured text, we may see his further thought: 'Ask Thou our questions for us, and then we shall never fail; then we shall be no desireless (anaêsha) men, spurned by the wailing kine as flinching champions (Y. XXIX, 9), but we shall be indeed Thy rulers, "speaking our mighty wish."

Like the isha-khshathra, whom she sought (Y. XXIX, 9), our wish shall work our will; it will accord with the will of God.'

11. He is, however, not blind to all that lies before him in accepting this call. He worships the bounty and majesty of Ahura while he is impressing his soul with the import of this conference, and that notwithstanding, and none the less, because His will, when obeyed in actions, will bring on earthly sufferings.

12. But notwithstanding all that may be in store for him, he hopes to make those doctrines treasures (Y. XXXIV, 7), that is, a spiritual wealth (compare also Ahura's îsti). One only qualification would he add: 'Wait only before Thou givest the word that I should go forth with Thy new truths (which bring such suffering to him who first pronounces them), wait till my obedient will, listening fully to all which Thou shalt say, shall come to me, and then shall that obedient reverence in me and my beloved, help on our effort, that we may spread abroad the tidings of Thy promised recompense to win the living to Thee (Y. XXXI, 3).' 13. 'And that I may know and make known (so he continues) the true aims and objects of desire to those to whom I am at Thy word to go, grant me for this long life within Thy Realm, although that life be full of bitterness (verse 11; and Y. XXXII, 10, 11; XLVI, 1), for those who propagate Thy cause.' 14. 'Yea, as a friend, both wise and powerful, gives to a friend, send to me not only Sraosha, an obedient listening will, but raf(e)nô frâkhshnenem, abundant grace. Then, and then only, shall I be flanked with a proper ally. Then with Thy Sovereign Power, like my Obedient will, as an angel sent forth from Thee, and inspired by Thy righteous Order in law and ritual, in thought, and word, and deed, then I will go out to arouse and head the chiefs, gathering into spiritual hosts the many believing priests who even now would bear in mind and celebrate Thy mysteries.'

15. And as he began with fearless severity, so he would end without a compromise. 'My patient suffering (so he implies as he proceeds (Y. XLVI, 1)) reveals its lesson to me. My mind is long-enduring, but that patience, although it may seem to some the cowardice of a pusillanimous protector (Y. XXIX, 9), yet it is not such in truth, for it declares within me, and forces me to say: Let no man please the wicked; this is our only prospect of success.'

16. And casting back his thoughts he (or another in his name) sums all up well: 'Thus doth Zarathustra choose the spirit, that spirit which animates the faithful in their chiefs (Y. XXXIII, 9),

and by his side every true believer utters his sympathising prayer: Let the Order of life and of the ritual become incarnate in our tribes, and strong because it has the valiant power of faithful men to obey and to defend it. And let Piety prevail till it covers our land blest with the favours of the sacred sun, and as she lives in the lives of true adherents, may she in sympathy with the Good Mind, thus grant rewards for all our deeds!'

Translation.

1. Salvation to this man[1], salvation to him whosoever (he may be[2])! Let the absolutely ruling Great Creator grant (us, He) the living Lord, the two eternal powers. Yea, verily[3], I ask it of Thee (O Ahura) for the maintaining[4] Righteousness. And may'st Thou also give it to me, (O inspiring) Piety! splendour[5] (as it is), holy blessings, the Good Mind's life[6].

2. Yea, to this one[7] may the man endowed with

---

[1] Ahmâi as=to us, does not seem to be good grammar here, as it necessitates a forced separation between it and yahmâi-kahmâi*k*î*t*. Cp. ahmâi yahmâi-kahmâi*k*î*t* in Y. XLIV, 16.

[2] I turn from the fine rendering of the Pahlavi with the greatest reluctance: Nadû*k* valman mûn zak î valman nadûkîh ka*d*ârzâî [aîgh ka*d*ârzâî an*s*utâ min nadûkîh î valman nadûkîh], happy is he whose benefit is for every one; [that is, for every man there is happiness from his benefit]; Ner. follows.

[3] There is a question whether the particle ga*t* (gha*t*?) may not have originated from gâ*t*. Barth. here follows the Pahlavi, reading gatôi (?)=pavan yâmtûni*s*nŏ. Lak may have been added, as often, to serve as an alternative rendering.

[4] Or 'I will,' so Prof. Jolly (infinitive for imper.).

[5] So also the Pahl. rayê-hômand, not as a rendering merely, but as a philological analagon. Otherwise 'riches.'

[6] Gaêm recalls sraê*s*ta gaya *g*(i)vai*n*ti.

[7] As ahmâi would more naturally mean 'to this one' in the previous verse, it is desirable to render it in the same way here.

glory[1] give that best of all things, the (spiritual) glory. And do Thou likewise (Thyself) reveal[2] Thine own[3] (gifts) through Thy most bountiful spirit, O Mazda! (And do Thou teach us) Thy wonderful thoughts of wisdom[4], those of Thy Good Mind, which Thou hast revealed (to us) by Thy Righteousness (within us) with the happy increase of (our joy[5]), and on a long life's every day[6].

3. And may that (holy man) approach toward that which is the better than the good[7], he who will show to us the straight paths of (spiritual) profit, (the blessings) of this corporeal life, and of that the mental[8], in those veritably real (eternal[9]) worlds, where dwells Ahura; (that holy man) an offerer of Thine[10], O Mazda! a faithful citizen[11], and bountiful of (mind).

---

[1] It is to the last degree improbable that *hv*âthrôyâ (*hv*âthravâ; 'y' miswritten for 'v') indicates a condition of ease and comfort here. The 'easy man' is the farthest possible from the thoughts of the composer. The 'best of all things' makes a word kindred to *hveng* (*hv*an) appropriate here.

[2] *Kîkî* (?), if an imperative (?), may mean guard over; but the Pahlavi translator gives us the better view; he has lak pê*d*âkînô; Ner. tvam prakâ*s*aya. Geldner's *kîk*îthwâ is important.

[3] Thwâ=thy properties. [4] The Pahl. has merely pa*d*mânô.

[5] This shade of meaning is expressed by the Pahlavi.

[6] Ayâr*e*, acc. pl.

[7] This expression seems to equal the summum bonum; so also 'worse than the evil' is the ultimate of woe.

[8] Cp. Y. XXVIII, 3.

[9] Does haithy*e*ng mean 'eternal,' with every passage in which it occurs considered?

[10] Thwâva*n*t may, however, like mava*n*t, simply express the personal pronoun here. The position of aredrô, &c. is awkward if thwâva*n*t=thy: 'Where dwells Ahura, Thyself, O Mazda! beneficent, wise, and bountiful.' But aredra is almost a special term for a zealous partisan.

[11] The Pahl. has khûp-dânâkîh, indicating a meaning which would

4. Yea, I will [1] regard Thee as mighty and likewise bountiful, O Ahura Mazda! when (I behold) those aids of grace (approach me), aids which Thou dost guard and nurture [2] as (Thy) just awards to the wicked (to hold him far from us), as well as to the righteous (for our help), Thy Fire's flame therewith so strong through the Holy Order [3], and when to me the Good Mind's power comes [4+5].

5. (For) so I conceived of Thee as bountiful, O Great Giver, Mazda! when I beheld Thee as supreme [6] in the generation of life, when, as rewarding [7] deeds and words, Thou didst establish evil for the evil, and happy blessings for the good, by Thy (great) virtue [8] (to be adjudged to each) in the creation's final change.

6. In which (last) changing Thou shalt come, and with Thy bounteous spirit, and Thy sovereign power,

---

better apply to Ahura than the one given, which cannot be applied to Him.

[1] Subjunctive (see Prof. Jolly, V. S. p. 28).

[2] 'By Thy hand.' [3] The holy Fire of the altar.

[4] *G*ima*t* may be regarded as an improper subjunctive here.

[5] The Pahlavi: 'and that too which renders justice to the wicked and also to the righteous. And this Thy Fire is burning, since by it the strength of him who lives in Righteousness is (maintained) when that violence which approaches with a good intention comes to me.'

[6] See Y. XXXI, 8, where the word is also rendered as = vornehmster.

[7] Literally, 'When Thou didst render deeds provided with rewards.' We are forced to put the action in the past on account of zãthôi, but the influences originally set in motion were to have their issue in the end of the world.

[8] I render hunarâ literally, and bring its Pahlavi translation to the same sense as necessarily. Otherwise hûnar would generally mean 'skill.' Ner. has tava gu*n*eshu. The Pahlavi would here be recognised by all reasonable scholars as striking in its closeness.

O Ahura Mazda! by deeds of whom the settlements are furthered through the Righteous Order. And saving regulations [1] likewise unto these shall Âramaiti utter, (she, our Piety within us), yea, (laws) of Thine understanding which no man may deceive [2].

7. Yea, I conceived of Thee as bountiful, O Great Giver Mazda! when he (Thy messenger, Obedience) drew near me, and asked me thus: Who [3] art thou? And whose is thine allegiance? And how to-day shall I show the signs that give the light on this (our) question, (signs) as to the lands (from whence thou camest) and in thyself?

8. Then to him I, Zarathustra, as my first answer, said: To the wicked (would that I could be) in very truth a strong [4] tormentor and avenger, but to the

---

[1] The word ratûs reminds one of the work of the Ratu for the afflicted kine. In the last changing, which shall complete the Frashakard, he, or his representatives, will appear as the last Saoshyant, introducing 'millennial' blessedness.

[2] I render the Pahlavi here as in evidence: 'Through Thee, O (?) bountiful Spirit! the changing comes [(later (?) gloss) from wickedness to goodness]. And it comes likewise through Aûharmazd's supremacy within a good mind, through whose action the progress of Aharâyîh's settlements is furthered, those which the master is instructing with a perfect mind [ ], and in which this Thy wisdom shall in no wise be deceived thereby.'

[3] As the kine thought little of her deliverer (see Y. XXIX, 9), so Sraosha, the obedient host, is here represented as inquiring as to the antecedents of the newly-appointed prophet. But he asks more properly concerning the settlements from which he comes than the lands. Gaêtha is not da*hv*(h)yu. An origin external to that of other chieftains is not at all necessarily indicated by the question.

[4] The Pahlavi sees a denominative in isôyâ (isôvâ; y for v); it is denom. in the Altiranisches Verbum. It differs, however, as to root. I offer an alternative in its sense. An open tormentor; [that is, I openly torment the wicked] even as much as I desire, do I torment (them) [(later (?) gloss) Ganrâk mînavad].

righteous may I be a mighty help and joy [1], since to preparations [2] for Thy Kingdom, and in desire (for its approach), I would devote myself so long as to Thee, O Mazda! I may praise, and weave my song.

9. Yea, I conceived of Thee as bountiful, O Ahura Mazda! when (Thine herald) with Thy Good Mind near approached me, and asked me thus: For what dost thou desire that thou may'st gain, and that thou may'st know it? Then for Thy Fire an offering of praise and holiness (I desired. And on that offering for myself)[3] as long as I have the power, will I meditate [4], (and for its holy power among Thy people will I plan [5]).

10. And may'st Thou likewise grant [6] me (Thy) Righteousness (within me), since I earnestly invoke that perfect readiness (of mind), joining in my prayer with Âramaiti (our Piety toward Thee. Yea, pray Thou Thyself within me through these holy powers). Ask Thou (Thyself) our questions, those which shall be asked by us [7] of Thee; for a question asked by

---

[1] We must be cautious in accepting the statement that the Pahlavi translations attempt to be literal. Here is one which is free and far from erroneous: Aêtûnŏ avŏ aharûbŏ min valman î aôg-hômand aîtŏ; [aîghas, râmînam].

[2] The Pahlavi here shows only the correct root. [3] Mâ=smâ?

[4] 'So long as I can, will I be of this mind,' seems hardly expressed here. Observe the nearly parallel construction in verse 8.

[5] The Pahlavi, Sanskrit, and Persian translations would here be regarded once more as extremely close even by opponents, if reasonable in their estimates. Manayâî seems to me hardly an infinitive, as it is comparatively seldom that an infinitive falls to the end of a sentence either in Gâthic or Vedic. I prefer the indication of the Pahlavi with Justi and Bartholomae (in the Altiranisches Verbum).

[6] Read perhaps daidhîs (later shortened to suit the metre).

[7] Or, 'ask us that we may be questioned by Thee.'

Thee (as its inspirer), is as the question of the mighty, whene'er Thy (?) ruler speaks his potent wish.

11. Yea, I conceived of Thee as bountiful, O Ahura Mazda! when (Thy messenger) with Thy Good Mind near approached me, and with your words I[1] first impressed (my soul). Woes then 'midst men Thy heart-devoted one[2] declared[3] (to be) my (portion); but that will I do[4] which Thou did'st[5] say was best.

12. And since Thou, coming thus, Thy legal Righteousness in fulness[6] spakest, then declare not to me words as yet unheard (with faith or knowledge; command me not) to go forth (with these upon my task) before Thy Sraosha[7] (Obedience) comes to me, to go on hand in hand with me with holy recompense and mighty splendour[8], whereby to

---

[1] The Pahlavi translation bears evidence to a less subtle, and therefore more probable sense here, but at the same time to a rarer grammatical form. It renders dîdainhê as a third person, indicating an instance of a third person in ê, and not in the perfect. It also recognises a reduplicated form by its pavan nikêzisnŏ nikêzêdŏ.

[2] The Pahlavi translator with a curious error, or still more curious freedom, has rûbâk-dahisnîh here and elsewhere. Possibly the Gâthic text before the last compiler differed from ours.

[3] I still prefer Professor Bartholomae's earlier rendering, after the Pahlavi, as more in harmony with mraotâ and mraos.

[4] Professor Jolly has the important rendering 'das will ich thun;' the infinitive in a future or imperative sense.

[5] 'Ye said.'

[6] The Pahlavi unvaryingly kabed.

[7] Here we probably have the missing subject in the other verses.

[8] Reading mãzâ rayâ. (Rayâ cannot well mean 'riches' here.) The Pahlavi also indicates the division by its free or erroneous mas ratû (rad). Sraosha, an obedient will personified, guides the soul as in the later Parsism. Cp. the Ardâ Vîrâf.

give the contending[1] throngs (?), as a blessing[2], (Your) spiritual gifts (of certainty and peace).

13. Thus I conceived of Thee as bounteous, O Ahura Mazda! when with Thy Good Mind (Sraosha, Obedience) approached me. (And I would therefore pray thus of Thee, that bounteous one.) In order that I may make known to men the true and sacred aims of their desires (in the rite or daily toil), grant Ye me long life[3] for this, (that blessing[4]) which none with daring may extort[5] from You, even this (gift) of that desired[6] place which has been declared to be within Thy Realm.

14. Yea, as the man enlightened[7] (in Thy law), and who has possessions, gives to his friend, (so give Ye) me, O Great Creator[8]! Thy rejoicing and

---

[1] Here we have the important reading rânôibyô as against the dual of K4, &c. (see Geldner). No mention of the fire occurs; and as the form does not agree with ara*n*i, we may well doubt that comparison in view of ãsay*a*u in Y. XXXI, 2, and the unvarying and uniform patkar*d*ârânŏ of the Pahlavi. The rendering 'with the sticks' is, however, admirably adapted, and must be considered as an emphatic alternative.

[2] The Pahlavi supports the reading vî for v*e*; it has barâ. Ashî might also mean merely 'holy,' as adjective.

[3] In Y. XXVIII, 7, he asks for it that he may crush the malice of the foe.

[4] Justi admirably suggested *y*ânem understood.

[5] The Pahlavi divides dâr*s*taitê, and, as I hold, mistakes the root as was inevitable. The ancient scribe feared to restore the severed fragments, which appeared, as so often, in the MSS. before him. I would read dar*s*aitê with Spiegel's c (?) (so Bartholomae, later, however, recurring to a division, with Geldner after the Pahlavi, for the sake of bringing out an infinitive).

[6] Vairy*a*u contracted from vairyay*a*u by a corrupting improvement to regulate the metre.

[7] So the Pahlavi indicates, Bartholomae following as against the rendering 'possessing.'

[8] With regard to Mazd*a*u and medhã́, I should perhaps long

abounding grace, when through Thy sovereign Power, and from (the motives of Thy cause of) Righteous Order, I stand forth[1] to go out to[2], or to arouse, the chiefs[3] of Thy (pure) proclamation, with all those (others) who recite Thy well-remembered[4] Mãthra word.

15. Yea, I conceived of Thee as bounteous, O Ahura Mazda! when with the Good Mind's grace Thy Sraosha (Obedience) approached me, (and said): Let the quiet and long-enduring better mind with understanding teach (thee); let not a foremost[5] man

---

since have stated that I object to the comparison, not only because medhā́ is a feminine, and, as Grassmann has supposed, possibly represented by the Zend madh, Greek math, but because 'wisdom' is an abstract (while su-medhā́s, as a compound, does not apply so directly). I hold, however, that mazdâ, the fem. noun in Y. XL, 1 = medhā́. It is also not impossible that this word may be represented (with differing shades of meaning) by both madh and mazdãm (fem.) in Zend.

[1] Read, perhaps, frâkh*s*tâ; or frâ*s*tâ, 'with Thine advancing kingdom I (am) to go forth to'; (frâ + as, participle.)

[2] Prof. Jolly has the important rendering, 'Ich will mich erheben;' the infinitive in a future or imperative sense.

[3] Chieftainships. Compare (not with exactness, however) *s*ár-dhâ*m*si.

[4] The idea of reciting from memory seems to be included in mar*en*tê.

[5] The rendering pourû*s* (?) as = pl. of pûrú*s* is attractive, but dreg-vatô hardly needs, and seldom has, a substantive. The wicked = wicked men; and, on the other hand, nâ constantly claims an accompanying word; (nâ ismanô; nâ vaêdemnô; hvô nâ-erethwô; nâ spe*n*tô, *y*e-nâ, k*e* vâ-nâ, &c.) Also it is improbable that the words nâ and pourû*s*, as = pûrávas, should come together; 'let not a man men evil ingratiate (?).' Compare for sense here purviâs in one or more of its applications. Possibly the meaning is, 'let not a man be foremost in conciliating the wicked.' The Pahlavi likewise has kabed (freely). Ner. has: Mâ nara*h** pra*k*ura*m* durgatinâm bhûyât* yathâ katha*mk*it satkartâ. An important rendering is that of Professor

conciliate the wicked (as sycophant desiring aid), for with that (quiet mind of faith), Thy saints have brought full many a sinner unto Thee (as convert, and in penitence[1]).

16. Thus, O Ahura Mazda! this Zarathustra loves[2] the Spirit[3], and every man most bounteous prays[4] (beside him): Be Righteousness life-strong, and clothed with body. In that (holy) Realm which shines (with splendour) as the sun, let Piety be present; and may she through the indwelling of Thy Good Mind give us blessings in reward for deeds[5]!

Jolly, V.S. s. 47, 'möchte es wenige Verehrer des Lügners geben.' Cp. Y. XLVI, 1, where the composer speaks of the chiefs as on their side, 'not contenting' him.

[1] Or, with the Pahl.: Mûn aêtûnŏ lak harvisp-gûnŏ aharûbânŏ pavan anâk yakhsenund, for they consider all Thy saints as wicked. The rendering above is less natural as conveying the idea of a conversion (comp., however, *yâ g(i)vantô vîspeng vaurayâ*), but it renders the grammatical forms more simply. It is bad policy to force a text to express what we happen to believe to be a more natural idea. Using the hint of the Pahlavi here in an understanding manner, we might then render 'for they hold all sinners as holy.'

[2] I had long since compared *verentê* with *vrinîte* (-devā̃nâin ávas); and am now sustained by Bartholomae's view.

[3] Possibly the Spenista mainyu of Ahura. (See also Y. XLIV, 2.)

[4] The Pahlavi, on the contrary, bears evidence to the meaning 'comes,' which I cannot accept as 'tradition' in view of the following precatives.

[5] Ner.: 'The kingdom becomes established (in a manner completely manifest) in sun-publicity through mental perfection [ ]; and upon the workers of righteousness the Good Mind bestows it.'

YASNA XLIV.

QUESTIONS ASKED OF AHURA WITH THANKFULNESS AND DEVOTION.

Many verses may here have fallen out, or, on the other hand, the piece having been made up of homogeneous, but not originally connected fragments, has been left with some abrupt transitions. These, however, occasion very little difficulty in exegetical treatment, and are also not displeasing. The formula, 'This I ask Thee, O Ahura! tell me aright' seems to have been suggested by Y. XXXI, 14. We might therefore look upon this piece as composed later than Y. XXXI, but not necessarily in a later generation, or even from another hand. In fact the style is thoroughly homogeneous in certain places with that of pieces which we ascribe without a doubt to Zarathustra, and the signs of struggle point to the earliest period. It is possible that the words in Y. XXXI, and the formula here were of common origin, neither having any extended priority to the other, or the words may be original here, and derived in Y. XXXI.

Whether Zarathustra, or another of the narrow circle of religious leaders, was the composer throughout depends upon the further questions already more than once broached, as to how far a corresponding intellectual cultivation was extended at the period in the community, and as to what is the probability of the existence of more than one man in the small group, endowed with the peculiar qualities everywhere manifested in these hymns (see remarks in the Introduction and elsewhere). It is safest to say that Zarathustra composed most of the matter here before us, and that the supplementary fragments were composed under his dominating, if not immediate, influence.

Verses 1 and 2 seem an introduction, but hardly give added emphasis to the fact that the following questions were expressions of devotion, and only in a few instances appeals for knowledge. Verses 3–5 are certainly questions intended to express veneration while naming particular objects of devout inquiry. Verse 6 stands somewhat apart. Verses 7–11 enter into details touching the moral and religious improvement of the people, 12–14 are polemical, 15 and 16 are prophetical, &c.

1. More closely; the composer beseeches Ahura to speak to him, and in a manner characteristic of Himself as in distinction from the falsifying utterance of the opposing religion, which was so familiarly described as the religion of 'Falsehood.' He is entreated to reveal, as is His wont, 'the holy truth.' And the first question propounded to Him by the composer, as comprehensive of all others, is how he may offer homage, the homage of God Himself or of His bountiful spirit; (see mainyû in verse 2). And he further asks that Ahura may speak to him, showing him by what ceremonial he may conciliate him, and by what helps of grace that spirit, or Ahura Himself, may be inclined to draw near to him in accordance with his frequent prayer.

2. Once more he asks how he may serve that Spirit as the foremost one of Heaven (compare Y. XXXI, 8, and the Parsi vahist) who seeks for this addition of praise to praise, for as the supreme claim to our veneration, He had, as a guardian (Y. XXXI, 13) like Ahura in yet another place, held off destruction from all believing saints and from all repentant men (Y. XXXI, 3), and that although as 'the chief of Heaven,' yet also as a benignant friend.

3. From these introductory petitions, inserted perhaps before many lost verses, he proceeds in another tone, although he may still be said to say what is homogeneous to the foregoing: 'Yea, I ask how I may serve Him, O Mazda! for He is indeed Thyself, and therefore, to show my fervent homage, I ask: Who was, not the first establisher alone, but the first father, of our holy Order as the personified Immortal, and that not by creation, but by generation, as the parent generates the child? Who fixed for stars and sun that "way," the undeviating path through space, long noticed and studied by our fathers, as no random course, or unknown progress save Thee?'

4. The laws of gravitation then become the theme of his praise still expressed in the form of questions, also the atmospheric phenomena, especially the clouds driven by winds, not like the Maruts beyond the mountains perhaps, but still terrible as winds can be. But he cannot leave even the sublime objects of nature without thinking once more of that spiritual power, the strength of righteous character, which was justly more impressive, although still more familiar, and which he designates, as ever, by the 'Good Mind.' Here this great Immortal is left an immortal thought, and is spoken of as 'created,' not 'born' like Asha (in verse third). 5. Beyond a doubt, recognising the satisfactions of energetic life as well as the solaces of slumber, and as forming by their contrast the necessary

change which builds up happiness, he alludes to the supreme arranger as 'well-skilled,' and asks: Who so wisely relieved the day by night? But, again, he cannot close without reverting to the course of moral duty. 6. Seized with a doubt which again only heightens the fervour of his assurance, he asks whether indeed the facts which he proclaims are really what they seem. Whether piety, although aided by the Good Mind, implanted through Ahura's grace within us, will indeed at last, or soon, assign the purified Realm to the servants of Ahura, who were there among the masses before his eyes (taêibyô), or to Ahura Himself as their sovereign controller (taibyô ?). And, as including all rural riches in herself, he asks for whom He had made the kine, not now wailing in her grief (Y. XXIX, 9), but 'delight-affording,' on account of the influence of Piety and Benevolence embodied in the Kingdom, inferring that God had made her for these same (the faithful masses). 7. And going yet further back; he asks who made that paternal and filial Piety itself, together with the Realm which it should leaven? Answering his own inquiries by an inference, he adds: I am pressing Thee with fulness in these questions, O Thou bountiful Spirit (compare mainyu*s*, or mainyû in verse 2), the maker of all (sun, stars, and holy qualities). 8. Turning now to verbal revelations, he asks by what means his soul may prosper in moral goodness, praying that it may indeed thus advance as the expected answer would declare. 9. He prays that he may know how he may still further sanctify that Religion which the King of the Holy Realm (compare angheu*s* vahi*s*tahyâ pourvîm), the one like Ahura (see Khshmâvatô and thwâvãs, verse 1) would teach, dwelling in the same abode (in which Ahura is also elsewhere said to dwell) with the holy Order, and the Good Mind (see Y. XLVI, 16).

10. Expressing all in a single word, he asks Ahura to reveal to him the Daêna, the Insight, the substance of that Religion which was 'of all things best,' and which alone could 'advance the settlements' with the holy ritual and moral Order as its ally, which would also render all their moral and ceremonial actions, and moral principles just by means of the divine Piety, which was their realisation in practice; and he closes with the exclamation that the wishes and desires of his soul, when most embued with wisdom, will seek for God.

11. Following out the influence of Âramaiti (that personified Piety), he asks to know by what practical means she may approach, and be realised as the characteristic of those to whom the holy Insight should be preached, avowing that God knows how prominent

he is in his devotion to the matter, and with what hatred seated 'in his spirit,' he views the opposing Gods. 12. Then casting a searching glance over the masses, and perhaps eyeing their several groups, each headed by its 'chieftainship' (sardenau senghahyâ), he cries, addressing Ahura formally, but the people really (so also elsewhere frequently), and says: 'Who is the righteous believer as regards these my questions asked of God to express my belief in Him, and who is the sceptic? Which man does the Angra Mainyu govern; or which is as evil as that chief himself?' And, recalling the galling fact that some are tolerated who not only do not assist but oppose his efforts, and perhaps having some half-convinced sections in full sight, he cries with bitterness: 'Why is this sinner, that chief who opposes me as Angra Mainyu opposed Ahura (compare paiti-eretê with âat môi paiti-eretê in Vendîdâd I), why is he not believed to be what in very truth he is? Why is he still countenanced?' 13. And then with a fierceness which reminds us of sâzdûm snaithishâ (Y. XXXI, 18), but which is deeper because proposing a less material remedy, he asks: 'Why must we abide the sight of these opposers, representing their Lie-demon as their Goddess? How can I drive her hence to Hell beneath, not to those who hesitate like these, pausing before they condemn the evil party, but to those who are already filled with their disobedience, and who, having no communion at all with us, receive no light, like these, from the reflected glory of the truth, and who have moreover neither sought nor shared like these, the counsels of Thy Good Mind. Yea, how,' he reiterates, 'can I deliver up that Lying Goddess, in the persons of her adherents, to the Holy Order, in the persons of the saints, into their hands, to slay her, not with the snaithis only, but to destroy her as a falsehood by the Mãthras of Thy doctrine, not barely to withstand these wicked corrupters, as we now do, enduring the silence of these masses at their deeds (verse 12), their fear of them, or their connivance with their creeds, but to spread slaughter among them to their total overthrow?'

15. He then presses on the coming collision, and prays to know to which of the hosts (compare ãsayau, Y. XXXI, 2) that claim the urvâtâ, Ahura will give the prize. 16. And who, he further asks, shall be the champion who shall lead the victors, the verethrem-gan (compare sargâ, Y. XXIX, 3) who will thus take up the snaithis and the Mãthra (verse 14), and so at once contend for 'both the worlds.' And he wishes him not alone pointed out, but approached, as Zarathustra was approached (Y. XLIII), by an obedient will, and moved to his holy work by the inspiring Good

Mind of Ahura, be that champion Ratu whosoever the Lord might wish. Salvation in the shape of success in his great attempt should be his portion (Y. XLIII, 1). 17. Half intimating that he himself may be the coming man, he begs to know when he can have that conference in which, as in the desired hemparsti and darsti of Y. XXXIII, 6, he may communicate more closely with Ahura, and through the revelation which might be vouchsafed, may become a protecting leader to secure the ever-named 'abiding two,' 'Weal' and 'Immortality,' which were the 'better than the good,' the 'vahista' of the saints.

18. A preliminary wish arising, he asks that he may receive the honorary gift of mated mares and a camel, as material for sacrifice before a battle (?), the highest interests of the people even, their lasting Welfare, demanding that he should receive this help. 19. For the monarch, or leading chief, who may withhold this justly deserved and needed help, or honour, he declares by the terms of his following question, that some instant judgment will be forthcoming, for the threats of the future condemnation seem for the moment only trite.

20. As a peroration, he appeals to the reason of the wavering groups, among the masses who still delay to call evil evil (verse 12), and he asks whether the Daêvas, as represented by their adherents, had ever been good rulers, when they had the power. Were not robbery and violence then the law with them as now? And did not the Kine, as representing the sacred herds and people, lift up her wailing voice?

(The piece from verse 12 seems to constitute a religious war-song. These verses seem not to have been originally connected with the calm and thankful contemplations in verses 1–10, but later united with them. Verses 12–20 stand in the closest connection with Y. XLVI, which has, however, preserved more of the elements of sorrow and discouragement which influenced the leader and his followers at times. See also XLIII, 11.)

Translation.

1. This I ask Thee, O Ahura! tell me aright; when praise is to be offered, how (shall I complete) the praise of the One like You [1], O Mazda? Let

[1] Some who seldom cite the Pahlavi follow it here; nîyâyisnŏ zak mûn aêtûnŏ nîyâyisnŏ î Lekûm [dînô]. Otherwise one might

the One like Thee declare it earnestly to the friend who is such as I, thus through Thy Righteousness (within us) to offer friendly help[1] to us, so that the One like Thee[2] may draw near[3] us through Thy Good Mind (within the soul).

2. This I ask Thee, O Ahura! tell me aright, how, in pleasing Him, may we serve the supreme one of (Heaven) the better world[4]; yea, how to serve that chief who may grant us those (blessings of His grace, and) who will seek for (grateful requitals at our hands); for He, bountiful (as He is) through the Righteous Order, (will hold off) ruin[5] from (us) all, guardian (as He is) for both the worlds, O Spirit[6] Mazda! and a friend.

---

read nemê with B.V.S. (variation) in Y. LVIII, 3, and render, 'how shall I bow myself in your worship?'

[1] The Pahl. hamkar*d*âr is likewise followed. The alteration to hâkôrenâ is very interesting, but, I think, hardly necessary.

[2] Observe the great difficulty in referring Khshmâvatô to a human subject. Here we have 'the homage of the One like You (of Yours(?)' some would say); in Y. XXXIII, 8 we have Yasnem Mazdâ (Ahurâ) Khshmâvatô; in Y. XXXIV, 2 Khshmâvatô vahmê; in Y. XLIX, 6 Tãm daênãm yâ Khshmâvatô Ahurâ. Khshmâvatô is sometimes merely a way of saying 'of Thyself,' as mavaitê=to me.

[3] Observe also the emphasis on his 'drawing near'; otherwise 'let Your one declare it to my friend' (?).

[4] See Roth, Y. XXXI, 8. See, however, also de Harlez's suggestion, perhaps after the hint of the Pahlavi: 'qu'elle a été l'origine?' Here we have another instance where an entire verse seems to allude to Ahura in the third person with an address to Him thrown in, or at the close. In connection with angh*e*u*s* vahi*s*tahyâ Ahura must be the pourvya, as in Y. XXXI, 8, where Roth renders vornehmster. The guardian is also Ahura (see Y. XXXI, 13).

[5] I cannot fully accept the hint of the Pahlavi here as others do who seldom heed it. I do not think that 'sin' is so much indicated as 'destruction.'

[6] Mainyû is suspiciously expressive as a vocative; perhaps 'by spiritual power' would be safer.

3. This I ask Thee, O Ahura! tell me aright: Who by generation[1] was the first father of the Righteous Order (within the world)? Who gave the (recurring) sun and stars[2] their (undeviating) way? Who established that whereby the moon waxes, and whereby she wanes[3], save Thee[4]? These things, O Great Creator! would I know[5], and others likewise still.

4. This I ask Thee, O Ahura! tell me aright, who from beneath hath sustained the earth and the clouds[6] above that they do not fall? Who made the waters and the plants? Who to the wind has yoked on the storm-clouds, the swift and fleetest two[7]? Who, O Great Creator! is the inspirer of the good thoughts (within our souls)?

---

[1] 'As a generator (?).'

[2] Bartholomae follows the Pahlavi here as rendered by Ner. putting hv*e*ng and star*e*m (-ãm) in the genitive, which is in itself far better than to regard dâ*t* as governing two accusatives. One would, however, rather expect hv*e*ng starãm adhvânem dâ*t*.

[3] All follow the Pahlavi here, which renders with allowable freedom. Nerefsaitî (=Pahl. nerefsê*d*; Ner. nimîlati; Persian kâhad) might possibly be explained as a nasalised form of an Aryan correspondent to arbha, as na*s*=a*s*.

[4] Possibly from thine influence (?).

[5] The infinitive vîduyê (=vîdvê) lies here in an unusual place, at the end of the sentence. It is because the word has no stress upon it. The emphasis rests on the objects which he desires to know about; the entire connection deals with 'knowing'; it has no prominence.

[6] This rendering is not supported by the Pahlavi, which seems to report a rendering from some text with an a privative, and a form of dar. The 'unsupported' object might mean the 'air-space.' See the suggestion of Bartholomae 'the earth and the air-space,' comparing the later Sanskrit.

[7] Or 'for velocity,' adverbially. Velocity, however, in the abstract as the object yoked-on, is rather too finely drawn. I should prefer

5. This I ask Thee, O Ahura! tell me aright; who, as a skilful artisan, hath made the lights and the darkness[1]? Who, as thus skilful, hath made sleep and the zest (of waking hours)? Who (spread) the Auroras, the noontides and midnight, monitors to discerning (man), duty's true (guides)[2]?

6. This I ask Thee, O Ahura! tell me aright these things which I shall speak forth, if they are truly thus. Doth the Piety (which we cherish) in reality increase[3] the sacred orderliness within our actions? To these Thy true saints hath she given the Realm through the Good Mind. For whom hast Thou made the Mother-kine, the producer of joy[4]?

7. This I ask Thee, O Ahura! tell me aright; who fashioned Âramaiti (our piety) the beloved, together with Thy Sovereign Power? Who, through his guiding wisdom[5], hath made the son revering the father? (Who made him beloved[6]?) With (ques-

---

the fleet ones, the lightnings. My rendering follows the indication of another, as a dual, but not as to full exegesis. One naturally supposes the yoking together of the winds and dark clouds to be meant.

[1] Recall svàr yád áśmann adhipā́ u ándho.—*R*v. VII, 88, 2.

[2] Ner.: 'Who gave us the lights with his keen discrimination? And who the darkness? Who, in his keen discrimination, gave (us our) sleep and waking; [that is, our diligence and activity?] Who is he who gave us the time of huśaina, and the time of rapithvana [ ], and the method and calculation of him who discerns by means of the just rule [ ]?'

[3] So also the Pahlavi indicates by 'stavar.'

[4] So I prefer; but the indication of the Pahlavi deserves an alternative 'giver of bounty'; skar=kar.

'Geu*s* azy*a*u' was later a common expression for a mature animal, but possibly vulgarised from its older special use here.

[5] Root nî (?).

[6] I thus add as the Pahlavi translator indicates such an element in uzemem.

tions such as) these, so abundant[1], O Mazda! I press Thee, O bountiful Spirit, (Thou) maker of all!

8. This I ask Thee, O Ahura! tell me aright, that I may ponder[2] these which are Thy revelations, O Mazda! and the words which were asked (of Thee) by Thy Good Mind (within us), and that whereby we may attain[3], through Thine Order, to this life's perfection. Yea, how may my soul with joyfulness[4] increase in goodness? Let it thus[5] be[6].

9. This I ask Thee, O Ahura! tell me aright, how to myself shall I hallow[7] the Faith of Thy people,

---

[1] Frakhshnî=in abundance (Pahl. kabed; Ner. pra*k*uram; Persian MS. bisyar). The thought refers back to anyâ*k*â vîduyê [-vê].

[2] Haug sagaciously renders as if me*n*dâidyâi were a miswriting for pe*n*dâidyâi, which is in itself very possible, as an 'm' ɕ looks much like an inverted ɘ in MSS. So the Pahlavi records the irregularity also, from which Haug derived his idea. But Haug explains the word as an allusion to the five prayer-hours of the day. I doubt very greatly whether the five prayer-hours existed at the date of the composition of this passage. Such regulations grew up much later. The Pahlavi translator indicates elsewhere an accusative (me*n*g=mãm) with an infinitive 'that I should give forth,' which is in itself far from impossible. He was aware (!) that me*n*g could also equal man; see Y. LIII, 5.

[3] Vaêdyâi is infinitively used for vôizdyâi.

[4] I do think that it is necessary on the whole to postulate two similar words here (although Geldner's suggestion is most keen and interesting). Urvâkh*s*anguha and urvâkh*s*ukhti do not favour a comparison with vrag here. The Pahlavi is indifferent: *K*îgûn denman î li rûbânô zak î *s*apîr hû-ravâkh-manîh? So Ner. uttamânanda*h*. Barth. beglückend.

[5] Kâ-tâ=kéna-téna.

[6] Or, 'let those things happen to me;' gam means 'come' more frequently than 'go,' here. Lit. 'let it thus advance.'

[7] *K*îgûn denman î li dînô yô*s*-dâsar î avê*g*ak yô*s*-dâsaryôm? Ner.: Katham ida*m* aha*m* yat* dîni*m* pavitratarâm pavitrayâmi; [kila, dîni*m* katha*m* pravartamânâ*m* karomi]? As Zarathu*s*tra is

which the beneficent kingdom's lord hath taught me, even the admonitions which He called Thine equal, hath taught me through His lofty (and most righteous Sovereignty and) Power, as He dwells in like abode[1] with Thine Order and Thy Good Mind?

10. This I ask Thee, O Ahura! tell me aright that holy Faith which is of all things best, and which, going on hand in hand with Thy people, shall further my lands in Asha, Thine order, and, through the words of Âramaiti (our piety), shall render actions just. The prayers of mine understanding will seek[2] for Thee, O Ahura!

11. This I ask Thee, O Ahura! tell me aright: how to these your (worshippers) may (that Piety once again and evermore) approach, to them to whom O Lord, Thy Faith is uttered? Yea, I beseech of Thee to tell me this, I who am known to Thee as Thy foremost[3] of (servants); all other (Gods, with their

represented as sanctifying the Fire (in Y. IX, 1), so here he would doubly sanctify the Faith itself. He would 'hallow its name' and meaning.

[1] Pavanas-hamdemûnîh-ketrûnê*d* [pavan hamkhadûkîh].

[2] I cannot regard the caesura in this verse as possessing ordinary importance, the ma*hvya*u (mahy*a*u) *k*istôi*s* is especially dependent on the following words. The Pahlavi translator hints at an important solution, which is, that a pause should be made before us*e*n; 'the wish of mine understanding wishes, and I wish (am wishing); Khûrsand hômanam = I am content. If we can accept a break (a possibility far too little recognised), the u*se*n as representing a nom. sing. would refer back to the meaning in ma*hvya*u (mahy*a*u). But reading îstî*s* (as irregular for î*s*tayô on account of the metre) we might regard us*e*n as a third pl. Or shall we take it as a quasi-third singular, us*e*n being usãn (*e*n = the nasal vowel; comp. û*k*ãm as a third sing. imper. after Barth.)? Let 'the wish (î*s*ti*s*) of my enlightened understanding wish for Thee.'

[3] Compare 'aêshãm tôi, Ahura! *e*hmâ pourutemâi*s* dastê.'

polluted worshippers), I look upon with (my) spirit's [1] hate [2].

12. This I ask Thee, O Ahura! tell me aright; who is the righteous one in that regard in which [3] I ask Thee my question? And who is evil? For which is the wicked? Or which is himself the (foremost) wicked one? And the vile man who stands against me (in this gain of) Thy blessing, wherefore [4] is he not held and believed to be the sinner that he is?

13. This I ask Thee, O Ahura! tell me aright, how shall I banish this Demon-of-the-Lie from us hence to those beneath who are filled [5] with rebellion? The friends of Righteousness (as it lives in Thy saints) gain no light (from their teachings), nor have they loved the questions which Thy Good Mind (asks in the soul [6])!

Auserkoren is a fine but a bold rendering. Election is, however, included in all divine prescience.

[1] I have no doubt whatever, but that mainy*eu*s and dvaêshanghâ belong together.

[2] The Pahlavi translation is as follows: 'That which I ask of Thee, tell me aright, O Aûharmazd! when shall the perfect mind come to those persons [that is, when does the mind of my disciples become perfect]? When shall it come to those who declare this Thy Religion, O Aûharmazd? Grant to me before these the proclamation of the truth. Against every other spirit which is malevolent I keep my guard.'

[3] Yâi*s* adverbially, or possibly, 'with whom I question.'

[4] *Kyanghat* is, I think, simply the equivalent for *k*î (?) angha*t* = quî fit, how does it happen that? 'Stands' free for 'comes.'

[5] The Pahlavi on the contrary takes peren*a*unghô in the sense of combating, pavan anyôkhshî*d*ârîh patkârênd = '(who) are opposing you through disobedience.' It is far from certain that he does not indicate some improvement in text, or rendering.

[6] Or, 'the counsels of holy men.'

14. This I ask Thee, O Ahura! tell me aright; how shall I deliver that Demon-of-the-Lie into the two hands of Thine Order[1] (as he lives in our hosts) to cast her down to death through Thy Mãthras of doctrine, and to send mighty destruction[2] among her evil believers, to keep those deceitful and harsh oppressors from reaching their (fell) aims[3]?

15. This I ask Thee, O Ahura! tell me aright. If through Thy Righteousness (within our souls) Thou hast the power over this for my[4] protection, when the two hosts shall meet in hate[5] (as they strive) for those vows which Thou dost desire to maintain, how, O Mazda! and to which of both wilt Thou give[5] the day[6]?

16. This I ask Thee, O Ahura! tell me aright,

---

[1] Ashâi with Geldner.

[2] The Pahlavi anticipates us in the correct general sense here. It has nas,hônisnŏ. The Persian MS. renders the Pahlavi, hamâvandî nîst dehand î darwand.

[3] Anâshê seems regarded as an infinitive by the Pahlavi translator, anayâtûnisnŏ. 'For the destruction of those deceivers' is an obvious alternative to the rendering above (â nâshê ?).

[4] Geldner and Roth render ma*t*=Sanskrit mad; otherwise 'with complete protection.' Or is ma*t* ablative for genitive: If thou rulest over me to afford me protection? The Pahlavi affords no indication.

[5] The Pahlavi translator erred widely in his attempt to render the word anao*k*anghâ. As it is certain that his MSS. differed from ours often, they probably did so here. The verse alludes beyond a question to some expected battle in a religious war, and perhaps in a religious civil war. It is the most positive allusion to the 'strife of the two parties' (Y. XXXI, 2) which has come down to us. It was a struggle concerning the religious vows, or doctrines; avâi*s* urvâtâi*s* yâ tû Mazdâ dîderegh*z*ô.

[6] The Pahlavi renders vananãm by 'good thing,' explaining 'the sovereign power.'

who smites with victory[1] in the protection (of all) who exist, and for the sake of, and by means of Thy doctrine? Yea, clearly reveal a lord having power[2] (to save us) for both lives. Then let (our) Obedience[3] with Thy Good Mind draw near to that (leader), O Mazda! yea, to him to whomsoever[4] Thou (shalt) wish that he should come.

17. This I ask Thee, O Ahura! tell me aright; how, O Mazda! shall I proceed to that (great) conference[5] with You, to that consummation of Your own, when my spoken wish[6] shall be (effected) unto me, (the desire) to be in the chieftainship[7] (and supported) by (the hope of) Weal and Immortality (those saving powers of Thy grace), and by that (holy) Mãthra (Thy word of thought) which fully guides our way through Righteousness (within).

---

[1] Verethrem-*g*â thwâ, following the Pahlavi with Westergaard, Geldner, and Bartholomae.

[2] Compare Y. XXIX, 2 and Y. XXVIII, 3; or it may mean 'promise to establish' (Barth.). *K*izdî, however, hardly seems to need an infinitive with it; it may mean 'appoint.' Compare dá*m*su (patnî) for a better sense than 'house-lord,' also for d*e*ng patôis.

[3] This casts additional light on the 'one that should come' in Y. XLIII, 7, 9, 11, 13, 15.

[4] This recalls ahmâi yahmâi us*t*â kahmâi*k*î*t*.

[5] The comparison with *g*ar has long circulated among Zendists. Many adopt it. It agrees admirably with the Pahlavi as to sense: Aîmat, Aûharmazd! damânŏ kar*d*ârîh î Lekûm, when is Your appointment of the time?

[6] The Pahlavi va mûni*k* zak î li gôbi*s*nŏ hômand khvâstar.

[7] Va sardâr yehevûni*s*nîh madam Haurvada*d* va Amerôdâ*d*; Ner. Svâmino bhavishyanti upari Avirdâde Amirdâde; comp. also Y. XLIX, 8 fraê*st*aunghô *a*unghâmâ. Professor Jolly compares bûzdyâi with φύεσθαι (Inf. s. 194). The long since circulated comparison with bhug seems to me hardly so probable. It may, however, deserve an alternative; 'to enjoy Weal and Immortality'; but accusatives

18. (And, having gained Thine audience and Thine Order's sacred chieftainship), then I ask of Thee, O Ahura! and tell me aright, how shall I acquire that Thy Righteous Order's prize, ten (costly) mares male-mated, and with them the camel[1] (those signs of honour and blessing for Thy chief. I ask Thee for these gifts for sacrifice). For it was told me for the sake of our Welfare (in our salvation), and of our Immortality, in what manner Thou[2] shalt give[3] to these (Thy conquering hosts) both of these Thy (gifts[4] of grace).

19. This I ask Thee, O Ahura! tell me aright; (in the case of the recreant, of him) who does not give this (honoured) gift to him who hath earned it; yea, who does not give it to this (veracious tiller of the earth, to him who in no respect shows favour to the Demon-of-the-Lie, even to the) correct speaker[5] (of Thy sacrificial word), what shall be his sentence at

do not fall so naturally to the end of the sentence in Gâthic or Vedic, without preceding related or qualifying words.

[1] Those suspected of no partisanship for the Pahlavi translation follow it here as against Haug, who translated the words u*s*trem*k*â by et amplius! It means a camel; so the Pahlavi translator rendered many centuries ago before Europeans even knew what the Indian ú*sh*/*t*ra meant, which simple analogy Neryosangh first drew. Horses were material for sacrifice among the Persians according to Herodotus. The reasons for the prayer are not fully expressed.

[2] So better than as a first person aorist subjunctive, if taêibyô is to be read. The Pahlavi, however, read taibyô, which is not lightly to be passed over.

[3] The rendering 'take' has long circulated. I do not, however, prefer it here.

[4] Weal and Immortality, but hî might refer to the two objects, 'the mares' and the 'camel.'

[5] The ideal Zarathu*s*trian; comp. Y. XXXI, 15; XLIX. 9.

the first (now at this time, and because of this false dealing? I ask it), knowing well his doom at last[1].

20. (And how as to our deluded foes?) Have Daêva-(worshippers) e'er reigned as worthy kings? (This verily I ask of Thee, the Daêva-worshippers) who fight[2] for these (who act amiss? Have they well reigned) by whom the Karpan and the Usi*g*(k) gave the (sacred) Kine to Rapine[3], whence, too, the Kavian in persistent strength[4] has flourished? (And these have also never given us tribal wealth nor blessings), nor for the Kine have they brought waters to the fields for the sake of the Righteous Order (in our hosts), to further on their growth (and welfare)!

---

[1] So also the Pahlavi followed by all. Ka*d*âr valman pavan zak vinâsis*n*ŏ aîtŏ fratûm; [aîga*s* pavan-vinâskârîh pâ*d*afrâs fratûm maman]? Âkâs hômanam zak mûn valman aîtŏ afdûm [mamana*s* darvandîh]? Ner. (with regard to him) who does not give the reward which has come for the one fitted for, or deserving of, it [to *G*arathustra's equal], (the reward) which the truthful man; [that is, the good man] is giving to him, what is the first thing which happens through this sin of his? [that is, what is his first chastisement in consequence of this fault?] (For) I am aware of what his punishment shall be in the end [ ].

[2] The Pahlavi translator either had a text with some form of pâ, or was otherwise misled. He renders mûn netrûnd, but gives the word the adverse sense of 'hindering' in the gloss. Ner., however, has pratiskhalanti which points to peshyêi*n*tî, and also tends to show that other MSS. of the Pahlavi (and among them the one used by Ner.) read differently from our three, K5, D. J., and the Persian transliteration. Kãm = Ved. kám with dat.

[3] See Y. XXIX, 1.

[4] Professor Wilhelm 'vigour' (De Infin. p. 14).

YASNA XLV.

THE DOCTRINE OF DUALISM. HOMAGE TO AHURA.

This hymn bears fewer traces of a fragmentary condition than others. It recalls Y. XXX, and, like it, appears to belong to a period, or to an interval, of political repose and theological activity. It is smoother and more artificial than is usual, and it goes straight on its way from beginning to end. A powerful adversary had just been crushed. It was the dussasti of Y. XXXII, 9. This may well have been the result of the conflict alluded to in Y. XLIV, 15, 16, and possibly in Y. LI, 9, 10, also urged on by the fierce Y. XXXI, 18 probably often repeated in lost hymns.

An assembly is addressed as in Y. XXX, 1, but this time as coming 'from near and from far.' It may very possibly have been the winning side in a late struggle. The first verse sounds like a congratulation.

It might be said to be intended to be sung, if not shouted, to a multitude whose outskirts were by no means within easy reach with the voice. At all events attention is summoned with three differing expressions. 'Awake your ears to the sound,' literally 'sound ye,' in a receptive sense; ('let the sound peal in your ears'), then 'listen' (sraotâ); and then 'ponder' (mãzdaunghôdûm). 'The Antizarathustra, the evil teacher par eminence, has been defeated,' he declares, 'and he will never again destroy the peace of our lives (Y. XXXII, 9, 11). His evil creed has been silenced, and his tongue can no longer shout out its periods of persuasion or invective (Y. XXXI, 12) beside our preachers.'

2. He then reiterates the chief doctrine for which the parties had been at war, and which they should now see clearly in the light of their victory. 'The foul evils of society do not lie within the control of the holy Ahura in such a manner as that he either originates, or tolerates them. They are, on the contrary, the product of the personified Anger of the Daêvas, the Mainyu in its evil sense, the Angra (angry ?) Spirit. Between this being, or personified abstraction, and Ahura, there is a gulf fixed. (Never do we see any aspersions upon Ahura's name, or a suspicion of His purity as shown by complicity with cruelty, or the toleration of evil passions.) It is also to be noted that the defeated dussasti may have possibly been a Daêva-worshipper chiefly as being a heretic from this Faith

of Ahura, believing Him to be implicated in the creation, or permission of sin and suffering, or, if the burial or burning of the dead was forbidden at this time, then possibly a heretic on these questions also. But yet, as a recreant Mazda-worshipper he may have claimed a rightful allegiance to the urvâtâ, and the future blessings, as well as temporal advantages, involved in a correct discipleship; and so he may have used the name of the sacred tenets of the Religion itself to help on a nefarious warfare. In fact he may have been a self-styled Mazda-worshipper, but not of 'Zarathustra's order,' not owned at all in any degree by the genuine adherents, and met as a real, if not an open, Daêva-worshipper.

The ardent prophet therefore declares the utter severance between the good and the evil, the God and the Demon. It is a popular corollary to Y. XXX, 3–6. The two spirits came together indeed at first to make life, and its negation, and they co-operate, if such a term can be applied to an irreconcilable antagonism out of whose antitheses and friction sentient existence alone becomes possible. Their union consists in opposition, for if they blend, they each cease to be what they are. They are, while upholders of existence, yet separate for ever, and that as to every attribute and interest.

3. And the sage goes on to assert that in this he is proclaiming the first Mãthra of this life which the all-wise Mazda had revealed to him. And, whether sure of the victorious masses before him, or whether on the contrary perfectly aware that many a group among them had been more convinced by the snaith*is* than by reason, he presses at once upon them that one terrible doctrine which seems unfortunately too needful for all successful and sudden propagandism, and he declares that they who do not act in a manner accordant with what he speaks, and even thinks, (having formerly announced it), to such delinquents this life should end in woe.

4. Proceeding in a happier vein, he then dwells upon the fatherhood of God. He will declare this world's best being who is Mazda Himself. He is the father of the Good Mind within His people, when that Good Mind is active in good works. So our piety, when it is practical, is His daughter, for no pretended good intention can claim relationship with Him, nor can any idle sentiment. He needs the 'ready mind' within His servant, and He is not to be deceived (compare Y. XLIII, 6).

5. Returning once more to the Mãthra, and this time to hold out rewards rather than to utter threats, he declares that Happiness and Immortality would be the portion of those who listened to, and

pondered his revelation, and that Ahura Himself would likewise approach them with the rewarding actions of His Good Mind, for Ahura was also in all good actions on the one hand, just as His Immortal Archangels on the other had their objective existence likewise in the believer's soul.

6. Turning from admonition to worship, he announces, not what he terms the 'first' (verse 3), nor the 'best' (verses 4 and 5), but the 'greatest,' element of all, implying that praise, which he now expresses, includes both prayer and doctrinal confessions, and he calls on Ahura both to listen and to teach. 7. It is the 'greatest' element indeed, for it concerns those spiritual blessings which not only the offerers who are now living will seek after, but those also who shall live in future; nay, even the spirits of the just desire them in the eternal Immortality. And these blessings are, according to a well-remembered law, woe to the wicked, and that, not only from outward discipline, but from inward grief. And Ahura had established, so he adds, the beneficent, but, as regards the wicked, still solemn regulations by the exercise of His Sovereign Power as the controller of all (Y. XXIX, 4). 8. Zarathu*s*tra (or his substitute) then professes his eagerness to serve the Lord with these words which he had called the 'greatest,' and because he had seen Him with his very eyes, which he explains as meaning that he had known Him through the Righteous Order in his soul, and therefore he prays and hopes to pronounce these greatest praises, not in the assembly (Y. LI, 3) alone, but in the 'Home of sublimity or song' (Y. L, 4).

9. And he desires all the more fervently to do homage to Ahura, because He approaches him with the Power of His divine Authority in weal or woe, blessing both men and herds so long as they multiplied under the influences of Piety. 10. As the praises were the 'greatest,' so he seeks to 'magnify' the Lord in the Yasnas of Âramaiti, Ahura being renowned by His unchanging purpose, for He will bestow the 'eternal two' in His holy Kingdom, when it shall have been made firm! 11. Yea, he would seek to magnify Him who contemns the Daêvas and their party as much as they, in their turn, profess to make little of Him and His religious Kingdom, contrasted as they were with Ahura's prophet, who honoured Him in the holy Insight, the Daêna of the Saoshya*n*t. And this Saoshya*n*t is declared to be the controlling master of every faithful worshipper, and he, or the faithful venerator of the reviled Ahura, is also as our friend, brother, nay, like Ahura Himself (verse 4), our very Father in the Faith.

Translation.

1. Yea, I will speak forth; hear ye; now listen, ye who from near, and ye who from afar have come seeking[1] (the knowledge). Now ponder[2] ye clearly all[3] (that concerns) him[4]. Not for a second time shall the false teacher slay our life (of the mind, or the body). The wicked is hemmed in with his faith and his tongue![5]

2. Yea, I will declare the world's two first[6] spirits, of whom the more bountiful thus spake to the harmful[7]: Neither our thoughts, nor commands, nor our

---

[1] Ish means 'to come seeking.' The bavihûnê*d* of the Pahlavi, followed by many, is by no means incorrect.

[2] The reading mãzd*a*unghôdûm was suggested to me by Dr. Aurel Stein previously (as I believe) to its announcement elsewhere. Before this the indication of the Pahlavi (which always hesitates to change a MS. regarded at the time as sacred) had been followed by all with its necessary error.

[3] The '*e*' in *k*ithr*e* must represent a nasalised vowel, as in m*e*hmaidî.

[4] Îm may be merely a particle.

[5] I would here strongly insist upon an alternative rendering in the sense of the Pahlavi. The rendering above is given on principle. A text should never be changed, if it is possible to render it as it is. Read, 'the wicked confessing (varetô, active sense) evil beliefs with his tongue.' The Pahlavi has zaka*s* sarîtar kâmakŏ va zaka*s* darvandîh pavan hûzvânŏ hêmnunê*d*. Many, with this view, would at once read varetâ without MSS.

[6] Observe the peculiar pouruyê (pourviyê, if not a locative), the two first things, principles, forces; so in Y. XXX, 3.

[7] Notice that vahyô akem*k*â (in Y. XXX, 3) necessarily apply to the mainyû, and not only because, as nominatives, the words fall to the end of the sentence. Here we have analogous adjectives applied unmistakably to the two. The neuters correspond with vahi*s*tem manô and a*k*i*s*tem manô, and are of capital importance as

understandings, nor our beliefs, nor our deeds, nor our consciences, nor our souls, are at one[1].

3. Thus I will declare this world's first[2] (teaching), that which the all-wise Mazda Ahura hath told me. And they among you who will not so fulfil and obey this Mãthra, as I now shall conceive and declare it, to these shall the end of life (issue) in woe.

4. Thus I will declare forth this world's best (being). From (the insight of His) Righteousness Mazda, who hath appointed these (things)[3], hath known (what He utters to be true; yea, I will declare) Him the father of the toiling Good Mind (within us). So is His

---

expressing that abstract conception which renders the Gâthas so much more impressive as the earliest documents of their kind.

[1] The Pahlavi thus glosses: I do not think what thou thinkest, [for I think what is pious, and thou thinkest what is impious]; nor our teachings, [for I teach what is pious, and thou, what is impious] —nor our religions, for mine is the Gâthic, and thine that of the sorcerer; nor our souls, [for he who takes his stand on my religion, and he who takes his stand on thy religion, are apart; their souls do not occupy the same position]. Ner.: na*k*a dînih [yato me dîni*h* gâthabhavâ te*k*a râkshasî*].

[2] The 'first teaching' was a prominent idea with the Zarathu*s*trians. Z. is called in the later Avesta the paoiryô*k*aêsha (sic). He hardly plays the rôle of a reformer in the Avesta. He is mentioned after others chronologically, not as repudiating them. He might better be termed reviver. Yãm is difficult; perhaps daênãm is to be understood, or *yem* (mãthrem) read; see verse 4, angh*eus* ahyâ vahi*s*tem. Neither pourvîm nor vahi*s*tem are adverbs.

[3] Some change the text here to another which corresponds to some of the terms better. It should, however, first be rendered as it stands; the obscurities may well be owing to idiosyncrasy in the composer; possibly also to an affectation of obscurity (or 'dark speech'). How can Mazda be said to 'know Himself?' or how could any but Ahura be spoken of as 'the Father of Vohu Manah and Âramaiti?' He recognised Himself as having generated V. M. and Â. He was conscious of the completed relation.

daughter through good deeds (our) Piety. Not to be deceived is the all-viewing[1] Lord.

5. Yea, thus I will declare that which the most bountiful One told me, that word which is the best to be heeded by mortals. They who therein grant me obedient[2] attention, upon them cometh Weal to bless, and the Immortal being, and in the deeds of His Good Mind cometh the Lord.

6. Aye, thus I will declare forth Him who is[3] of all the greatest, praising through my Righteousness, I who do aright, those who (dispose of all as well aright). Let Ahura Mazda hear with His bounteous spirit, in whose homage (what I asked) was asked[4] with the Good Mind. Aye, let Him exhort me through His wisdom (which is ever) the best.

7. (Yea, I will declare Him) whose blessings the offerers will seek for, those who are living now, as well as those who have lived (aforetime), as will they

---

[1] Hishas looks irresistibly like a nom. sing., but may it not be a nom. actoris from the redup. root? Compare hîshasa*t* (although the Pahlavi renders with a different cast of meaning). What Indian word to compare here is hard to say. I prefer Bartholomae's earlier view (as to the meaning) with the Pahlavi harvispŏ nikîrî*d*ar. By dropping the later glosses, the sense of the Pahlavi comes out as usual, much closer to the Gâtha.

[2] Observe the vigour possessed by 'Sraosha.' It designates the angel of Obedience; and at the same time it is the only word which can here bring out the sense when it is understood in its actual meaning; so continually with the words Vohu Manah, Asha, &c.

[3] Lit. 'Him who I, doing aright, (praising Him with His immortals) who (all likewise) are (beneficent).' Or it may be 'that which.'

[4] So with many who hold the least to the hints of the Pahlavi. Otherwise I would render 'there is furtherance,' comparing afrashîma*n*tô.

also who are coming [1] (hereafter. Yea, even) the soul(s) of the righteous (will desire) them in the eternal [2] Immortality. (Those things they will desire which are blessings to the righteous) but woes to the wicked. And these hath Ahura Mazda (established) through His kingdom, He, the creator (of all).

8. Him in our hymns of homage and of praise would I faithfully serve, for now with (mine) eye, I see Him clearly, Lord of the good spirit [3], of word, and action, I knowing through my Righteousness Him who is Ahura Mazda. And to Him (not here alone, but) in His home of song [4], His praise we [5] shall bear.

9. Yea, Him with our better Mind we seek to honour, who desiring (good), shall come to us (to bless) in weal and sorrow [6]. May He, Ahura Mazda, make us [7] vigorous through Khshathra's royal power,

---

[1] Bvai*n*ti*k*â (sic) seems, as elsewhere, to express 'those who are becoming.'

[2] The Pahlavi uniformly errs, or is strangely free, with this word. The sense 'continuous' is here admirably adapted.

[3] This word seems evidently used almost in a modern sense of 'character,' 'disposition.' Elsewhere we are in doubt whether to refer it to the Spe*n*i*s*ta Mainyu of Ahura, or to Ahura Himself.

[4] Paradise; possibly 'home of sublimity.'

[5] The change from singular to plural is frequent. Ner. varies from the Pahlavi in the last verse, improving upon it: Evam tasmai pra*n*âmam antar Garothmâne nidadâmahe. This was probably an intentional improvement, as the Persian MS. follows our Pahlavi text. His MS. of the Pahlavi probably read barâ yehabûnd.

[6] Or, 'who has created weal and sorrow for us with good intention, (and as our discipline);' but this is hardly probable. Ahura did not originate evil. Spe*nk*â, aspe*nk*â are used adverbially (see Y. XXXIV, 7).

[7] I hardly agree to reading vereze*n*y*a*u (sic) here in the sense of 'homes.' The meaning is 'endow us with efficiency' in the pursuit of the objects mentioned in the context. Or 'the propitiation and

our flocks and men in thrift to further, from the good support and bearing[1] of His Good Mind, (itself born in us) by His Righteousness.

10. Him in the Yasnas of our Piety we seek to praise with homage, who in His persistent energy[2] was famed to be (in truth) the Lord Ahura Mazda, for He hath appointed in His kingdom, through His holy Order and His Good Mind, both Weal and Immortality, to grant[3] the eternal mighty pair to this our land (and the creation).

11. (Him would we magnify and praise) who hath despised the Daêva-gods and alien men, them who before held Him in their derision. Far different are (these) from him who gave Him honour. This latter one is through the Saoshya*n*t's bounteous Faith, who likewise is the Lord of saving power[4],

---

reverential honour' may have been more directly in the composer's mind; 'may He endow our (worship) with efficiency that it may accomplish its desired result.' See the positions of the words.

The Pahlavi translation also bears witness to the rendering above, with its erroneous or free varzî*d*âr avŏ lanman.

[1] As it is impossible for those who have studied the subject to believe that the Pahlavi translator did not know the meaning of amavandîh in Zend, we must suppose him to have had some form like hazah before him instead of huzã(thwâ*t*).

[2] The Pahlavi translator, rendering this word in the two other places by pavan astûbîh, had evidently some reason for seeing a form of nãman here. The natural conclusion is that his MS. read differently in this place. Ner. renders him appropriately.

[3] Dãn looks like an accusative infinitive here (Bartholomae); otherwise the two verbs must be regarded as having indefinite pronouns understood, 'one assigns,' and 'they grant.'

[4] I cannot see the applicability of Agni's title 'house-lord' here; compare dá*m*supatni as adj. referring to páti.

a friend, brother, or a father to us, Mazda Lord[1]!

YASNA XLVI.

Personal Sufferings, Hopes, and Appeals.

In treating this most valuable section, we can as usual presuppose that the several verses were not originally composed in the order in which they now appear. Verses 1–3 seem like a cry 'from the depths.' In verse 4 animosity appears; and an appeal to the energy of some of his warlike adherents seems to prove that, with verses 5 and 6, the composer addressed it to an assembly; 7–10 are questions and appeals to Ahura, but, as a matter of course, they are none the less really intended to impress the hearers, as well as to animate the mind of the reciter. Verses 11 and 12 were again intended to be delivered to adherents.

Verse 13 is addressed to them in terms. Verse 14 would be regarded by some as little suited to the connection, and the rest seem spoken to an assembly of chiefs. However different they may be as to the particular time or circumstances of their origin, they are in general so homogeneous even as to pitch of intensity, that, with a little exercise of the mind, we can as usual see the reasons why they were put together, or were consecutively composed; and in poetic diction sudden changes neither displease nor surprise us. 1. Beyond a doubt the leading prophet is the figure in the first and second verses; and those verses are so free from imagery that we hold them as describing beyond any reasonable

[1] He who despised the Daêvas, they returning the contempt is probably the same person expressed by the two hôi in the previous verse. It is therefore Ahura, but the words which mean friend, brother, father, are grammatically connected with *ye*—mainyâtâ, the one who reverenced Ahura. The expression 'father' gives a strong impression that Ahura is referred to, notwithstanding the vocative. Particularly as we have father in verse 4. The word 'brother,' however, inclines one to the more closely grammatical view.

question, together with many other passages in the Gâthas, the afflictions and discouragements of Zarathustra himself. He knows not whither to turn, although he speaks as a public person and in command of forces which are scanty indeed (verse 2), but yet still able to take the field (Y. XLIV, 15, 16); and his movements also concern large districts ('lands'). He is not driven from his house, but from his country. It is superfluous to say that religion, although blended with a natural ambition, is his leading motive. How he shall satisfy Ahura is the one problem which he aims to solve; but his case at this particular juncture shows every discouragement.

2. Not supposing that his yâ=yéna is merely lost in the meaning 'that,' we see that in relieving his burdened mind he exclaims, not that he knows that he is poor in means and troops, but that he knows why it is thus. It is the dregvant's work, whom we may also well understand as the drugvant, the accursed enemy, who holds back (verse 4) the bearers of the Holy Order from all success in their efforts to gain a righteous livelihood from the favoured cattle culture (Y. XXIX, 2), and who, as he with grief long since foresaw, should he attain to power, would deliver up home, village, district, and province to ruin and death (Y. XXXI, 18). He therefore cries to Ahura in common with the Kine herself (Y. XXIX, 9), and his 'behold' is only a changed expression for her exclamations (Y. XXIX, 1).

As a friend, he would have the good Mazda to regard him as seeking an especial form of grace; and he would beseech Him to fill up his need (Y. XXVIII, 11) in his extremity, teaching him, not the value of flocks and followers alone, but of that isti which lay deeper than the material wealth which he yet lamented, even the blessings of the Holy Order in every home. 3. And therefore he continues: Teach me and tell me of those great thoughts, the khratavô, the salvation-schemes of the Saviours, elsewhere also spoken of as the khratu of life (Y. XXXII, 9); for these saving helpers would, through a severe conflict and after many a reverse, at last bring on 'Completed Progress.'

4. But he must arouse himself from the relief and indulgence of his grief, he therefore springs to action, and with a cry which we hear elsewhere (Y. LIII, 9), and which was in all probability often uttered in hymns now lost to us, he urges the reward for the chief, who at the head of his retainers, shall expel the world-destroyer, the dussasti (Y. XLV, 1), from power and from life. And what is that reward? It seems to be merely the recognition and confirmation of merit among the faithful. The man who shall

expel, or destroy, the heretical tyrant shall be eminent in the recognition of his services in the support of the people and their sacred agricultural civilisation.

That was to be reward enough, and even that prestige (pourvatâtem) was to be given back to God in offering for still further service (Y. XXXIII, 14).

5. And every righteous official is urged to repeat the proclamation as a warning to every polluted Daêva-worshipper whom he can discover, or to whom his voice can reach, as well as to those secret adherents who would seem to need encouragement. The charged official is to assail the destructive opponent (Y. XXXII, 6–8), only after careful discrimination. He is to approach the evil chief, the hostile *hv*aêtu (of the blood), as distinct from the inferior noble, or the peasant clansman, and he is to tell him fully of the price set on his head. 6. 'And the superintendent who has the power, and does not thus carry out these instructions, shall himself be delivered over to the bonds of that Lie-demon whom the evil "kinsman" serves. For there is no compromise in the dualistic moral creed. The man who favours the evil is as the evil, and the friend of the good is as the good himself; so had the Lord ordained.'

7. Then, as so often elsewhere, he turns his thoughts to the outward emblem as the sign of inward grace, the sacramental Fire without which the masses would have had no help to fix the eye, or draw prostrations, and he asks with the question of profound devotion: Whom have they (Thy Saoshya*n*ts, verse 3) set me, as strengthener in these storms, save Thee and Thy symbolic flames? Yet even here he names the Good Mind with them, and the Order.

8. 'But,' he continues, 'may he who would destroy my settlement find every influence and power combined to form his ruin; may all things keep him back from prosperity, and may nothing keep him back from harm.'

9. He calls, then, for a leading helper who may help him magnify Ahura, not merely in religious celebrations, but in that universal advance of the sacred 'cause,' which follows Ahura's 'conciliation' (verse 1).

10. As if to hinder the discouragement of those who hear his own unburdenings of grief, he declares that he will never leave the faithful few who follow him; he will go with them to the 'dread assize' itself, as if to help them pass the last of tests.

11. But the 'wicked,' open or concealed, should not share these hopes; their conscience, ever the remorseless executioner, shall curse them, as they try to pass the Judgment Bridge; and hurled

from that narrow path (it becomes narrow to the faithless), they shall fall to 'eternal' Hell.

12. Their destruction is not, however, yet decided; there is not only hope for the tribesmen of Ahura, but for the pagan, and not for the 'alien' only, but for the Turanian enemy, whose very name had been a synonym for suffering. If these even shall repent, they may be blest; and some had already turned. The converted tribe Fryâna offered many pious proselytes. These would help on the righteous order together with the holy people, and God would dwell with them as well.

13. Rhetorically referring to himself as in the third person, or else representing some second speaker who names his name, he can still offer his reward to any prince who will yet come up with his retainers to his cause, not kept back by the many refusals which he had met (verse 1), nor discouraged by the scant numbers of his bands; and that reward is one which might yet be efficacious to induce self-sacrificing succour, for in addition to what had been said (see verse 4) he could declare spiritual life from Ahura to be the portion of every faithful follower, and with it future temporal wealth. And he should declare this true recruit the 'good mate' in the service, the first helper (verse 9) of the tribes.

14. Here we have what seems a question conceived as uttered by some one in the throng, or else simply rhetorically thrown in: 'Who is that friend, that powerful coadjutor who is thus offered this reward, and for such a service?' Zarathustra names the king. But he diverts the minds of hearers from a pernicious trust in individuals.

He would appeal, so he implies, not to one man only, although that one be Vîstâspa, the heroic, but to all whom Ahura would recognise in His assembly, through the inspired suffrage of the mass.

15. And first he addresses the group made up chiefly of his family, the Spitâmas; they were, as he implied, enlightened in the sacred lore, and among the foremost therefore of the Ar(e)dra. 16. He then calls on Frashaostra, with the Hvôgvas, exhorting all to continue in their righteous course, in harmony with those whom they wish for as Saviours for the land, assuring them that they will reach at last that sacred scene where the 'Immortals' dwell with God. 17. 'That scene,' he further adds, 'where the faithful sing their praises in perfection, using the true metres' (as sacred as the Vedic). And he declares that Ahura, who discerns the truth infallibly, will heed and answer; for the praises sung there will be those of obedient men who offer to the cause. 18. He once

more holds out his spiritual rewards as the best gifts of the inspired revelation, threatening as usual commensurate visitation upon the oppressing clans, while both promises and threats are in harmony with Ahura's will, for that alone has been his guide in every statement. 19. After all complaints, and threats, and stern injunctions, he closes with the once more repeated word 'reward,' and that for every man who shall aid in 'his great affair' (Y. XXX, 2), and he appeals to God Himself, asserting His inspiration for all that he has said.

Translation.

1. To what land to turn[1]; aye, whither turning shall I go? On the part of[2] a kinsman (prince), or allied peer, none, to conciliate, give[3] (offerings) to me (to help my cause), nor yet the throngs of labour, (not) even such as these[4], nor yet (still less) the evil

[1] The Pahlavi translator sees the usual meaning in nemôi and nemô. He also accepts kãm zãm adverbially after the constant Greek usage. 'In what land shall I establish my religion (as it is here rejected); whither with my praises (of the true God) shall I go?' The rendering is so much richer that I turn from it with great reluctance.

[2] It is to be regretted that able scholars should so hastily change the Gâthic text here without first trying to render it as it is. This is all the more necessary, as each independent writer disputes emendations. Pairî I think ought to stand. The *hv*aêtu, airyaman, and vereze*n*em are also elsewhere alluded to, as appertaining to the hostile party sometimes, and therefore not among those from among whom (parâ?) the prophet would be expelled.

[3] Dadaitî as a third plural has long been suggested with the eagerness of discovery. Its subjects would then be khshnâu*s*, and that implied in yâ vereze*n*â. But the construction is difficult thus, and it may be greatly doubted whether we had not better alter our discovery back into the singular with the Pahlavi. I am greatly confirmed in my view of the grammatical form of khshnâu*s* by Bartholomae's decision for a nominal form. Otherwise it would be a third singular, with loss of the final dental.

[4] He*k*â seems to be an irregular form (see Y. LVIII, 4). I can

tyrants of the province. How then shall I (establish well the Faith, and thus) conciliate Thy (grace), O Lord?

2. This know I, Mazda! wherefore I am thus unable to attain my wish[1], and why my flocks are so reduced in number, and why my following is likewise scant. Therefore I cry to Thee; behold it, Lord! desiring helpful grace for me, as friend bestows on friend. (Therefore to meet my spirit's need, and this as well) declare and teach[2] to me the Good Mind's wealth.

3. When come, Great Giver! they who are the day's enlighteners[3], to hold the Righteous Order of the world upright, and forward pressing? When are

---

only make an exclamatory isque=talisque of it. The Pahlavi renders freely as if some form of hi=to bind were before him (recall hôis?), or perhaps he read hakâ, rendering as=these all together, hamsâyakik; Ner. ye svasrenayo.

[1] So the Kine complained of him in Y. XXIX, 9 as anaêsha; so also the Pahlavi, explaining akhvâstar [aîgham denman atûbânikîh maman râî khavîtûnam]. He proceeds li amat kam ramak va amatik kam-gabrâ hômanam, explaining anaêshô as not being an îshâ-khshathra. Mâ=smâ notwithstanding position (?).

[2] 'Nim wahr' has long since circulated as a rendering for âkhsô; and with îstîm in the sense of 'prayer,' it has afforded the admirable sense 'observe, take heed of the desire of the pious.' But we have a positive proof of the meaning 'teach,' 'declare' for khsa; see Y. LXV, 9 (Wg.). So also in Y. XXVIII, 5. That Ahura possessed an îsti is clear from Y. XXXIV, 5. And if the sage could ask, 'What is your îsti (wealth)? what is your kingdom (power over possessions)?' it is certainly not strained to suppose that he could say here; 'tell me concerning your wealth,' especially as he bewails his poverty. Îsti is in antithesis to the idea expressed in kamnafshvâ and kamnânâ. So also the Pahlavi as translated by the Persian 'hezânah.

[3] Ukshâno would seem to be an ancient error for ushâno, as the Pahlavi translator renders as if reading ushâ in Y. L, 10, and

the schemes of the saviour Saoshya*n*ts with (their) lofty revelations (to appear)? To whom for help does he (their chief) approach, who has Thy Good Mind (as his fellow-worker[1])? Thee, for mine exhorter and commander, Living Lord! I choose.

4. (But e'er these helpers come to me, all rests as yet in gloom.) The evil man is holding back[2] those who are the bearers of the Righteous Order from progress[3] with the Kine, (from progress with the sacred cause) within the region, or the province[4], he, the evil governor, endowed with evil might[5], consuming[6] life with evil deeds. Wherefore, whoever hurls him from his power, O Mazda! or from life, stores for the Kine in sacred wisdom shall he make[7].

---

not ukhshâ. Otherwise 'increasers of the days' is a fine expression, but suspicious in view of the Pahlavi rendering in Y. L, 10. Ner.'s *vikâ*s*ayitryo (sic) is striking, but I cannot claim for it all that it seems to offer, as Ner. elsewhere renders forms of vakhsh by those of kas. The Persian follows the Pahlavi.

[1] Comp. Y. XLIV, 1.

[2] Pâ in the sense of 'keeping back from welfare' as well as in that of 'protection,' a sense first taught us by the Pahlavi writers, is now at last generally acknowledged. It now, like many other suggestions of the Pahlavi, actually casts light in the rendering of the analogous Vedic word.

[3] So the mass of MSS. with the Pahl. min fravâmi*s*nŏ; Persian az raftan. The expression might refer to the 'going of the kine,' as representing the people in her 'path.'

[4] Comp. Y. XXXI, 18.

[5] Pahl. zak î pavan dû*s*-stahamak; Ner. dush*t*o balâtkârî. The elements seem to be duz + hazô + bâo(=vâo).

[6] Ush in Iranian seems to have the sense of destruction combined with it sometimes; hence aoshah, aoshi*s*nŏ.

[7] *K*ar can well mean 'attain to.' Pathme*n*g as=paths (so I formerly rendered) gives a far feebler sense than that indicated by the first Zendist, the Pahlavi writer. The 'wisdom' of preparing stores for the kine, even if we suppose an animal only to be meant

5. (Yea), he who, as ruler, treats no coming applicant with injury[1], as a good citizen (or nobly wise) in sacred vow and duty, and living righteously in every covenant, who, as an uncorrupted judge, discerns the wicked (that leader who, rejecting me, would keep back those who propagate the Faith), let him, (this righteous judge,) declare (the vengeance) to that (hostile[2]) lord, (my) kinsman. Yea, let him crush him when he sallies forth[3] (to approach us for our harm)!

6. (And he who leaves him in his guilty error has my curse.) Yea, he who has the power[4], and will not thus (with stern reproof[5]) approach him, shall go to

---

is obvious. The Iranian winter was something very different from that in India. But the kine is not alluded to without a certain figurative meaning: she represents the people, and as such she cried aloud; and Zarathustra received the commission to relieve her sufferings as such. That the word hu*k*i*s*tôi*s* stands in the genitive should not disturb us. The 'care for the kine' was a matter of national importance, and 'wisdom' could not better be exercised than in this direction.

[1] Or we may render 'he who as ruler does not bestow favours upon him who approaches with injury.' The hint of the Pahlavi favours this.

[2] *H*vaêtavê is here, as in Y. XXXIII, 4; Y. XXXII, 1, and the first verse of this chapter, the hostile chieftain called 'kinsman' in an aristocratic sense by Zarathustra and his group.

[3] I compare uzûithy*a*us*k*a which is used of the breaking forth of water. The Pahlavi translator seems to have had some such idea 'mûn lâlâ hengî*d*ô,' but with him the entire line, which divides all writers, favours the sense 'in saving him from his impiety.' Khrûnyâ*t* is a verbal form (with Bartholomae).

[4] The Pahlavi translator sees the root is=to wish in ismanô, 'who does not willingly approach him;' or 'who does not approach desiring (and seeking?) him.'

[5] I am gratified to see that another takes nearly this view of this line. He has 'verfolgt.'

the abode of the Lie, (and) the enchainer[1]. For he is evil who is the best one to the evil, and he is holy who is friendly to the righteous, as Thou didst fix the moral laws[2], O Lord!

7. Whom, then, as guard, O Mazda! hast Thou[3] set me[4] then when that wicked one still held[5] me for his hate? Whom (had I) then but Thee, Thy Fire and Mind, Ahura! by deeds performed in which Thy Righteous rule is saved and nurtured? Therefore that spiritual power[6] (vouchsafing me) for the (holy) Faith (its truths) declare.

8. And as to him who (now by evil power) delivers up my settlements to harm, let not his burning (wrath) in deeds attain[7] me. But bearing back[8] the (evil will and evil influence of such), let these things come (back) to him in anger. Let that to his body come which holds from[9] welfare; but let no (help)

---

[1] Haêthahyâ, as a masculine, is awkward, as would be baêthahyâ, so the Pahl. (of the terrifier). A loc. of haithya may be correct, taking dâmãn also as a loc. Otherwise 'to the creatures of the Lie, and the enchainer (or terrifier).'

[2] Or, 'as Thou didst make the souls at first.'

[3] So with K6, K9 (Barth.).

[4] Some render 'me' here, who seem elsewhere loath to translate thwâva*n*t as=like thee, thee. Khshmâvatô, thwâvãs, and mavaitê, in Y. XLIV, 1, may be rendered, 'of you,' 'thou,' and 'to me.'

[5] So the Pahlavi indicates. I have, however, elsewhere, as against tradition, rendered as if the root were dar(e)s; 'has set his eye on me for vengeance.'

[6] One might be tempted to read ta*t* môi dãs tv*e*m; 'that granting me, do Thou speak forth for the faith.'

[7] The Pahlavi translator indicates the root sâ by his rêsh; so read as alternative, 'let him not wound us.'

[8] The meaning 'but contrariwise' has been ventured on. The indication of the Pahlavi is 'in opposing;' pavan pa*d*îrak yâmtûni*s*nŏ.

[9] The Pahlavi here misses the point, and taking pâyâ*t* in its usual

at all (approach him, which may) keep him back from misery. (And let this happen as I speak) from (vengeful) hate, O Lord!

9. But who is the freely helping one who will teach me foremost[1] how we may adore Thee, Thou the well to be invoked[2] as in Thy deeds, the holy[3], bountiful Ahura? What (words) the Kine's creator[4] spake for Thee by aid of, and to aid, the Righteous ritual Order, these words of Thine, (Thy people coming) with Thy Good Mind, are seeking[5] now (to gain and learn from) me[6], O Mazda Lord!

---

sense, falls into confusion. The ancient scholars, like some of their successors, could not always believe that pâ could mean 'to hold back from good' as well as from evil. They recognised it sometimes, giving us our instruction on the subject, but not here.

[1] Did the composer appeal to some powerful coadjutor here, or does he rhetorically express his perplexity?

[2] Zevîstîm must equal forms of hû; but from the constant evidence of the Pahlavi to the meaning 'endearing,' one is much inclined to suggest a reading as if from zush.

[3] Ashavanem is applied to Ahura, and cannot so well mean 'righteous' here. 'Holy' is the more proper term in this connection, while spe*n*tem is necessarily excluded from that meaning by its occurrence with ashavanem in immediate connection.

[4] Notice that the word tashâ occurs here with no mention of wounding in the connection (see note 6 on page 6).

[5] I am here recalled to the Pahlavi by some who rarely name it. I had rendered, 'these words are inciting me (in duty) through Thy Good Mind;' so ish often in the Veda. The Pahlavi translator, like his successors, scandalised at the difficult forms, also anticipated his successors (as elsewhere often) in getting free from the difficulty. He did what is exactly equivalent to what is now practised by scholars (sometimes too often). He rendered the text as if changed from what he could not understand to what he could understand, adhering to the right roots however, which I now follow. He knew that ishe*n*tî mâ did not mean, 'I am seeking,' but he could not credit the words before him.

[6] We have now a suggestion which must often have presented itself to those who read the *Ri*g-veda constantly, and that is (so

10. Whoever, man or woman, shall give to me those (gifts) of life which Thou hast known [1] as best, O Mazda! and as a holy blessing through (Thy) Righteous Order, a throne (established) with (Thy) Good Mind, (with these I shall go forth; yea, those) whom I shall (accompany and so) incite [2], to the homage of such as You [3] (on earth), forth to the Judge's Bridge (itself) with all of them shall I lead on [4] (at last).

11. (And they and I have every need for help, for now) the Karpan and the Kavi will join in governments [5] to slay the life of man with evil deeds, they whom their own souls and their own conscience will becry [6]. And when they approach there where the Judge's Bridge (extends, unlike the believing ones of God, who go so firmly forth with me as guide and helper, these shall miss their path and fall [7]), and

Bartholomae) that mâ may equal smâ here and often elsewhere. It is well possible, as the 's' often disappears.

[1] Notice once more the expression, 'Thou hast known;' so in Y. XXVIII, 11, the composer confides the very direction of his petitions to the discrimination of the Deity. We gain from this the true sense of peresâ n*a*u yâ tôi *e*hmâ par*s*tâ; Ahura's question and prayer are mighty when repeated by us, because He has known what is best, and what are the true dâth*en*g for which we should ask.

[2] This sense corresponds admirably with the connection; Ner. utthâpayâmi.

[3] Such as you=you as in the plural of majesty, or as referring to Ahura and His Bountiful Immortals (so often).

[4] 'Go forth.'

[5] Or, 'with kings;' but the Pahlavi has, avŏ khû*d*âyîh ayûgênd mûn Kîk va Karapŏ.

[6] So the Pahlavi indicates. Otherwise 'will harden,' or, if khraodat is read, 'will rage (against).'

[7] Inserted to shed light on the last line; so the later Parsism.

in the Lie's abode for ever shall their habitation[1] be.

12. (But for the penitent there is yet hope; for all our former foes shall not thus fall, as from the *K*inva*t* Bridge to woe, for) when from among the tribes and kith of the Turanian, even among the more powerful ones of the Fryâna, those shall arise[2] who further on the settlements of Piety with energy and zeal, with these shall Ahura dwell together through His Good Mind (in them), and to them for joyful grace deliver His commands[3].

13. Yea, he who will propitiate Zarathu*s*tra Spitâma[4] with gifts midst men, this man is fitted for the proclamation, and to him Ahura Mazda will give the (prospered) life. And he will likewise cause the settlements to thrive in mental goodness. We think[5] him, therefore, Your good companion to (further and maintain) Your Righteousness (and meet for Your approach).

---

[1] I am again brought back to the Pahlavi, having formerly rendered 'bodies,' which I would now put in the second place.

[2] The Pahlavi, although as usual free or erroneous as to forms, gives us the valuable hint of heng*î*-aît for uz*ge*n (sic=*g*ayen).

[3] Here we have the clear evidence of the conversion of a border tribe. The Zarathu*s*trians had saved some Turanian clan from plunder or annihilation, and so secured their friendship. These became known as the 'friendly people.' That true Zarathu*s*trian piety may have arisen among them is of course possible.

[4] It need hardly be said that this reference to Z. in the third person, does not prove that the composer was not Z. himself. One might even say that his authorship was even not less probable on this account.

[5] Let it be noted that the Pahlavi translator gives us our first critical knowledge as to the true writing and meaning of m*e*hmaidî; or will scholars object that he renders in the singular? Valman pavan zak î Lekûm Aharâyîh hamîshak minâm khûp hamkhâk; Ner. dhyâyâmi *s*uddha-sakhâya*m*.

(A voice from among the Chiefs.)

14. (But where is such an one ?) Whom hast thou Zarathustra[1] ! thus a holy friend for the great (effort of the) cause ? Who is it who thus desires to speak it forth ? (Zarathustra answers. Aye, such an one I have.) It is our Kavi Vîstâspa[2], the heroic; (and not he alone, but all) whom thou shalt (as in Thy prophet) meet[3] in the assembly, O Ahura Mazda ! these likewise will I call (to my attempt), and with Thy Good Mind's words.

15. O ye Haêkat-aspas, Spitâmas ! to you will I now address my words, since ye discern the things unlawful, and the lawful, for these your actions to establish[4] (firmly on its base) for you the Righteous Order through those which are the Lord's primeval laws.

16. (And to the Hvôgvas would I likewise speak.) Thou Frashaostra Hvôgva (whom I see)[5]; go thou

---

[1] Shall we regard this verse as misplaced because the subject is in the second person? It is probable (as of very many verses) that it was often recited by the composer, or others, in a different connection, and perhaps originally so; but it was a happy thought for the effect to introduce it here. Let it be supposed that this and the previous verse were arranged to be spoken by another voice during the public recital. We see that the interest is much increased by the intruding strophe.

[2] This passage may be regarded as recording the call of Vîstâspa to the holy work. Zu=hû need not always express the invocation of the gods.

[3] Others, 'unite.'

[4] Or, 'ye take to you the righteous character to yourselves,' as the infinitive is difficult; but in that case Khshmaibyâ becomes awkward. The translation of dâ as 'take' has long been familiar.

[5] Obviously composed for an occasion when the several parties would be present.

(forth) with the generous helpers[1], with those whom we are praying for as for salvation to the land. Go thou where Piety joins hand in hand with the Righteous Order, where are the wished-for Realms of Good Mind, where Mazda in His most honoured[2] home abides,

17. Where in your measured verse[3] I will declare aloud (the praises), not in unmeasured lines, *G*âmâspa Hvôgva! but songs of homage (will I weave) with ever gained Obedience in offering. (And unto Mazda) will I chant them, yea, to Him who will discern aright what things are lawful (or) unlawful[4] (which I thus do, or utter), and with His wonder-working thoughts[5] of Righteousness (attend).

18. (For) whosoever (offers) sanctity[6] to me, to him shall be the best gifts whatsoever. Yea, of my

---

[1] Ar(e)dra seems to be especially applied, and might be left unrendered.

[2] I see no impossibility whatever in such a rendering, literally in 'his choice-abode;' so also the Pahlavi indicates: tamman aîgh Aûharmazd pavan kâmak dên demânô ketrûnê*d*. The question is of 'going' and 'dwelling,' and the meaning 'abode' is quite in point. As to var, see î*s*tâ khshathrâ; and compare mazdâvarâ. Aside from this, vardmãm = in blessing.

[3] The Pahlavi again, with its followers, gives us our first hint at the general meaning here. What else can his pa*d*mân and apa*d*mânîk mean, but the regularity, that is, the rhythm and cadence of the words?

[4] Dâthem*k*â adâthem*k*â would be 'the truth and the heresy' in general.

[5] If ma*n*tû is taken as an instrumental, (can it be an act. imper.?) vistâ might occupy the place of a preterit, but it looks far more like a participle, and might be regarded as forming a compositum with vahm*eng*. Supply the dat. (?) pers. pron. understood before *ye*.

[6] The alteration to yau*s*, considered as an aorist, has long circulated, but seems now, like so many of the bolder conceptions, to be given up. Yao*s* is the sister word of the Vedic yós, and

(spirit's) wealth will I bestow on him through Thy Good Mind (which I give), but oppressions will I send on him who as oppressor will deliver us to anguish, O Mazda! desiring, as I do, to satisfy Your choice by righteous (vengeance). This is the decision of mine understanding and my will.

19. (Yea, this I earnestly announce.) He who from Righteousness (in mind and life) shall verily perform for me, for Zarathustra, that which is thus most helpful (for my cause) according to my earnest wish (and through my words of urgent zeal) on him shall they bestow reward(s) beyond this earth, with all the mental[1] blessings gained through the sacred mother-kine[2]. And these things (all) did'st Thou (Thyself) command to me, O Mazda, Thou most wise[3]!

---

shows us that some shade of sanctity may inhere in that word. The Pahlavi renders more indefinitely by 'yân'=a helpful blessing.

[1] The Pahlavi translator, however, saw *menâ*, rendering avŏ li. His text may well have justified him.

[2] Bearing; or is it 'fit to drive?'

[3] The Pahlavi here reports another text.

(SUPPLEMENTARY NOTES. *Askît*, in verse 18, may equal 'verily indeed.' Vahistâ, &c.='the best things of my wealth will I assign to him through the Good Mind.' The meaning 'wealth' seems much called for here, and if here, then in verse 2. Vasnâ in verse 19 may mean 'through grace.')

THE GÂTHA(Â) SPE*N*TÂ MAINYÛ (SPE*N*TÂMAINYU(Û)).

This Gâtha, consisting of Yasna XLVII–L, takes its name from its commencing words. Like the other Gâthas it owes its existence as a collection to the nature of its metre, as its matter is homogeneous with that of the others. Its metre may be said to be Trish*t*up, as its lines have each eleven syllables, and are arranged in stanzas of four.

A general view precedes each chapter. The grouping of hymns in this Gâtha has, as usual, little or nothing to do with the question of their relative age.

YASNA XLVII.

The Bountifulness of Ahura.

As in every instance, we may have here only the fragments of a more extended piece; but also, as ever, the circumstance does not diminish the value of what remains. Although some signs of authorship apart from Zarathu*s*tra are present, the later verses are not at all remote, so far as the period of time which they indicate is concerned, from the Zarathu*s*trian verses, and are therefore of nearly equal interest, possessing the advantage moreover of affording data for estimating the progress of change.

1. The Spe*n*tâ mainyû here is not identical with Ahura, but is, as so often, His spirit. It is more than possible that the memorable application of the word spe*n*ta to the seven, giving us the Ameshôspends, the Amshaspands of literature, derives its origin from the first verse here before us, or from lost verses of a similar character. All the seven seem purposely and artificially grouped here, although 'His Spirit' is of course not one of them. The commencing word spe*n*ta further attracted attention in so far as to form the theme for a sort of play upon words in the later epilogue of Visparad XIX. By means of this His indwelling Spirit (which idea, or expression, has probably no direct connection with the 'Holy Spirit' of the Old and New Testaments, but which, as giving the designation 'spirit' to the Ameshôspends, may well have been the original of the 'seven spirits which are before the throne of God'), by means of this

blessed spirit, that is, in accordance with his inmost thoughts, Ahura bestows a gift upon the ideal saint (verses 4, 5), upon him who works the best results for Zarathustra (Y. XLVI, 19), the Ratu, and the prophet (Y. XXIX, 6, 8). And this gift is declared to be the inseparable two, Happiness in every particular, and then both the prospect and realisation of the continuance of that Happiness in Immortality. And these He bestows, not through His immediate action, which no human intellect, or susceptibility, could take in unaided, but by His especially revealed Benevolence, His Best Mind, as His representative, in accordance with His plan of Order and Purity, pervading every moral as well as every spiritual regulation, and by the exercise of His Royal Power, sent forth as the 'archangel' Khshathra, and embodied in the polity of the sacred Zarathustrian state, and this as influenced in all its relations, public and domestic, by practical piety called Âramaiti, Ahura's daughter (the ready mind). Such a revelation of the component parts of the mind and will of the Deity, the simplest labouring class could understand for the moment, and for some decades; but all was, as a matter of course, soon to be overgrown with the old weeds of superstition and of myth.

2. Falling into detail and varying expressions, the composer prays that Ahura may carry out His holy scheme into action by the busy hands and fingers of domestic piety, and by the preached and recited words of the Good Mind from the mouth and tongue of faithful priests. So, and so only, would He become the Father of Asha, the divine Order, and of moral and ritual regularity among men.

3. From discourse concerning God, he arises, as so often, to an address to Him. That Spirit (referred to in the verses 1, 2) is Ahura's own, for He is the One who makes it bounteous; He is the bountiful One who has created the sacred symbolic Kine, the emblem and the substance of 'joy,' representing at once the possessions of the holy people, and those people themselves. And He it is who, in answer to her wail (Y. XXIX, 1, 9), has spread for her the meadows 'of Piety' as arranged in the consultations (Y. XXXIII, 6) made on her behalf.

4. And this 'Spirit,' as might be expected, does not confine its attention to the inspiration of Piety alone. The justice of Mazda is vindicated. The wicked are afflicted under its influence with a long wounding (Y. XXX, 11) for their sins, and for their cynical preference for prosperous men of bad and dishonest character as well as of heretical faith.

5. But he expresses his confidence that Ahura Mazda will, in the end, set all aright. He will, unlike the persons just mentioned, give unto the ashavan, not kasu alone, but paru, (not a meagre share, but fulness) of whatever is the best, while the dregvant and the aka (verse 4), the faithless and the wicked, although they may be isvanô, prosperous, will only taste the enjoyment of their wealth aside from God, and therefore marred. So long as they pursue their usual course, they live in actions inspired not by the bountiful spirit, but by the Evil Mind, a mind as aka as the person alluded to in the words paraos (kâthê) akô dregvaitê in the previous verse.

6. But, as ever, the moral appeals, and ascriptions of praise, lofty as they are, are not left without the support and service of the ritual. God will give these gifts, and all which are the best, but in connection with His Fire imparted to these struggling sides (Y. XXXI, 2), the believing and the faithless (verses 4, 5), through the increase of His Piety and Order; for that piety, as ever the instructress, will convert all those who come to her, and seek her light (Y. XXX, 1; Y. XLV, 1). Nay, she will cause all the living to choose and believe in God (Y. XXXI, 3).

(If the first two verses here are more like the work of a disciple, the last four show again the original tone. It must never be forgotten, however, that later and even interpolated portions are, in their sense, also original, and differ but slightly in their great age from pieces more directly from the first composer.)

Translation.

1. And to this[1] (man, His chosen saint), Ahura Mazda will give[2] both the two (greatest gifts, His)

[1] Or, 'to us;' but in that case it would be the Kine who 'took counsel' as mentioned in the third verse. This is, however, far from impossible, as she is mentioned as uttering her wail, and being answered by her maker in Y. XXIX, 1, 2. So understanding, 'to us' becomes an admirable rendering for verse 1; but in verse 3, it is strained, as the Kine for whom (Y. XXIX, 9) Zarathustra was appointed, could not so readily be declared to be the one which was given to 'us,' she representing 'us' in that place to a great extent. There is a certain plausibility about the rendering 'to us,' but I think ahmâi refers to ashaonê understood (see verses 4 and 5). The Pahlavi, moreover, is against a first person.

[2] Dãn (Geldn.) seems to be a 3rd plural aorist subjunctive; the

Universal Weal and Immortality, by means of His bountiful Spirit, and with His Best Mind, from (the desire to maintain His) Righteous moral Order in word and deed, and by the (strength and wisdom) of His Sovereign Power, (established) in Piety (among His folk).

2. Aye, (that blessedness, which is the) best[1] (creation) of this most bounteous spirit, Ahura Mazda will bring forth in action with words from the mouth and tongue of His Good Mind (within His seers), and by the two hands[2] of Âramaiti (His Piety as she lives within the soul). And by such[3] wise (beneficence is) He the father of the righteous Order (within our worship and our lives).

3. And Thou art therein, O Ahura Mazda! the bountiful One who appertains to, and who possesses, that (most bounteous) spirit in that Thou art He who for this[4] (man, in whom this spirit works) hath made the joy-creating Kine. (And as to her), for her, as

---

plural being owing to the fact that Ahura gives with the other Ameshôspends. Dã might also be the relic of the proper word which represents the participle; comp. dãs (sic).

[1] The idea of the summum bonum seems to have early developed itself, and from this constant use of this word in the neut. singular and plural, and also with anghu.

[2] Notice once more the pronounced personification of both Vohu Manah and Âramaiti; see Y. XXX, 8, and Y. XLIV, 14, &c. The Pahlavi translation notices the dual form pavan kolâ II yadman.

[3] The Pahlavi seems to lead those who regard ôyâ as=a form of ava; it has zak î.

[4] This is the ahmâi of the first verse, (but always possibly='to us,' if the verses are not to be brought into any kind of connection.) Otherwise it obviously refers to ashâunê* in 4 and 5; so the Pahlavi throughout. See ahmâi and hôi in LI, 6.

joyful meadows[1] of her peace, wilt Thou bestow (Thine) Âramaiti (who is our Piety as earth considered), since he[2] (for her) hath taken counsel with Thy Good Mind, Lord!

4. (But this Thy bounteous spirit doth not alone bestow rewards and blessings on the good.) The wicked (foemen of the Faith) are harmed, and from (the motives which move) that bounteous spirit (of Thine own), O Mazda[3]! but not thus the saints. (And yet the ruler's pride would ever slight the righteous.) The feeble man alone stands free to give in kindly obligation[4] to Thy saint, but having wealth and ruling power, the evil (man) is (at the service) of the wicked, and for much[5].

---

[1] Many would say that we have here an instance in which the identity of Âramaiti with the earth is recognised in the Gâthas. I would say, on the contrary, that here we have an instance in which a poetical conception gave rise to a later error or fantastical association. Piety, with frugal virtue, induced a thorough husbandry; and secured the hushiti, peaceful home-life. She gave meadows to the Kine; at the next step she poetically represents the meadows, and then the earth. If vâstrâi, it would be for 'nurture.'

[2] Or 'she,' as she once bewailed in a colloquy. Otherwise the person who was appointed to care for her interests is meant. Compare Y. XXXIII, 6, where the righteous Zaotar speaks as desiring counsels (*h*emparstôi*s*) in the interest of the pastures, and the laws of the sacred agriculture. Cp. also the later reproduction of the idea in an extended form in the Vendîdâd. The zaotar of Y. XXXIII, 6, may have been the ashavan of verses 4 and 5.

[3] Voc. with K5 (Barth.).

[4] The Pahlavi gives us, as usual, our first surmise as to the meaning of 'kâthê;' I follow Geldner with regard to it as against Haug. The expressions here are not literal.

[5] Isvâ*k*î*t* connects only indirectly with kas*e*u*s*/*k*î*t*, as kâthê intervenes. I regard parao*s* akô dregvâitê as presenting the true antithesis to kas*e*u*s*/*k*î*t* nâ ashâunê. The isvâ may have *k*î*t* merely from the influence of jingle, being at the head of the line like kas*e*u*s*; isvâ means

5. But Thou wilt give these gifts, and through Thy (most blessed and most) bounteous spirit, O Ahura Mazda! to this[1] Thy holy saint, for they are whatsoever is the best; but far[2] from Thy love the wicked has his portion, abiding in the actions of the Evil Mind.

6. Aye, these things wilt Thou give (to him), O Thou Ahura Mazda! and through Thy bounteous spirit, (and) by Thy Fire as in a good bestowal to

---

of itself 'possessing means.' Paraos may depend on kâthê understood, as kaseus depends on it expressed. Moreover, hãs in all the instances in which it is used ends the sense, and here is separated by the caesura from paraos, which, however, is of no great importance. The discourse is of the wicked; the holy are incidentally mentioned, and here their ill-treatment is signalised. Akô cannot well mean 'hostile' here; see also akâ*t* in the following verse. Isvâ*k*î*t*, if understood with nâ, alters nothing. 'A man was desirous of little for the service of the saint, but even when he himself was rich, (in the desire) of much was the evil for the evil.' Or, taking kas*e*us*k*î*t* as governed by isvâ*k*î*t* understood with kâthê as before understood in the last line: 'Only a man (men) (possessed) of little was at the service of the righteous, while an evil man (men) possessed of much (was at the service) of the wicked.' The other translation is: 'Even a man of little means stands to the willing service of the saint, but a man even of large means is hostile (?) to the wicked.' This is very glib and so attractive, but I cannot accept it in view of the context. Gâthic expression is often unfortunately far from glib; but cramped, awkward, and apt to contain more thought than could be conveniently expressed within the counted number of syllables. The glib rendering needs other language than that in the MSS. See the following verse, which directly contrasts the treatment of the good and evil by Ahura Himself.

[1] See ahmâi in verse 1, and ashaunê in verse 4. Ahura treats the saint in a manner the reverse from that practised by the nâ kas*e*us* and akô, not giving sparingly to the good, nor much to the wicked.

[2] The Pahlavi gives us our first surmise here, as usual, by *gavîd* min hanâ î lak dôshis*n*ih.

the two striving[1] (throngs) through the prosperous increase of our Piety, and of the Righteous ritual and moral Truth; for that (Piety of ours instructing) doth teach[2] the many coming ones who seek her (face)!

YASNA XLVIII.

ANTICIPATED STRUGGLES AND PRAYERS FOR CHAMPIONS AND DEFENDERS.

This chapter divides itself quite naturally into sections. 1–4 belong together, then 5 and 6, 7 seems less closely connected; then follows 8–12.

1. A struggle is evidently at hand, whether the same as that to which allusion is more than once made, by incitation, as in Y. XXXI, 18; with anxious expectation, as in Y. XLIV, 15, 16; or as if in a sense of victory, as in Y. XLV, 1; or of defeat, as in Y. XLIX, is difficult, or rather impossible to determine. But with the verses 10, 11, 12 in view, together with the dispirited, Y. XLIX, 1, we shall say at once that, if this verse was intended to connect with them, an armed struggle had been expected, whether the decisive one or not, we need not say.

The saint, that is, the pious adherent to the Holy Order, whatever may be the result of the preliminary struggles, is encouraged by a view of the end. 2. But the burdened worshipper craves still further reassurance before the storms of battle came once more upon him. 3. For little as the assurances of Ahura are valued

[1] Or, 'by the two ará*n*i;' but compare the ăsay*a*u in Y. XXXI, 2 just preceding ranôibyâ; so here the ashavan and dregva*n*t are mentioned in a preceding verse. The Pahlavi is unvarying with patkardârânŏ. I will not positively decide as to this point; generally, however, the preferred rendering is in the text, while on very many questions there is nearly an even balance of probabilities.

[2] Or, 'chooses to herself;' but a causative sense may be expressed by an intensive form; the Pahlavi also here bears evidence in the same sense to a causative by hêmnunê*d*, itself, however, meaning only the object caused; namely, the belief.

by the heretic, to the man who understands the true relations, what Ahura declares by means of His inspired prophets, the secret-announcers, this is, of all things, best; (he need not ask as elsewhere, Y. XXXI, 17). 4. And whoever would hope for spiritual growth and purity must turn his mind to that word of the Deity, and pursue its teachings faithfully, and so at last his fears will vanish, for his doubts will disappear. He will understand as the Lord has taught.

5. This verse seems a prayer to Âramaiti; when the long struggles shall have found their issues, and the one party or the other wins the day, let not that party be the evil alliance with its monarch. For, if the government is set up, and carried on with all the prescribed ceremonial and moral exactness of the wise *K*isti; if men who toil for the sacred Kine, and with the virtue of those who cultivate her, hold the reins of power, and can so suppress the predatory raids on defenceless, as well as unoffending victims, then no gift of Ahura, since the tribes became a nation, could be looked upon as a greater, or as so great a blessing, as the correct Authority, and the Order of the Faith.

6. For that sacred Kine, as so often already implied or stated, was all in all to the pious worshipper. It was she, representing, as she did, all wealth in herds, who alone could sustain the home-life of happy industry. And this is the reason why Ahura had originally caused the herbage to grow for her support.

7. Urging the overthrow of the spirit of Rapine in accordance with the Kine's complaint, he exhorts the armed masses to energetic and offensive valour.

8. He then vehemently, although only rhetorically, asks how he may use the proper prayers to rally the needed coadjutors among the chiefs (Y. XLVI, 9) to carry on the struggle. 9. Again he utters a cry for relief in his suspense, and of entreaty for light as to the rewards, which did not concern this life for its own sake (verse 1) merely or chiefly; but which were spiritual blessings received here in preparation for the spiritual world. 10. 'When,' he repeats as one among similar questions four times repeated, 'when shall the ideal men appear whose thoughtful plans (Y. XLVI, 3) shall drive hence the polluted schemes of the false priests and of the tyrants (Y. XLVI, 1)? 11. And when shall Âramaiti, the kindly piety of home, appear, she who, like the earth, spreads pastures for the peaceful kine, when shall she appear with holy Khshathra (later well called an angel, or archangel) the personified Authority of God over home and state, without which

an anarchy as bad as that of the Evil Authority (verse 5) might continue or recur; and who was the champion-chief who would give them peace through blood (Y. XLVI, 4; LIII, 9)? In a word, to whom, as to the coadjutors of such a leader, would the light of reason, and the true faith come to inspire and to guide them?' 12. There is but one only class of human combatants whom he would thus match against that Demon of furious Rapine (v. 6), toward whom the evil on their part at their first creation rushed as to their leader (Y. XXX, 6), and these are the saving Saoshya*n*ts, the vicegerents of the Immortals upon earth, the religious princes Vî*s*tâspa, *G*âmâspa, Frashao*s*tra, and with them, as the greatest among all, he who was, with much probability, the speaker in the passage, that is, the Ratu appointed by Ahura for the kine and for men, Zarathu*s*tra Spitâma elsewhere and later called, with hyperbole, the first tiller, warrior, and priest.

Translation.

1. If through his action[1] in the offering of gifts in accordance with the Righteous Order, (Thy saint[2]) shall smite the Demon-of-the-Lie (the inspiring spirit of our foes), when that in very truth shall come[3], which has been (and is still yet) proclaimed as a deceit[4], (when it shall come) in the Immortal life, regarding (as it does both) men (to bless), and Daêvas[5] (to afflict them), then shall (Thy faithful worshipper) increase thereby the celebration of Thy praise, O Lord! and with it blessings[6] (for Thy folk).

2. Tell me then, Lord! (the end), for Thou dost

---

[1] The Pahlavi has also pavan zak dahi*s*nô; but a false gloss gives an erroneous concrete [pavan tanû î pasînô]. Recall âdâi paitî.

[2] See ashaônô, ashâunê (sic) (Y. XLVII, 4, 5).

[3] Read 'as âshûtâ'=has been pushed on, enacted. I correct here as seems so evidently necessary; but the Pahlavi anticipates with its amat zak yâmtûnê*d*.

[4] Pavan frîftârîh.

[5] See Y. XXIX, 4.

[6] See Y. XXX, 11, sava*k*â ashavabyô.

know it. (Tell me to grant me strength and courage) before those conflicts come which shall encounter me[1] (as leader of Thy tribes); shall the champion of Thy holy Order, O Ahura! smite (at last) the evil heretic, and when? (I ask Thee this); for this if it be gained (is known) to be the (one) good consummation[2] of (our) life.

3. (Yea, tell me then this), for to the enlightened[3] man is that the best of teachings which the beneficent Ahura doth proclaim, and through (the revelations of) His holy Order, bounteous as he and wise with His intelligence, as well as they[4] who declare to us (still other) secret sayings (in His name). The one like Thee (their chieftain[5]) is, O Mazda! endowed with Thy Good Mind's understanding thoughts.

---

[1] M*en*g=mãm or man; *-en*g is the nasalised vowel. Man is suspiciously significant here; 'mental battles' is rather advanced for the circumstances. It is, however, not impossible. The Pahlavi favours mãm (?) here; it has avŏ li. We might even read m*e*nâ on its evidence. The Pahlavi indicates the meaning 'crises' under the figure of the 'Bridge,' which was the last great crisis to every man in the eye of the earlier, as well as of the later, Faith; so also in Y. LI, 12. The 'straits of life' would be an admirable meaning; I differ with hesitation.

[2] Pahlavi kar*d*ârîh.

[3] See Y. XLIII, 14.

[4] Yaê*k*î*t* gûzrâ-s*e*ngh*a*unghô. Or, 'knowing also those who are the teachers of secret doctrines.'

[5] We may, with some effort, connect thwâvãs with vaêdemnâi. Spe*n*tô vîdv*a*u, however, must refer to the immediately foregoing Ahurô, especially in view of the tv*e*m vîdv*a*u, Ahurâ, of verse 2. 'The one like Thee' might even, as in other cases, be only an oblique way of rendering 'Thyself;' but the expression 'with the understanding of Vohu Manah' induces me to refer the word Thwâvãs to the servant of Ahura; in this case, however, this last line must of course be drawn to verse 4, although not mechanically separated from verse 3.

4. (Yea, tell me the secret of the future struggle[1]; for that enlightened man) must[2] follow close[3] the holy Faith (for which that struggle had its toil and effort). Yea, O Mazda! he who would bend his mind (till it attains to) that which is the better and more holy, must pursue the Daêna close in word and action. His will and wish must be consistent with his chosen creed and fealty, and in Thine Understanding (which discerneth all) shall he in many ways[4] be (versed) at last!

——————[5].

5. (But while I as yet know not the issue, I can yet hope and pray.) Let the good kings obtain the rule. Let not the evil monarchs govern us[6], (but let the righteous gain the day and rule us), with deeds done in a good discernment, O thou pious wisdom, Âramaiti! sanctifying to men's minds the best of blessings for (their) offspring[7]. Yea, for the Kine, (O Âramaiti[5]!)

---

[1] See verse 2.

[2] Present for imperative, as sometimes in modern languages in giving directions.

[3] The words are anticipated from the third line.

[4] I follow the Indian sense here with great reluctance. Nanâ may well be, in Iranian, equivalent to 'each several one,' and in fact may not impossibly teach us the origin of the word ('man, man:' comp. nar*e*m,* nar*e*m*). The Pahl. trlr. is so decided for a personal sense, that he renders gabrâ n*e*sman=man and woman. Did he suppose 'woman' to be literally (!) expressed in the text?

[5] Âramaiti is addressed, unless indeed an instrumental is read without MSS. An instrumental is of course preferable.

[6] The Pahlavi has, with admirable freedom, zakatŏ hû-khû*d*âî pâ*d*akhshâyînis*n*, va al lanman zak î dû*s*-khû*d*âî *s*alîtâ yehavûnâ*d*ŏ. I read hukhshathrâ khshaye*n*tãm, mâ n*e* dû*s*-khshathrâ, to bring the metre somewhat into order, as some gross irregularity is present; the caesura only, not the sense, is affected by the change.

[7] Or, 'from the birth-hour on;' so the Pahlavi. Its gloss reads [akhar min zerkhûnis*n*ŏ avinâsîh pâhlûm].

let (Thy) toil be given [1], and may'st Thou cause her to prosper for our life.

6. For she will grant us pleasing homes [2], and, (while we live) in this Thy Good Mind's longing [3] prayer (to gain her welfare), she grants us likewise lasting strength (for every deed which that Thy Good Mind moves us to perform), and therefore hath Mazda caused the plants [4] to flourish for her (nurture), He, Ahura, in the generation of primeval life.

---

7. (Then in our coming strife [5] let both her mortal foes be slain.) Let the Wrath-demon of rapine be cast down. Smite ye against the envy (which would plot against our Throne [6]), O ye who, abiding by the Good Mind, and in accordance with our holy Order, desire to hold that refuge [7] fast, to whose sacred bond the bounteous man belongs. And therefore,

---

[1] So Bartholomae, who now holds to a third singular here, leaving the text undisturbed, and explaining as an optative.

[2] The Pahlavi seems to render 'comfort' here, using khvârîh in that sense.

[3] So the Pahlavi correctly indicates by its arzûk; Ner. priyataram.

[4] Compare Y. LI, 7. Are the plants here mentioned as in connection with Âramaiti in her figurative association with the earth?

[5] See verses 1, 2.

[6] Or, 'against the blow,' Y. XXIX, 1. The Pahlavi translator here renders pa*d*îrak î arêshak, while in Y. XXIX, 1 he renders î rêshkûn. The variations are probably not real; the renderings referring to some forgotten differences of text; or, as often, he may have anticipated modern freedom, and 'changed his text;' that is, rendered it as if changed to a seemingly more intelligible form; so in a throng of similar cases. This is the only rational explanation of some of his errors. (He was able to render, and has rendered, most grammatical forms in different places.)

[7] The Pahlavi has, however, navîdîh. Did he read vidhyãm, in itself a very possible text?

O Ahura! (to save Thy struggling saint who toils with changing lot) will I place (that refuge) for him in Thy world.

8. (And how shall I beseech Thee for this victory and gift?) What is the (potent[1]) prayer to bring on that Thy holy Reign[2]? What for Thy sacred reward and blessing for my (soul)? How shall I seek the open helpers for (the spread and maintenance of) Thy (great) Order[3], while I myself live[4] on in Thy Good Spirit's deeds?

9. (Aye, when shall faith be changed to sight[5]); and when shall I in verity discern if Ye indeed have power over aught, O Lord! and through Thy Righteous Order (guarding here on earth), O Thou within whose (power lie) my griefs[6] and doubts? Let then Thy saving prophet find and gain aright (for) my delight[7] Thy Good Mind's wonder-

---

[1] Compare *e*mava*n*tem aêshem, also peresâ n*a*u yâ tôi *e*hmâ par*s*tâ. Observe that the Pahlavi translator distinguishes the two senses of î*s*ti. In Y. XLVI, 2 he transcribes the Gâthic word, the Persian rendering 'hezânah; Ner. pu*n*yalakshmîm; here, however, he has: Ka*d*âr lak, Aûharmazd, zak î *s*apîr khvahî*s*n î khû*d*âyîh.

[2] Compare verse 5.

[3] Ashâ might certainly equal á*k*h*â here (so Bartholomae) if the constant and intentional repetition of the name and idea of Asha, = the personified Order, would not have caused confusion.

[4] The Pahlavi translator renders a word which occupied the place of *g*avarô by yakhsenunî*d*ârîh; Ner. following as to root (freely as to form). As he, however, renders related forms elsewhere by 'living,' 'live,' our only safe conclusion is that he had a different word from *g*avarô (*g*ivarô) before him in his MS.

[5] Compare Y. XXVIII, 6.

[6] I am very far from certain that we do not seriously blunder in not following the indication of the Pahlavi here. See remarks Y. XXXII, 16.

[7] Or, 'let me enjoy as my own;' but môi is difficult. Û*k*ãm might otherwise be a first personal form in the sense of the Vedic u*k*.

working grace[1]; yea, let Thy Saoshyant see how gifts of recompense may be his own.

10. When, Mazda! shall the men of mind's perfection come[2]? And when shall they drive[3] from hence, the soil of this (polluted) drunken joy[4], whereby the Karpans with (their) angry zeal would crush us[5], and by whose inspiration the tyrants of the provinces (hold on) their evil rule[6]?

11. Yea, when shall our perfected Piety appear

Bartholomae's third sing. imper. is also of course well possible; but were not the originally abnormal third singulars in -âm, duhâm sayâm, vidâm, taken over from third pl. subj. '-âm' really equalling the nasal vowel merely*? Comp. also Indian ádrisram, ábudhram, ásrigram, Zend vavazirem, -am=an. 'Tradition' has, Pahl. zîvisnîh; Ner. gîvitam; Pers. zîstan, for ûkâm, as if rendering 'enjoyment,' 'experience of life.' * (âm=tâm is more difficult.)

1 Comparing vápus; otherwise, with the Pahlavi, 'knowing the destruction (of the evil) which Vohûman works;' see Y. XXIX, 6, where the rendering of the Pahlavi is supported by the previous verse.

2 Comp. Y. XLVI, 3. Kadâ Mazdâ frârentê*—saoshyantâm khratavô?

3 Compare Y. XXXII, 15.

4 Is Soma-intoxication here referred to? And was the Haoma-worship in abeyance at the time? The Pahlavi seems to have understood 'magic' here, and in the evil sense, that is, judging from the perhaps later gloss. Aside from the gloss, however, the Pahlavi may well have been, nay, more probably was, intended to be read madîh as=madahyâ.

5 As to this word, we cannot do better than follow Justi (although his work is now a score of years old). The Indian várpas, in the sense of deceit, has also been compared. The last Pahlavi translator was probably confused by finding this word, as so often, divided in his MS. He rendered as best he could, or rather he handed down the shattered documents, or oral teachings, of his predecessors with his own too often lame additions, the whole mass being rich in the relics of the truth.

6 See verse 5.

together with[1] Thy Righteousness? When shall she come, as having the amenities of home for us, and provided (like our land) with pastures[2] (for the kine)? And who shall give us quiet[3] from the cruel (men) of evil life and faith? To whom shall Thy Good Mind's sacred wisdom come (to guide them in their toil to rescue and avenge us)?

12. (To whom? The answer lieth near.) Such shall be the Saviours of the Provinces, and they who, through Thy Good Mind's grace, shall go on hand in hand with mental keenness[4] (as it spreads among Thy saints) by the doing every deed of Thy commandment, O Ahura! through the help of, and in accordance with, Thy Holy Order; for such as these are set (for us), as steadfast foes of hate!

YASNA XLIX.

Reverses and Hopes. Honour to Frashaostra and other Chiefs.

The chapter divides itself naturally into sections 1–5, 6–11. Verse 12 belongs with chapter L. One of the struggles in the holy cause seems to have gone against the party of Asha. I say 'one

---

[1] Ma*t* following Ashâ shows that we may also have the preposition in pôi ma*t*.

[2] As Âramaiti is here spoken of as 'having pasture,' that is, as inspiring the thrifty husbandmen who cultivate the meadows by irrigation, or drainage, she became associated herself with those meadows, and so later with the earth; see Y. XLVII, 2.

[3] The Pahlavi sees in râmãm enforced quiet not 'from' but 'to' the wicked; 'who shall deal the finishing blow to the wicked?'

[4] So also the Pahlavi, shnâsinî*d*ârîh.

of the struggles,' for from the account of a reverse which we have here, and from that of a success which meets us in chapter XLV, 1, and again from reverses in XLVI, 1, 2, &c., we naturally conclude that 'the cause' saw many vicissitudes, in which the last Gâtha still leaves us. Whether Y. XLV, 1 records a victory which was subsequent to the reverse before us, referring to a battle alluded to in Y. XLIV, 14, 15, also possibly anticipated in Y. XXXI, can never be decided; the order of the statements in the sequence of our present MSS. has little or nothing to do with the possible order of the events.

1. A border chief, B*en*dva by name, had proved himself too formidable (mazi*s*tô) for the moment, and the holy Faith knows how to beg for vengeance on the armed Drû*g*-worshipper. The weapons of Ahura were not spiritual only, any more than those of Israel were, or those of Mohammed. The death of an armed religious enemy was devoutly to be desired for every moral and political, as well as for every personal reason. 2. For judicial as well as priestly decisions hung on the issue. And this B*en*dva had his functionaries and a system, and they were in full and active operation. And this was, beyond a doubt, a rival and settled system, and not merely an upstart and insurrectionary one. It had caused the true prophet many an hour of thought as well as anger. Its functionaries gave him pause (mânayêitî). Falsity in religion was as ever his opportunity; and invective follows. 'The priestly judge himself who served the Drû*g*-worshippers was a cheat.' 'The holy Order was his foe, and not his helper.' And he did not contribute at all to the spread of Piety as the Zarathu*s*trians conceived of it, nor indeed really in another sense for the reason that he even repudiated the source of pious wisdom, which is holy counsel. 3. But, however, the evil functionaries might resort to subterfuge and strategy, the opposing powers themselves, the Righteous Order on the one side, and the power of the Lie-demon on the other, were planted in the opposing systems with dualistic clearness, to benefit or injure. There was no compromise, as doubtless the Drû*g*-party may have wished.

And so the poet cries once more for the divine Benevolence to be his guardian; or perhaps he may have intended a particular chief who represented the Good Mind, while at the same time he swept the entire throng and company who adhered to the Lie-demon, with his interdict, away from his consideration. 4. He declares them closely allied to the Daêva-worshippers, or else he puts their worship of the Daêvas in the place of climax as their highest offence, not failing to point out what should conciliate sympathy with him always; that is, that those who brought the Daêvas, and opposed Asha, were the devotees of Rapine (aêshmem vareden); for murderous rapine seems to have been, apart from Asha, the universal sin. By this these Daêva-worshippers gained a stolen livelihood, and spent their ill-gotten means in idle waste (fshuyasû afshuya*n*tô). 5. But he who defended the holy Daêna was as meat and drink to the people, wise and faithful, as a settled citizen, and trained in the habits of the holy State.

6. He therefore prays once more for right discernment as to how he may propagate the Faith. 7. And he calls on the steady citizen to listen, beseeching God Himself to give an ear, and to tell him who the faithful prince, or peer, or villager, may be, who may take the lead (see sar*e*) in giving forth (see srâvayaêmâ) that holy Daêna, with its frasasti, to the masses who await it. 8. But he asks the question as if only to give emphasis to his naming a chief and venerated friend. Frashao*s*tra is the man. He is the one fitted for the hearing, apt to proclaim the truth (frasrûidyâi erethwô). And he begs that they both (compare Y. XXVIII, 9) may be lastingly prominent in that holy Realm which was to counteract the depraved polity whose chief had for the moment gained the upper hand (verses 1, 2). 9. But the case is in so far uncertain and undecided, that he cries for help once more to the ideal citizen himself, fearing that he may yet be induced to share the power with the heretic, and still declares that men's souls may reach the reward of priority only through the holy System of Ahura, and under the rulers of His choice.

10. He therefore confides the result to Ahura, and with it, his dependents, those living and those dead. And his thoughts, being turned to heaven (11), they also revert as if by antithesis (the key-note of the Daêna) to future retribution. Those who may be wavering, half-inclined to adhere to the opposing party (verse 9), are warned in words of peculiar meaning. Those that choose the evil sovereign, a du*s*sasti, as in Y. XXXII, 9, or as the sastars of Y. XLVI, 1, will not go forward with the saints to the *K*inva*t* (Y. XLVI, 10), nor will they be met by their consciences under pleasing images, and later by the souls of saints who had gone before, but the wicked dead shall meet them in the home of Lies, with poisoned food, and sneering words. And this shall be a self-inflicted vengeance.

Translation.

1. Be*n*dva [1] has ever fought with me; (yea, since he first appeared at hand to threaten, and alas to his advantage in the strife). He is the most powerful (in brutal might), and (in his predominance) would crush my strength as I seek to win back the disaffected (in my host) through Righteous [2] (zeal), O Mazda! Come then with gifts of (vengeful [3]) good to (meet) my sorrow [4]. Through (Thine inspiring) Good Mind obtain (for me [5]) that (Be*n*dva's) death [6]!

2. (Aye, he is indeed the greatest [7]), for that

[1] If this word does not simply mean 'a band,' one might suspect a relation of root with bãnayen. The Pahlavi has expressively and freely badtûm here, and vîmarîh in the next verse, with a like word in Y. XXX, 6. This enemy may have been roughly dubbed 'the polluted,' or even 'diseased one;' analogous occurrences are not wanting.

[2] I cannot agree to rendering ashâ 'really,' when applied in an evil sense. The sacred word may mean 'really' when applied to the righteous, but then, in that case, the reality indicated has an element of sanctity in it, and that of no low order. I am also not aware that *ri*téna is applied in an evil sense in the *Ri*g-veda. The use of Asha, like that of Vohu Manah and Khshathra, &c., is obvious in the Gâtha; the six sacred words were, like the theme of a symphony, brought in at every opportunity, with all shades of meaning from those of proper names to those of adverbs. With slight change of text to a nom., we might render, 'He who seeks to please the evil-minded, O Thou A.!'

[3] Comp. Y. XXXIII, 2.

[4] I cannot agree that arapâ should be read rapâ for the sake of a syllable in the metre. The line has more than eleven syllables here, as the Vedic Trish*t*up often has. Moreover the ancient writing before the Pahlavi translator read likewise arapâ, and the sense demands it.

[5] Or, 'may I obtain.' [6] See Y. LIII, 9. [7] See the first verse.

B*en*dva's evil judge doth cause me to hesitate and ponder (in my earnest course of propagation and reform), a deceiver as he is, (estranged) from the Righteous Order, and receiving[1] from it (not happiness) but many a wound. The bountiful and perfect Piety he has not maintained nor strengthened for this[2] land, nor questions with Thy Good Mind hath he asked[3] (to gain him light), O Lord!

3. But (all is not yet lost!); for this religious choice[4] (our holy creed, for which our last lost[5] battle has been fought), O Mazda! Thy blessed Order (our guardian help) has yet been set to save and bless us. (But) for (that evil) Judge, the Demon-of-the-Lie, (is set) to deal (for him) her wounds[6]. Therefore do I pray (the more) for the sheltering leadership of Thy Good Mind (within our folk and our commanders). And all the allies of the wicked I abjure[7].

4. They who with evil scheme and will shall cherish and help on the Wrath of Rapine, and with her Râma[8], and (not by silent favour, but) with their

---

[1] I would gladly accede to a subjunctive 2nd singular intensive here in a causative sense, but a 3rd singular precedes, and a 3rd singular follows. I cannot therefore recognise a subjunctive in a precative, or imperative, sense here. I think the word is a nominative, as its position in the verse corresponds well to that form. It may mean 'delivering against us many a wound.'

[2] Possibly 'for us in (this) land.'

[3] Comp. Y. XLIV, 13.

[4] Comp. Y. XXX, 2.

[5] See mazi*s*tô in the first verse.

[6] The Pahlavi mûn rêshînê*d* pavan Drû*g*.

[7] The Pahlavi translator gave as our first rendering here: Andarg harvîsp-gûnŏ darvandânŏ min hamkhâkîh andarg yemalelûnam; [aîgh, min dôstîh î levatman valman*s*ân *g*avî*d*âk yehevûnam].

[8] The Pahlavi has arêshkŏ=envy.

very tongues, whose will and wish[1] (run) not with good but evil deeds. These settle and support the Daêvas (in their power, not the Lord). It is[2] the wicked's Faith and Insight (so to do. Their faith is the perverted).

5. But he, O Mazda! is our abundance and our fatness[3], who (will yet dare these unbelieving foes) and guard the Faith (against that envious Wrath[4]), and with the Good Mind's power. For every man of Piety is a wise citizen[5] in accordance with the holy Order, and so are all who are (in truth) within Thy Realm, O Lord!

6. And now, will I beseech of You, O Mazda, and Righteousness (within Thy Mãthra) speaks[6] (to tell me) what lies within Your will's intention, that (having discerned Your Insight as the enlightened

---

[1] The Pahlavi gave us our first surmise as to the general meaning of vãs; it renders kâmak.

[2] Or, 'by that which is the evil's Faith.'

[3] The Pahlavi translator gave us our first general indication here as elsewhere; he has shîrînîh and *k*arpîh. Reading 'Mazd*a*u,' we have 'Mazda (is our source of) abundance and refreshment.'

[4] See the fourth verse.

[5] The Pahlavi has, however, khûp shinâsakîh. I differ with hesitation; possibly views may be harmonised.

[6] Compare Y. XXIX, 3, where Asha answers. I cannot well accept mrûitê as an infinitive. Geldner has keenly pointed out that fraêshyâ is inclined to unite with an infinitive, but so are other forms of ish and vas. Moreover the infinitive does not so naturally fall to the end of the sentence in Gâthic or Vedic. (See above, note on Y. XXXIV, 1.) If an infinitive is insisted upon (so long since) let us at least bring the word into more usual shape, using the Pahlavi translator, as in one of his most valuable offices, as an indirect evidence, where his translation is at fault as a rendering. He has: Frâzŏ avŏ zak î Lekûm farmâyêm, Aûharmazd, va Ashavahi*st*ŏ*k* râî yemalelûnam. He had 'mrûvê' before him, which might be an infinitive.

ever must), I may as well discern aright how we can herald forth those (truths), and that pure Daêna (with them) which is the Faith of Him who is Thyself[1], O Lord.

7. And (as we speak it forth as taught by Asha) then let the (zealous[2] citizen) give heed, and with Thy Good Mind, O Ahura Mazda! Yea, let him give ear in accordance with (the dictate of) the Holy Order, and do Thou hear alike as well[3]. Who shall be the ally; and who the kinsman-lord himself, who, with his gifts and (legal rules), shall institute and settle for the serving mass a worthy praise (for God[4])?

8. (And I do not ask in vain, for such an one is found for us, and near at hand.) To Frashaostra hast Thou given that most favouring guardian power, the headship[5] of the Holy Order (for us), O

---

[1] I think that khshmâvatô equals simply 'yourself' here, as often (so mava*n*t=me); otherwise 'of your disciple,' which would be feeble. Professor Jolly has, V. S., s. 97, 'damit wir ihn verkündigen möchten den Glauben, welcher der euere ist, o Ahura.'

[2] See the ninth verse.

[3] Ahura is elsewhere addressed in close connection with human beings; here the human subject is half lost in Vohûman and Asha. I hardly think that it is wise to change the text without MSS. A lost verse may have relieved all difficulty.

[4] Others 'the good doctrine,' or again 'the good repute;' but as to the latter, frasasti is coupled so constantly in the later Avesta with yasna, and vahma, &c., that I do not feel at liberty to depart from that sense. The Pahlavi has also vâfrîgânîh, quite in harmony with the connection.

[5] This verse is clearly an answer to the questions contained in verse 7. It is a half answer, even if we render d*a*u (dâo) as a subjunctive. As the question in verse 7 certainly concerns a chief of some kind, I cannot see how we can avoid rendering sar*e*m analogously. We need one who gives a refuge rather than one who receives it. Compare the Pahlavi, and also the Persian, sar. The Pahlavi

Ahura! This therefore would I pray of Thee (to confirm to him that gracious gift), and for myself likewise, would I now seek as well that sheltering headship which is within Thy Realm; yea, most blest and foremost[1] may we both for ever be within it.

9. Aye, let the zealous and thrifty husbandman, so formed for giving help and blessings[2], give heed and listen when I call, (O Mazda!) Let not the truthful (tiller, he who hears and speaks Thy word[3]), be he who takes[4] that sheltering chieftainship together with the wicked. Let the believing natures (only) join in that best recompense. And thus in the course of the holy Order are in the fact so joined those two, *G*âmâspa and the 'hero'[5].

10. (And since these champions thus join in that reward), then therefore will I place as well in Thy

translation gives its evidence without intermission for this meaning, a fact largely overlooked.

[1] I think that the connection fairly proves this meaning; and it has likewise the powerful support of the Pahlavi translation: Hamâi vad avŏ vîspŏ farmânpatŏ hômanânî [aîgh, Frasho*s*tar [ ] vad tanû î pasînŏ hamâî *s*alîtâîh yehabûn].

[2] It is not to be forgotten that su is the root of Saoshya*n*t.

[3] Comp. Y. XXXI, 15.

[4] Or 'gives;' compare peresâ ava*t* yâ maini*s* *ye* dregvâitê khshathrem hunâitî. Professor Jolly, V. S., s. 36: 'Nicht soll wer das Rechte redet, die Herrschaft dem Lügner überlassen.'

[5] Yâhî remains a singular, whereas we should expect a dual; (can it be such, the form being altered, as so often by later reciters, to accommodate the metre?) For *G*âmâspâ and yukhtâ as duals compare utayûitî tevîshî. Yâhî probably refers to Vî*s*tâspa (Y. XLVI, 14). Was it an especial epithet for the kings? The later Persian kings took prominent places in battle. If the duals are not admitted, my rendering would be, 'the souls are united with the reward through the (influence and example of the) valiant *G*âmâspa.' Perhaps *G*âmâspô is to be read.

protection (Thy) Good Mind[1] (in the living) and the spirits (of the dead. Yea, I confide our very) self-humbling praises, (which we offer, unto Thee), by which (Thine) Âramaiti (who is our Piety, exists), and likewise sacrificing zeal. And this would we do to further Thy great Sovereign Power (among Thy folk), and with undying[2] (?) strength.

11. (But as to faithless reprobates); the souls (of the evil dead) shall meet those evil men who serve their evil rulers, who speak with evil words, and harbour evil consciences, these souls (in Hell) shall come with evil food[3] (to welcome them), and in the Lie's abode their dwelling[4] verily shall be[5]!

YASNA XLIX, 12 — L.

The most striking circumstance here, after the rhetorical and moral-religious peculiarities have been observed, is the sixth verse; and as to the question of Zarathustrian authorship, it is the most striking in the Gâthas or the Avesta. In that verse we have Zarathustra, not named alone, which might easily be harmonised

---

[1] This is probably the foundation for the later identification of Vohû Manah and the faithful disciple.

[2] Here all is conjectural. The Pahlavi reports an adjective from a form of man (or a participle). They who think upon the throne (to seize it) do so with dying power. Wilder conjectures have been made; but the Pahlavi translators seldom wilfully guessed. They took the shattered results of their predecessors, and worked them feebly over; hence their great value, and the unimportance of their errors. They used what intelligence they possessed in re-delivering what they heard and read. Vazdanghâ cannot well be taken in an evil sense, as it is used in a good sense elsewhere. The connection mãzâ with râ has long circulated; mãzâ avêmî râ (?). As the souls of the departed are thought of, perhaps 'undying' is the meaning; compare avemîra (for form) with the Zend avimithris.

[3] See Yast XXII by Darmesteter, as supplemented.

[4] So the Pahlavi; otherwise 'their bodies shall so lie.'

[5] Verse 12 belongs to the next chapter.

with his personal authorship, nor have we only such expressions as 'to Zarathustra and to us' (Y. XXVIII, 7), but we have Zarathustra named as 'mahyâ râzeng sâhît,' 'may he declare my regulations, which could only be said, without figure of speech, by some superior, if not by the prime mover himself. Were these verses then written by the prime mover? And was he other than Zarathustra? If so, the entire mass of the Gâthas was of course written by him, or else their style and character may be regarded as of such a character that they could have been composed by four or five closely connected individuals. But while verses here and there are doubtless the productions of secondary persons, the mass of the Gâthas cannot be regarded as the work of several different composers. They are one man's work, directly or indirectly. If then the present section, which is especially original in its tone, was not from Zarathustra, the man whose heart and soul, and, we may add, whose power were in Zarathustrianism, was not Zarathustra, but some unnamed individual far more important. (See note on Y. XXVIII, 7.) The prominence of the name of Zarathustra was in that case solely owing to the personal activity of Zarathustra supported by the social rank of the Spitâmas. Zarathustra was a princely disciple, on the hypothesis mentioned, and nothing more. The real author of Zarathustrianism was, in that case, in no sense Zarathustra; compare 'to Zarathustra and to us:' nor yet Vîstâspa; compare 'to Vîstâspa and to me:' nor Frashaostra; compare 'to Frashaostra and to us;' and, we may also say, not Gâmâspa, for he is addressed in the vocative. He was mentally and personally the superior of all of them. In fact he was the power behind both throne and home, and yet without a name! But, in that case, what becomes of Y. XXIX, 6, 8? Is it probable that the founder of a religion (or of a new departure in a religion) would describe another as the chosen of God, if he were not in fact supposed to be thus eminent? Or, if a popular and sincerely enthusiastic religious composer were about to chant a hymn at a meeting of the religious masses, would he be likely to name a person to the animated throngs, whom they themselves did not feel to be the life of their religious faith? especially, if that person were not prominent from the arbitrary circumstance that he was the reigning prince? I do not think that this is at all probable. But if Zarathustra had, as described, the leading name, and composed a portion of the hymns with their lost companions, is it probable that he possessed no decided prominence in this matter above Vîstâspa, Frashaostra, and Gâmâspa? Was there no central poet, who composed the mass of the metrical lore, dominating by his influence those who added portions here and there, or was there a quaternion of seers, four Zarathustras, as one might say? As we have said, the hymns decide it. One man's soul is in them, as a composer's feelings are in his compositions, or a master's feelings are in the lines of his disciples. But if there was one central figure instead of four, and he is mentioned as Zarathustra, and as the spokesman in many portions of the Gâthas, being likewise known by inference to be the composer of nearly all of them, how can we account for the words, 'let him, Zarathustra, teach or proclaim my regulations?' Can the verse be regarded as put into the mouth of Ahura, as elsewhere? Hardly, for Ahura is addressed in it. I can therefore only repeat of this verse, as of the others which present analogous questions in Y. XXVIII (with which this chapter L stands in the closest connection), that this thoroughly original piece was composed by Zarathustra as by far the most prominent individual in the religious struggle, dominating his party essentially and positively, and that these verses (6–11) were simply rhetorically put into the mouth of the monarch from the exigency of the style of composition. And I conclude that Vîstâspa was supposed to speak them, because in the presence of Zarathustra, it is extremely improbable that any one but the titular head of the State should have been represented as saying of Zarathustra, 'mahyâ râzeng sâhît.'

1. The piece from Y. XLIX, 12 to Y. L, 1–5 joins well on with Y. XLIX, although the tone is brighter. As he begins with questions in Y. XLVIII, 8–11, after the prospective prayers of Y. XLVIII, 1–7, in which he looks forward to a crisis in the armed struggle, so now after the hostile chief has got the upper hand, he cries out once more with interrogatives, uttering the questions, not of curiosity, but of mournful devotion.

'The storm has broken over us,' so he would seem to say, 'and I have prayed for grace to know how we may administer (Y. XLIV, 9) the all-powerful means of help, the Daêna, in which Thy Righteous Order is set (Y. XLIX, 3). I have cried to Thee for chief and peer (verse 7), naming Frashaostra, Gâmâspa, and the Yâhin, and now, while I invoke you, praying for what in your selection is the best (Y. XXVIII, 11; Y. XLIV, 10), I would more than ever declare that I have none other help than Thee and Thy saving Order.' 2. And he asks once more to know how he who seeks to further the sacred herds, as the emblem of the moral thrift of the provinces, should proceed in his allotted work. 3. Answering his own question, he says that it is by advance upon the enemy; he declares that the heroic settler who pushes the holy system to the utmost verge of the sacred territory or still further, was the man 'to gain the Kine' for the seeking prophet. 4. But in the midst of struggles, he anticipates Garôdman with its praises. 5. For they were all prepared for both worship and work, since God had approached to aid His prophet, encouraging His discouraged spirit. 6. Here Vîstâspa is represented as intervening; and he addresses Ahura literally, but Zarathustra really, exhorting him indirectly to continue on in his work of propagation, undismayed by present circumstances. 7. And with Zarathustra, he would re-engage the other powerful helpers, whom he would yoke on as steeds to gain God's praise in Heaven by passing over every bridge of trial safely. 8. Having heard from Zarathustra his metric words, he will approach with them to pray, and, as in Y. XXVIII, 2, 3, 'with hands stretched out' with homage, and with vigour. 9. And he looks to attain the object of his prayers by religious self-control, and faithful action. 10. His efforts vie with the heavenly bodies in their praise of God. 11. Therefore he will persevere, and as a praiser-king (so the Pahlavi in one place); and he beseeches that Ahura, the life-giver, may help on the all-engrossing cause.

Translation.

Y. XLIX, 12[1]. What aids of grace hast Thou for Thine invoking Zarathustra, (O Ahura Mazda!) to grant him through Thy Righteous Order? Yea, what (aids of[2] grace hast thou for me as) through Thy Good Mind given (within my soul), for me who will (still) pray to Thee with praises, O Great Creator! beseeching what in accordance with Your wished-for aim is best?

Y. L, 1. Aye, doth my soul indeed obtain assisting

[1] This verse is placed here as obviously more closely related to chapter L than to chapter XLIX. Lost verses may, however, have intervened between it and Y. L, 1.

[2] Another rendering, regarding kat as a purely interrogative participle, would be, 'Are they (tôi) helpful to the invoking Zarathustra?' But kat tôi is a familiar form; see Y. XXXIV, 12, where it must mean quid tibi.

grace, and which of Thy blessings is that gift to me, O Lord? What saving champion is found to save both flocks and herds? And who for myself other than Thy Righteous Order, and Thyself, Ahura? Tell me[1], O (ye) invoked ones! Or what of grace is there for me save Thy Best Mind (itself)?

2. (And if Thy guardian is verily to save our wealth) how shall he (obtain, and by what means shall he) seek after[2] that joy-creating Kine (who is the living symbol of our peace[3])? (How shall that man obtain his wish) who shall desire to see her provided with pastures for (the welfare of) this land? (That only way is righteousness.) Do Thou then grant me lands (so would I ask of Thee) which live in justice in the many[4] splendours of the sun, and lands which openly[5] thus live, and which are to be

[1] I should be far from denying that azdâ may equal addhấ, but a strengthening adverb seems to me of no particular force here. I formerly rested at the simple explanation az + dâ = dhâ = desire-exciting, much desired one. But the Pahlavi translator affords an explanation which may surpass that of his successors. He sees the meaning: 'When I shall call upon You,' (that is, freely, 'being invoked,') 'cause Thou (sic) me to understand fully.' This is the remnant of some predecessor's work, who rendered 'tell ye me;' az = ah, otherwise lost in Zend. The plural follows the singular too often to excite much doubt; azdâ = tell ye; so zdî is from az, as syôdûm is from as (recall the well-known Indian analogies). See also the explanation of the Pahlavi at Y. XXXI, 17. If a plural cannot be admitted, then consider a form extended by d.

[2] The Pahlavi translates freely, bavîhûnam.

[3] The Kine must represent the people as well as their live-stock. The raids concerned the owners more than their cattle. In answer to the cry of the Kine, Zarathustra was sent to the people.

[4] I can hardly agree to the rendering 'among people who see the sun' without a needless reconstruction of the text. The Pahlavi likewise has pavan khvârîh; for general meaning, compare Khshathrôi *hveng* daresôi, not as equivalent however.

[5] Âskârak stî.

sought and gained by me (as conquests for the cause). Give Thou this gift!

3. (Yea, let that joy-creating one) be his possession through the Righteous Order (which he helps to bring, that living sign) which (the most valiant citizen) may give to him (at once reward and charge), and in accordance with Thy Sovereign Authority. (May that heroic settler grant him this gift) he who may make the (last imperilled) farm to flourish in the vigour of Thy blest prosperity, the tract which lies the nearest (to the fields) which our foeman holds as his[1].

4. (And therefore both in thankfulness and hope) will I give sacrifice to You with praises, O Ahura Mazda! together with Thine Order and Thy Best Mind (in Thy saints), and in accordance with Thy sacred Sovereign Power, by whose help the wisher (heavenbound) may stand upon the (certain) pathway[2], and in Thine Home-of-song shall I (by means of these my Yasnas offered here) there hear the praises of Thine offering saints who see Thy face[3].

5. And we[4] are in readiness as well (to fulfil Your praises and declare your words), O Ahura Mazda! through Your (grace, and) in accordance with Your Holy Order, since Ye advance with friendliness[5] to cheer the speaker of Your Măthra-word with open acts of visible relief, as if with hand sent forth,

[1] The Pahlavi translation, as usual, not literally exact, still furnishes the correct clue, Zak î nazdistô (?) gêhânŏ min valman î darvand bakhshê*d* [aîga*s* zak dên dâri*s*n barâ yansegûnyên].

[2] Frô tâi*s* vîspâi*s* *K*învatô frâ peretûm.

[3] Âk*a*u (compare the Indian âkê); 'who approach, and are therefore evident (âshkârak) to God, and seeing Him.' Comp. âk*a*u in Y. LI, 13, which has been thought a loc.

[4] See n*a*u.

[5] To vra*g*.

whereby that Mãthra-speaker of Your truth may bring us on, and settle us, in weal and bliss[1].

6. (Therefore will I incite him to his task the more. Let him indeed proclaim the righteous way[2]) he who already lifts his voice in Mãthras, O Ahura Mazda! he, Zarathustra[3], the faithful friend in accordance with the Holy Order, and with self-abasing worship, giver of understanding for this land, voice-guider (of the way to glory[4]), let him indeed proclaim and teach my regulations, and in accordance with Thy Good Mind (as his law).

7. (And together with that chief speaker of your word I would engage yet others in the cause). Your well-incited[5] and swift[6] (servants), O Ahura! would I yoke[7] on (as steeds to take their holy course toward heaven), gaining[7] thereby (at last) the Bridges[8] where

[1] See the previous verse, where the wisher stands on the path, seeking to reach Garô*d*man. It seems therefore probable that *hv*âthrê refers to demânê garô.

[2] Compare Y. LIII, 2, *d*aunghô erezû*s* pathô.

[3] As remarked, this entire piece recalls Y. XXVIII. Here the monarch is represented as speaking precisely as spokesmen are introduced in any other composition. We have no reason to suppose the piece to be the composition of some leading person other than Zarathu*s*tra, because of the words 'let Zarathu*s*tra speak forth my regulations.' (See page 169.)

[4] Îshô st*a*ungha*t* â paithî.

[5] Consider a suffix ish*t*i.

[6] Here the Pahlavi translator gives us both text and translation, aurvatô = arvand.

[7] Or, 'yoke Thou, may'st Thou gain.'

[8] The *K*inva*t* Bridge, either literally or figuratively. Compare 'the bridge of the earth' (Y. LI, 12). The crises of effort, or temptation, are meant, as the *K*inva*t* Bridge was the last crisis before salvation or perdition. The souls of the good and of the evil were met by their own consciences on the Bridge, and encouraged or reviled.

'When the soul of the pious passes over that Bridge, the width of

Your adoration (rules and is complete). Yea, I (?) yoke on your mighty ones, and with Thy Holy Order, and Thy Good Mind. And with these may Ye drive on; aye, be Ye for my help!

8. (And as I yoke on Your Mãthra-speakers for their course, then) would I (myself) approach You in the (highest) deed of worship[1], and with these sacred metric feet (of Zarathustra and his peers[2]), those which are heard and famed afar, as the metric feet of zealous worship, and with my hands stretched[3] out (in supplicating prayer). Yea, You (would I approach), O Mazda! in union with Your sacred ritual Truth, and with the homage of a freely-giving helper[4], and with the good virtue of (Your) Good Mind (in my soul).

9. Yea, with these Yasnas of Your sacrifice would I approach You, praising back to You (in answer to Your mercies), O Ahura! and Thou, O Righteousness! in (the holy) actions of Your Good Mind, (as he moves within us), so long indeed as I shall have the power, commanding at my will o'er this my sacred (privilege) and gift. (And doing as) the wise man (thus), may I (like him) become a supplicant who gains[5] his ends.

10. (Mine every wish and prayer is this), then therefore whatsoever I shall do, and whatsoever deeds

---

that Bridge becomes about one league' (West, Mainyô-î Khard,* p. 134). Possibly the extension of the Bridge for the pious arose from the plural use here.

[1] Compare Y. XXVIII, 3. [2] See Y. XXVIII, 9.

[3] See Y. XXVIII, 2. [4] See Y. XLVI, 9.

[5] The Pahlavi translator accepts a sense of acquisition here as well as of desire: Aêtûnô zak î valman î avŏ hû-dânâk pavan khvahîsnŏ grîftâr hômanânî [mozd]. I accede to its indication, holding that gardh certainly has such an element in its meaning.

(of ritual and truth I shall yet further do) on account of, (and to make full[1]) these (prior deeds of worship), yea, whatsoever (holy works) shine bright[2] as having worth in (all) men's eyes through Thy Good Mind (whose character they share; these as) the stars, suns, and the Aurora which brings on the light[3] of days, are all, through their Righteous Order, (the speakers) of Thy[4] praise, O Thou Great Giver, Lord!

11. Your praiser then (by eminence) would I be named, and (more), would be it, so long as by (Thine inspiring) Righteousness I am thus able and may have the power. And may the maker of the world give help through (His implanted) Good Mind (in my fellow-servants). And may that (all) be done[5] (to further us) which through His veritable grace is most promotive (for the cause)!

---

[1] I can here only follow the words as they are written; the meaning is clear enough although rather advanced. Reconstructions on a large scale are seldom of value.

[2] Judging from the context, we may render arga*t* thus.

[3] The Pahlavi translator here renders as if he read ushâ. In Y. XLVI, 3 he translates ukhshânô. Professor Wilhelm, preferring as above, still recalls the Homeric usage favouring 'increaser.' The Pahlavi has vakhshînî*d*âr in Y. XLVI, 3. Here hôsh zak î arûs dên bâm I. Ner. alone understood arûs.

[4] 'Your.'

[5] An imperative has long been recognised in var*s*tãm; or read: 'Let him cause that which is the most furthering of deeds to grow influential through veritable grace.' So perhaps better.

THE GÂTHA(Â) VOHÛ KHSHATHREM (VOHUKHSHATHRA(Â)).

This Gâtha consists of the single chapter Y. LI. It has lines of fourteen syllables with caesura in the middle.

YASNA LI.

INSTRUCTIONS AND APPEALS TO AN ASSEMBLY OF THE FAITHFUL.

It is hardly possible that we have here a continuous whole. The thoughts, however, harmonise well enough, and the changes give little trouble. 1. As so often the Sovereign Authority of Ahura, His reign over the hearts and in the minds of His faithful worshippers, is the leading theme. That sovereign Power, when it is established, will produce every good thing with it, and repress every evil, and the composer prays that he may never pause at any moment in his efforts to bring that kingdom on. 2. Accordingly, as the foremost of objects, he beseeches for both its blessings and its protection, and names Âramaiti as the especial representative of Ahura in this case to grant the Kingdom as a Realm established in spiritual wealth, and whose first effect should be the glory of God through the agency of holy dispositions in men.

3. The spirit of the Daêna is public and prophetic rather than occult and mysterious. The people therefore gather to hear Gâthas recited, and religious harangues delivered as on political occasions, and all the more because the Mãthras are declared to be the results of direct inspiration from Ahura. 4. The present recitations are invocations calling for the four energising Immortals, the guiding Order, the active Piety, the inspiring Benevolence, and the Power-wielding Kingdom, and, in using these names, the multitude are also beseeching, by the voice of their spokesman, for the Ratu, the Saoshya*n*t cried for by the Kine, looked for by Asha himself, and promised by Ahura.

5. And the men who press this prayer are, each of them, for the moment (nû*k*î*t*), as the Ratu himself. Wise in his homage, he seeks to gain the kine, like the ideal husbandman, both as property and as emblem, and he desires to establish the Ratu, understood as a person, or as the law, which may judge between the two sides (Y. XXXI, 2), and, by the expulsion of the evil, give quiet to the land (Y. XLVI, 4; Y. LIII, 9). 6. Declaring Ahura to be the awarder of the highest good and deepest evil, (7) he calls on Him to grant the 'eternal two,' the rewarding Immortals (not named in the former verse), but only by means of the inspired teachings. 8. And as these inculcations are effective for himself, he will declare forth their threats and promises to others, being repaid for his zealous fidelity in the very act. 9. Recalling the hopes of vengeance, he beseeches Ahura to give forth a sign, or instrument, from the holy Fire, which may settle the disputes by the forged blade of justice. 10. For he declares that the man who murderously assaults his adherents in the opposing interest (see Y. XXXII, 10, &c.) is inherently and originally perverted in his motives, a very son of the Lie, and of the seed of Akôman.

11. While in terms he addresses Ahura, he in reality challenges the devotion of the chieftains, as he calls aloud to the Deity.

12. Here a temptation of Zarathustra is narrated, as in the Vendîdâd, here dwelling on his youth, there on his maturer manhood. But the verse shows marked signs of later age.

13. And the soul of the righteous is encouraged by the recorded example; he shall come off the conqueror, as Zarathustra did.

14. But the Karpans (priestly chiefs?) of the opposing party, following the typical destroyer (as in Y. XXXII), would bring the world to ruin, and the creatures to Hell.

15. The true disciples will however infallibly receive the promised recompense.

16. And as for that *K*isti, conceived by Mazda to give the saving knowledge in the sacred verse, the King of the Realm had acquired it. It will be stored in the memory of faithful priests under his care and rule; and he will give his subjects a good worship (Y. XLIX, 7) in accordance with it. 17. A female saint, also illustrious in rank, is celebrated with honourable mention; she is, as it were, the *K*isti in her person, as she is named in this connection.

18. Another devoted friend arrests the speaker's eye, as he stands in the assembly; (19) and still another. 20. Then, as if taking in all with his view, and with an expression which shows

his identification with the people, he declares that the 'Archangels' are of one mind with Mazda in bestowing spiritual blessings, the chief of which are inspired words, the source of their discipline, and the guide of their hopes.

21. And with assurances as to the greatness of the spiritual blessings implied in all that he has said, he prays Ahura all the more earnestly to grant them to His elect. 22. And he declares that Ahura knows and observes the man who fulfils every command that he has uttered, as well as believes every doctrine which he has divulged, and that, knowing Him, He also marks Him as the object of His grace. And he ends by expressing once more his desire to approach the Bountiful Immortals, not as naming them alone, but naming them, as we may well suppose, with a full appreciation of all that is meant by the sacred words which belong to them as names.

Translation.

1. The good Government (of Ahura[1]) is to be chosen (among all wished-for things[2]) as that lot which most of all brings on (our happiness). Actions that oppress us it opposes[3], through the holy Order (which pervades it), and with the pious zeal (of its true servants). Therefore, O Great Creator! let me

---

[1] It is far better to take Khshathra in its usual and often necessary sense. And it is especially desirable not to confound it with shôithra=kshétra.

[2] The choice one.

[3] One is somewhat inclined to regard vîdushemnâis as a monstrous form of vid, which has crept into the text under the influence of the two words vîdushê in verse 8, and owing to an attempt to fill out the metre, the original word having been vîdemnâis. The Pahlavi gives no indication except for a form of dû=to give. Leaving the MSS. intact, I compare dush+vi.

I render as above on the principle that the text in the MSS. should not be violated where it is possible to translate it at all. Reading vîdemnâis we might render, 'that kingdom's privileges are shared (it is entered and penetrated) by men who act (by actions) in a manner to further its security, (by actions gaining it).'

produce, and help bring on (that Sovereign Power) which is the best for us at every present hour.

2. And first I will ask for[1] these two blessings of Your own, O Thou Great Creator, and thou His Righteous Order! and I also ask of thee, Our Piety (personified, as well); and grant me this Your Sovereign Rule over our desired wealth (to give and to preserve it; and likewise) those spiritual blessings which are advantageous for our worship (of Ahura) through (the inspiration of His) Good Mind (within the soul).

3. (And it is not I alone who thus appeal to You; I speak for all) who are guarded in the (ceremonial and moral) actions of Your (law), and by those (inspired) words (which proceed) from the tongue of Thy Good Mind (as he speaks within Thy Mãthra). Yea, these are all assembling (each) to hear You, of whom Thou, O Ahura Mazda! art the foremost guide[2] and light.

4. (And they cry aloud to Thee, O Mazda! I speaking with them, and in their name): Where is the (promised[3]) lord of our thrift (the embodied law, saving us from the most dreaded dangers that we fear[4], the thrift-lord) of (our) ready zeal? Where

---

[1] I have rather reluctantly read yê*k*â with long ê. Having in mind Y. XXX, 1, where Sp.'s B. reads yaê*k*â, and reading yaĉ*k*â here, we might regain the lost dual neuter of the pronoun here as in Y. XXX, 1, and so render, 'and which two things belong to thee, the possession (rule) of wealth and the blessings.'

Roth, cited by Geldner, changes to ashayaê*k*â here and in Y. XXX, 1; and it is certainly striking that ashâ yê*k*â should occur twice. I render as above, first, as nearer our MSS., and as affording a good sense.

[2] See Y. XXXI, 17.

[3] See verse 5.

[4] See Y. XXIX, 1; Y. XXXII.

does he stand to (show us) mercy? Whither are (Thy) Righteousness and the Bountiful Âramaiti (our Piety) approaching? From what direction comes Thy Best Mind (to inspire and to guide)? And whence (again), O Great Creator! Thy Sovereign Power (to be our ruler and defence[1])?

5. And it is the tiller of the earth who asks this of Thee, O Ahura! (Thy chosen saint himself); he has asked this all of Thee, striving to discover how he may gain to himself the sacred Kine (and with all wealth in herds beside. And he would seek this) moved by the motives which flow from Thy Righteous Order (and Thy cause), upright as he is in actions, and wise in his self-humbling worship (of that[2] One) who, as a righteous ruler, has appointed a just controlling guide for those whom He has made.

6. (And in partial answer to his question, and to solve his doubt, I now declare the truth): He who gives to this (good citizen) that which is better than the good[3]; yea, He who bestows on him in accordance with his religious choice is (our) Ahura Mazda (and not

---

[1] It is hardly necessary to call attention to the fact that these abstracts are personified here, as in so many other places in the Gâthas. We may indeed doubt whether the idea of personification was ever wholly absent, the original meaning being likewise never lost. Professor Wilhelm prefers taking Ashem as an accusative, 'how does one (do they) come to Asha?' This is admirable; but I am, on the whole, inclined to regard Ashem as a nominative with fseratu*s*, Âr(a)maiti*s*, &c., taking the plurals yasô *hvy*e*n* (hy*e*n) as irregularly extending to the other subjects.

[2] So Wilhelm (by letter), taking a form of the pronoun as understood. It is difficult to suppose that the vâstrya could be referred to as appointing the Ratu through the influence of his devotion and pious supplications; as Wilhelm justly says, the third line must apply to Ahura.

[3] See Y. XLIII, 3; notice ahmâi as referring to hôi.

a false god of the Daêvas[1]). And this will He bestow through His divine Authority (established in preparation here), while on the withholder of the sacrifice, who offers nothing to His (cause), He will send worse than the evil (and that not here alone, but) in the last turning of the creation in its course!

7. (And as Thou wilt bestow thus graciously on him), so grant me also, O Thou most bountiful Spirit Mazda, Thou who hast made both the Kine and the waters and the plants[2] (for her support)! both Immortality and Welfare, those two eternal powers, and through Thy Good Mind in the doctrine (which is revealed through his inspired words[3]).

8. (Yea, grant me these two inseparable gifts, for having them in store) I will speak for Thee, O Mazda! because to the man of understanding[4] one should declare for Thee that which is woe to the wicked, but salvation to him who has maintained the holy Order (in Thy folk and in his soul). For he is (repaid in his deed, and) rejoiced by the Mãthra who declares it to the wise.

9. (And when I shall speak, I will declare for You that mental) keenness (which reaches the decision), and which Thou hast bestowed upon the two striving sides[5], (in Thy satisfying word). And this

[1] See Y. XXXI, 17 where the faith of the dregva*n*t is sufficiently recognised to form the basis for a question, rhetorical indeed, but still a question.

[2] From this and similar occurrences of the 'water and the plants' beside 'Immortality and Welfare' probably arose the later peculiar identification of those names with water and plants.

[3] Compare perhaps verse 20.

[4] Otherwise; 'I will speak for Thee, O Lord! for the (all)-wise one should speak.'

[5] Or, 'from the two ara*n*i;' see notes on Y. XXXI, 3 and Y. XLIII, 12.

I will announce by means of Thy flaming Fire; yea, I will declare it for the bestowal of that sword of justice which is forged from steel [1], and wrought for both the worlds [2]. And for the wounding of the wicked (with its blade) may'st Thou [3], O Ahura Mazda! bless and prosper Thine (avenging) saint [4]!

10. (Yea, let Thy believer wound the wicked to the quick), for he, who totally estranged from this (our holy rule [5]), O Mazda! seeks to destroy my life, is a son [6] of the Lie's creation, and belongs to the miscreants; (but as for me), I call on Asha (Thy Righteous Order to be my help); and may he come with Thy good blessing.

11. (And ye who throng the great assembly [7], it is of you I speak while, with my lips, I now address the Lord): Who, O Ahura! is a loyal friend to the Spitâma [8], to Zarathustra? Who has asked his question of the divine Righteousness, (as he approached [9])?

---

[1] Compare Y. XXXII, 7, *hv*aênâ ayanghâ (lit. iron).

Others see the ordeal of fire here, and the bath of melted metal from which the righteous suffers nothing, but in which the sinner is consumed, but râshayanghê seems to point to injury produced otherwise than by dipping, and dakhshta certainly designates a metallic instrument elsewhere; 'sign' is, however, the original meaning.

[2] So several times; comp. Y. XXVIII, 3, where the depth is unmistakable; see also Y. XXXI, 18 with ahûbî*s* in the next verse.

[3] The Pahlavi while not strictly correct, affords the indication of a causative, sû*d*înê*d*.

[4] From this verse probably arose the later association of khshathra-vairya and metal founding and forging.

[5] As invoking Asha is in the antithesis, I regard ashâ*t* as understood here. Ga*t* seems a particle, but also not impossibly=gâ*t*. As it is twice followed by tê (tôi), the interesting change is suggested to gatê, infin.

[6] Or a proper name.

[7] See the third verse.

[8] See Y. XLVI, 9, 14.

[9] See the fourth verse.

By whom is the bounteous Piety (received and cherished)? Or who has been regarded as upright and fitted for the great cause of Thy Good Mind?

12. ('Who is worthy?' would I ask, for Zarathustra was ever such, and from earliest days. He was no polluted wretch.) Paederast never gained his ear, nor Kavi-follower on this (temptation-)bridge of earth, when his body was (maturely) grown, when they both hasten(ed) to him with the bosom's[1] impure power[2].

13. (And he will be likewise victorious on the veritable Judgment Bridge, for) the righteous man's conscience will truly[3] crush the wicked man's (spirit) while his soul rages[4] fiercely on the open *K*invat Bridge[5], as he strives by his actions, and his tongue's

---

[1] Some other portion of the human body, suggested by the context, may be meant by aodares. The word looks like a verbal form, 3rd pl., but see the preceding dual.

[2] I render the Pahlavi of this most difficult verse as follows: Far from satisfying me is the Kîk, the paederast, in regard to both of the two particulars [food and clothing] on the path of winter; (far from satisfying me) who am Zartûsht, the Spîtâman, with whom he is; that is, (or 'where') he incites me with his incitation in my bodily (?) (sensations; reading astak (?)); [that is, a person comes, and thus also they, or he, would do it to me]; and this one who (is doing) [that to us] is also leading us on, even in our progress in the cold [of a winter] of accustomed sin, (or in the cold iniquitous winter). This verse seems a very ancient interpolation.

[3] Haithîm is an adverb; its position also does not so much favour an accusative substantive.

[4] So our texts; but the Pahlavi translator saw khraozhdaitî (see Y. XLVI, 11) in his MSS., rendering khrûsisnŏ yehabûnd=utter cries: 'while his soul cries fiercely.'

[5] The occurrence of peretau(âo) in this verse sheds light upon the peretô in the previous one. Âkau(âo) seems to be an attracted form for a loc. as elsewhere. Perhaps it is miswritten.

(cursing speech) to reach[1] (and to pollute) Asha's paths (where the faithful souls come).

14. (And as are those lost spirits, so are our foes.) No friends to the creatures[2] are the Karpans, (not granting) complete (harvests) from the fields with complete (pasture) for the Kine (chief objects for our prayer), bringing woe[3] by their deeds and their teachings. And they[4] will deliver these (beings[5] whom they lead) at the last (?) by their doctrine(s) in the Home of the Lie.

15. But this is the reward which Zarathu*s*tra declared before (to his friends who counsel with Asha), and are fitted for the cause[6]; Ahura Mazda will come the first[7] into His Song Home, Garô*d*man,

---

[1] Nãsv*a*u(âo) would naturally mean 'reaching'; but the word is also elsewhere used in an evil sense, 'reaching to harm.' Y. LIII, 7. The Pahlavi, however, indicates the reading nasv*a*u by its nasînênd. Does the Avesta show an original evil sense to nas = to reach? May the two nas possibly have some original connection? That *h*vâi*s* *s*kyaothnâi*s* means here 'by means of' rather than 'because of' is the more probable from the same words in the next verse, and this notwithstanding Y. XXXI, 20.

[2] So general a term as 'creatures' should be avoided where possible; but see y*e* dâthaêibyô ere*s* ratûm khshayãs ashav*a*u *k*istâ (verse 5).

[3] As to the grammatical structure, all depends on se*n*dâ. Shall we bring down nôi*t* from the verse above; or shall we regard se*n*dâ as in an evil sense from sad as in sadrâ? The Pahlavi favours the former, as also in Y. XXXVIII, 5 (Sp. 15). The general result is not, however, affected. Read as alternative: No friends to the creatures are the Karpans as to perfect (harvests) from the fields, (not) blessing us in the matter of perfect (care and fodder) for the cattle, &c.; (sad in the sense of blessing with nôi*t*).

[4] Free. [5] Or, 'doctrines.' [6] See the eleventh verse.

[7] Alternatives would be, 'Ahura will meet these engagements (?) made when the reward was promised;' or, 'the reward which Zarathu*s*tra promised before Ahura came into Garô*d*man.' Ac-

and then these gifts will be given you by the Good Mind (within you), and with blessings for the cause of the Righteous Order (in His hosts).

16. (And one of you, the greatest, has indeed attained to that wisdom which is thus blessed with a promise), Kavi Vîstâspa has reached it in the Realm of our great cause (of devotion [1]), and moved in his toil by the chants of the Good Mind (who speaks in the Mãthra [2]); yea, he hath attained to that wisdom which the bountiful Ahura conceived in accordance with Asha, thus to teach us salvation.

17. (And not alone amidst our princes hath sanctity been marked), Frashaostra, the Hvôgva, hath presented a blest and an endeared form (his child [3]); and may Ahura Mazda, who has the Sovereign Power, grant her (to us), who is so much to be beloved. And for the (progress of the) good Religion [4] do ye, O ye people! receive her with desire [5], and for the gaining of Asha; (she will help the great cause).

18. Yea, that (holy) wisdom, O *G*âmâspa the Hvôgva [6]! these (pious throngs) are choosing through

cording to the general form of the Gâthic sentence, *k*ôist parâ go more naturally together than if the force of the parâ was extended to *g*asa*t*. The coming of Ahura is elsewhere mentioned; here He enters His audience-chamber before His approaching saints.

[1] Maga may have some such cast of meaning. I have, moreover, more than once suspected that the origin of 'magian' may, notwithstanding the môghu of the later Avesta, be simply this maga so often used in the Gâthas to designate 'the cause.'

[2] See verse 20.

[3] So also the Pahlavi translator in his gloss; aîgham bartman pavan nêsmanîh barâ yehabûnê*d*ô.

[4] So also of Zarathustra's daughter, Y. LIII, 4.

[5] Or, 'cry ye for the gaining of Asha,' as in Y. XXIX, 1.

[6] Or, reading a nominative, '*G*âmâspa is choosing,' which is itself

their Righteousness as the (true) splendours of riches (these pious men who are) gaining the kingdom where the Good Mind (doth govern). And grant me also, O Mazda! that which these with glad wishes[1] receive from Thy grace[2].

19. (And this prayer is already and beforehand heard.) This established Sovereign Power the heroic (Kavi Vîstâspa has given), O Maidhyô-mâh the Spitâma. He who is wise through the Religion, and who seeks (the true) life, he is granting it to us[3]; yea, he has pronounced the laws of Ahura our Maker, and declared that which is for (our) life's actions (beyond all other things) best.

20. And, that gift of blessedness for you, all (the Bountiful Immortals) with one consent in sympathy to help us (are disposed[4]) to grant; (and may they likewise make) the Holy Order (firm) for us through the Good Mind (in our folk); and may they reveal to us the words with which Piety likewise (speaks her truths). And receiving sacrifice with homage (from our praises), may they seek[5] for us Ahura Mazda's grace.

21. (Yea, this Kavi Vîstâspa) the man of Âramaiti is bounteous, and with understanding in his words and his actions. (And as a reward) may Ahura give

---

well possible, as var is also conjugated with n; but rapen seems a plural, and vîdô likewise.

[1] I concede this shade of meaning to the indications of the Pahlavi.

[2] The Pahlavi gives us our first indication here.

[3] If Gâmâspô (nom.) is read in verse 18, ahmâi might here refer to him; 'to this one.'

[4] Or, 'let them grant;' infinitive as imperative.

[5] Seeking; a dual is here disapproved by the source from which the suggestion originated.

him that Righteousness which is blest, (but) with the Religion (alone), and that Sovereign Power which is established through the Good Mind (in His folk). And this same blessing would I pray from His grace[1].

22. For Ahura Mazda knoweth the man whose best gift for the sacrifice is given unto me, and from the motive of Righteousness; (and in thankfulness for all, and in prayer for yet still further grace), I will worship (the eternal ones); yea, I will worship those who have ever lived, and who still live, and by their own (holy) names, and to their (thrones[2]) will I draw near with my praise!

THE GÂTHA(Â) VAHISTÂ ÎSTIS (VAHISTÔISTI(Î)).

This Gâtha, named from its first words, consists of chapter LIII of the Yasna. While its matter is homogeneous with that of the other Gâthas, it bears some evidence of having been composed in the latter portion of Zarathustra's life. It is, as usual, separated from the other Gâthas by its metre, which shows four lines with two half lines. The first two have eleven or twelve syllables; the third seems to have fourteen plus a half line with five, so also the last. Irregularities seem frequent. The composition has for its substance a marriage song, but one of a politically religious character.

The piece â-airyemâ-ishyô, Y. LIV, 1, has been considered by some as susceptible of a similar metrical arrangement, and it certainly looks as if it originally belonged to Y. LIII. It is, however,

[1] I refer tem to Ahura, supposing it to stand; reading tãm, I would refer it to ashi.

[2] Compare Vend. XIX, 31.

otherwise divided by Bartholomae (see Arische Forschungen, 2ter heft, s. 23). From the past form of srâvî, some have thought that Zarathustra was no longer living when this hymn was composed, but the word may only mean '(his prayer) has been, or is heard.' If we must, however, render 'was heard,' this does not determine the certainty of Zarathustra's death. The expression Zarathustris Spitâmô also gives the impression that some heir to Zarathustra's office and prestige existed, but even this is not decisive, for a future successor may be for a time a contemporary, while, on the contrary, the nuptials of Zarathustra's daughter, with the mention of his name, and the reference to her 'father' as the one from whom her bridegroom obtained her, indicate that Zarathustra may well have been still living. The later forms Zarathustrahê and fedhrô remain as the indications of a later origin than the actual period of Zarathustra's lifetime; but these circumstances may be owing to accidental causes.

The style has freshness and vigour throughout, and would indicate Zarathustrian influence, if not authorship. That Zarathustra does not speak in the first person, has no importance whatever in the question. The piece is not of course a whole; but it may well be a whole out of which parts have fallen. That the subject passes on to the old polemical vehemence in the last verses, is far from unnatural. The marriage festival of Zarathustra's child must have been, if without intention, a semi-political occasion, and the bard would express himself, as naturally, with regard to the struggle which was still going on. This latter fact also shows an early date; the passages referring to the struggle are strongly kindred with some in Y. XLVI, and elsewhere.

Verses 1 and 2 form an admirable introduction; the transition to the marriage occasion was, however, contained in lost verses. Verses 3, 4, and 5 hang well together; and 6 and 7 are not at all remote from them; the warlike close, although far from surprising us, must have been introduced by one or more now missing stanzas.

1. As the object of the 'great cause,' next to the preservation of its adherents, was the extension of its influence, first over hesitating parties (Y. XLIV, 12), and then over all the living (Y. XXXI, 3), it is not surprising that the central prayer of Zarathustra should have culminated in a desire for the conversion of opponents. Even Turanians had been known to come over to the holy creed, and help prosper the settlements which their kith had so often plundered (Y. XLVI, 12); he had therefore prayed that those who

had heretofore injured the holy Daêna might become its disciples by a genuine conversion. 2. Having observed the fidelity of converts and original disciples, the king and his chief nobles would celebrate their devotion by hymns, ceremonies, and sacrifices, as the symbols of every moral virtue, laying down for the people the moral law of the Saviour. 3. As it would be pushing rather far to suppose the Saoshyant to be referred to in *temkâ*, and as moreover, according to Geldner's admirable suggestion, that title may here well refer to Zarathustra, it is better to accept a loss of verses, and to suppose a person alluded to as the bridegroom, who, if not one so eminent as to merit the imposing name of Saoshyant, was still at least one of his more prominent satellites, for the ancient poet goes on to address a daughter of Zarathustra as a bride. She is the youngest, and her name is as pious as that of a maid of ancient Israel, for she is called 'full of the religious knowledge.' Her husband is to be a support in holiness, and she is to take counsel with piety. 4. Her response is appropriate; she will vie with her husband in every sacred affection, as well as in every domestic virtue. 5. The priestly thaliarch then addresses the bridesmaids and the pair with suitable admonitions to piety and affection. 6. Turning now to the assembly, possibly after the recital of some stanzas long since vanished, he proceeds with warnings and encouragements. He will exorcise the Demon who was especially the slave of the Daêvas; but he warns all men and women against the evil Vayu, the spirit of the air. 7. Charitably concluding that they would come forth as conquerors from the trials which still awaited them, he next warns them against all solicitations to vice. 8. Having named profane Demons, his polemical zeal becomes fully inflamed. Anticipating with fierce delight the sufferings of the wicked, he calls vehemently for the champion, who may, in alliance with neighbouring potentates, deliver up the murderous false-leader, giving peace to the masses; and he entreats that all haste may be used. 9. To arouse the great chiefs to their duty, he recalls (as in Y. XXXII) the successes of the foe; and he calls for the prince who may overthrow and expel him, but, as if well aware that the human arm could not alone bring salvation, he attributes to Ahura the Sovereign Power, which alone can guard helpless innocence against lawless plunder and oppression.

Translation.

1. That best prayer has been answered[1], the prayer of Zarathustra Spitâma, that Ahura Mazda might[2] grant him those boons, (the most wished-for) which flow from the good Order, even a life that is prospered[3] for eternal duration, and also those who deceived[4] him (may He likewise thus grant him) as the good Faith's disciples in word and in deed[5].

2. And may Kavi Vîstâspa, and the Zarathustrian Spitâma[6], and Frashaostra too with them, offer propitiation to Mazda in thought, word, and deed, and

---

[1] Some lay stress upon the literal form 'was heard,' and regard the expression as indicating the fact that Zarathustra was no longer living (see the remarks in the summary).

[2] Free.

[3] I follow the Pahlavi with all; it has hû-âhûînâd.

[4] I follow the frîftâr of the Pahlavi, as the conversion of those formerly hostile is suggested by vaurayâ and Fryâna, not to speak of the primary rendering of duserethrîs kikhshnushâ. The Pahlavi also has, 'even he who is the deceiver is to be instructed in the word and deed of the good religion.' The MSS. should not hastily be abandoned.

[5] That more than a ritualistic sanctity is meant is certain (see Y. XXX, 3); but that no sanctity could be recognised apart from worship is equally undeniable.

[6] Who was the Zarathustrian Spitâma? Some change the text after the Pahlavi translator, reading Zarathustra Spitâma; but I would not follow this evil example in a first translation of a translatable text. Why should a Spitâma, who was not Zarathustra, be called Zarathustrian? Were some of the Spitâmas not in sympathy with their great kinsman, Spitâmas who were Mazdayasnians, but not 'of Zarathustra's order?' One would however suppose that some one of Zarathustra's family was meant who occupied the position of his especial representative and natural successor.

Yasna confessions[1] as they render Him praise, making straight paths[2] (for our going), even that Faith of the Saoshyant which Ahura will found[3].

(The master of the feast.)

3[4]. And him will they give Thee, O Pourukista, Haêkat-aspid and Spitâmi! young[5] (as thou art) of the daughters of Zarathustra, him will they[6] give thee as a help in the Good Mind's true service, of Asha's and Mazda's, as a chief and a guardian[7]. Counsel well then (together[8]), with the mind of Ârmaiti, most bounteous and pious; and act with just action.

(She answers.)

4. I will love[9] and vie with him, since from (my) father[10] he gained (me). For the master and toilers, and for the lord-kinsman (be) the Good Mind's bright

---

1 Free.

2 Recall the 'path made for the Kine,' and 'the way' which 'Thou declarest to be that of the Good Mind.'

3 That is, will permanently found, establish.

4 Verses have here fallen out, as some allusion must have been made to the bridegroom.

5 So more according to the hint of the Pahlavi and the statement of the Bundahis; West, XXXII, 5. So Geldner, K. Z. 28, 195.

6 Or, 'will he, the Saoshyant, the bride's father.'

7 A chieftain, a protecting head.

8 It is, perhaps, safer to refer this 'questioning' to the pair; but forms of ham with pares are also used of consultations with the Deity (see Y. XXXIII, 6). Y. XLIV, 13 nearly necessitates the wider and less concrete view here.

9 Varânî looks somewhat like a gloss, but the metre seems to demand it.

10 Her father's sanction was a reason for devotion to the man to whom he had given her.

blessing[1], the pure for the pure ones, and to me (be[2]) the insight (which I gain from his counsel[3]). Mazda grant it, Ahura for good conscience for ever.

(The priestly master of the feast.)

5. Monitions for the marrying I speak to (you) maidens, to you, I who know them; and heed ye my (sayings): By these[4] laws of the Faith which I utter obtain ye the life of the Good Mind (on earth and in heaven). (And to you, bride and bridegroom[5]), let each one the other in Righteousness cherish; thus alone unto each shall the home-life be happy.

6. [Thus real are these things, ye men and ye women[6]!] from the Lie-demon protecting, I guard o'er my (faithful), and so (I) grant progress (in weal and in goodness). And the hate of the Lie (with the hate of her) bondsmen (?) I pray from the body, (and so would expel it[7]). For to those who bear Vayu[8], (and bring him to power), his shame[9] mars the glory. To these evil truth-harmers by these means he reaches. Ye thus slay the life mental (if ye follow his courses[10]).

---

[1] The Pahlavi translator has sîrîh here.

[2] B*et*=bâ*d* lies certainly nearer than b*eet*=bava*t*.

[3] See the previous verse.

[4] Or, 'being zealous.'

[5] These words do not seem adapted to the bridesmaids.

[6] *G*aini is elsewhere used in an evil sense.

[7] I can only render thus literally: From the Drû*g* as a generous guide (I) who (compare *ye* in Y. XXVIII) (for) mine, (mê) a watching guardian (I guide as a râthema; nom. sing. with verbal force) increasing prosperity, i.e. progress, of the Drû*g* I pray (forth*; I exorcise) of the bond (?) (of the Drû*g*) the malicious injuries* from the body or person. * yêsê-parâ. * to 3rd pî.

[8] 'If ye bear, or promote, the interests of Vayu.'

[9] Or, 'evil food.'

[10] Some line here is gloss; the first thought would be to eliminate

7. But yours be the recompense, (O ye righteous women!) of this great cause. For while lustful desire heart-inflamed from the body[1] there beyond goeth down where the spirit of evil reaches (to ruin, still) ye bring forth the champion[2] to help on the cause, (and thus conquer temptation). So your last word is 'Vayu'; (ye cry it in triumph[3]).

8. And thus let the sinners by these means be foiled[4]; and consumed[5] be they likewise. Let them shriek in their anger. With good kings let (our champion[6]) deliver[7] the smiter[8] (as a captive in

the difficult second line; but the third line might be an effort (by the poet himself, or an associate, see the metrical form) to explain, or relieve, the awkward second line. Reading *yemâ* and râthemâ, and taking *genayô* as in an evil sense, with spasuthâ as a second plural, we might render as a question: 'Do ye, O ye twain, ye helpers of the Drûg; do ye regard promotion (as thus to be gained)?' But in that case verses 6 and 7 should be regarded as separated by many lost verses from the fifth verse. But is not the first line the gloss? It is merely an address.

[1] Free. [2] Lit. 'the greatness.'

[3] The difficulty here lies in the first line which seems to declare a reward in a good sense. Mîzdem is hardly used of retribution. It must therefore be taken in a good sense. The following evil results must be supposed to have been avoided; and 'Vayu' to be uttered in triumph. Vayu is used in an evil sense in verse 6.

If mîzdem could be supposed to express retribution, then evil men and women would be threatened, and Vayu would be a cry uttered in woe. As to Vayu with his two natures, see part ii as per index.

[4] The foiling of the evil here recalls âdebaomâ.

[5] The Pahlavi translator seems to me too free in rendering za*h*v*y*â*k*â (zahyâ*k*â), zani*s*n-hômand. It also makes a curious imitation of letters in *g*êh va mar for *g*enarãm. It is of course far from certain that he had our present text.

[6] See verse 9; also Y. XLVI, 4.

[7] Recall the delivering of the evil into the two hands of Asha (Y. XXX, 8, and Y. XLIV, 14).

[8] Khrûnerãm*k*â must be a gloss.

battle), giving peace to our dwellings, and peace to our hamlets. Let him charge[1] those deceivers, chaining death as the strongest[2]; and swift be (the issue).

9. Through false believers the tormentor makes Thy helpers[3] refusers[4]; (those who once helped our heroes shall no longer give succour). The estranged thus desires, and the reprobate[5] wills it, with the will that he harbours to conquer our honour[6]. Where is then the Lord righteous who will smite them from life[7], and (beguile) them of license? Mazda! Thine is that power, (which will banish and conquer). And Thine is the Kingdom[8]; and by it Thou bestowest the highest (of blessings) on the right-living poor[9]!

---

[1] 'Let him "rout" or "stir" them.'

[2] Comp. mazista=the strongest in Y. XLIX, 1, 'the prevailer.' Lit. 'with the chaining of death the greatest.'

[3] For narpîs I can only suggest the suspiciously simple nar=hero (comp. the frequent nâ) and pî=nourish, support. The Pahlavi translator seems likewise to have had some such rendering in mind, for he translates dastôbar.

[4] As to rigîs, the Pahlavi translation, which is here more than usually difficult, hints in the direction above followed, by a word which I would restore as rêgînênd.

[5] The Pahlavi translator erroneously sees 'bridge' in peshô, or is free with his tanâpûharkânŏ hômand. See Geldner, Stud. 3.

[6] See Geldner, Stud. 54. [7] See Y. XLVI, 4.

[8] Comp. the Ahuna-vairya which takes its last line from this place, and Y. XXXIV, 5. Vahyô is a variation for vangheus vahyô.

[9] Here I have endeavoured to imitate the swing of the rhythm by breaking up the sentences, especially in the second line. Literally it would be, 'with the desire, with the virtue-conquering (desire) of the reprobate.' Such freedom as the above is often a critical necessity in the attempts to reproduce the warmth of the original.

THE YASNA.

It is now hardly necessary to say that the Yasna is the chief liturgy of the Zarathustrians, in which confession, invocation, prayer, exhortation, and praise are all combined as in other liturgies. Like other compositions of the kind, it is made up of more or less mutually adapted fragments of different ages, and modes of composition. The Gâthas are sung in the middle of it, and in the Vendîdâd Sâdah, the Visparad is interpolated within it for the most part at the ends of chapters.

We have no reason to suppose that the Yasna existed in its present form in the earlier periods of Zarathustrianism, but we have also no reason to doubt that its present arrangement is, as regards us, very ancient. The word Yasna means worship including sacrifice. Introductory excerpts occur in several MSS., and are now printed by Geldner. They are to be found in Y. I, 23; Y. III, 25; Y. XI, 17, 18; Y. XXII, 23–27; Y. XXVII, 13, 14; Ny. I, 2.

YASNA I.

The Sacrifice Commences.

1. I announce[1] and I (will) complete (my Yasna) to Ahura Mazda, the Creator, the radiant and glorious, the greatest and the best, the most beautiful (?) (to our conceptions), the most firm, the wisest, and the one of all whose body[2] is the most perfect, who

---

[1] Or, 'I invite;' but the word seems equal to âvaêdhayêma; compare the Vedic vid + ni. Comp. also nî tê vaêdhayêmi and nî vô vaêdhayêmi in Y. I, 21, 22. The Pahlavi favours 'I invite.'

[2] Not that Ahura was conceived of as having a body proper. The stars are elsewhere poetically described as his body, as other

attains His ends the most infallibly, because of His Righteous Order, to Him who disposes our minds aright[1], who sends His joy-creating grace afar; who made us, and has fashioned us, and who has nourished and protected us[2], who is the most bounteous Spirit[3]!

2. I announce and I (will) complete (my Yasna) to the Good Mind, and to Righteousness the Best, and to the Sovereignty which is to be desired, and to Piety the Bountiful, and to the two, the Universal Weal and Immortality, to the body of the Kine, and to the Kine's Soul, and to the Fire of Ahura Mazda, that one who more than[4] (all) the Bountiful Immortals has made most effort (for our succour)!

3. And I announce and I (will) complete (my Yasna) to the Asnya, the day-lords of the ritual order, to Hâvani the holy, the lord[5] of the ritual order; and I celebrate, and I (will) complete (my Yasna) to Sâvanghi and to Vîsya, the holy lord(s) of the ritual order. And I announce and (will) complete (my Yasna) to Mithra of the wide pastures, of the thousand ears, and of the myriad eyes, the Yazad of the spoken[6] name, and to Râman *Hv*âstra.

---

divinities are said to be tanu-mãthra, having the Mãthra as their body; that is, incarnate in the Mãthra.

[1] 'Disposing aright as to mind.'

[2] Pahlavi parvar*d*.

[3] Elsewhere the Spe*n*ta Mainyu is spoken of as His possession.

[4] The Fire seems almost spoken of as one of the Amesha Spe*n*ta.

[5] Lords of the ritual because ruling as chief at the time of their mention, and in this sense regarded as genii protecting all ritual seasons and times of their class. Vîsya presides over the Vîs; Sâvanghi, over cattle.

[6] Having an especial Yast.

4. I announce and (will) complete (my Yasna) to Rapithwina, the holy lord of the ritual order, and to Frâda*t*fshu, and to Za*n*tuma, the holy lord(s) of the ritual order; and I celebrate and complete (my Yasna) to Righteousness[1] the Best, and to Ahura Mazda's Fire[1].

5. I announce and complete (my Yasna) to Uzayêirina the holy lord of the ritual order, and to Frâda*t*-vîra and to Da*hv*yuma[2], the holy lord(s) of the ritual order, and to that lofty Ahura Napâ*t*-apãm (the son of waters), and to the waters which Ahura Mazda[3] made.

6. I announce and complete (my Yasna) to Aiwisrûthrima (and) Aibigaya[4], the holy lord(s) of the ritual order, and to Zarathu*s*trôtema, and to him who possesses and who gives that prosperity in life which furthers all. And I celebrate and complete (my Yasna) to the Fravashis of the saints, and to those of the women who have many sons[5], and to a prosperous home-life which continues without reverse throughout the year, and to that Might which is well-shaped and stately[6], which strikes victoriously, Ahura-made, and to that Victorious Ascendency (which it secures).

7. I announce and I complete (my Yasna) to Ushahina, the holy lord of the ritual order, and to Bere*g*ya (and) Nmânya, the holy lord(s) of the ritual order, and to Sraosha (who is Obedience) the blessed, endowed with blessed recompense (as a thing com-

[1] Constantly associated together in the later Avesta.

[2] *hv*=h before y.

[3] As opposed to those which might belong to Angra Mainyu.

[4] Or, 'who furthers life.'

[5] 'Men and herds?'

[6] 'Well-grown.'

pleted[1]), who smites with victory, and furthers the settlements, and to Rashnu[2], the most just, and to Arstât[3], who advances the settlements, and causes them to increase.

8. And I announce and I complete (my Yasna) to the Mâhya, the monthly festivals, lords of the ritual order, to the new and the later[4] moon, the holy lord of the ritual order, and to the full moon which scatters night.

9. And I announce and complete (my Yasna) to the Yâirya, yearly feasts, the holy lords of the ritual order. I celebrate and complete (my Yasna) to Maidyô-zaremya[5], the holy lord of the ritual order, and to Maidyô-shema, the holy lord of the ritual order, and to Paitishahya, and to Ayâthrima the advancer, and the spender of the strength of males[6], the holy lord of the ritual order, and to Maidhyâirya, the holy lord of the ritual order, and to Hamaspathmaêdhaya, the holy lord of the ritual order; yea, I celebrate and complete my Yasna to the seasons, lords of the ritual order.

10. And I announce and complete (my Yasna) to all those who are the thirty and three[7] lords of the ritual order, which, coming the nearest, are around about Hâvani, and which (as in their festivals) were

[1] I should say that the suffix has this force here as in close connection with ashyô.

[2] Genius of rectitude. [3] Rectitude in another form.

[4] Literally, 'to the moon within,' showing little light.

[5] See the Âfrînagân. [6] The rutting season.

[7] Haug first called attention to the striking coincidence with the Indian. In the Aitareya and Satapatha Brâhmanas, in the Atharvaveda, and in the Râmâyana, the gods are brought up to the number thirty-three. The names differ somewhat however. (See Essays, ed. West, 2nd edition, p. 276; see also *Rv.* 240, 9; 250, 2.)

inculcated by Ahura Mazda, and were promulgated by Zarathustra, as the lords of Asha Vahista, who is Righteousness the Best.

11. And I announce and complete (my Yasna) to the two, to Ahura[1] and to Mithra, the lofty, and the everlasting, and the holy, and to all the stars which are Spenta Mainyu's creatures, and to the star Tistrya, the resplendent and glorious, and to the Moon which contains the seed of the Kine, and to the resplendent Sun, him of the rapid steeds, the eye[2] of Ahura Mazda, and to Mithra the province-ruler. And I celebrate and complete my Yasna to Ahura Mazda (once again, and as to him who rules the month[3]), the radiant, the glorious, and to the Fravashis[4] of the saints.

12. And I announce and complete my Yasna to thee, the Fire, O Ahura Mazda's son! together with all the fires, and to the good waters, even to all the waters made by Mazda, and to all the plants which Mazda made.

13. And I announce and complete (my Yasna) to the Bounteous Mãthra, the holy and effective, the revelation given against the Daêvas[5]; the Zarathus-

---

[1] The star Jupiter has been called Ormuzd by the Persians and Armenians, and it may be intended here, as stars are next mentioned, but who can fail to be struck with the resemblance to the Mitra-Varuna of the *Rig*-veda. Possibly both ideas were present to the composer.

[2] Recall *K*akshur Mitrasya Varunasya Agneh.

[3] The first day of the month is called Ahura Mazda.

[4] The first month is called Fravashi. These are put for the particular day of celebration.

[5] This was the Vendîdâd, the name being a contraction of vîdaêvâ-dâta. It will not be forgotten that the Vendîdâd, although later put together, contains old Aryan myths which antedate

trian revelation, and to the long descent[1] of the good Mazdayasnian Faith.

14. And I announce and complete (my Yasna) to the mountain Ushi-darena[2], the Mazda-made, with its sacred brilliance, and to all the mountains glorious with sanctity[3], with their abundant Glory Mazda-made, and to that majestic Glory Mazda-made, the unconsumed[4] Glory which Mazda made. And I announce and complete (my Yasna) to Ashi the good, the blessedness (of the reward), and to *K*isti, the good religious Knowledge, to the good Erethe (Rectitude[5]?), and to the good Rasãstâ*t* (persisting zeal[6]?), and to the Glory and the Benefit which are Mazda-made.

15. And I announce and complete (my Yasna) to the pious and good Blessing of the religious man[7], the holy, and to the curse of wisdom, the swift and redoubted Yazad of potency (to blight).

16. And I announce and complete (my Yasna) to these places and these lands, and to these pastures, and these abodes with their springs of water (?)[8], and

---

Zarathu*s*tra, although in its present greatly later form, Zarathu*s*tra is a demi-god in it, and his name is involved in myth.

[1] 'The long tradition;' so Spiegel.

[2] From this mountain the Iranian kings were later supposed to have descended; hence the mention of the 'glory.'

[3] Observe the impossibility of the meaning 'comfort,' or mere 'well-being' here.

[4] Or possibly 'the unseized,' the Pahlavi agrift (?); Ner. ag*ri*hîtâ*m*; *hv*ar, to eat, may have meant 'seize' originally.

[5] Erethe (*ri*ti ?) seems without inflection.

[6] The state of activity (?).

[7] Shall we say, 'of the departed saint' here?

[8] The Pahlavi with its afkhvâr points here perhaps to a better text. Recall awzhdâtem*k*a, awzhd*a*unghô, awrem.

to the waters, land, and plants, and to this earth and to yon heaven, and to the holy wind, and to the stars, moon, and sun, and to the eternal stars without beginning[1], and self-disposing[2], and to all the holy creatures of Spe*n*ta-Mainyu, male and female, the regulators of the ritual order.

17. And I announce and complete (my Yasna) to that lofty lord who is the ritual Righteousness[3] (itself), and to the lords of the days in their duration, and of the days during daylight, to the moons, the years, and the seasons which are lords of the ritual order at the time of Hâvani[4].

18. And I announce and complete (my Yasna) to the Fravashis of the saints, the redoubted, which overwhelm (the evil), to those of the saints of the ancient lore, to those of the next of kin, and to the Fravashi of (mine) own[5] soul!

19. And I announce and complete (my Yasna) to all the lords of the ritual order, and to all the Yazads, the beneficent, who dispose (of all) aright, to those both heavenly and earthly, who are (meet) for our sacrifice and homage because of Asha Vahi*s*ta, (of the ritual Order which is 'the best').

20. O (thou) Hâvani, holy lord of the ritual order, and Sâvanghi, Rapithwina, and Uzayêirina, and Aiwisrûthrima, (and) Aibigaya, (thou that aidest

[1] Meaning 'without beginning to their course,' and so 'fixed' (?).

[2] Self-determining, not satellites, having the laws of their own motion in themselves.

[3] The divine Order par eminence, expressed in the ritual and the faith.

[4] Not 'to the chief of Hâvani,' possibly 'in the lordship,' the time when it is especially the object of worship. Thus each object of worship becomes in its turn a 'lord or chief' of 'the ritual order.'

[5] The soul of the celebrant or his client is intended.

life!) if I have offended you, and thou, O Ushahina, holy lord of the ritual order!

21. If I have offended thee[1], whether by thought, or word, or deed, whether by act of will, or without intent or wish, I earnestly make up the deficiency of this in praise to thee. If I have caused decrease[2] in that which is Thy Yasna, and Thy homage, I announce (and celebrate[3]) to thee (the more for this)!

22. Yea, all ye lords, the greatest ones, holy lords of the ritual order, if I have offended you by thought, or word, or deed, whether with my will, or without intending error[4], I praise you (now the more) for this. I announce to you (the more) if I have caused decrease in this which is your Yasna, and your praise.

23. I would confess myself a Mazda-worshipper, of Zarathustra's order, a foe to the Daêvas, devoted to the lore of the Lord, for Hâvani, the holy lord of the ritual order, for (his) sacrifice, homage, propitiation, and praise, for Sâvanghi, and for Vîsya, the holy lord of the ritual order, for (his) sacrifice, homage, propitiation and praise, and for the sacrifice, homage, propitiation and praise of the lords of the days in their duration, and of the days during daylight, for

---

[1] Compare *Rv.* VII, 86, 3-6.

[2] Practised, or induced neglect, or omitted portions of it.

[3] 'I invite for Thee' (?).

[4] That the thought, word, and deed here were more than the mere semi-mechanical use of faculties in reciting the liturgy, is clear. At the same time all morality was supposed to be represented in the liturgy. The evil man would offend in thought, word, and deed, if he recited it carelessly, or with bad conscience, and as guilty of any known and unrepented sins. The moral and ceremonial laws went hand in hand.

those of the monthly festivals, and for those of the yearly ones, and for those of the seasons!

YASNA II.

The Sacrifice continues.

1. I desire to approach[1] the Zaothras[2] with my worship. I desire to approach the Baresman with my worship. I desire to approach the Zaothra conjointly with the Baresman in my worship, and the Baresman conjointly with the Zaothra. Yea, I desire to approach this Zaothra (here), and with this (present) Baresman, and I desire to approach this Baresman conjoined with this Zaothra with my praise[3]; and I desire to approach this Baresman with praise provided with its Zaothra with its girdle, and spread with sanctity.

2. And in this Zaothra[3] and the Baresman I desire to approach Ahura Mazda with my praise, the holy

---

[1] Referring yâs to its more original sense. Or read, 'I desire the approach of' the various objects of worship, which may be correct, as we understand the genius of each several object to be invoked. Aside from this, a desire 'to approach' seems quite necessary to fill out the sense here. Many of the objects referred to were already present, although some, like 'the mountains,' needed to be spiritually approached, or indeed invoked.

[2] Zaothra seems to me hardly a vocative here. If declined as other nouns, it would seem to be exceptionally a masculine; compare ahmya zaothrê below. I should feel constrained to regard it here as a masc. plural accusative (comp. haoma).

[3] If zaothrê is not a loc. masc. it may be used with the loc. masc. pronoun irregularly. It would then equal Zaothraya. The letter ‹Avestan letter› is often simply the Pahlavi ‹Pahlavi letter› a little lengthened and equivalent to ya (aya). ‹Avestan letter› does not merely stand for ya (aya), but it is sometimes the correct writing for those letters. (Useless repetitions are curtailed.)

lord of the ritual order, and the Bountiful Immortals, (all) those who rule aright, and who dispose of all aright, these also I desire to approach and with my praise.

3. And in this Zaothra with this Baresman I desire to approach the Asnya with my praise. I desire to approach the Hâvani with my praise, the holy lord of the ritual order, and Sâvanghi and Vîsya, the holy lords of the ritual order. And in this Zaothra with this Baresman I desire to approach Mithra with my praise, of the wide pastures, of the thousand ears, and of the myriad eyes, the Yazad of the spoken name, and Râman *Hv*âstra with him, the holy lord of the ritual order.

4. And in this Zaothra and with the Baresman I desire to approach Rapithwina with my praise, the holy lord of the ritual order; and Frâda*t*-fshu and Za*n*tuma, the holy lords of the ritual order; and in this Zaothra with this Baresman I desire to approach toward Righteousness the Best with my praise, and with him the Fire, Ahura Mazda's son.

5. And in this Zaothra with this Baresman I desire to approach Uzayêirina with my praise, and Frâda*t*-vîra and Da*hv*yuma[1], the holy lords of the ritual order; and with them that lofty lord, the kingly and brilliant Apãm-napâ*t*[2], of the fleet horses, and likewise the water Mazda-made and holy,

6. And Aiwisrûthrima, (and) Aibigaya, the holy lord(s) of the ritual order, and Frâda*t*-vîspãm-hu*g*âiti, and Zarathu*s*trôtema, the holy lord, and the good, heroic, and bountiful Fravashis of the saints, and the women who have many sons, and a peaceful and prosperous home-life that continues without reverse throughout the year, and Force well-shaped and

[1] *hv*=h before y.

[2] Sometimes Napâ*t*-apãm.

stately, and the Victorious-blow Ahura-given, and the Victorious Ascendency (which it secures), and (7) Ushahina, the holy lord of the ritual order, Beregya and Nmânya, the holy lords of the ritual order, and Sraosha, Obedience, the blessed and the stately, who smites with the blow of victory, furthering the settlements, the holy lord of the ritual order, and Rashnu, the most just, and Arstât, who furthers the settlements, and causes them to increase.

8. And in this Zaothra with this Baresman I desire to approach the Mâhya, the monthly festivals with my praise, the new moon and the waning moon (the moon within), the holy lords of the ritual order, and the full moon which scatters night, (9) and the Yearly festivals, Maidhyô-zaremaya, the holy lord of the ritual order, and Maidhyô-shema, and Paitishahya, and Ayâthrima, the promoter, who spends the strength of males, and Maidhyâirya and Hamaspathmaêdhaya, and the seasons, the holy lords of the ritual order.

10. And in this Zaothra with this Baresman I desire to approach all the lords of the ritual order with my praise, the three and thirty who come the nearest round about our Hâvanis, who are those lords (and seasons) of Righteousness the Best, which were inculcated by Mazda, and spoken forth by Zarathustra.

11. And in this Zaothra with this Baresman I desire to approach Ahura and Mithra with my praise, the lofty, eternal, and the holy two; and I desire to approach the stars, moon, and sun with the Baresman plants, and with my praise, and with them Mithra the governor of all the provinces, and Ahura Mazda the radiant and glorious, and the good, heroic, bountiful Fravashis of the saints, (12) and thee, the Fire,

Ahura Mazda's son, the holy lord of the ritual order, with all the fires! And I desire to approach the good waters in this Zaothra with this Baresman with my praise, all best waters, Mazda-made and holy, and all the plants which are Mazda-made and holy.

13. And I desire to approach the bounteous Māthra in this Zaothra with this Baresman, and with my praise, the most glorious as it is, and with it the law instituted against the Daêvas; yea, I desire to approach the Zarathustrian law with my praise, and (with it) its long descent, and the good Mazdayasnian Religion (as complete).

14. And I desire to approach Mount Ushi-darena in this Zaothra, with this Baresman with my praise, Mazda-made, and glorious with sanctity, the Yazad-(mount). And I desire to approach all the mountains with my praise, glorious with sanctity as they are, and with abundant glory, Mazda-made, and holy lords of the ritual order; and I desire to approach the mighty kingly Glory Mazda-made and unconsumed; yea, (even) the mighty unconsumed Glory Mazda-made. And I desire to approach Ashi Vanguhi (the good blessedness) in my praise, the brilliant, lofty, powerful, and stately, saving by inherent power. Yea, I desire to approach the Glory Mazda-made with my praise; and I desire to approach the Benefit conferred by Mazda.

15. And in this Zaothra with this Baresman I desire to approach the Blessing, pious and good, and the pious and holy man who utters it, and the mighty and redoubted Curse of the wise, the Yazad.

16. And in this Zaothra with this Baresman I desire to approach these waters with my praise, and these lands and plants, and these places, districts,

and pastures, and these dwellings with their springs of water[1], and this land-ruler, who is Ahura Mazda.

17. And in this Zaothra with this Baresman I desire to approach all the greatest lords with my praise, the day-lords, and the month-lords, those of the years, and of the seasons, and the good, heroic, bountiful Fravashis of the saints.

18. And in this Zaothra with this Baresman I desire to approach all the holy Yazads with my praise; yea, even all the lords of the ritual order, Hâvani at his time, and Sâvanghi at his time, and all the greatest lords of the ritual at their proper times.

YASNA III.

The Yasna advances to the Naming of the Objects of Propitiation.

1. With a Baresman brought to its appointed place accompanied with the Zaothra at the time of Hâvani, I desire to approach the Myazda-offering with my praise, as it is consumed, and likewise Ameretatâ*t*[2] (as the guardian of plants and wood) and Haurvatâ*t* (who guards the water), with the (fresh) meat[3], for the propitiation of Ahura Mazda, and of the Bountiful

---

[1] See note on Y. I, 16.

[2] Spiegel has observed with truth that Ameretatâ*t* and Haurvatâ*t* may represent severally all the fruits and the liquids offered.

[3] The modern Parsis, Haug following, render 'butter'; but Spiegel is inclined to discredit this later tradition, holding that 'flesh' was originally intended; but on its becoming disused in India, milk was substituted, hence the error.

Gau*s* hudh*a*u, in its primary sense, meant of course 'the Kine of blessed endowment.' (Repetitions are again curtailed.)

Immortals, and for the propitiation of Sraosha (who is Obedience) the blessed, who is endowed with sanctity, and who smites with the blow of victory, and causes the settlements to advance.

2. And I desire to approach Haoma and Parahaoma[1] with my praise for the propitiation of the Fravashi of Spitâma Zarathustra, the saint. And I desire to approach the (sacred) wood with my praise, with the perfume, for the propitiation of thee, the Fire, O Ahura Mazda's son!

3. And I desire to approach the Haomas with my praise for the propitiation of the good waters which Mazda created; and I desire to approach the Haoma-water, and the fresh milk[2] with my praise, and the plant Hadhânaêpata, offered with sanctity for the propitiation of the waters which are Mazda-made.

4. And I desire to approach this Baresman with the Zaothra with my praise, with its binding[3] and spread with sanctity for the propitiation of the Bountiful Immortals. And I desire with (?) my voice the thoughts well thought, and the words well spoken, and the deeds well done, and the recital of the Gâthas as they are heard. And I desire to approach the well-said Mãthras with my praise, and this (higher) lordship with this sanctity, and this exact regulation[4] (of the Ratu), and the reverential prayer for blessings (spoken at the fitting hour); and I desire to approach them for the contentment and propitiation

---

[1] The Haoma-juice.

[2] So better than 'fresh meat.' Fluids are the chief objects of attention here.

[3] With its girdle.

[4] Anghuyãm—rathwãm stand related as ahû and ratu; so also the Pahlavi ahûôîh and ra*d*ih, and Ner. svâmitâ*mk*a gurutâ*mk*a.

of the holy Yazads, heavenly and earthly, and for the contentment of each man's soul.

5. And I desire to approach the Asnya with my praise, the lords of the ritual order, and the Hâvani and Sâvanghi and Vîsya, the holy lords of the ritual order. And I desire to approach with the Yast[1] of Mithra of the wide pastures, of the thousand ears, of the myriad eyes, the Yazad of the spoken name, and with him Râman *Hv*âstra.

6. And I desire to approach Rapithwina with my praise, the holy lord of the ritual order, and Frâda*t*-fshu and Za*n*tuma, and Righteousness the Best, and Ahura Mazda's Fire.

7. And I desire to approach Uzayêirina, and Frâda*t*-vîra and Da*hv*yuma* with my praise, with that lofty Ahura Napâ*t*-apãm, and the waters Mazda-made,

8. And Aiwisrûthrima, and Aibigaya, and Frâda*t*-vîspãm-hu*g*aiti, and Zarathu*s*trôtema with the Ya*s*t of the Fravashis of the saints[2], and of the women who have many sons, and the year long unchanged prosperity, and of Might, the well-shaped and stately, smiting victoriously, Ahura-made and of the Victorious Ascendency (which it secures).

9. And I desire to approach Ushahina, Bere*g*ya, and Nmânya with the Ya*s*t of Sraosha (Obedience) the sacred, the holy, who smites with the blow of victory, and makes the settlements advance, and with that of Rashnu, the most just, and Ar*s*tâ*t*

[1] Ye*s*tî seems used of an especial Ya*s*t here, and subsequently, as genitives intrude among datives, the form possibly taking the place of the words 'for the propitiation of'; here Ya*s*t X may be referred to.

[2] Ya*s*t XIII.

who furthers the settlements, and causes them to increase.

10. And I desire to approach the monthly festivals, the lords of the ritual order, and the new moon and the waning moon, and the full moon which scatters night,

11. And the yearly festivals, Maidhyô-zaremaya, Maidhyô-shema, Paitishahya, and Ayâthrima the breeder who spends the strength of males, and Maidhyâirya, and Hamaspathmaêdhaya, and the seasons, lords of the ritual order, (12) and all those lords who are the three and thirty, who approach the nearest at the time of Hâvani, who are the Lords of Asha called Vahishta (and whose services were) inculcated by Mazda, and pronounced by Zarathustra, as the feasts of Righteousness, the Best.

13. And I desire to approach Ahura and Mithra, the lofty and imperishable two, the holy, and with the Yast of those stars which are the creatures of Spenta Mainyu, and with the Yast of the star Tistrya, the radiant, the glorious, and with that of the moon which contains the seed of cattle, and with that of the resplendent sun, the eye of Ahura Mazda, and of Mithra, province-lord of the provinces, and with that of Ahura Mazda (as He rules this day) the radiant, the glorious, and with that of the Fravashis of the saints, (who rule this month),

14. And with thy Yast, the Fire's, O Ahura Mazda's son! with all the fires, and to the good waters with the Yast of all the waters which are Mazda-made, and with that of all the plants which Mazda made.

15. And I desire to approach with the Yast of the

Mãthra Spe*n*ta, the holy, the effective, the law composed against the Daêvas, the Zarathu*s*trian, and with that of the long descent of the Religion which Mazda gave.

16. And I desire to approach with the Ya*s*t of Mount Ushi-darena, Mazda-made, and of all, glorious with sanctity, and abundant in brilliance, and with that of the Kingly Glory, Mazda-made; yea, with that of the unconsumed glory which Mazda made, and with that of Ashi Vanguhi, and *K*i*s*ti Vanguhi, and with that of the good Erethe, and the good Rasãstâ*t*, and the good Glory, and of the Benefit which Mazda gave.

17. And I desire to approach with the Ya*s*t of the good and pious Blessing of the pious man and of the saint, and with that of the awful and swift Curse of the wise, the Yazad-curse, (18) and to these places, regions, pastures, and abodes, with their water-springs, and with that of the waters, and the lands, and the plants, and with that of this earth and yon heaven, and with that of the holy wind and of the stars, moon, and sun, and with that of the stars without beginning, self-determined and self-moved, and with that of all the holy creatures which are those of Spe*n*ta Mainyu, male and female, regulators of the ritual order, (19) and with that of the lofty lord who is Righteousness (himself, the essence of the ritual), and with that of the days in their duration, and of the days during daylight, and with that of the monthly festivals, and the yearly festivals, and with those of the several seasons which are lords of the ritual at the time of Hâvani.

20. And I desire to approach the meat-offering with a Ya*s*t, and Haurvatâ*t* (who guards the water), and Ameretatâ*t* (who guards the plants and wood), with

the Yast of the sacred flesh for the propitiation of Sraosha (Obedience) the blessed and the mighty, whose body is the Māthra, of him of the daring spear, the lordly, the Yazad of the spoken name.

21. And I desire to approach both Haoma and the Haoma-juice with a Yast for the propitiation of the Fravashi of Zarathustra Spitâma, the saint, the Yazad of the spoken name. And I desire to approach the wood-billets with a Yast, with the perfume for the propitiation of thee, the Fire, O Ahura Mazda's son! the Yazad of the spoken name.

22. And I desire to approach with a Yast for the mighty Fravashis of the saints, the overwhelming, the Fravashis of those who held to the ancient lore, and of those of the next of kin.

23. And I desire to approach toward all the lords of the ritual order with a Yast, toward all the good Yazads, heavenly and earthly, who are (set) for worship and for praise because of Asha Vahista (of Righteousness the Best).

24. I will confess myself a Mazdayasnian, of Zarathustra's order, a foe to the Daêvas, devoted to the lore of the Lord for Hâvani, the holy lord of the ritual order, for sacrifice, homage, propitiation, and for praise, and for Sâvanghi and Vîsya, the holy lord(s) of the ritual order, and for the sacrifice, homage, propitiation, and praise of the day-lords of the days in their duration, and of the days during daylight, and for the month-regulators, and the year-regulators, and for those of the (several) seasons, for their sacrifice, and homage, their propitiation, and their praise.

(The Zaotar speaks[1]): As the Ahû to be

[1] So at least the rubric. One would think that the sentence was intended to be dictated to the Ratu to be repeated; that is, if the

(revered and) chosen, let the priest speak[1] forth to me.

(The Ratu responds): As the Ahû to be (revered and) chosen, let him who is the Zaotar speak[1] forth to me.

(The Zaotar again): So let the Ratu from his Righteousness, holy and learned, speak forth!

YASNA IV.

The Offering takes place.

1. These good thoughts, good words, and good deeds[2], these Haomas, meat-offerings, and Zaothras, this Baresman spread with sanctity, this flesh, and the two, Haurvatâ*t* (who guards the water) and Ameretatâ*t* (who guards the plants and wood), even the flesh, the Haoma and Haoma-juice, the wood-billets, and their perfume, this sacred lordship[3] and chieftainship[3], and the timely prayer with blessing, and the heard recital of the Gâthas, and the well-said Mãthras, these all we offer, and make known with celebrations (here).

2. Yea, these do we announce with celebrations, and we present them to Ahura Mazda, and to Sraosha

---

rubric is correct. The sentence as uttered by the priest seems difficult.

[1] Present, or infin. for imperative (?).

[2] The fact that somewhat of a more technical sumatí, sûktá, suk*ri*tá adheres to these expressions in this place must not for a moment induce us to suppose that their deeper meaning was lost. All good thoughts, words, and deeds culminated in the ritual, as in an enlightened high ecclesiasticism. They were nourished by it, and not lost in it. (Expressions are here varied.)

[3] The prominence and supremacy of each deity, or genius, while he is especially the object of worship in the ritual order, the expressions being taken from the Ahuna-vairya.

(Obedience) the blessed, and to the Bountiful Immortals, and to the Fravashis of the saints, and to their souls, and to the Fire of Ahura Mazda, the lofty lord of the entire creation of the holy, for sacrifice, homage, propitiation, and praise.

3. Yea, further, we present (them to the Bountiful Immortals with an especial gift) these thoughts well thought, these words well spoken, these deeds well done, these Haomas, Myazdas, Zaothras, and this Baresman spread with sanctity, the flesh, and Haurvatâ*t* (who guards the water), and Ameretatâ*t* (who guards the plants and wood), even the flesh, Haoma and Parahaoma, the wood-billets, the perfume, and this their lordship and their sanctity, and this chieftainship, this prayer for blessing, the heard recital of the Gâthas, and the well-said Mãthras.

4. We offer with our celebrations, and we announce them (of a verity) to the Bountiful Immortals, those who exercise their rule aright, and who dispose (of all) aright, the ever-living, ever-helpful, the male divinities among their number who dwell with the Good Mind [1], [and the female [2] ones as well].

5. And we announce them in our celebrations as more propitious for this house [3], and for the furtherance of this house, of its herds, and of its men, of those now born, and of those yet to be born, the holy, yea, for the furtherance of that house of which these (men) are thus.

6. And we present these offerings to the good

---

[1] Vohu Manah, Asha, and Khshathra.

[2] Âramaiti, Haurvatâ*t*, and Ameretatâ*t*.

[3] It would seem that the Yasna must have been at the time celebrated in the houses of the worshippers. Hence perhaps some of the priests were pairigathans.

Fravashis of the saints who are mighty and overwhelming for the succour of the saints.

7. Yea, we present these hereby to the Creator Ahura Mazda, the radiant, the glorious, and the heavenly spirit, for the sacrifice, homage, propitiation, and praise of the Bountiful Immortals (all).

8. And we present these hereby to the Day-lords of the ritual order, to Hâvani, to Sâvanghi, and to Vîsya, the holy lords of the ritual order, for sacrifice, homage, propitiation, and for praise, and to Mithra of the wide pastures, and the thousand ears, and the myriad eyes, the Yazad of the spoken name,

9. And to Rapithwina, Frâda*t*-fshu, and Za*n*tuma, the holy lords of the ritual order, and to Righteousness the Best, and to Ahura Mazda's Fire,

10. And to Uzayêirina, Frâda*t*-vîra, and Da*hv*yuma[1], the holy lords of the ritual order, and to that lofty lord Napâ*t*-apãm, and to the water Mazda-made,

11. And to Aiwisrûthrima, the life-furtherer[2], and to Frâda*t*-vîspãm-hu*g*yâiti and Zarathu*s*trôtema, the holy lords of the ritual order, and to the Fravashis of the saints, and to the women who bring forth many sons, and to the Prosperous home-life which endures without reverse throughout the year, and to Force, well-shaped and stately, and to the Blow of victory which Mazda gives, and to the Victorious Ascendency which it secures, for their sacrifice, homage, their propitiation, and their praise,

12. And to Ushahina, with Bere*g*ya and Nmânya, and Sraosha (Obedience) the blessed, smiting with the blow of victory and furthering the settlements, and to Rashnu, the most just, and to Ar*s*tâ*t*, furthering the settlements, and causing them to increase.

---

[1] Dahyuma. [2] Aibigaya.

13. And these we announce and we present hereby to the Month-lords of the ritual order, to the new moon and the waning moon (the moon within), and to the full moon which scatters night, the holy lord of the ritual order, for (their) sacrifice, homage, their propitiation, and their praise.

14. And these we announce hereby and we present to the Yearly festivals, to Maidhyô-zaremaya, Maidhyô-shema, Patishahya, and to Ayâthrima, to Maidhyâirya, Hamaspathmaêdhaya, and to the Seasons as holy lords of the ritual order, for sacrifice, homage, propitiation, and for praise.

15. And these we announce and we present hereby to all those lords who are the three and thirty lords of the ritual order, who approach the nearest around about our Hâvani, and which are the festivals of Righteousness the Best, inculcated by Mazda, and uttered forth by Zarathustra for their sacrifice, homage, propitiation, and praise.

16. And these we announce and we present to Ahura and to Mithra, the lofty, and imperishable, and holy two, to the stars, the creatures of Spenta Mainyu, and to the star Tistrya, the radiant, the glorious, and to the Moon which contains the seed of cattle, and to the resplendent Sun, of the swift horses, Ahura Mazda's eye, and to Mithra, the lord of provinces, for their sacrifice, homage, their propitiation and their praise; yea, these we present hereby to Ahura Mazda (as he rules this day) and to the Fravashis of the saints (as they rule this month), for their sacrifice, homage, their propitiation and their praise.

17. And these we announce hereby to thee, the Fire, O Ahura Mazda's son! with all the fires for

thy sacrifice, homage, propitiation, and praise, and to the good waters for the sacrifice, homage, propitiation, and praise of all the waters Mazda-made, and to all the plants which Mazda made,

18. And to the Mãthra Spe*n*ta, the holy, the effective, the law against the Daêvas, the Zarathus*t*rian statute, and to the long descent of the good Mazdayasnian religion.

19. And these we announce and we present hereby to Mount Ushi-darena, Mazda-made, brilliant with sanctity, and to all the mountains shining with their holiness, abundantly luminous, and Mazda-made, and to the Kingly glory, the unconsumed[1] glory Mazda-made, and to the good Blessedness, and the good Religious-knowledge, and the good Rectitude, and to the good Rasãstâ*t*, and to the Glory and the Benefit which Mazda created.

20. And these we offer and present to the pious and good Blessing of the pious, and to the swift and dreadful Yazad, the Curse of wisdom.

21. And to these places, pastures, and dwellings with their springs of water, their rivers, to the lands and to the plants, to this earth and yon heaven, to the holy wind, to the stars, moon, and sun, to the stars without beginning, self-disposed, and to all the holy creatures of the Spe*n*ta Mainyu, male and female (the rulers as they are of the ritual order).

22. And these we announce and we present hereby to that lofty lord who is Asha, the ritual righteousness itself, to the Day-lords, and the Month-lords, the Year-lords, and the Seasons who are the lords of the ritual at the time of Hâvani, and for

[1] Unseized (?).

their sacrifice, homage, their propitiation and their praise.

23. Yea, these we announce and we present to Sraosha, the blessed and mighty, whose body is the Mãthra, him of the daring spear, the lordly one, and to the holy Fravashi of Zarathustra Spitâma, the saint.

And these we announce and we present to thee, the Fire, O Ahura Mazda's son! for thy sacrifice, homage, thy propitiation, and thy praise.

24. And these we announce and we present to the Fravashis of the saints, the mighty and overwhelming, of the saints of the ancient lore, and of the next of kin.

25. And these we announce and we present hereby to all the good Yazads, earthly and heavenly, who are (meet) for sacrifice, homage, propitiation, and for praise, because of Asha Vahista (who is Righteousness the Best).

We worship the Bountiful Immortals who rule aright, and who dispose of all aright.

26. And that one of beings (do we worship) whose superior (service) in the sacrifice Ahura Mazda knows, and from his righteousness (which he maintains, and those of all female beings do we worship) whose (higher service is thus likewise known; yea, all) male and female beings do we worship (who are such)[1]!

YASNA V.

This chapter is identical with Yasna XXXVII.

---

[1] Elsewhere with slight verbal change.

YASNA VI[1].

THE SACRIFICE CONTINUES WITH FULLER EXPRESSION.

1. We worship the Creator Ahura Mazda with our sacrifice, and the Bountiful Immortals who rule aright, and who dispose of all aright.

2. And we worship the Asnya with our sacrifice, and Hâvani, Sâvanghi and Vîsya, the holy lords of the ritual order, and Mithra of the wide pastures, of the thousand ears, and myriad eyes, the Yazad of the spoken name, and we worship Râman *Hv*âstra.

3. And we worship Rapithwina with our sacrifice, and Frâda*t*-fshu, and the Za*n*tuma, and Righteousness the Best, and the Fire, Ahura Mazda's son, holy lords of the ritual order.

4. And we worship Uzayêirina, and Frâda*t*-vîra, and Da*hv*yuma*, the holy lord of the ritual order, and that kingly Ahura, the radiant Napâ*t*-apãm, of the fleet horses, and the water holy, and Mazda-made.

5. And we worship Aiwisrûthrima and Aibigaya in our sacrifice, the holy lord of the ritual order, and Frâda*t*-vîspãm-hu*g*yâiti and the Zarathu*s*trôtema, the holy lord of the ritual order, and the good, heroic, bountiful Fravashis of the saints, and the women who bring forth many sons, and the Prosperous home-life which endures without reverse throughout the year, and Force which is well-shaped and stately, and the Blow which brings the victory, which is Ahura-given, and the Victorious Ascendency (which it secures).

6. And we worship Ushahina with our sacrifice, and

[1] This chapter differs from Y. II only in having yazamaidê instead of the formula ahmya zaothrê baresmanaê*k*a—âyêsê yê*s*ti. Expressions for the same Zend words are purposely varied.

Beregya, and Nmânya, and Sraosha (Obedience) the blessed and the stately who smites with victory, and makes the settlements advance, and Rashnu, the most just, and Arstât who makes the settlements advance and causes them to increase, the holy lords of the ritual order.

7. And we worship the Mâhya in our sacrifice, the new moon and the waning moon (the moon within) and the full moon which scatters night, the holy lord of the ritual order.

8. And we worship the Yearly festivals in our sacrifice, Maidhyô-zaremaya, Maidhyô-shema, Paitishahya, and Ayâthrima, the furtherer (or breeder), the spender of virile strength, and Maidhyâirya, the holy lord of the ritual order, and Hamaspathmaêdhaya, and the Seasons (in which they are).

9. And we worship with our sacrifice all the lords of the ritual order, who are the thirty and three who approach the nearest around about us at Hâvani, who are the lords of Righteousness the Best, and whose observances were inculcated by Ahura Mazda, and uttered forth by Zarathustra.

10. And we worship Ahura and Mithra with our sacrifice, the lofty, and imperishable, and holy two, and the stars, moon, and sun, among the plants of the Baresman, and Mithra, the province-lord of all the provinces, even Ahura Mazda, the radiant, the glorious, and the good, valiant, and bountiful Fravashis of the saints.

11. And we worship thee, the Fire, Ahura Mazda's son, together with all the fires, and the good waters, the best and Mazda-made, and holy, even all the waters which are Mazda-made and holy, and all the plants which Mazda made.

12. And we worship the Mãthra Spenta with our sacrifice, the glorious and of a truth, the law revealed against the Daêvas, the Zarathustrian law, and we worship with our sacrifice its long descent, and the good Mazdayasnian Religion.

13. And we worship Mount Ushi-darena, the Mazda-made, the glorious Yazad, shining with holiness, and all the mountains that shine with holiness, with abundant brilliance, Mazda-made, the holy lords of the ritual order. And we worship the mighty Kingly glory Mazda-made, the mighty glory, unconsumed and Mazda-made, and the good Sanctity, the brilliant, the lofty, the powerful and the stately, delivering (men) with its inherent power. Yea, we worship the Glory, and the Benefit which are Mazda-made.

14. And we worship the pious and good Blessing with our sacrifice, and the pious man, the saint, and that Yazad, the mighty Curse of wisdom.

15. And we worship these waters, lands, and plants, these places, districts, pastures, and abodes with their springs of water, and we worship this lord of the district with our sacrifice, who is Ahura Mazda (Himself).

16. And we worship all the greatest lords, the Day-lords in the day's duration, and the Day-lords during daylight, and the Month-lords, and the Year-lords.

17. And we worship Haurvatât (who guards the water) and Ameretatât (who guards the plants and the wood), and Sraosha (Obedience) the blessed and the stately, who smites with the blow of victory, and makes the settlements advance, the holy lord of the ritual order.

18. And we worship Haoma with our sacrifice

and the Haoma-juice. And we worship the sacred Fravashi of Zarathustra Spitâma the saint.

And we worship the wood-billets, and the perfume and thee, the Fire, Ahura Mazda's son, the holy lord of the ritual order.

19. And we worship the good, heroic, bountiful Fravashis of the saints.

20. And we worship all the holy Yazads, and all the lords of the ritual order at the time of Hâvani, and Sâvanghi, and all the greatest lords at their (proper) time. (The Yênhê hâtãm follows.)

21. The Ratu. As an Ahû (revered and) to be chosen, the priest speaks forth to me.

The Zaotar. So let the Ratu from his Righteousness, holy and learned, speak forth!

YASNA VII.

Presentation of Offerings by the Priest with the Object of Propitiation named.

1. With a complete and sacred offering[1] I offer and I give this meat-offering, and (with it) Haurvatâ*t* (who guards the water), and Ameretatâ*t* (who guards the plants and the wood), and the flesh of the Kine of blessed gift, for the propitiation of Ahura Mazda, and of the Bountiful Immortals (all, and) for the propitiation of Sraosha (Obedience) the blessed, endowed with sanctity, who smites with the blow of victory, and who causes the settlements to advance.

[1] With Ashi; possibly 'for a blessing,' as Ashi often has the sense of 'reward,' but scrupulous sanctity and completeness seem to be the sense here. (Expressions here are as usual varied.)

2. And I offer the Haoma and Haoma-juice with a complete and sacred offering for the propitiation of the Fravashi of Zarathustra Spitâma the saint, and I offer the wood-billets with the perfume for Thy propitiation, the Fire's, O Ahura Mazda's son!

3. And I offer the Haomas with a complete and sacred offering for propitiation [to the good waters] for the good waters Mazda-made. And I offer this Haoma-water with scrupulous exactness and with sanctity, and this fresh milk, and the plant Hadhânaêpata uplifted with a complete and sacred offering for the propitiation of the waters which are Mazda-made.

4. And I offer this Baresman with its Zaothra (and with its binding) for a girdle spread with complete sanctity and order for the propitiation of the Bountiful Immortals, and I offer with my voice the thoughts well-thought, the words well-spoken, and the deeds well-done, and the heard recital of the Gâthas, the Mãthras well-composed and well-delivered, and this Lordship, and this Sanctity, and this ritual mastership, and the timely Prayer for blessings, with a complete and sacred offering for the propitiation of the holy Yazads, heavenly and earthly, and for the contentment of the individual soul!

5. And I offer to the Asnya with a complete and sacred offering, as lords of the ritual order, and to Hâvani, and to Sâvanghi and Vîsya, holy lords of the ritual order, and to Mithra of the wide pastures, of the thousand ears, and myriad eyes, the Yazad of the spoken name, and to Râman *Hv*âstra.

6. And I offer with a complete and sacred offering to Rapithwina, the holy lord of the ritual order; and I offer to Frâda*t*-fshu and to the Za*n*tuma, and to

Asha Vahista (who is Righteousness the Best) and to Ahura Mazda's Fire.

7. And I offer with a complete and sacred offering to Uzayêirina, Frâdat-vîra, and to the Dahvyuma*, the holy lord of the ritual order, and to that lofty Ahura Napât-apãm, and to the waters which Mazda created.

8. And I offer with a complete and sacred offering to Aiwisrûthrima, the life-furtherer, and to Frâdat-vîspâm-hugyâiti, and to the Zarathustrôtema, and to the Fravashis of the saints, and to the women who have many sons, and to the Prosperous home-life which endures (without reverse) throughout the year, and to Force, the well-shaped and stately, and to the Blow which smites with victory Ahura-given, and to the Victorious Ascendency (which it secures).

9. And I offer with a complete and sacred offering to Ushahina, the holy lord of the ritual order, and to Beregya, and Nmânya, and to Sraosha (Obedience) the blessed, endowed with sanctity, who smites with the blow of victory, and makes the settlements advance, and to Rashnu the most just, and to Arstât who furthers the settlements and causes them to increase.

10. And I offer with a complete and sacred offering to the Mâhya, lords of the ritual order, to the new and the waning moon (the moon within), and to the full moon which scatters night, holy lords of the ritual order.

11. And I offer with a complete and sacred offering to the Yearly festivals, the lords of the ritual order, to Maidhyô-zaremaya, and Maidhyô-shema, to Paitishahya, and to Ayâthrima the furtherer (the breeder), the spender of the strength of males, and

to Maidhyâirya and Hamaspathmaêdhaya, holy lords of the ritual order, and I offer with sanctity to the several seasons, the lords of the ritual order.

12. And I offer with a complete and sacred offering to all those lords who are the thirty and three, who approach the nearest round about our Hâvani, and who are the lords of Asha (the ritual by-eminence), of Righteousness who is (the Best), whose observances are inculcated as precepts by Mazda, and uttered forth by Zarathustra.

13. And I offer with a complete and sacred offering to Ahura and Mithra, the lofty and imperishable, and holy two, and to the stars which are the creatures of Spenta Mainyu, and to the star Tistrya, the radiant, the glorious, and to the Moon which contains the seed of cattle in its beams, and to the resplendent Sun of the fleet horses, the eye of Ahura Mazda, and to Mithra, the lord of the provinces. And I offer with a complete and sacred offering to Ahura Mazda, the resplendent, the glorious, (who rules this day), and to the Fravashis of the saints (who name the month).

14. And I offer with a complete and sacred offering to thee, the Fire, O Ahura Mazda's son! together with all the fires, and to the good waters, even to the waters which are Mazda-made, and to all the plants which Mazda made.

15. And I offer with a complete and sacred offering to the Mãthra Spenta, the holy, the effective, revealed against the Daêvas, the Zarathustrian law, and to the long descent of the good Religion, of the Mazdayasnian faith.

16. And I offer with a complete and sacred offering to Mount Ushi-darena, the Mazda-made, brilliant

with holiness, and to all the mountains shining with holiness, of abundant brightness, and which Mazda made, and to the Royal glory unconsumed and Mazda-made. And I offer with a complete and sacred offering to Ashi Vanguhi, and to *K*isti Vanguhi, and to Erethe, and to Rasâstâ*t*, and to the Glory (and the) Benefit which Mazda made.

17. And I offer with a complete and sacred offering to the good and pious Prayer for blessings of the pious man, and to that Yazad, the swift and dreadful Curse of the wise.

18. And I offer with a complete and sacred blessing to these places, districts, pastures, and abodes with their springs of water, and to the waters and the lands, and the plants, and to this earth and yon heaven, and to the holy wind, and to the stars, and the moon, even to the stars without beginning (to their course), the self-appointed, and to all the holy creatures of Spe*n*ta Mainyu, be they male or female, regulators (as they are) of the ritual order.

19. And I offer with a complete and sacred blessing to that lofty lord who is Righteousness (the Best), and the Day-lords, the lords of the days during their duration, and to those of the days during daylight, and to the Month-lords, and the Year-lords, and to those of the seasons, the lords who are lords of the ritual, and at the time of Hâvani.

20. And I offer the Myazda meat-offering with a complete and sacred offering, and Haurvatâ*t* (who guards the water), and Ameretatâ*t* (who guards the wood), and the flesh of the Kine of blessed gift, for the propitiation of Sraosha (Obedience) the blessed, whose body is the Mãthra, him of the

daring spear, the lordly, the Yazad of the spoken name.

21. And I offer the Haoma and the Haoma-juice for the propitiation of the Fravashi of Zarathustra Spitâma the saint, the Yazad of the spoken name.

And I offer the wood-billets with the perfume for Thy propitiation, the Fire's, Ahura Mazda's son, the Yazad of the spoken name.

22. And I offer with a complete and sacred offering to the Fravashis of the saints, the mighty and overwhelming, to those of the saints of the ancient lore, and to those of the next of kin.

23. And I offer with a complete and sacred offering to all the lords of the ritual order, and to all the good Yazads heavenly and earthly who are (meet) for sacrifice and homage because of Asha who is Vahista (of Righteousness who is the Best).

24. May that approach to us, and with a sacred blessing (O Lord!) whose benefits the offerers are seeking for. Thy praisers and Mãthra-speakers, O Ahura Mazda! may we be named; we desire it, and such may we be. What reward, O Ahura Mazda! adapted to myself Thou hast appointed unto souls,

25. Of this do Thou Thyself bestow upon us for this world and for that of mind; (yea, do Thou bestow) so much of this as that we may attain to Thy ruling protection and to that of Righteousness for ever.

26. We sacrifice to the Ahuna-vairya, and to the veracious word correctly uttered, and to the good and pious prayer for blessings, and to the dreadful curse of the wise, the Yazad, and to Haurvatât and Ameretatât, and to the flesh of the Kine of blessed gift, and to the Haoma and Haoma-juice, and to the wood-billets, and the perfume, for the praise of the pious and good prayer for blessings.

The Yênhê hâtãm.

27. (To that one) of beings do we sacrifice whose superior (fidelity) in the sacrifice Ahura Mazda knows through his Righteousness (within him, yea, even to those female saints do we sacrifice) whose (superior sanctity is thus known. We sacrifice to all) both males and females whose (superiority is such). (The Ratu speaks.) As an Ahû (revered and) to be chosen, he who is the Zaotar speaks forth to me.

(The Zaotar.) So let the Ratu from his Righteousness, holy and learned, speak forth!

YASNA VIII.

Offering of the Meat-offering in particular. The Faithful Partake.

1. A blessing is Righteousness (called) the Best.
It is weal; it is weal to this (man),
When toward Righteousness Best there is right.

I offer the Myazda (of the) meat-offering with a complete and sacred offering; and I offer Haurvatâ*t* (who guards the water), and Ameretatâ*t* (who guards the plants and the wood), and the flesh of the blessed Kine; and I offer the Haoma and the Haoma-juice, the wood-billets and the perfume for the praise of Ahura Mazda, and of the Ahuna-vairya, the veracious word, and for that of the pious and beneficent Prayer for blessings, and for the redoubted Curse of the wise, and for the praise of the Haoma, and of the Mãthra of the holy Zarathu*s*tra; and may it come to us with sacred fulness (to accept and to recompense our gift).

2. (The Ratu speaks.) Eat, O ye men, of this Myazda, the meat-offering, ye who have deserved it by your righteousness and correctness!

3. O ye Bountiful Immortals, and thou, the Mazdayasnian law, ye just men and just women, and ye Zaothras, whoever among these Mazdayasnians would call himself a Mazdayasnian desiring to live in the practice of the liberality of Righteousness [for by sorcery the settlements of Righteousness are ruined], do ye cause (such an one) to be (still further) taught, (ye), who are the waters, the plants, and the Zaothras!

4. And whoever of these Mazdayasnians, adults, when he invokes with earnestness, does not adhere to these words, and (so) speaks, he approaches to that (word) of the magician; (but, as against that magician's word) 'a blessing is Righteousness (called) the Best.'

5. May'st Thou, O Ahura Mazda! reign at Thy will, and with a saving rule over Thine own creatures, and render Ye the holy (man) also a sovereign at his will over waters, and over plants, and over all the clean and sacred (creatures) which contain the seed of Righteousness. Strip ye the wicked of all power!

6. Absolute in power may the holy be, bereft of all free choice the wicked! Gone (may he be), met as foe, carried out from the creatures of Spe*n*ta Mainyu, hemmed in[1] without power over any wish!

---

7. I will incite, even I who am Zarathu*s*tra[2], the

[1] Or 'shut out,' which would seem better adapted.

[2] This piece is a reproduction, or close imitation, of some earlier fragment. It sounds like an exhortation delivered while the Faith was still new.

heads of the houses, villages, Za*n*tus, and provinces, to the careful following of this Religion which is that of Ahura, and according to Zarathu*s*tra, in their thoughts, their words, and their deeds.

8. I pray for the freedom and glory of the entire existence of the holy (man) while I bless it, and I pray for the repression and shame [1] of the entire existence [2] of the wicked.

9. Propitiation to Haoma who brings righteousness (to us) for sacrifice, homage, propitiation, and for praise. (The Zaotar ?) As the Ahû to be (revered and) chosen, the Zaotar speaks forth to me. (The Ratu.) As an Ahû to be (revered and) chosen, the Zaotar speaks forth to me. (The Zaotar.) So let the Ratu from his Righteousness, holy and learned, speak forth!

YASNA IX.

THE HÔM YA*S*T.

The Haoma-ya*s*t has claims to antiquity (owing to its subject, but not to its dialect), next after the Srô*s*-ya*s*t. H(a)oma=Soma, as a deity, flourished not only before the Gâthas, but before the *Ri*ks of the Veda, in Aryan ages before Iranian and Indian became two peoples.

The astonishing circumstance has been elsewhere noted that a hymn, which is a reproduction of an Aryan original, should, notwithstanding its earlier characteristics, be necessarily assigned to

[1] The Pahlavi translator, as I think, had a text before him which read du*zh*vâthrem; I so correct. Against the keen and most interesting suggestion of du*z* + âthrem, I am compelled to note a*hv*âthrê, showing a compositum a- + *hv*âthra, which seems not probable if = a + hu + âthra. Du*z*âthra, not a*hv*âthrê, would have been written. Cp. *hv*eng=*hv*an for root.

[2] Possibly 'house.'

a date much later than the Gâthas in which H(a)oma worship is not mentioned.

Probably on account of bitter animosities prevailing between their more southern neighbours and themselves, and the use of Soma by the Indians as a stimulant before battle, the Iranians of the Gâthic period had become lukewarm in their own H(a)oma worship. But that it should have revived, as we see it in this Yast, after having nearly or quite disappeared, is most interesting and remarkable. Was it definitively and purposely repudiated by Zarathustra, afterwards reviving as by a relapse? I do not think that it is well to hold to such deliberate and conscious antagonisms, and to a definite policy and action based upon them. The Soma-worship, like the sacramental acts of other religions which have become less practised after exaggerated attention, had simply fallen into neglect, increased by an aversion to practices outwardly similar to those of 'Daêva-worshippers.' The Yast is, of course, made up of fragments, which I have endeavoured to separate by lines. In the translation I have given a rhythmical rendering, necessarily somewhat free. It was difficult to import sufficient vivacity to the piece, while using a uselessly awkward literalness. The freedom, as elsewhere, often consists in adding words to point the sense, or round the rhythm. (Expressions for identical Zend words have been here, as elsewhere, purposely varied.)

1. At the hour of Hâvani[1]. H(a)oma came to Zarathustra, as he served the (sacred) Fire, and sanctified (its flame), while he sang aloud the Gâthas.

And Zarathustra asked him: Who art thou, O man! who art of all the incarnate world the most beautiful in Thine own body[2] of those whom I have seen, (thou) glorious [immortal]?

2. Thereupon gave H(a)oma answer[3], the holy one who driveth death afar: I am, O Zarathustra

[1] In the morning from six to ten.

[2] Or, 'beautiful of life.'

[3] 'Me,' omitted as interrupting rhythm, seems to be merely dramatic; or did it indicate that there was an original Zarathustrian Haoma Gâtha from which this is an extension?

H(a)oma, the holy and driving death afar; pray to me, O Spitâma, prepare me for the taste. Praise toward me in (Thy) praises as the other [Saoshyants] praise.

3. Thereupon spake Zarathustra: Unto H(a)oma be the praise[1]. What man, O H(a)oma! first prepared thee for the corporeal world? What blessedness was offered him? what gain did he acquire?

4. Thereupon did H(a)oma answer me, he the holy one, and driving death afar: Vîvanghvant[2] was the first of men who prepared me for the incarnate world. This blessedness was offered him; this gain did he acquire, that to him was born a son who was Yima, called the brilliant, (he of the many flocks, the most glorious of those yet born, the sunlike-one of men[3]), that he made from his authority both herds and people free from dying, both plants and waters free from drought, and men could eat imperishable food.

5. In the reign of Yima swift of motion was there neither cold nor heat, there was neither age nor death, nor envy[4] demon-made. Like fifteen-yearlings[5] walked the two forth, son and father, in their stature and their form, so long as Yima, son of Vîvanghvant ruled, he of the many herds!

6. Who was the second man, O H(a)oma! who

---

[1] Might not the entire sixteenth verse be placed here?

[2] The fifth from Gaya Maretan the Iranian Adam, but his counterpart, the Indian Vivasvat, appears not only as the father of Yama, but of Manu, and even of the gods, (as promoted mortals?).

[3] Compare svar-d*ri*sas pávamânâs.

[4] So the Pahlavi.

[5] Males, like females, seem to have been considered as developed at fifteen years of age.

prepared thee for the corporeal world? What sanctity was offered him? what gain did he acquire?

7. Thereupon gave H(a)oma answer, he the holy one, and driving death afar: Âthwya[1] was the second who prepared me for the corporeal world. This blessedness was given him, this gain did he acquire, that to him a son was born, Thraêtaona[2] of the heroic tribe,

8. Who smote the dragon Dahâka[3], three-jawed and triple-headed, six-eyed, with thousand powers, and of mighty strength, a lie-demon of[4] the Daêvas, evil for our settlements, and wicked, whom the evil spirit Angra Mainyu made as the most mighty Drug(k) [against the corporeal world], and for the murder of (our) settlements, and to slay the (homes) of Asha!

9. Who was the third man, O H(a)oma! who prepared thee for the corporeal world? What blessedness was given him? what gain did he acquire?

10. Thereupon gave H(a)oma answer, the holy one, and driving death afar: Thrita[5], [the most helpful of the Sâmas[6]], was the third man who prepared me for the corporeal world. This blessedness was given

---

[1] Comp. Tritá âptiá.

[2] Comp. the Indian Traitaná connected with Tritá.

[3] Let it be remembered that Tritá smote the Ahi before Indra, Indra seeming only to re-enact the more original victory which the Avesta notices. Concerning Azhi Dahâka, see Windischmann's Zendstudien, s. 136.

[4] Free.

[5] In the *Rig*-veda âptyá seems only an epithet added to the name Tritá*; and the two serpents of the Avesta are suspicious. Two names seem to have become two persons, or has the Avesta the more correct representation?

[6] Have we the Semites here? They certainly penetrated as conquerors far into Media, and it seems uncritical to deny their leaving traces. The gloss may be very old.

* And to that of other gods.

him, this gain did he acquire, that to him two sons were born, Urvâkhshaya and Keresâspa, the one a judge confirming order, the other a youth of great ascendant, ringlet-headed[1], bludgeon-bearing.

11. He who smote the horny dragon swallowing men, and swallowing horses, poisonous, and green of colour, over which, as thick as thumbs are, greenish poison flowed aside, on whose back once Keresâspa cooked his meat in iron caldron at the noonday meal; and the deadly, scorched, upstarted[2], and springing off, dashed out the water as it boiled. Headlong fled affrighted manly-minded[3] Keresâspa.

12. Who was the fourth man who prepared thee,

[1] Comp. Kapardínam.

[2] I abandon reluctantly the admirable comparison of hvîs with the Indian svid (Geldner), also when explained as an inchoative (Barth.), but the resulting meaning is far from natural either here or in Vend. III, 32 (Sp. 105). That the dragon should begin to sweat (!) under the fire which was kindled upon his back, and which caused him to spring away, seems difficult. The process was not so deliberate. He was scorched, started, and then sprang. Also in Vend. III, 32 when the barley is produced the demons hardly 'sweat (with mental misery).' The idea is too advanced for the document. Burnouf's and Haug's 'hiss' was much better in both places. But I prefer the hint of the Pahlavi lâlâ vazlûn*d*. In Vend. III, 32 (Sp. 105), khîst-hômand. Ner. tapta*s*k*a sa n*ri*sam*sa*h* k*ukshubhe [dvipâdo * babhûva]. Whether *hv*îsat*k*a=hîsat*k*a (?) has anything to do with hiz or khiz=Pahlavi âkhîzîdanŏ †, N. P. 'hîzîdan, is a question. I follow tradition without etymological help; perhaps we might as well write the word like the better known form as a conjecture.

[3] The Pahlavi translator makes the attempt to account for the epithet 'manly-minded' as applied to Keresâspa while yet he fled affrighted; he says: Hôman*d* mar*d*mîni*s*nîh hanâ yehevûn*d*, aîgha*s* libbemman pavan gâsdâ*s*t; Ner. asya paurushamânasatvam * ida*m* babhûva yad asau *k*aitanya*m* sthâne dadhau, 'his manly-mindedness was this, that he kept his wits on the occasion.' See the same story treated somewhat differently in the Ya*s*ts by Darmesteter (p. 295, note 2).

† Or, âkhêzîdanŏ.

O H(a)oma! for the corporeal world? What blessedness was given him? what gain did he acquire?

13. Thereupon gave H(a)oma answer, he the holy, and driving death afar: Pourushaspa[1] was the fourth man who prepared me for the corporeal world. This blessedness was given him, this gain did he acquire, that thou, O Zarathustra! wast born to him, the just, in Pourushaspa's house, the D(a)êva's foe, the friend of Mazda's lore, (14) famed in Airyêna Vaêgah; and thou, O Zarathustra! didst recite the first the Ahuna-vairya[2], four times intoning it, and with verses kept apart [(Pâzand) each time with louder and still louder voice].

15. And thou didst cause, O Zarathustra! all the demon-gods to vanish in the ground who aforetime flew about this earth in human shape (and power. This hast thou done), thou who hast been the strongest, and the staunchest, the most active, and the swiftest, and (in every deed) the most victorious in the two spirits'[3] world.

16. Thereupon spake Zarathustra: Praise to H(a)oma. Good is H(a)oma, and the well-endowed, exact and righteous in its nature, and good inherently, and healing, beautiful of form, and good in deed, and most successful in its working[4], golden-hued, with bending sprouts. As it is the best for drinking, so (through its sacred stimulus) is it the most nutritious[5] for the soul.

---

17. I make my claim on thee, O yellow one! for

[1] Son of Pâîtirasp or Spêtârasp; Bundahis XXXII, 1, 2, &c.

[2] The Ahuna-vairya is in the Gâthic dialect, and in the Ahunavaiti metre; it may have been composed by Z. It named the Gâtha.

[3] Comp. Y. XXX, 6?

[4] Free.

[5] Comp. pathmeng gavôi.

inspiration[1]. I make my claim on thee for strength; I make my claim on thee for victory; I make my claim on thee for health and healing (when healing is my need); I make my claim on thee for progress and increased prosperity, and vigour of the entire frame, and for understanding[2], of each adorning kind, and for this, that I may have free course among our settlements, having power where I will, overwhelming angry malice, and a conqueror of lies.

18. Yea, I make my claim on thee that I may overwhelm the angry hate of haters, of the D(a)êvas and of mortals, of the sorcerers and sirens[3], of the tyrants[4], and the Kavis, of the Karpans, murderous bipeds, of the sanctity-destroyers, the profane apostate bipeds, of the wolves four-footed monsters, of the invading host, wide-fronted, which with stratagems[5] advance.

---

19. This first blessing I beseech of thee, O H(a)oma, thou that drivest death afar! I beseech of thee for (heaven), the best life of the saints, the radiant, all-glorious[6].

This second blessing I beseech of thee, O H(a)oma, thou that drivest death afar! this body's health (before that blest life is attained).

This third blessing I beseech of thee, O H(a)oma, thou that drivest death afar! the long vitality of life.

---

[1] Or, is madhem related to medhâ as well as mazdâ (fem.)?

[2] Pahl. farzânakîh.

[3] Hardly 'witches;' outwardly attractive, but evil female beings.

[4] Pahl. sâstârânô.

[5] Pahl. pavan frîftârîh; Ner. pratâra*n*atayâ.

[6] Vîspô-*hv*âthrem does not mean 'comfortable' here. *Hv*an is the root; comp. *hveng*=sun.

20. This fourth blessing I beseech of thee, O H(a)oma, thou that drivest death afar! that I may stand forth on this earth with desires gained[1], and powerful, receiving satisfaction, overwhelming the assaults of hate, and conquering the lie.

This fifth blessing, O H(a)oma, I beseech of thee, thou that drivest death afar! that I may stand victorious on earth, conquering in battles[2], overwhelming the assaults of hate, and conquering the lie.

21. This sixth blessing I ask of thee, O H(a)oma, thou that drivest death afar! that we may get good warning of the thief, good warning of the murderer, see first the bludgeon-bearer, get first sight of the wolf. May no one whichsoever get first the sight of us. In the strife with each may we be they who get the first alarm!

---

22. H(a)oma grants to racers[3] who would run a course with span both speed and bottom (in their horses). H(a)oma grants to women come to bed with child a brilliant offspring and a righteous line.

H(a)oma grants to those (how many!) who have long sat searching books, more knowledge and more wisdom.

23. H(a)oma grants to those long maidens, who sit at home unwed, good husbands, and that as soon as asked, he H(a)oma, the well-minded.

24. H(a)oma lowered Keresâni[4], dethroned him from his throne, for he grew so fond of power, that

---

[1] Pahl. min *hv*âstâr. [2] Pahl. vânî*d*âr pavan kûshânŏ.

[3] Arva*n*tô=aurva*n*tô; so the Pahl. arvand.

[4] Comp. the Vedic K*ri*s*â*nu, archer and demi-god who guarded the Soma. Ner. seems to notice that the name recalls that of the Christians.

he treacherously said: No priest behind[1] (and watching) shall walk the lands for me, as a counsellor to prosper them, he would rob everything of progress, he would crush the growth of all!

---

25. Hail to thee, O H(a)oma, who hast power as thou wilt, and by thine inborn strength! Hail to thee, thou art well-versed in many sayings, and true and holy words. Hail to thee for thou dost ask no wily questions, but questionest direct.

26. Forth hath Mazda borne to thee, the star-bespangled girdle[2], the spirit-made, the ancient one, the Mazdayasnian Faith.

So with this thou art begirt on the summits of the mountains, for the spreading of the precepts, and the headings[3] of the Mãthra, (and to help the Mãthra's teacher),

27. O H(a)oma, thou house-lord, and thou clan-lord, thou tribe-lord, and chieftain of the land, and thou successful learned teacher, for aggressive strength I speak to thee, for that which smites with victory, and for my body's saving, and for manifold delight!

28. Bear off from us the torment and the malice of the hateful. Divert the angry foe's intent!

What man soever in this house is violent and wicked, what man soever in this village, or this tribe, or province, seize thou away the fleetness from

[1] So the Pahlavi, before others, read apãs; comp. frãs.

[2] Haug's keen-sighted suggestion, pourvanîm = paurva = the Pleiades + nî = leading the P., looks doubtful, and seems refuted by Yast XXIV, 29, where Darmesteter renders a word probably akin, as 'the many.' I would here render 'the former.'

[3] The 'grasp,' the 'summary of them.'

his feet; throw thou a veil of darkness o'er his mind; make thou his intellect (at once) a wreck!

29. Let not the man who harms us, mind or body, have power to go forth on both his legs, or hold with both his hands, or see with both his eyes, not the land (beneath his feet), or the herd before his face.

---

30. At the aroused and fearful[1] Dragon, green, and belching forth his poison, for the righteous saint that perishes, yellow H(a)oma, hurl thy mace[2]!

At the (murderous) bludgeon-bearer, committing deeds unheard of[3], blood-thirsty, (drunk) with fury, yellow H(a)oma, hurl thy mace!

31. Against the wicked human tyrant, hurling weapons at the head, for the righteous saint that perishes, yellow H(a)oma, hurl thy mace!

Against the righteousness-disturber, the unholy life-destroyer, thoughts and words of our[4] religion well-delivering, yet in actions never reaching, for the righteous saint that perishes, yellow H(a)oma, hurl thy mace!

32. Against the body of the harlot, with her magic minds o'erthrowing with (intoxicating) pleasures[5], to the lusts her person offering, whose[6] mind as vapour wavers as it flies before the wind, for the righteous saint that perishes, yellow H(a)oma, hurl thy mace!

---

[1] Pahl. sakhmakan; Ner. bhaya*m*kare.

[2] Or, 'strike thy club.'

[3] 'Deeds apart,' 'evil deeds.'

[4] Free.

[5] Or, 'holding.'

[6] Yênhê must be an error; otherwise 'offering the person to him whose mind as vapour wavers.'

YASNA X.

1. Let the Demon-gods and Goddesses fly far away [1] from hence, and let the good Sraosha make here his home! [And may the good Blessedness here likewise dwell], and may she here spread delight and peace within this house, Ahura's, which is sanctified by H(a)oma, bringing righteousness (to all).

2. At the first force of thy pressure, O intelligent! I praise thee with my voice, while I grasp at first thy shoots. At thy next pressure, O intelligent! I praise thee with my voice, when as with full force of a man I crush thee down.

3. I praise the cloud that waters thee, and the rains which make thee grow on the summits of the mountains; and I praise thy lofty mountains where the H(a)oma branches spread [2].

4. This wide earth do I praise, expanded far (with paths), the productive, the full bearing, thy mother, holy plant! Yea, I praise the lands where thou dost grow, sweet-scented, swiftly spreading, the good growth of the Lord. O H(a)oma, thou growest on the mountains, apart on many paths [3], and there still may'st thou flourish. The springs of Righteousness most verily thou art, (and the fountains of the ritual find their source in thee)!

---

[1] The Pahlavi as corrected by the MS. of Dastur Hoshanggi *G*âmâspgi has barâ akhar min latamman pa*d*ênd barâ shêdâ-; Ner. *R*ite pa*s*kât asmât prapatanti, *r*ite devâ*h* *r*ite devasahâyâ*h* devyâ*h*, uttama*h* *S*roso nivasati.

[2] Or, 'where, O Haoma! thou hast grown,' reading—i*s*a with Barth. as 2nd sing. perf. pret. middle.

[3] Or, 'on the pathways of the birds.'

5. Grow (then) because I pray to thee on all thy stems and branches, in all thy shoots (and tendrils) increase thou through my word!

---

6. H(a)oma grows while he is praised, and the man who praises him is therewith more victorious. The lightest pressure of thee, H(a)oma, thy feeblest praise, the slightest tasting of thy juice, avails to the thousand-smiting of the D(a)êvas.

7. Wasting doth vanish from that house, and with it foulness, whither in verity they bear thee, and where thy praise in truth is sung, the drink of H(a)oma, famed, health-bringing (as thou art). [(Pâzand) to his village and abode they bear him.]

8. All other toxicants go hand in hand with Rapine of the bloody spear, but H(a)oma's stirring power goes hand in hand with friendship. [Light is the drunkenness of H(a)oma (Pâzand).]

Who as a tender son caresses H(a)oma, forth to the bodies of such persons H(a)oma comes to heal.

9. Of all the healing virtues, H(a)oma, whereby thou art a healer, grant me some. Of all the victorious powers, whereby thou art a victor, grant me some. A faithful praiser will I be to thee, O H(a)oma, and a faithful praiser (is) a better (thing) than Righteousness the Best; so hath the Lord, declaring (it), decreed.

10. Swift[1] and wise hath the well-skilled[2] Deity created thee; swift and wise on high Haraiti did He, the well-skilled, plant thee.

11. And taught (by implanted instinct) on every

---

[1] Having immediate effect, and giving wisdom.
[2] Comp. Y. XLIV, 5.

side, the bounteous[1] birds have carried thee to the Peaks-above-the-eagles[2], to the mount's extremest summit, to the gorges and abysses, to the heights of many pathways[3], to the snow-peaks ever whitened.

12. There, H(a)oma, on the ranges dost thou grow of many kinds. Now thou growest of milky whiteness, and now thou growest golden; and forth thine healing liquors flow for the inspiring of the pious. So terrify away from me the (death's) aim of the curser. So terrify and crush his thought who stands as my maligner.

13. Praise be to thee, O H(a)oma, (for he makes the poor man's thoughts as great as any of the richest whomsoever.) Praise be to H(a)oma, (for he makes the poor man's thoughts as great as when mind reacheth culmination.) With manifold retainers dost thou, O H(a)oma, endow the man who drinks thee mixed with milk; yea, more prosperous thou makest him, and more endowed with mind.

14. Do not vanish from me suddenly like milk-drops in the rain; let thine exhilarations go forth ever vigorous and fresh; and let them come to me with strong effect. Before thee, holy H(a)oma, thou bearer of the ritual truth, and around thee would I cast this body, a body which (as all) may see (is fit for gift and) grown[4].

15. I renounce with vehemence the murderous woman's[5] emptiness, the *G*aini's, hers, with intellect

---

[1] Possibly 'the birds taught by the bounteous one;' the 'God-taught birds.'

[2] Elsewhere and here also possibly a proper name.

[3] Or the 'pathways of the birds;' so Haug, following Spiegel and Justi. Gugrati, as above.

[4] Which is seen as mine well-grown.

[5] *G*aini seems always used in an evil sense in the later Avesta.

dethroned[1]. She vainly thinks to foil us, and would beguile both Fire-priest and H(a)oma; but she herself, deceived therein, shall perish. And when she sits at home[2], and wrongly eats of H(a)oma's offering, priest's mother will that never make her, nor give her holy[3] sons!

16. [4]To five do I belong, to five others do I not; of the good thought am I, of the evil am I not; of the good word am I, of the evil am I not; of the good deed am I, and of the evil, not.

To Obedience am I given, and to deaf disobedience, not; to the saint do I belong, and to the wicked, not; and so from this on till the ending shall be the spirits' parting. (The two shall here divide.)

17. Thereupon spake Zarathustra: Praise to H(a)oma, Mazda-made. Good is H(a)oma, Mazda-made. All the plants of H(a)oma praise I, on the heights of lofty mountains, in the gorges of the valleys, in the clefts (of sundered hill-sides) cut for the bundles bound by women. From the silver cup I pour Thee to the golden chalice over[5]. Let me not thy (sacred) liquor spill to earth, of precious cost.

18. These are thy Gâthas[6], holy H(a)oma, these

[1] I would correct to a form of khratu.

[2] Compare the avoiding the service mentioned by the Pahlavi translator on Y. LIII, 5.

[3] Or, more safely, 'many sons.'

[4] Haoma speaks.

[5] Here the priest evidently manipulates the cups containing the Haoma-juice.

[6] The application of this term here seems to point to a high antiquity for the Haoma Yast; if not in the present piece, which is not so old as the Gâthas, then in previous hymns to Haoma of which this Yast is an improvement, or extension.

thy songs, and these thy teachings[1], and these thy truthful ritual words, health[2]-imparting, victory-giving, from harmful hatred healing giving.

19. These and thou art mine, and forth let thine exhilarations flow; bright and sparkling let them hold on their (steadfast) way; for light are thine exhilaration(s), and flying lightly come they here. Victory-giving smiteth H(a)oma, victory-giving is it worshipped; with this Gâthic word we praise it.

---

20. Praise to the Kine; praise and victory (be) spoken to her! Food for the Kine, and pasture! 'For the Kine let thrift use toil; yield thou us food[3].'

21. We worship the yellow lofty one; we worship H(a)oma who causes progress, who makes the settlements advance; we worship H(a)oma who drives death afar; yea, we worship all the H(a)oma plants. And we worship (their) blessedness, and the Fravashi of Zarathustra Spitâma, the saint[4].

YASNA XI.

PRELUDE TO THE H(A)OMA-OFFERING[5].

1. Three clean creatures (full of blessings) curse betimes while yet invoking, the cow, the horse, and then H(a)oma. The cow cries to her driver[6] thus:

---

[1] Ner. possibly figuratively *yâh kaskit* asvâdanâh.

[2] Ner. saundaryam.

[3] See Y. XLVIII, 5.

[4] The Yênhê hâtãm follows.

[5] This characteristic fragment is repeated and extended in the later literature of the Parsis. The curse of the cow, horse, and of Haoma (scilicet the priest) when they are stinted, was extended to all domestic animals. It has been difficult to avoid the full metrical rhythm of the original with its jingling cadence. A full freedom is also not avoided.

[6] Not 'to the priest;' Ner. grihîtâram.

Childless be thou, shorn of offspring, evil-famed, and slander-followed, who foddered[1] fairly dost not use me, but fattenest me for wife or children, and for thy niggard selfish meal.

2. The horse cries to his rider thus: Be not spanner[2] of the racers; stretch no coursers to full-speed; do not stride across the fleetest, thou, who dost not pray me swiftness in the meeting thick with numbers, in the circuit thronged with men.

3. H(a)oma speaks his drinker thus: Childless be thou, shorn of offspring, evil-famed, and slander-followed, who holdest me from full outpouring, as a robber, skulls in-crushing. No head-smiter[3] am I ever, holy H(a)oma, far from death[4].

4. Forth my father gave an offering, tongue and left eye chose Ahura, set apart for H(a)oma's meal.

5. Who this offering would deny me, eats himself, or prays it from me, this which Mazda gave to bless me, tongue with left eye (as my portion).

6. In his house is born no fire-priest, warrior ne'er in chariot standing, never more the thrifty tiller. In his home be born Dahâkas, Mûrakas of evil practice, doing deeds of double nature.

7. Quick, cut off then H(a)oma's portion, gift of flesh for doughty H(a)oma! Heed lest H(a)oma

[1] 'Who dost not give me cooked (food)' seems improbable. If *hvâstãm* means fodder, why is it fem., especially here with a feminine correlative? I think that 'having good food' is the meaning of the word, as an adjective, and agreeing with gãm understood. Possibly, 'who dost not bestow upon me as the one well-foddered.'

[2] Dialectically used.

[3] 'Light is the intoxication of Haoma;' (other toxicants smite the head).

[4] 'Having death afar.'

bind thee fettered, as he bound the fell Turanian Frangrasyan[1] (the murderous robber) fast in iron close-surrounded in the mid-third[2] of this earth! 8. Thereupon spake Zarathustra[3]: Praise to H(a)oma made by Mazda, good is H(a)oma Mazda-made.

---

9. [4]Who to us is one hereupon to thee (becomes) two, to be made to three, for the five[5]-making of the four, for the seven-making of the sixth, who are your nine in the decade (?), who serve you and with zeal[6].

---

10. [7]To thee, O holy H(a)oma! bearer of the ritual sanctity, I offer this my person which is seen (by all to be) mature, (and fit for gift); to H(a)oma the effective do I offer it, and to the sacred exhilaration which he bestows; and do thou grant to me (for this), O holy H(a)oma! thou that drivest death afar, (Heaven) the best world of the saints, shining, all brilliant.

---

[1] A Turanian king.

[2] Observe the threefold division of the earth; see it also in Vend. II.

[3] A poetical reproduction. Z. had been long among the ancient dead.

[4] The Raspi at present hands the Haoma-cup to the priest at this point; the efficacy of the liquor is supposed to be multiplied.

[5] Pe*n*daidyâi is to be read as of course; the letter ɞ, not unlike ɕ in a MS. when turned, was probably half inverted.

[6] This seems rendered by the Pahlavi as an interlude between the Ratu and the Zaotar; comp. Y. XXVIII, 11. Several broken sentences from other parts of the Avesta are here doubtfully recalled, perhaps as having especial sanctity.

[7] The Raspi brings the Haoma-vessel to the Baresman at this point; and touching its stand, the Mâh-rû, lays a cloth on the right hand of the Zaotar, who, looking at the vessel, proceeds to recite as follows in verse 10.

11. (The Ashem Vohû, &c.)

12–15. May'st Thou rule at Thy will, O Lord[1]!

16. I confess myself a Mazdayasnian of Zarathustra's order[2].

17. [3]I celebrate my praises for good thoughts, good words, and good deeds for my thoughts, my speeches, and (my) actions. With chanting praises I present all good thoughts, good words, and good deeds, and with rejection I repudiate all evil thoughts, and words, and deeds. 18. Here I give to you, O ye Bountiful Immortals! sacrifice and homage with the mind, with words, deeds, and my entire person; yea, (I offer) to you the flesh of my very body (as your own). And I praise Righteousness. A blessing is Righteousness (called) the Best, &c.

YASNA XII (Sp. XIII).

The Mazdayasnian Confession[4].

1. I drive[5] the Daêvas hence; I confess as a Mazda-worshipper of the order of Zarathustra, estranged from the Daêvas, devoted to the lore of

[1] See Y. VIII, 5–8. [2] See Y. III, 24, 25.

[3] This piece is in the Gâthic dialect, and therefore an especially fitting prelude to the Confession of faith in Y. XII.

[4] This piece in the Gâthic dialect has claims to higher antiquity next after the Haptanghâiti. Its retrospective cast shows that it is later than the original period. Verse 7 savours of a later date with its reference to the plants and waters. That Zarathustra, Kavi Vîstâspa, Frashaostra, and *G*âmâspa are named by no means proves that they were still living. Still, they are not mentioned with any fanciful or superstitious exaggeration; they are not yet demi-gods.

[5] As a partial explanation of nâismî* from nas, compare the aorist nesat. Possibly also from nad, 'I curse the demons.'

the Lord, a praiser[1] of the Bountiful Immortals; and to Ahura Mazda, the good and endowed with good possessions, I attribute all things good, to the holy One, the resplendent, to the glorious, whose are all things whatsoever which are good; whose is the Kine, whose is Asha (the righteous order pervading all things pure), whose are the stars, in whose lights the glorious beings and objects are clothed[2].

2. And I choose Piety, the bounteous and the good, mine may she be[3]. And therefore I loudly deprecate all robbery[4] and violence against the (sacred) Kine, and all drought[5] to the wasting of the Mazdayasnian villages.

3. Away from (?) their thoughts do I wish to lead (the thought of) wandering at will, (away the thought of) free nomadic pitching of the tent, for I wish to remove (?) all wandering from[6] (their) Kine which abide in steadfastness upon this land; and bowing down in worship to Righteousness I dedicate my offerings with praise so far as that. Never may I stand as a source of wasting, never as a source of withering to the Mazdayasnian villages, not for the love[7] of body or of life.

4. Away do I abjure the shelter and headship of the

[1] And sacrificer.

[2] A genuine citation from the Gâthas (see Y. XXXI, 7).

[3] A genuine allusion to the Gâthas (Y. XXXII, 2).

[4] This preserves the proper reading of tâyus*k*a (so the Pahlavi) in Y. XXIX, 1.

[5] Viyâpa*t* as beyond a doubt; so viyâpem in verse 3.

[6] Frâ has the same force as in fra perenaoiti (?), to fill forth, to empty. Otherwise, 'forth to their thoughts I offer in my prayer free ranging at their choice, and a lodging where they will, together with their cattle which dwell upon this land.'

[7] Comp. nâiri-*k*inanghô, khratu-*k*inanghô, and shaêtô-*k*inanghô.

Daêvas, evil as they are; aye, utterly bereft of good, and void of virtue, deceitful in their wickedness, of (all) beings those most like the Demon-of-the-Lie, the most loathsome of existing things, and the ones the most of all bereft of good.

5. Off, off, do I abjure the Daêvas and all possessed by them, the sorcerers and all that hold to their devices, and every existing being of the sort; their thoughts do I abjure, their words and actions, and their seed (that propagate their sin); away do I abjure their shelter and their headship, and the iniquitous of every kind who act as Rakhshas act!

Thus and so in very deed might Ahura Mazda have indicated[1] to Zarathustra in every question which Zarathustra asked, and in all the consultations in the which they two conversed together. 6. Thus and so might Zarathustra have abjured the shelter and the headship of the Daêvas in all the questions, and in all the consultations with which they two conversed together, Zarathustra and the Lord.

And so I myself, in whatsoever circumstances I may be placed, as a worshipper of Mazda, and of Zarathustra's order, would so abjure the Daêvas and their shelter, as he who[2] was the holy Zarathustra abjured them (once of old).

7. To that religious sanctity[3] to which the waters appertain, do I belong, to that sanctity to which the plants, to that sanctity to which the Kine of blessed gift[4], to that religious sanctity to which Ahura Mazda, who made both Kine and holy men, belongs,

---

[1] Reading adakhshayaêtâ; otherwise khshayaêtâ, commanded.

[2] The Pahlavi structure 'he who' foreshadowed, as often.

[3] Not in the sense of recompense here.

[4] Observe this original meaning; 'butter' is here impossible.

to that sanctity do I. Of that creed which Zarathustra held, which Kavi Vîstâspa, and those two, Frashaostra and Gâmâspa; yea, of that religious faith which every Saoshyant who shall (yet come to) save (us), the holy ones who do the deeds of real significance, of that creed, and of that lore, am I.

8. A Mazda-worshipper I am, of Zarathustra's order; (so) do I confess, as a praiser and confessor, and I therefore praise aloud the well-thought thought, the word well spoken, and the deed well done;

9. Yea, I praise at once the Faith of Mazda, the Faith which has no faltering utterance [1], the Faith that wields the felling halbert [2], the Faith of kindred marriage, the holy (Creed), which is the most imposing, best, and most beautiful of all religions which exist, and of all that shall in future come to knowledge, Ahura's Faith, the Zarathustrian creed. Yea, to Ahura Mazda do I ascribe all good, and such shall be the worship of the Mazdayasnian belief!

YASNA XIII (Sp. XIV).

Invocations and Dedications.

1. I address (my invocation to) Ahura Mazda. And I invoke (among guardian beings) the chief [3] of

---

[1] Fraspâvaokhedhrãm; 'y' miswritten for 'v.' Fra seems to be prohibitive 'speech without falling, or hesitation;' better as adj.

[2] Comp. Y. XXXI, 18.

[3] This Ratu is the description and representation of the Nmânôpaiti as occupying the attention of the worshippers chiefly at the time of his mention in the course of the ritual. (I vary the expression 'chief' with that of 'lord' here for the sake of change.) Once established as a Ratu in the ritual, he became a guardian genius Nmânya; so of the others. (Y. XIII is in the Gâthic dialect.)

the house-lord, and the chief of the Vîs-lord[1], and the chief of the Zantu-lord[2]. And I invoke the chief of the province-lord[3]. And the chief of women I invoke, the Mazdayasnian Faith, the blessed and good Parendi[4], her who is the holy one of human-kind[5]. And I invoke this (holy) earth which bears us.

2. And I invoke the friendly and most helpful person's[6] lord, the Fire of Ahura Mazda, and also the most energetic lords of holy men, those who are most strenuous[7] in their care of cattle and the fields, and the chief of the thrifty tiller of the earth. And I invoke the steady settler[8] of sanctity, (and) the chief of the charioteer.

3. And I invoke the chief of the fire-priest by means of the most imposing sciences of the Mazdayasnian Faith. And I invoke the chief of the Âtharvan, and his pupils I invoke; yea, the lords of each of them. I invoke these lords, and I summon the Bountiful Immortals here, and the Prophets who shall serve us, the wisest as they are, the most scru-

[1] Vîsya. [2] Zantuma. [3] Dahvyuma = Dahyuma.

[4] The goddess of riches.

[5] Lit. biped; see elsewhere where quadruped means merely beast.

[6] Or, 'households.'

[7] Ashethwôzgatemã (several manuscripts have ashe) finds its explanation from the Pahlavi of Dastur Hoshanggi Gâmâspgi's MS. It may be read kabed rang rasisntûm instead of kabed yôm rasisntûm. The ancient error of yôm arose from the fact that the copyist had before him a form which might be read either rôg or rang, the characters being identical for either word. He could not reconcile himself to rang in the sense of effort, and so decided for rôg; but in order to guide his successors aright, he changed it for its synonym yôm, which, as Spiegel well remarks, affords but little sense. But the word is rang, as I believe, and this is at once corroborated by Ner.'s bahuklesa. Read as + thwakhsa + gatemã = kabed + rang + rasisntûm, the most progressing with painful energy.

[8] Or, 'steadiest forces.'

pulous in their exactness (as) they utter words (of doctrine and of service), the most devoted (to their duties likewise), and the most glorious in their thoughts (?)[1]. And I invoke the most imposing forces of the Mazdayasnian Faith, and the fire-priests I invoke, and the charioteers, the warriors, and the thrifty tillers of the soil.

4. And to You, O Ye Bountiful Immortals! Ye who rule aright, and dispose (of all) aright, I offer the flesh of my very frame, and all the blessings of my life.

Thus[2] the two spirits[3] thought, thus they spoke, and thus they did;

5. And therefore as Thou, O Ahura Mazda! didst think, speak, dispose, and do all things good (for us), so to Thee would we give, so would we assign to Thee our homage; so would we worship Thee with our sacrifices. So would we bow before Thee with these gifts, and so direct our prayers to Thee with confessions of our debt.

6. By the kinship of the good kindred[4], by that of Righteousness the good (Thy righteous servant's nature) would we approach Thee, and by that of the good thrift-law, and of Piety the good.

7. And we would worship the Fravashi of the Kine of blessed gift[5], and that of the holy Gaya Maretan, and we would worship the holy Fravashi[6]

[1] I should think that the reference was here to khratavŏ, Y. XLVI, 3. See Y. XXXII, 14, as alternatively rendered.

[2] A portion of the text has here fallen out.

[3] The recognition of a strong dualism here is imperative. Ahura alone is praised.

[4] Or, 'of the good kinsman, the lord (?).'

[5] Elsewhere meaning 'meat,' just as Ameretatâ*t* and Haurvatâ*t* mean wood and water.

[6] Or, 'sanctity and the Fravashi.'

of Zarathustra Spitâma, the saint. Yea, that one of beings do we worship whose better (service) in the sacrifice Ahura Mazda knows; (even those women do we worship) whose[1] (better service thus is known). Yea, both (holy) men and women (do we worship whom Ahura Mazda knows[2]). As the Ahû is excelling, so is our Ratu, one who rules from the Righteous Order, a creator of mental goodness, and of life's actions done for Mazda; and the Kingdom is to Ahura which to the poor (may offer) nurture[2].

A blessing is the Right called the best, there is weal, there is weal to this (man), when toward Righteousness Best (he does) right[2].

8. We worship the Ahuna-vairya; and we worship Asha Vahista the best (?), the bountiful Immortal. And we sacrifice to the Hâ fraoreti, even to the confession and laudation of the Mazdayasnian Faith!

YASNA XIV (Sp. XV).

Dedications.

1. I will come to You, O Ye Bountiful Immortals! as a praiser and a priest, and an invoker and sacrificer, as a memorising reciter and a chanter, for Your sacrifice and homage, which are to be offered to You, the Bountiful Immortals, and for our dedication and sanctification; (yea, for ours) who are the holy prophets (destined to benefit the saints).

2. And to You, O Ye Bountiful Immortals[2]! would I dedicate the flesh of my very body[3], and all the blessings of a prospered life[4].

3. In this Zaothra with this Baresman, I desire to

[1] Feminine.

[2] Elsewhere with verbal difference.

[3] See Y. XXXIII, 14.

[4] Verses 1, 2 are Gâthic.

approach the holy Yazads with my praise [1], and all the holy lords of the ritual order at their times, Hâvani at his time, and Sâvanghi and Vîsya at their times. 4. I confess myself a Mazdayasnian, and of Zarathustra's order [2].

5. The Zaotar speaks: As an Ahû (revered and) chosen, the Zaotar (?) speaks forth to me (?).

The Ratu speaks: As an Ahû (revered and) to be chosen, the Zaotar speaks forth to me.

The Zaotar: So let the Ratu from his Righteousness, holy and learned, speak forth!

YASNA XV (Sp. XVI).

The Sacrifice continues.

1. With precept, praise, and with delight produced by grace [3], I call upon the Bountiful Immortals the good, and also therewith the beautiful by name [4]; and I sacrifice to them with the blessing of the good ritual, with the earnest blessings of the good Mazdayasnian Faith.

2. Whose best gift from his Righteousness is mine in the offering Ahura this knoweth; who have lived, and live ever, by their names these I worship, while I draw near with praises [5]. The Good Kingdom is to be chosen, that lot which most of all bears on (our blessings [6]).

3. Let Sraosha (Obedience) be here present for

[1] See Y. II, 18. [2] See Y. III, 24, 25.

[3] Root rap=rabh, a reception of grace, or being received by grace.

[4] Namãn may be meant for a locative; 'with the beautiful things in their name (?).'

[5] See Y. LI, 22. [6] See Y. LI, 1.

the sacrifice of Ahura Mazda, the most beneficent, the holy, who is so dear to us as at the first, so at the last; yea, let him be present here[1].

4. As the Ahû (revered and) to be chosen, the Âtarevakhsha thus speaks forth to me.

(Response): So let the Ratu from his righteousness, holy and learned, speak forth!

YASNA XVI (Sp. XVII).

The Sacrifice continues with increased fulness of expression.

1. We worship Ahura Mazda, the holy lord of the ritual order, who disposes (all) aright, the greatest Yazad, who is also the most beneficent, and the one who causes the settlements to advance, the creator of good creatures; yea, we worship Him with these offered Zaothras, and with truthfully and scrupulously delivered words; and we worship every holy Yazad of the heaven (as well)!

2. And we worship Zarathustra Spitâma in our sacrifice, the holy lord of the ritual order with these Zaothras and with faithfully delivered words; and we worship every holy earthly Yazad as we worship him; and we worship also the Fravashi of Zarathustra Spitâma, the saint. And we worship the utterances of Zarathustra and his religion, his faith and his lore.

3. And we worship the former religions of the world[2] devoted to Righteousness which were insti-

[1] This fragment in the Gâthic dialect might more properly be placed before the Srôsh Yast.

[2] So the Pahlavi translator, probably reading angheus; otherwise

tuted at the creation, the holy religions of the Creator Ahura Mazda, the resplendent and glorious. And we worship Vohu Manah (the Good Mind), and Asha Vahista (who is Righteousness the Best), and Khshathra-vairya, the Kingdom to be desired, and the good and bountiful Âramaiti (true piety in the believers), and Haurvatâ*t* and Ameretatâ*t* (our Weal and Immortality).

4. Yea, we worship the Creator Ahura Mazda and the Fire, Ahura Mazda's son, and the good waters which are Mazda-made and holy, and the resplendent sun of the swift horses, and the moon with the seed of cattle (in his beams[1]); and we worship the star Tistrya, the lustrous and glorious; and we worship the soul of the Kine of blessed endowment, (5) and its Creator Ahura Mazda; and we worship Mithra of the wide pastures, and Sraosha (Obedience) the blessed, and Rashnu the most just, and the good, heroic, bountiful Fravashis of the saints, and the Blow-of-victory Ahura-given (as it is). And we worship Râman *Hv*âstra, and the bounteous Wind of blessed gift, (6) and (its) Creator Ahura Mazda, and the good Mazdayasnian Religion, and the good Blessedness and Arstâ*t*.

And we worship the heaven and the earth of blessed gift, and the bounteous Mãthra, and the stars without beginning (to their course), self-disposing as they are.

7. And we worship the glorious works of Righteousness in which the souls of the dead find satisfaction and delight [(Pâzand) which are the Fravashis

'of the conscience that loves the right.' In Yast XIII, 118 the word is a proper name through an error.

[1] Possibly in allusion to the menses. The moon is masc.

of the saints], and we worship (Heaven) the best world of the saints, shining, all glorious.

8. And we worship the two, the milk-offering and the libation, the two which cause the waters to flow forth[1], and the plants to flourish, the two foes who meet the Dragon[1] demon-made; and who are set to meet, to defeat, and to put to flight, that cheat[2], the Pairika, and to contradict the insulting malice of the Ashemaogha (the persecuting heretic) and that of the unholy tyrant full of death[3].

9. And we worship all waters and all plants, and all good men and all good women. And we worship all these Yazads, heavenly and earthly[4], who are beneficent and holy.

10. And we worship thee (our) dwelling-place who art the (earth, our) bounteous Âramaiti[5], and Thee, O Ahura Mazda, O holy Lord of this abode[6]! which is the home of healthy herds and healthy men, and of those who are both endowed with health and lover(s) of the ritual right.

(Response of the individual worshipper (?).) Wherefore whichever of persons, or whatever of bodily influences, is most helpful and preserving in that abode (thus owned by Mazda) let this meet me in mine abode, and there may it abide for summer and for winter. (Or[7] let that one meet me in all my house,

---

[1] We cannot mistake a connection here with yó áhi*m* *g*aghanva—avâs*rig*at sártave saptá síndhûn.

[2] Or is it possible that a plague of mice is meant, mû*s* being here indeclinable?

[3] Ordering the execution of many of his subjects.

[4] Gaêthyâ*k*a with J 3, K 11.

[5] Later association of Â. and the earth.

[6] Originally recited in private houses.

[7] Alternative.

in whom are what of influences are the most mighty power for the body and the person's life; yea, let that one meet me there, and there abide for summer and for winter (for my help)!)

YASNA XVII.

To the Fires, Waters, Plants, &c.

1–10[1], 11. We worship thee, the Fire, O Ahura Mazda's son! We worship the fire Berezi-savangha (of the lofty use[2]), and the fire Vohu-fryâna (the good and friendly[3]), and the fire Urvâzista (the most beneficial and most helpful[4]), and the fire Vâzista (the most supporting[5]), and the fire Spenista (the most bountiful[6]), and Nairya-sangha the Yazad of the royal lineage[7], and that fire which is the house-lord of all houses and Mazda-made, even the son of Ahura Mazda, the holy lord of the ritual order, with all the fires.

12. And we worship the good and best waters Mazda-made, holy, all the waters Mazda-made and holy, and all the plants which Mazda made, and which are holy.

---

[1] See chapter VI, which is nearly identical with XVII, 1–10.

[2] This fire is that before Ahura Mazda and the kings.

[3] This fire dwells in the bodies of men and beasts (animal heat).

[4] This is in trees and plants.

[5] This in the clouds (lightning).

[6] This is the fire which is applied in the world (Bundahis, West, page 61).

[7] That N. is here referred to as connected with the fire, seems certain; this fire corresponds with that of Vâhrâm in places of worship.

13. And we worship the Mãthra-spe*n*ta (the bounteous word-of-reason), the Zarathu*s*trian law against the Daêvas, and its long descent.

14. And we worship Mount Ushi-darena which is Mazda-made and shining with its holiness, and all the mountains shining with holiness, and of abundant glory, and which Mazda made —.

15. And we worship the good and pious prayer for blessings, (16) and these waters and (these lands), (17) and all the greatest chieftains, lords of the ritual order[1];

18. And I praise, invoke, and glorify the good, heroic, bountiful Fravashis of the saints, those of the house, the Vîs, the Za*n*tuma, the Da*hv*yuma[2], and the Zarathu*s*trôtema, and all the holy Yazads[3]!

YASNA XVIII[4].

1. Grant me, Thou who art maker of the Kine, plants and waters, Immortality, Mazda! Grant, too, Weal, Spirit bounteous —.

YASNA XIX.

Zand or Commentary on the Ahuna-vairya Formulas[5].

(As the Ahû is excellent, so (is) the Ratu (one who rules) from the righteous Order, a creator of mental goodness and of life's actions done for Mazda; and

[1] 1–17 occur also in MSS. as Y. LIX, 1–17.

[2] Dahyuma.

[3] The Yêṅhê hâtãm follows.

[4] See Y. LI, 7, and Y. XLVII.

[5] The obvious errors contained in this ancient comment cannot

the Kingdom (is) for Ahura which to the poor shall offer a nurturer.)

1. Zarathustra asked of Ahura Mazda: O Ahura Mazda, Thou most bounteous Spirit! maker[1] of the corporeal worlds, the holy One! which was that word which Thou did'st declare to me, (2) which was before the sky, and before the water, before the earth, and before the cattle, before the plants, and before the fire, and before the holy man, and the Demon-gods (the Daêvas), before the Khrafstra-men[2], and before all the incarnate world; even before all the good creatures made by Mazda, and which contain (and are) the seed of righteousness?

3. Thereupon Ahura Mazda said: It was this piece[3], the Ahuna-vairya, O Spitama Zarathustra! which I pronounced as thine (4) before the sky, and before the waters, before the land, and before the cattle and the plants, and before the fire, Ahura Mazda's son, before the holy man[4], and before the Daêvas, and Khrafstra-men, and before the entire corporeal world, even before the good creatures made by Mazda, which contain (and are) the seed of righteousness.

5. It was these part(s) of the Ahuna-vairya, O Spi-

destroy its great interest as a specimen of early exegesis. Where I hold it to be erroneous may be seen from my rendering of the Ahuna without further observations. The Ahuna-vairya is in the Gâthic dialect, and the Ahunavaiti metre. This Zand is in the Zend (sic). Ahû gives better sense as a nom.

[1] See daunghôit para below.

[2] May not khrafstra be a degeneration from kehrp-astar? While the term may be applied to wild beasts, one is strongly inclined to hold that foul insects are chiefly referred to.

[3] This part of the Ahuna (?), meaning its several parts.

[4] Tradition naturally specifies Gaya Maretan.

tama Zarathustra! which especially belongs to me, and when each is intoned aloud without the (needless) repetition[1] of verses and of words, and without their omission, it is worth a hundred of their other stanzas, even although they are prominent in the ritual, and likewise equally as well recited without additions or omissions; nay, further, when it is intoned imperfectly but added to, and with omissions, it is even then in effect equivalent (not to a hundred indeed, but) to ten other (stanzas) that are prominent.

6. And whoever in this world of mine which is corporeal shall mentally recall, O Spitâma* Zarathustra! a portion of the Ahuna-vairya, and having thus recalled it, shall undertone it, or beginning to recite it with the undertone, shall then utter it aloud, or chanting it with intoning voice, shall worship thus, then with even threefold (safety and with speed[2]) I will bring his soul over the Bridge of *K*inva*t*, I who am Ahura Mazda (I will help him to pass over it) to Heaven (the best life), and to Righteousness the Best, and to the lights of heaven[3].

7. And whoever, O Spitama Zarathustra! while undertoning the part(s) of the Ahuna-vairya (or this piece the Ahuna-vairya), takes ought therefrom, whether the half, or the third, or the fourth, or the fifth, I who am Ahura Mazda will draw his soul off

[1] I do not think that mispronunciation is here intended; the Pahlavi has abarâ shûtakîh; aîghas barâ lâ khelmûnê*d*; Ner. na sete. I am strongly inclined to read anapashûta for anapishûta.

[2] Three times seems to me to lack meaning, but it may have given rise to a foolish belief that the soul went three times before death to heaven.

[3] Vahistaêibyô retaining this sense here.

from the better world; yea, so far off will I withdraw it as the earth is large and wide; [and this[1] earth is as long as it is broad[2]].

8. And I pronounced this saying which contains its Ahû and its Ratu[3] before the creation of this heaven, before the making of the waters, and the plants, and the four-footed kine, before the birth of the holy biped man, before this sun with its body made for the acquisition of the creation of the Bountiful Immortals[4].

9. [5]And the more bountiful[6] of the two Spirits (Ahura) declared to me[7] (Zarathustra) the entire creation of the pure, that which exists at present, that which is in the course of emerging into existence[8], and that which shall be, with reference to the performance and realisation 'of the actions of a life devoted to Mazda[9].'

10. And this word is the most emphatic of the words which have ever been pronounced, or which are[10] now spoken, or which shall be spoken in future; for (the eminence of) this utterance is a thing of such a nature, that if all the corporeal and living world

---

[1] Îm here equals iyám. [2] Pâzand.

[3] So, referring to the wording of the Ahuna.

[4] Enabling us to receive the blessings which they bestow through the influence of the sun. 'The sun-shaped matter' would give us a materialism. The Pahlavi has 'levînŏ min zak khurkhshê*dŏ* brînŏ (?) kerpŏ tanû î khûrkhshê*d* pavan barâ ayâpakîh î ameshôspendânŏ yehabûn*d*.'

[5] I hold that Ahura speaks no further here.

[6] See Y. XLV, 1.

[7] Of course fictitious, as Z. had long been among the dead.

[8] Does bavai*n*ti*k*a mean 'past?'

[9] Through the state of action; *s*kyaothananãm angh*eus* Mazdâi.

[10] Can mruyê(-vê) be a third singular like ghnê, isê?

should learn it, and learning should hold fast by it, they would be redeemed from their mortality!

11. And this our word I have proclaimed as a symbol to be learned [1], and to be recited, as it were, to every one of the beings under the influence of and for the sake of Righteousness the Best.

12. And 'as' (the worshipper has) here spoken it forth, when he has thus 'appointed' the 'Lord and regulator [2],' so (by thus reciting these authoritative words), he acknowledges Ahura Mazda (as prior to, and supreme) over, those creatures who have 'the mind' [3] as their first. 'As' he acknowledges Him as the greatest of them all, 'so' he assigns the creatures to Him (as to their originator).

13. As he undertones the third sentence, he thereby announces that 'all the amenities of life appertain to the 'good' Mazda [4], (and come) from Him. As he recites 'dazda mananghô,' 'the creator of mind,' he acknowledges Him as superior and prior to mind; and as he makes Him the one who indicates (the truth) to mind, (saying) 'mananghô of mind,' which means that by this much he makes Him (its director), and then he makes Him 'the lord of actions [5].'

14. And when he acknowledges Him for the creatures thus, 'O Mazda [6]!' he acknowledges Him (as

---

[1] Or, 'it has been declared to us, the learner, and the one in charge of the ritual.'

[2] In the words yathâ ahû vairyô, athâ ratu*s*.

[3] See dazda mananghô, coming 'before' *s*kyaothananãm angh*e*u*s*, khshathrem, and vâstârem.

[4] Can the Ahuna have lost words, and is Mazd*a*u hugîtî*s* vangh*e*u*s* a citation? At all events, the Zandist errs in separating vangh*e*u*s* from mananghô. He attributes mystical meaning to every word.

[5] Comp. ahû-*s*kyaothananãm. [6] Reading Mazda (?).

their ruler) when he assigns the creatures to Him thus. He then assigns the Kingdom to Ahura[1], saying: 'Thine, O Mazda! is the Kingdom.' And he assigns a nourisher and protector to the poor, saying: Yim drigubyô dada*t* vâstârem; that is, as a friend to Spitama[2]. This is the fifth sentence, (and it concludes) the entire recital and word, (even) the whole of this word of Ahura Mazda[3].

15. He who is the best (of all) Ahura Mazda, pronounced the Ahuna-vairya, and as He pronounced it as the best, so He caused it to have its effect[4], (He, ever) the same, (as He is).

The evil one at once[5] arose (to oppose Him), but He (Ahura) repelled that wicked one with His interdict, and with this repelling renunciation: Neither our minds are in harmony, nor our precepts, nor our comprehensions, nor our beliefs, nor our words, nor our actions, nor our consciences, nor our souls[6]!

Catechetical Zand[7].

16. And this saying, uttered by Mazda, has three stages, or measures[8], and belongs to four classes (of men as its supporters), and to five chiefs (in the political world, without whom its efficiency is

---

[1] Khshathremk*â* Ahurâi â.

[2] As having the interest of the poor at heart.

[3] Supposing Ahura (?) to be meant by Ahû and Ratu; see Mazdâi Ahurâi. The Zandist may have rendered: As Ahura is the (first) to be chosen, so He is our Ratu from His righteousness, the creator of Vohûman (including all good creatures), &c.

[4] 'Praised' (?).

[5] Reading haithwa*t*; Pahlavi tîz; possibly 'being present.'

[6] See Y. XLV, 2.

[7] This Zand differs, as to the application of Ahû and Ratu, from the former.

[8] Afsman elsewhere applies to metre.

marred), and it has a conclusion ending with a gift. (Question.) How are its measures (constituted)? (Answer.) The good thought, the good word, and the good deed. 17. (Question.) With what classes of men? (Answer.) The priest, the charioteer (as the chief of warriors), the systematic tiller[1] of the ground, and the artisan[2]. These classes therefore accompany the religious man throughout his entire duty[3] with the correct thought, the truthful word, and the righteous action. These are the classes and states in life which give attention to the rulers[4], and fulfil the (laws) of religion; (yea, they are the guides and companions of that religious man) through whose actions the settlements are furthered in righteousness.

18. (Question.) How are the chiefs (constituted)? (Answer.) They are the house-chief, the village-chief, and the tribe-chief, the chief of the province, and the Zarathustra[5] as the fifth. That is, so far as those provinces are concerned which are different from, and outside of the Zarathustrian regency, or domain. [Ragha[6] which has four chiefs (only) is the Zarathustrian (district)]. (Question.) How are the chiefs of this one constituted? (Answer.) They (are) the house-chief, the village-chief, the tribe-chief, and the Zarathustra as the fourth. 19. (Question.) What is the thought well thought? (Answer.) (It is that which the holy man thinks), the one who holds the holy thought to be before all other things[7]. (Question.)

[1] These are 'the poor,' but not mendicants.

[2] A class not in the Gâthas; observe the rise of a caste system.

[3] Or, 'experience.'

[4] Or, 'the ritual.'

[5] The title of a governor.

[6] It did not need the fifth. It was a centre of rule.

[7] Ashavan manas paoiryô.

What is the word well spoken? (Answer.) It is the Mãthra Spe*n*ta[1], the bounteous word of reason. (Question.) What is the deed well done? (Answer.) It is that done with praises[2], and by the creatures who regard Righteousness as before all other things. 20. (Question.) Mazda made a proclamation, whom did He announce? (Answer.) Some one who was holy, and yet both heavenly and mundane[3]. (Question.) What was His character, He who made this sacred enunciation? (Answer.) He who is the best (of all), the ruling one. (Question.) Of what character (did He proclaim him the coming one)? (Answer.) As holy and the best, a ruler who exercises no wanton or despotic power[4].

21. We sacrifice to the (several) part(s) of the Ahuna-vairya. We sacrifice to the memorised recital of the Ahuna-vairya, and its regular chanting and its use in the full Yasna.

YASNA XX.

Zand, or Commentary, on the Ashem Vohû.

1. A blessing is Righteousness (called) the best; there is weal, there is weal to this man when the Right (helps) the Righteousness best, (when the pious man serves it in truth[5]). Ahura Mazda spake forth: Ashem vohû vahi*s*tem astî. To this Asha, the holy ritual sanctity, one attributes the

[1] Probably the Gâthas with their lost portions, also the Vendîdâd.

[2] Ritual strictness based upon practical piety.

[3] The Saoshya*n*t.

[4] The latter part of this Zand shows that the Ratu was recognised as a human ruler in it.

[5] Elsewhere verbally different; 'when Asha is for A.V.'

qualities of 'good' and 'best,' as one attributes property to an owner; thus this sentence vohû vahistem astî is substantiated (at once[1]).

2. Ustâ astî ustâ ahmâi; by this attribution of blessedness (the praiser) assigns every person (or thing) of a sacred nature to every holy person, and as one usually (?) and regularly (?)[2] assigns every person or thing (?)[3] that is holy to every holy man.

3. Yyat ashâi vahistai[4]; by these words the worshipper ascribes the entire Mãthra (to Asha Vahista), and ascribes all to the Mãthra, as one ascribes the kingdom to Righteousness, and as one ascribes righteousness to the invoking saint; yea, as one ascribes righteousness to us who are the prophets (who shall help and bless the people). The three maxims of the sentences (are thus fulfilled). And every word (in its detail), and the entire utterance in its proclamation, is the word of Ahura Mazda.

Catechetical Addition[5].

4. Mazda has made a proclamation. (Question.) Whom did He announce? (Answer.) That holy one who is both heavenly and earthly. (Question.) Of what character is He who has thus announced Him? (Answer.) He is the best, and the one who is exercising sovereign power. (Question.) Of what character is the man whom He announced? (Answer.)

[1] It is carried into effect; possibly 'rendered fit for praising' (?).

[2] The Pahlavi indicates nâ stâitya (?).

[3] Ashavanem here and in Y. XIX, 19 might be a neuter from a transition, or addition.

[4] 'Ashem.'

[5] This Catechetical addition is identical with that in Y. XIX. The wording alone is slightly altered in the translation to relieve the sameness.

The holy and the best, the one who rules with no capricious tyranny.

We sacrifice to the (several) part(s) of the Asha Vahista (prayer). We sacrifice to the heard-recital of the Asha Vahista, to its memorising, its chanting, and its sacrificial use[1]!

YASNA XXI.

Catechetical Zand, or Commentary upon the Yênhê hâtãm[2].

(The Yênhê. (To that one) of beings do we offer, whose superior (fidelity) in the sacrifice Ahura Mazda recognises by reason of the sanctity (within him; yea, even to those female saints also do we sacrifice) whose (superior fidelity is thus likewise known; thus) we sacrifice to (all, to both) the males and females (of the saints)!)

---

[1] The Yênhê hâtãm follows.

[2] The expressions in this prayer were suggested by Y. LI, 22; but the Zand does not consistently follow the thoughts in the Gâtha. Tem understood should be supplied as an object for yazamaidê in connection with yênhê, as well as tauskâ for yaunghãm. In Y. LI, 22, it is, however, by no means certain that yazâi applies to a tem yêhyâ. Holding the twenty-first verse in mind, I am obliged to refer yêhyâ to nâ spentô. Here, however, men and women are worshipped, as it is improbable that the 'Immortals' whose names are in the feminine are meant. The prayer is in the Gâthic dialect, and ancient metre would hardly contain so artificial a formation. It can only be defended from the teng yazâi hvâis nâmenîs of Y. LI, 22.

Or did the composer of the prayer correctly render Y. LI, 22, and boldly write his succinct words as being clear to his hearers from explanations which are now lost? Such explanations (oral or written) as a matter of course existed from the first. No composer fails to discuss his productions.

1. A word for the Yasna by Zarathustra, the saint. Yênhê, &c. Here the worshipper indicates and offers the Yasna (which is the sacrificial worship) of Mazda as by the command (or as the institution) of Ahura[1]. Hâtãm. Here the worshipper offers the sacrificial worship as if with the beings who are among those who are destined to live[2]. 2. Yaunghãm. Here he indicates and offers the sacrificial worship of those holy females who have Âramaiti at their head[3], as homage to the Immortals. These are the three sentences which comprehend all the Yasnian speech. (Question.) To whom is this Yasna addressed? (Answer.) To the Bountiful Immortals (in the course of the Yasna). 3. Thereupon spake Mazda: Salvation to this one, whosoever he may be! May the absolute ruler Ahura grant it. (Question.) 4. Whom did He answer with this answer? (Answer.) He answered: The state of salvation; and with this answer, 'the state of salvation,' he answered every saint who exists, every one who is coming into existence, and every one who shall exist in the future. (Question. Who answered thus? Answer.) The best One. (Question. What did He answer?) (Answer.) The best thing. (That is,) the best One, Mazda, answered the best and the holy (answer) for the better and the holy man. 5. We sacrifice to this piece, the Yênhê hâtãm, the prominent and holy Yast.

---

[1] Referring yênhê to Ahura (?). [2] Fit to live, clean.

[3] The Ameshôspends whose names are in the feminine; so the Zandist erroneously.

YASNA XXII.

THE SACRIFICE CONTINUES.

1. With the Baresman brought hither together with the Zaothra, for the worship of the Creator Ahura Mazda, the resplendent, the glorious, and for that of the Bountiful Immortals, I desire to approach this Haoma with my praise, offered (as it is) with punctilious sanctity (or, for a blessing), and this fresh milk, and this plant Hadhânaêpata. 2. And, as an act of worship to the beneficent waters, I desire to approach these Zaothras with (my) praise offered (as they are) with punctilious sanctity, having the Haoma with them, and the flesh, with the Hadhânaêpata. And I desire to approach the Haoma-water with my praise for the beneficent waters; and I desire to approach the stone mortar and the iron mortar with my praise. 3. And I desire to approach this plant for the Baresman with my praise, and the well-timed prayer for blessings, that which has approached (to accept our homage), and the memorised recital and the fulfilment of the good Mazdayasnian Faith, and the heard recital of the Gâthas, and the well-timed and successful prayer for blessings, that of the holy lord of the ritual order. And I desire to approach these wood-billets and their perfume with my praise,—thine, the Fire's, O Ahura Mazda's son! Yea, I desire to approach all good things with my praise, those which Mazda made, and which have the seed of sanctity (within them), (4) for the propitiation of Ahura Mazda and of the Bountiful

Immortals, and of Sraosha the blessed, and of Ahura Mazda's Fire, the lofty ritual lord[1]!

20. And I desire to approach this Haoma with (my) praise, that which is thus lifted up with sanctity, and this milk (fresh as it is, and as if) living and lifted up with sanctity, and this plant the Hadhânaêpata lifted up with sanctity. 21. And I desire to approach these Zaothras with (my) praise for the beneficial waters, these Zaothras which have the H(a)oma with them and the milk with them, and the Hadhânaêpata, and which are lifted up with sanctity. And I desire to approach the Haoma-water with (my) praise for the beneficial waters, and the two mortars, the stone one and the iron one, (22) and I desire to approach this branch for the Baresman with my praise, and the memorised recital and fulfilment of the Mazdayasnian law, and the heard recital of the Gâthas, and the well-timed and persistent prayer for blessings (uttered) by the holy lord[2] of the ritual order, and this wood and perfume, even thine, O Fire, Ahura Mazda's son, and all good objects Mazda-made (23) for the propitiation of Ahura Mazda, the resplendent, the glorious, and of the Bountiful Immortals, and of Mithra of the wide pastures, and of Râman *Hv*âstra[3], (24) and of the resplendent sun, immortal, radiant, of the fleet horses, and of Vayu, (of predominant influence and) working on high, set over the other beings in the creation [(Pâzand); that is for thee thus (O Vayu) when thine influence is that which apper-

[1] 5–19=Y. III, 5–19; 20–23=1–4 from imem.

[2] The priest? (Repetitions are, as everywhere, curtailed and varied.)

[3] For closer rendering of details, see verses 2, 3, 4, which differ chiefly in the final dedication.

tains to Spe*n*ta Mainyu [1]], and for the propitiation of the most just knowledge Mazda-given, and of the holy and good Religion, the Mazdayasnian Faith; (25) for the propitiation of the Mãthra Spe*n*ta, (the bounteous) and holy, and the effective, instituted against the Daêvas, the Zarathu*s*trian law, and of the long descent of the good Mazdayasnian Faith [2] [the holding in mind and devotion to the Mãthra Spe*n*ta, and knowledge of the Mazdayasnian Religion] for the propitiation of the understanding which is innate and Mazda-made, and of that which is heard by the ear; (26) and for thy propitiation, the Fire's, O Ahura Mazda's son! [(Pâzand); (yea) thine, the Fire's, O Ahura Mazda's son] with all the fires, and for the propitiation of Mount Ushi-darena, the Mazda-made, radiant with sanctity; (27) and of all the holy Yazads, spiritual and earthly, and of the holy Fravashis, the redoubted and overwhelming, those of the ancient lore, and those of the next of kin and of the Yazad of the spoken name!

YASNA XXIII.

THE FRAVASHIS OF THE SAINTS; PRAYERS FOR THEIR APPROACH [3].

1. I desire to approach with my praise [4] those Fravashis which have existed from of old, the Fravashis of the houses, and of the villages, of the communities, and of the provinces, which hold the

[1] And not the evil Vayu, which appertains to Angra Mainyu.
[2] Insert, 'and of the good Zarathu*s*trian devotion.'
[3] This chapter is said to be reserved for funeral occasions.
[4] Or, 'I pray for the approach.' See Y. XXVI.

heaven in its place apart, and the water, land, and cattle, which hold the children in the wombs safely enclosed apart so that they do not miscarry. 2. And I desire to approach toward the Fravashi[1] of Ahura Mazda, and with my praise, and for those of the Bountiful Immortals, with all the holy Fravashis which are those of the heavenly Yazads. And I desire to approach the Fravashi of Gaya Maretan (the life-man) in my worship with my praise, and for that of Zarathustra Spitâma, and for those of Kavi Vîstâspa, and of Isat-vâstra[2], the Zarathustrian, with all the holy Fravashis of the other ancient counsellors as well. 3. And I desire in my worship to approach toward every holy Fravashi whosesoever it may be, and wheresoever dead upon this earth (its possessor may have lain), the pious woman, or the girl of tender years, the maiden diligent (among the cattle) in the field (who) may have dwelt (here; yea, all) which are now worshipped from this house[3], which are attentive to, and which attain to (our) good Yasnas and (our) homage. 4. Yea, I desire to approach the Fravashis of the saints with my praise, redoubted (as they are) and overwhelming, the Fravashis of those who held to the ancient lore, and the Fravashis of the next-of-kin; and I desire to approach toward the Fravashi of mine own[4] soul in my worship with my praise; and I desire therewith to approach toward all the lords of the ritual, and with

[1] Fravashi seems a dative; comp. ûtî.

[2] Zarathustra's eldest son by his wife Padokhshah; he was the chief of priests according to tradition.

[3] This Yasna was recited from house to house.

[4] The 'own' soul; notice the seeming distinction between Fravashi and soul.

praise; and I desire to approach all the good Yazads with my praise, the heavenly and the earthly, who are meet for sacrifice and homage, because of Righteousness the Best!

YASNA XXIV.

Presentations.

1. (And having approached these Haomas with our worship), we present them to Ahura Mazda; (yea, we present) these Haomas, Myazdas, Zaothras, and the Baresman spread with punctilious sanctity, and the flesh, and the milk, fresh as if living, and lifted up with punctilious sanctity, and this branch the Hadhânaêpata likewise lifted up with sanctity.

2. (And having approached these Zaothras in our worship), we present them to the good waters having the Haoma with them, and the milk, and the Hadhânaêpata, and lifted up with scrupulous sanctity; and (with them) we present the Haoma-water to the good waters, and both the stone and the iron mortar.

3. And we present this plant of the Baresman, and the timely prayer for blessings, which has approached in the due course of the ritual, and the recollection and practice[1] of the good Mazdayasnian Religion, and the heard recital of the Gâthas, and the timely prayer for blessings which has approached as the prayer of the holy lord of the ritual order; and these wood-billets, and the perfume, (even) thine, the Fire's, O Ahura Mazda's son! and all good objects Mazda-made, which have the seed of righteousness, we offer and present. 4. And these we present hereby to Ahura Mazda, and to Sraosha (Obedience) the

[1] Or the memorised recital and performance of its rites.

blessed (and Righteous), and to the Bountiful Immortals; and to the Fravashis of the saints, even to the souls of the saints, and to the Fire of Ahura Mazda, the lofty lord of entire holy creation, for sacrifice, homage, propitiation, and for praise.

5. And these we present hereby to the Fravashi of Zarathustra Spitâma, the saint, for sacrifice, propitiation, and for praise, and to that of the people[1] who love Righteousness, with all the holy Fravashis of the saints who are dead and who are living, and to those of men who are as yet unborn, and to those of the prophets who will serve us, and will labour to complete the progress and renovation of the world[2].

6. And we present these Haomas, Myazdas, Zaothras, and the Baresman spread with sanctity, and the flesh, and the milk (fresh as if) living, and lifted up with sanctity, and the Hadhânaêpata branch.

7. And we present these Zaothras to the beneficial waters having the Haoma with them, and the flesh, and the Hadhânaêpata lifted up with sanctity, and the Haoma-water, to the good waters, with the stone and iron mortars, (8) and this plant of the Baresman, (and) the timely Prayer and the recollection and practice of the good Mazdayasnian Faith[3], and these wood-billets, and the perfume, thine, the Fire's, O Ahura Mazda's son! and all objects which are Mazda-made, and which have, and are, the seed of Righteousness, these we offer and present.

9. (Yea,) we present these hereby to the Bountiful Immortals who rule aright, and who dispose of all

[1] Elsewhere perhaps, erroneously, as a proper name: or read angh*eus*.

[2] Pahlavi frashakar*d* kar*d*ârân.

[3] 'And the heard recital of the Gâthas.'

aright, the ever-living, ever-helpful, who abide with the Good Mind (of the Lord and of His folk[1])!

YASNA XXV.

1. And we worship the Bountiful Immortals with our sacrifice, who rule aright, and who dispose of all aright; and we worship this Haoma, this flesh and branch, (2) and these Zaothras for the good waters, having the Haoma with them, and the flesh with them, and Hadhânaêpata, and lifted up with sanctity, and we worship the Haoma-water for the beneficial waters; and we worship the two, the stone mortar and the iron mortar; (3) and we worship this plant for the Baresman and the well-timed prayer for blessings which has approached (in its proper place within the ritual course), and also both the remembrance and the practice[2] of the good Mazdayasnian Religion, and the heard recital of the Gâthas, and the well-timed prayer for blessings of the holy lord of the ritual order which has approached, and these wood-billets with the perfume, (even) thine, the Fire's, O Ahura Mazda's son! and we worship all good objects which are Mazda-made, and which contain (and are) the seed of Righteousness.

4. And we worship Ahura Mazda with our sacrifice, the resplendent, the glorious, and the Bountiful Immortals who rule aright, and who dispose (of all) aright, and Mithra of the wide pastures and Râman *Hv*âstra; and we worship the shining sun, the resplendent, the immortal, of the fleet horses.

---

[1] See Y. IV, 4–25, which is repeated here. Expressions are curtailed.

[2] Or the memorised recital and fulfilment.

5. And we worship the holy wind which works on high, placed higher than the other creatures in the creation; and we worship this which is thine, O Vayu! and which appertains to the Spe*n*ta Mainyu within thee; and we worship the most true religious Knowledge, Mazda-made and holy, and the good Mazdayasnian law.

6. And we worship the Mãthra Spe*n*ta verily glorious (as it is), even the law pronounced against the Daêvas, the Zarathu*s*trian law, and its long descent[1]; yea, we worship the good Mazdayasnian Religion, and the Mãthra which is heart-devoted and bounteous (imparting heart's devotion to the saint); yea, we worship the Mazdayasnian Religion maintained in the understanding[2] of the saint; and we honour that science which is the Mãthra Spe*n*ta, and the innate understanding Mazda-made, and the derived understanding, heard with ear, and Mazda-made.

7. Yea, we worship thee, the Fire, Ahura Mazda's son! the holy lord of the ritual order; and we worship all the Fires, and Mount Ushi-darena (which holds the light[3]) Mazda-made and holy, the Yazad mount, brilliant with sanctity. 8. And we worship every holy spiritual[4] Yazad; and every holy earthly Yazad (who exists)!

---

[1] Its long tradition.

[2] Or maintaining the understanding.

[3] A sunrise or sunset mountain; see the word applied intellectually just previously, also previous notes on it.

[4] That is, heavenly.

YASNA XXVI.

The Fravashis; Sacrifice and Praise to them.

1. I praise, invoke, and weave my hymn to the good, heroic, and bountiful Fravashis of the saints; (and having invoked these, then) we worship the Nmânyas, and the Vîsyas, and the Za*n*tumas, and the Da*h*v*y*umas[1], and the Zarathu*s*trôtemas.

2. And of all these prior Fravashis, we worship here the Fravashi of Ahura Mazda, which is the greatest and the best, the most beautiful and the firmest, the most wise and the best in form, and the one that attains the most its ends because of Righteousness. 3. And (having invoked them) hither, we worship the good, heroic, bountiful Fravashis of the holy ones, those of the Bountiful Immortals, the brilliant, of effective glance, the lofty, the devoted, the swift ones of the creatures of Ahura who are imperishable and holy.

4. And (having invoked them) hither, we worship the spirit and conscience, the intelligence and soul and Fravashi of those holy men and women who early heard the lore and commands (of God[2]), and loved and strove after Righteousness, the ritual truth; and we worship the soul of the Kine of blessed gift. 5. And (having invoked it) hither, we worship the Fravashi of Gaya Maretan the holy, and the sanctity and Fravashi of Zarathu*s*tra Spitâma the saint; and we worship the Fravashi of Kavi Vî*s*tâspa the holy, and that of Isa*t*-vâstra the Zarathu*s*trian, the saint.

---

[1] Dahyumas.

[2] 'Of the early religion.'

6. And (having invoked them) hither, we worship the life, conscience, intelligence, soul and Fravashi of the next of kin, of the saints male and female who have striven after the ritual truth, which are those of the dead and living saints, and which are those also of men as yet unborn, of the future prophets who will help on the renovation, and complete the human progress, with them all.

7. And (having invoked them) hither, we worship the souls of the dead [(Pâzand) which are the Fravashis of the saints [1]]; and of all the next of kin who have passed away in this house, of the Âêthrapaitis (the teachers) and of the disciples; yea, of all holy men and women; (8) and we worship the Fravashis of all the holy teachers and disciples; and of all the saints both male and female.

9. (And having invoked them) hither we worship the Fravashis of all the holy children who fulfil the deeds of piety; and we worship the Fravashis of the saints within the province; and those of the saints without the province. 10. We worship the Fravashis of (those) holy men and holy women; we worship all the good, heroic, bountiful Fravashis of the saints from Gaya Maretan (the first created) to the Saoshya*n*t, the victorious [2].

11. Yea, we worship all the Fravashis of the saints, and we worship the souls of the dead [(Pâzand) which are the Fravashis of the saints]!

---

[1] Whether a real distinction existed in the minds of these early writers, between a Fravashi and a departed soul, is hard to say. That a Fravashi was worshipped as existing before the person to whom it appertained was born, may be owing to a poetical, and not a dogmatic, anticipation.

[2] From the Iranian Adam to the Christ of the resurrection; see Yast XIX, 89, 91.

YASNA XXVII.

Prelude to the Chief Recital of the Ahuna-vairya.

1. This is to render[1] Him who is of all the greatest, our lord[2] and master[3] (even) Ahura Mazda. And this to smite[4] the wicked Angra Mainyu, and to smite Aêshma of the bloody spear, and the Mazainya Daêvas, and to smite all the wicked Varenya Daêvas.

2. And this is to further Ahura Mazda, the resplendent, the glorious, to further the Bountiful Immortals, and the influences of the star Tis*t*rya, the resplendent, the glorious, (and) to the furtherance of the holy man, and of all the (bountiful and) holy creatures of the Bounteous Spirit.

3–5[5]. 6. The Haomas are crushed, O Mazda, Khshathra, and Asha, O ye Lords! Good is Sraosha who accompanies the sacrifice with the great glory[6], and may he be present affording strenuous help.

7. We are offering saving acts of wisdom and of worship with the sacred gift of the Ahuna-vairya intoned with sanctity, and of the two mortars here

---

[1] Dazdyâi would be an infin. for an imperative; but it here refers to the Ahuna. We might say, 'Let this render,' &c.

[2] See Y. XXXIV, 5.

[3] Referring to the Ahû and Ratu of the Ahuna, but with erroneous application.

[4] Comp. Vend. XIX, 9 (Wg.).

[5] The Ahuna appears here in the MS. with Y. XXXIV, 5, the â airy*e*mâ, and the Ashem Vohû.

[6] Mãzâ rayâ; otherwise mãzarayâ, with greatness (see Y. XLIII, 12).

brought forward[1] with holy act, and with that of the correctly uttered words likewise; and therefore may they be to us the more saving in their wise significance.

8–12[2]. 13. As the Ahû is excellent, so is the Ratu (one who rules) from (his) sanctity, a creator of mental goodness, and of life's actions done for Mazda; and the Kingdom (is) for Ahura, which to the poor may offer a nurturer. 14. (What is Your Kingdom, Your riches; how may I be Your own in my actions, to nourish Your poor, O Mazda? Beyond; yea, beyond all we declare You, far from Daêvas and Khrafstra-accursed mortals[3]!)

15. We worship the Ahuna-vairya. We worship Asha Vahista, the most beautiful[4], the Bountiful Immortal[5].

YASNA XXXV.

Yasna Haptanghâiti.

With the Yasna of the 'Seven Chapters' which ranks next in antiquity after the Gâthas, we already pass into an atmosphere distinct from theirs. The dialect still lingers, but the spirit is changed. We have advanced personification of the Bountiful Immortals; that is, their personification seems more prominent, while the ideas of which they are the personification already, and to a proportionate degree, have grown dim. The name Amesha Spenta occurs: the Fravashis appear; the Fire is worshipped, the Earth, and the Grass.

To the waters, to the Soul of the Kine, and to all holy or clean

---

[1] Here the Parsi priests now manipulate the mortars.

[2] See Y. XXXIII, 11–14; and Y. I, 23, and Y. XII.

[3] See Y. XXXIV, 15. The Ashem follows.

[4] Or, 'the best.'

[5] The Yênhê hâtãm follows. For Y. XXVIII–XXXIV, see the Gâtha Ahunavaiti above, pp. 2–194.

beings, the very word yazamaidê is applied for the first time. On the other hand, many later objects of worship are totally absent, the six seasons of the creation, the five divisions of the day, the five Gâthas, Zarathustra, the Baresman, the Haoma, &c. A considerable period of time must have elapsed since the Gâthas had been composed, and a lengthy period must also be supposed to have passed before the Avesta of the later type began to be sung and recited. The chapter numbered XLII in the Vendîdâd Sâdah of Brockhaus (1850), and in the edition of Westergaard (1852), and numbered XLI, 18–35 in Spiegel's edition, seems a later addition; but it cannot be very much later, as it preserves the dialect and general features. An intentional imitation is not probable. Spiegel has included it with chapter XLI to preserve the number 'seven;' and if the entire section is to be called 'the Yasnas of the Seven Chapters,' it should most certainly not be numbered XLII! I so number merely to follow Westergaard, as do the first two parts of these translations from the Avesta. This portion should neither be incorporated with chapter XLI, nor numbered as a separate one; it should be noted as a supplement. The name 'Seven Chapters' was of course given to the pieces long after their composition.

Praise to Ahura and the Immortals; Prayer for the Practice and Diffusion of the Faith.

1. We sacrifice to Ahura Mazda, the holy Lord of the ritual order, and to the Bountiful Immortals, who rule aright, who dispose of all aright; and we sacrifice to the entire creation of the clean, the spiritual and the mundane, with the longing blessing of the beneficent ritual, with the longing blessing of the benignant Religion, the Mazdayasnian Faith.

2. We are praisers of good thoughts, of good words, and of good actions, of those now and those hereafter[1] [(Pâzand) of those being done, and of those

[1] The Pahlavi translator, as so often, first saw the proper explanation here.

completed]. We implant[1] (?) them (with our homage, and we do this) the more, and yet the more since we are (praisers) of the good (from whom they spring).

3. That, therefore, would we choose, O Ahura Mazda! and thou, O Righteousness the beauteous! that we should think, and speak, and do those thoughts, and words, and deeds, among actual good[2] thoughts, and words, and actions, which are the best for both the worlds; (4) and together with these gifts (?) and actions which are thus the best, we would pray for the Kine (which represents the pure creation), that she may have comfort and have fodder from the famed, and from the humble, from the potent and the weak.

5. To the best of good rulers (is) verily the Kingdom, because we render and ascribe it to Him, and make it thoroughly His own (?), to Mazda Ahura do we ascribe it, and to Righteousness the Best. 6. As thus both man or woman knows (the duty), both thoroughly and truly, so let him, or her, declare it and fulfil it, and inculcate it upon those who may perform it as it is. 7. We would be deeply mindful of Your sacrifice and homage, Yours, O Ahura Mazda! and the best, (and we would be mindful) of the nurture of the Kine. And that let us inculcate and perform for You according as we may, and (for) such (praisers as we are).

8. Under the shelter[3] of the ritual Order let us do so in the active fulfilment[3] of its (precepts) toward every one of the (clean) and better creatures which

---

[1] Or, we are 'purifiers,' or 'adorners.' Tradition 'spreading from man to man,' so thoroughly implanting themselves; comp. perhaps nî*d*.

[2] Hâtãm in this sense.

[3] Or, 'in the house and stall.'

are fit to live[1], with a gift for both the worlds. 9. Yea, those words and sayings, O Ahura Mazda! we would proclaim as Righteousness, and as of the better mind (?); and we would make Thee the one who both supports (us in our proclamation) of them, and who throws still further light upon them (as they are),

10. And by reason of Thy Righteous Order, Thy Good Mind, and Thy Sovereign Power, and through the instrumentality of our praises of Thee, O Ahura Mazda! and for the purpose of (still further) praises, by Thy spoken words, and for (still further) spoken words, through Thy Yasna, and for (still further) Yasnas (would we thus proclaim them, and make Thee the bestower of our light).

YASNA XXXVI.

To Ahura and the Fire.

1. We would approach You two, O (Ye) primeval ones in the house[2] of this Thy holy Fire, O Ahura Mazda, Thou most bounteous Spirit! Who brings pollutions to this (Thy flame) him wilt Thou cover with pollutions (in his turn). 2. But as the most friendly do Thou give us zeal, O Fire of the Lord! and approach us[3], and with the loving blessing of the most friendly, with the praise of the

[1] Or, 'live-stock.'

[2] Or, 'in the service of the Fire;' so the Pahlavi: consider also the occurrence of forms of var(e)z in the other sense in the close proximity. Fire temples did not exist; some shelter, however, must have been afforded. Also the dual pouruyê(-ve) may refer to Ahura and the Fire. Comp. Y. XXX, 3. Or, is it 'at first?'

[3] Possibly, 'but most favoured is he whom (yem).'

most adored. Yea, may'st thou approach to aid us in this our greatest (undertaking) among the efforts of our zeal.

3. The Fire of Ahura Mazda art thou verily[1]; yea, the most bounteous one of His Spirit, wherefore Thine is the most potent of all names (for grace), O Fire of the Lord! 4. And therefore we would approach Thee, (O Ahura!) with the help of Thy Good Mind (which Thou dost implant within us), with Thy (good) Righteousness, and with the actions and the words inculcated by Thy good wisdom!

5. We therefore bow before Thee, and we direct our prayers to Thee with confessions of our guilt, O Ahura Mazda! with all the good thoughts (which Thou dost inspire), with all the words well said, and the deeds well done, with these would we approach Thee. 6. And to Thy most beauteous body[2] do we make our deep acknowledgments, O Ahura Mazda! to those stars (which are Thy body); and to that one, the highest of the high, [such as the sun was called]!

YASNA XXXVII.

To Ahura, the holy Creation, the Fravashis of the Just, and the Bountiful Immortals.

1. Thus therefore do we worship Ahura Mazda, who made the Kine (the living creation), and the (embodied) Righteousness (which is incarnate in the clean), and the waters, and the wholesome plants, the stars, and the earth, and all (existing) objects

[1] Vôi looks as if it represented vâî here.

[2] See Y. I, 1.

that are good. 2. Yea, we worship Him for His Sovereign Power and His greatness, beneficent (as they are), and with priority among the Yazads[1] who abide beside the Kine (and care for her protection and support).

3. And we worship Him under His name as Lord, to Mazda dear, the most beneficent (of names). We worship him with our bones, and with our flesh, (with our bodies and our life). And we worship the[2] Fravashis of the saints, of holy men, and holy women; (4) and Righteousness the Best do we worship, the most beauteous, the Bountiful Immortal and that which is endowed with light in all things good.

5. And we worship the Good Mind (of the Lord), and His Sovereign Power, and the Good Faith, the good law of our thrift, and Piety the ready mind (within Thy folk)!

YASNA XXXVIII.

To the Earth and the Sacred Waters.

1. And now we worship this earth which bears us, together with Thy wives[3], O Ahura Mazda! yea, those Thy wives do we worship which are so desired from their sanctity. 2. We sacrifice to their zealous wishes, and their capabilities, their inquiries (as to duty), and their wise acts of pious reverence,

---

[1] Or, 'with the priority in the Yasnas, (we who are they) who abide.'

[2] Tem is interpolated; or shall we render: 'We worship Him' as in the F. with adverbial use as in the Greek, and often here?

[3] Compare the Indian gnā́s. The waters are wives, as is the earth; below they are mothers.

and with these their blessedness, their full vigour and good portions, their good fame and ample wealth. 3. O ye waters! now we worship you, you that are showered down, and you that stand in pools and vats, and you that bear forth (our loaded vessels?) ye female Ahuras of Ahura, you that serve us (all) in helpful ways, well forded and full-flowing, and effective for the bathings, we will seek you and for both the worlds! 4. Therefore did Ahura Mazda give you names, O ye beneficent[1] ones! when He who made the good bestowed you. And by these names we worship you, and by them we would ingratiate ourselves with you, and with them would we bow before you, and direct our prayers to you with free confessions of our debt. O waters, ye who are productive[2], and ye maternal ones, ye with heat[3] that suckles the (frail and) needy (before birth), ye waters (that have once been) rulers of (us) all, we will now address you as the best, and the most beautiful; those (are) yours, those good (objects) of our offerings, ye long of arm to reach our sickness, or misfortune[4], ye mothers of our life!

YASNA XXXIX.

To the Soul of the Kine, &c.

1. And now we sacrifice to the Kine's soul, and to her created body, and we sacrifice to the souls

[1] Vanguhîs with K4, &c.

[2] Compare azi as applied to the Kine.

[3] Compare agnáyas, reading agnayô. Or is it agnivau with a suffix va?

[4] Or, 'our sicknesses and welfare.'

of cattle who are fit to live[1] (for us), and whose (we ?) are, such as are the same to them.

2. And we worship the souls of those beasts which are tame and broken in, and of wild herds, and the souls of the saints wherever they were born, both of men and of women, whose good consciences are conquering in the strife against the Daêvas, or will conquer, or have conquered.

3. And now we worship the Bountiful Immortals (all) the good, and both those male[2], and those female[3] (by their names). The males among them do we worship, ever living, and ever helpful, who dwell beside the pious, and the females thus the same. 4. As Thou, O Ahura Mazda! hast thought and spoken, as thou hast determined, and hast done these things (effecting) what is good, therefore do we offer to Thee, therefore do we ascribe to Thee our praises, and worship Thee, and bow ourselves before Thee; and therefore would we direct our prayers to Thee, Ahura! with confessions of our sin.

5. And we thus draw near to Thee together with the good kinship of our kindred, with that of Righteousness the blessed, and the good law of thrift and energy and the good Piety, the ready mind (within Thy folk)!

YASNA XL.

Prayers for Helpers.

1. And now in these Thy dispensations, O Ahura Mazda! do Thou wisely[4] act for us, and with abun-

---

[1] Live-stock. [2] Yôi. [3] Y*a*us*k*â.

[4] A fem. noun mazdâ=medhá.

dance with Thy bounty and Thy tenderness[1] as touching us; and grant that reward which Thou hast appointed to our souls, O Ahura Mazda! 2. Of this do Thou Thyself bestow upon us for this world and the spiritual; and now as part thereof (do Thou grant) that we may attain to fellowship with Thee, and Thy Righteousness for all duration.

3. And do Thou grant us, O Ahura! men who are righteous, and both lovers and producers of the Right as well. And give us trained beasts for the pastures, broken in for riding[2], and for bearing, (that they may be) in helpful[3] companionship with us, and as a source of long enduring vigour, and a means of rejoicing grace to us for this[4].

4. So let there be a kinsman lord for us, with the labourers of the village, and so likewise let there be the clients (or the peers[5]). And by the help of those may we arise.

So may we be to You, O Mazda Ahura! holy and true[6], and with free giving of our gifts.

YASNA XLI.

A Prayer to Ahura as the King, the Life, and the Rewarder.

1. Praises, and songs, and adorations do we offer to Ahura Mazda, and to Righteousness the Best; yea, we offer and we ascribe them, and proclaim them. 2. And to Thy good Kingdom, O Ahura Mazda!

[1] Otherwise, 'understanding which protects' (?).

[2] So the Pahlavi and Ner. [3] Bezvaitê. [4] May we be rejoicing (?).

[5] Hakhemã (=-a) replacing the airyaman of the Gâthas, and throwing light upon its meaning. The form is irregular.

[6] Or, 'holy *ri*shis' (ereshayô ?).

may we attain for ever, and a good King be Thou over us; and let each man of us, and so each woman, thus abide, O Thou most beneficent of beings, and for both the worlds! 3. Thus do we render Thee, the helpful Yazad, endowed with good devices, the friend of them (who worship Thee) with (well-adjusted) ritual; so may'st Thou be to us our life, and our body's vigour, O Thou most beneficent of beings, and that for both the worlds!

4. Aye, let us win and conquer (?) long life, O Ahura Mazda! in Thy grace, and through Thy will may we be powerful. May'st Thou lay hold on us to help, and long, and with salvation, O Thou most beneficent of beings!

5. Thy praisers and Mãthra-speakers may we be called[1], O Ahura Mazda! so do we wish, and to this may we attain[2]. What reward most meet for our deserving Thou hast appointed for the souls, O Ahura Mazda! (6) of that do Thou bestow on us for this life, and for that of mind[3]. Of that reward (do Thou Thyself grant this advantage), that we may come under Thy protecting guardianship, and that of Righteousness for ever. We sacrifice to that brave Yasna, the Yasna Haptanghâiti[4], the holy, the ritual chief!

YASNA XLII.

A Supplement to the Haptanghâiti[5].

1. We worship You, O Ye Bountiful Immortals! with the entire collection of this Yasna, Haptanghâiti

[1] See Y. L, 11. [2] Or, 'abide.' [3] See Y. XXVIII, 3.

[4] Here the Haptanghâiti once ended.

[5] Of not greatly later origin.

(as we sum up all). And we sacrifice to the fountains of the waters, and to the fordings of the rivers, to the forkings of the highways, and to the meetings of the roads.

2. And we sacrifice to the hills that run with torrents, and the lakes that brim with waters, and to the corn that fills the corn-fields; and we sacrifice to both the protector and the Creator, to both Zarathustra and the Lord.

3. And we sacrifice to both earth and heaven, and to the stormy wind that Mazda made, and to the peak of high Haraiti, and to the land, and all things good.

4. And we worship the Good Mind (in the living) and the spirits of the saints. And we sacrifice to the fish of fifty-fins[1], and to that sacred beast the Unicorn[2] (?) which stands in Vouru-kasha, and we sacrifice to that sea of Vouru-kasha where he stands, (5) and to the Haoma, golden-flowered, growing on the heights; yea, to the Haoma that restores us, and aids this world's advance. We sacrifice to Haoma that driveth death afar, (6) and to the flood-streams of the waters, and to the great flights of the birds, and to the approaches of the Fire-priests, as they approach us from afar[3], and seek to gain the provinces, and spread the ritual lore. And we sacrifice to the Bountiful Immortals all[4]!

[1] See, however, Bundahis (West), p. 66.

[2] See Bundahis, chap. XIX, also Darmesteter, Ormuzd and Ahriman (pp. 148–150).

[3] Yôi yêyã dûrâ*t* points to a migration of Zaroastrianism, coming West (?).

[4] For Yasna XLIII–LI, see above, pp. 98–187.

YASNA LII (Sp. LI).

A Prayer for Sanctity and its Benefits.

1. I pray with benedictions for a benefit, and for the good, even for the entire creation of the holy (and the clean); I beseech for them for the (generation which is) now alive, for that which is just coming into life[1], and for that which shall be hereafter. And (I pray for that) sanctity which leads to prosperity, and which has long afforded shelter[2], which goes on hand in hand with it[3], which joins it in its walk, and of itself becoming its close companion as it delivers forth its precepts, (2) bearing every form of healing virtue which comes to us in waters[4], appertains to cattle, or is found in plants, and overwhelming all the harmful malice of the Daêvas, (and their servants) who might harm this dwelling[5] and its lord, (3) bringing good gifts, and better blessings, given very early, and later (gifts), leading to successes, and for a long time giving shelter[6]. And so the greatest, and the best, and most beautiful benefits of sanctity fall likewise to our lot (4) for the sacrifice, homage, propitiation, and the praise of the Bountiful Immortals, for the bringing prosperity to this abode, and for the prosperity of the entire creation of the holy,

---

[1] Or, 'for that which is past?' bavãithyâi*k*a.

[2] Dareghô-vârethmanem is treated as a feminine; see also dareghô-vârethmanô in verse 3.

[3] Have we hvô-aiwishâ*k*îm, as representing some more regular form?

[4] Medicinal springs.

[5] This Yasna was celebrated from house to house.

[6] Vârethmanô.

and the clean, (and as for this, so) for the opposition of the entire evil creation. (And I pray for this) as I praise through Righteousness, I who am beneficent, those who are (likewise of a better mind)[1]. 5–8. (See Y. VIII, 5–8.) (For Y. LIII, see Gâthas, pp. 190–194.)

YASNA LIV[2] (Sp. LIII).

The Airyemâ-ishyô.

1. Let the Airyaman, the desired friend and peersman, draw near for grace to the men and to the women who are taught of Zarathustra, for the joyful grace of the Good Mind, whereby the conscience may attain its wished-for recompense. I pray for the sacred reward of the ritual order which is (likewise so much) to be desired; and may Ahura Mazda grant[3] it, (or cause it to increase).

---

2. We sacrifice to the Airyemâ-ishyô, the powerful, the victoriously smiting, the opponent of assaulting malice, the greatest of the sentences of the holy ritual order. And we sacrifice to the bounteous Gâthas that rule supreme in the ritual, the holy (and august). And we sacrifice to the Praises of the Yasna which were the productions of the world of old[4].

---

[1] Citation from the Gâthas (Y. XLV, 6).

[2] This piece in the Gâthic dialect, and in a metre supposed by some to be identical with that of the Vahistôisti, is very old, and ranks with the Ahuna-vairya and Ashem Vohû in importance.

[3] Or, can masatâ (sic) equal 'with his liberality, or majesty,' leaving yantu to be understood with Ahurô?

[4] The later Avesta notes the antiquity of the older.

YASNA LV (Sp. LIV).

The Worship of the Gâthas as concluded, and that of the Staota Yêsnya[1] as beginning.

1. We present hereby and we make known, as our offering to the bountiful Gâthas which rule (as the leading chants) within (the appointed times and seasons of) the Ritual, all our landed riches, and our persons, together with our very bones and tissues, our forms and forces, our consciousness, our soul, and Fravashi.

2. That which Gâthas (may) be to us, which are our guardians and defenders, and our spiritual food, yea, which (may) be to our souls both food and clothing, such are these Gâthas to us, guardians, and defenders, and (spiritual) food, even such they are, both food and clothing to the soul.

And (may) they be to us (for this our offering) abundant givers of rewards, and just and righteous ones, for the world beyond the present, after the parting of our consciousness and body. 3. And may these (Praises of the Offering) come forth, and appear for us with power and victorious assault, with health and healing, with progress, and with growth, with preparation and protection, with beneficence and sanctity, and abounding with gifts[2] toward him who can understand; yea, let them appear (with free liberality to the enlightened), let them appear as

[1] Staota Yêsnya seems to designate that part of the Yasna which begins with the Srôsh Yast.

[2] Frârâiti; or possibly 'to the freely giving,' (the term. '-ti' as a dative).

Mazda, the most beneficent, has produced them, He the one who is victorious when He smites, and who helps the settlements advance, for the protection, and the guarding of the religious order of the settlements which are now being furthered, and of those which shall bring salvation to us, and for the protection of the entire creation of the holy (and the clean).

---

4. And may'st thou, (O Asha! who abidest within the Gâthas[1]), give to every holy man who comes with this prayer for a blessing, and endeavouring to help himself[2], according to his good thoughts, and words, and deeds.

5. We are therefore worshipping both the (divine) Righteousness and the Good Mind, and the bountiful Gâthas, that rule as the leading chants within (the times and the seasons of) the holy ritual order.

---

6. And we worship the Praises of the Yasna which were the production of the ancient world, those which are (now) recollected and put in use[3], those which are now learned and taught, those which are being held (in mind, and so) repeated, those remembered and recited, and those worshipped, and thus the ones which further the world through grace in its advance.

And we worship the part(s)[4] of the Praises of the Yasna, and their recitation as it is heard, even their memorised recital, and their chanting, and their offering (as complete).

---

[1] Conjectural; see Ashem below. [2] Pahlavi avŏ nafsman.
[3] Recited from memory, and used in the ceremonial.
[4] The part, 'each part.'

YASNA LVI (Sp. LV).

Introduction to the Srôsh Yast.

1. Let Sraosha (the listening Obedience) be present here for the worship of Ahura Mazda, the most beneficent, and holy, of him) who is desired by us as at the first, so at the last; and so again may attentive Obedience be present here for the worship of Ahura Mazda, the most beneficent and the holy who (is so) desired by us.

2. (Yea), let Sraosha (the attentive Obedience) be present here for the worship of the good waters, and for the Fravashis of the saints which are so desired by us, [and for (their [1]) souls], as at the first, so at the last.

And thus again may Sraosha (the listening Obedience) be present here for the worship of the good waters, and for the Fravashis of the saints, which are so desired by us, [(and) for (their) souls].

3. Let Sraosha (the listening Obedience) be present here for the worship of the good waters; yea, let the good Obedience be here for the worship of the good and bountiful Immortals who rule aright, and dispose (of all) aright, the good, and for the worship of the good Sanctity, or Blessedness, who is closely knit with the Righteous Order, to perfect us, and to incite us. May Sraosha (Obedience) be here present for the worship of the good waters, he the good and the holy [2], as at the first, so at the last.

---

[1] One might be inclined to render 'who are so desired by us for our souls.' But I think that the words are Pâzand to the preceding.

[2] Or, 'endowed with recompense.'

4. And so again may Sraosha, (Obedience) the good, be present here for the worship of the good waters, and of the good[1] and bountiful Immortals, and of Blessedness the good who is closely knit with the Righteous Order to perfect and to incite us[2]. Yea, we worship Sraosha the blessed and the stately, who smites with victory, and who furthers the settlements in their advance, the holy lord of the ritual order[3].

YASNA LVII (Sp. LVI).

The Srôsh Yast[4].

1. A blessing is Righteousness (called) the Best, &c.

Propitiation be to Sraosha, Obedience the blessed, the mighty, the incarnate word of reason, whose body is the Mãthra, him of the daring spear, devoted to the Lord, for (his) sacrificial worship, homage, propitiation, and praise.

---

[1] Of the female (feminine) names.

[2] Or, 'give to us.' The Ahuna and Ashem Vohû follow here.

[3] The Yênhê hâtãm, &c. follows.

[4] As Sraosha is the only divinity of the later groups mentioned in the first four Gâthas, this Yast would seem to have claims to antiquity next after the pieces in the Gâthic dialect. The name Sraosha does not appear to have lost its meaning as an abstract quality, notwithstanding the materialistic imagery. With Y. XXVIII, 6 in view, where Sraosha 'finds the way' to Ahura, or 'finds His throne,' we may understand that the worshippers, who first heard this Yast, praised listening obedience, or repentance, as they did nearly all the remaining abstract qualities, together with their principal prayers, and hymns themselves. The rhythm of the original has been somewhat imitated in the rendering given, as it is difficult to avoid doing so, and to avoid other objectionable features at the same time.

I.

2. We worship Sraosha, (Obedience) the blessed, the stately, him who smites with the blow of victory, and who furthers the settlements, the holy, (ruling) as the ritual lord. Him do we worship, who in[1] the creation of Mazda the first adored Ahura, with the Baresman spread, who worshipped the Bountiful Immortals[2] (first), who worshipped both the protector and the Creator, who are[3] (both) creating all things in the creation.

3. For his splendour and his glory, for his might, and the blow which smites with victory, I will worship him with the Yasna of the Yazads, with a Yasna loud intoned, him Obedience the blessed, with the consecrated waters, and the good Blessedness, the lofty, and Nairya-sangha, the stately; and may he draw near to us to aid us, he who smites with victory, Obedience the blessed!

4. We worship Sraosha, Obedience the blessed, and that lofty Lord who is Ahura Mazda Himself, Him who has attained the most to this our ritual, Him who has approached the nearest to us in our celebrations. And we worship all the words of Zarathustra, and all the deeds well done (for him), both those that have been done (in times gone by),

[1] So 'tradition.'

[2] Sraosha was not reckoned as one of the Ameshôspends at the time of the composition of this verse.

[3] Comp. Y. XXX, 4; but Ahura and some one of the Immortals, or possibly Zarathustra (see Y. XLII, 2), must be meant here. Angra Mainyu could not have been worshipped as either protector or creator. Observe the present tense.

and those which are yet to be done (for him in times to come).

II.

5. We worship Sraosha (Obedience) the blessed and the stately, him who smites with the blow of victory, who prospers the settlements, the holy ritual lord, (6) who first spread forth the Baresman, and the three bundles, and the five bundles, and the seven bundles, and the nine, till it was heaped for us knee-high, and to the middle of the thighs [1], for the Bountiful Immortals, for their worship, and their homage, and their propitiation, and their praise.

For his splendour and his glory, for his might, and the blow which smites with victory, I will worship him with the Yasna of the Yazads, with a Yasna loud intoned, him Obedience the blessed, with the consecrated waters.

III.

7. We worship Sraosha (Obedience) the blessed, the stately, who smites with the blow of victory, who furthers the settlements, the holy ritual chief.

8. Who first chanted the Gâthas, the five [2] Gâthas of Zarathu*s*tra, the Spitâma, the holy (with the fashion) of their metres [3], and after the well-constructed order of their words, together with the Zand which they contain, and the questions [4] which they

[1] Le Barsom est de cinq branches dans les Darouns ordinaires. Il est de sept branches pour le Daroun No naber, pour le Freoueschi, et pour le Gâhânbâr. Il est de neuf branches pour le Daroun des Rois, et pour celui du Mobed des Mobeds (Anquetil).

[2] This proves that the Gâthas were greatly older than this Ya*s*t. That the Gâthas were originally five seems improbable; yet they had become reduced to that number at this time.

[3] Nom. sing.?

[4] Comp. ta*t* thwâ peresâ, &c.; 'questions back and forth.'

utter, and the answers which they give, for the Bountiful Immortals, for their sacrifice and homage, their propitiation, and their praise.

For his splendour and his glory, for his might . . . .

IV.

9. We worship Sraosha (Obedience) the blessed and the stately, who smites with the blow of victory, and who furthers the settlements, the holy ritual chief, (10) who for the poor among (our) men and women built a mighty house[1], who after sunset, and with his levelled battle-axe, smites Aêshema bloody wounds, and having struck the head, casts him lightly (?)[2] (to the earth), as the stronger (smites) the weaker.

For his splendour and his glory, for his might . . . .

V.

11. We worship Sraosha, Obedience the blessed and the stately, him who smites with the blow of victory, who furthers the settlements, the holy ritual chief, as the energetic, and the swift, the strong, the daring (and redoubted) hero, (12) who comes back from all his battles (and comes from them) a conqueror, who amid the Bountiful Immortals sits as companion at their meeting[3].

For his splendour and his glory, for his might . . . .

---

[1] One of the earliest notices of the kind.

[2] Hu + angh, or can sas = to be inactive, indicate a change?

[3] This is possibly the origin of a later view which established Sraosha as one of the Immortals, to fill up the number seven without including Ahura. The original 'seven spirits' included Ahura.

VI.

13. We worship Sraosha (Obedience) the blessed, who is the strongest and most persistent of the youths, the most energetic, and the swiftest, who of all the youths strikes most with terror[1] from afar (?). [Be ye desirous, O ye Mazdayasnians! of the Yasna of Obedience the blessed[2].]

14. Far from this house, this village, and this tribe, and from this country, the evil and destructive terrors (shall) depart. In the dwelling of that man in whose abode Obedience the blessed, who smites victoriously, is satisfied and welcomed, there is that holy man who thus contents him (most) forward in the thinking better thoughts, in the speaking truthful (ritual) words, and in the doing holy deeds[3].

For his splendour and his glory, for his might . . . .

VII.

15. We worship Sraosha (Obedience) the blessed and the stately, who is the conqueror of the Kayadha, and the Kâidhya, who was the smiter of the Lie-demon of the Daêvas, the one veritably powerful, the destroyer of the world, who is the guardian and watchman over all the migrations (?) of the tribes.

16. Who sleeplessly and vigilant guards the creatures of Ahura, who sleeplessly and with vigilance

---

[1] =kat-tarestemem, comp. for form katpayãm.

[2] Possibly an ancient interpolation. Repetitions are curtailed.

[3] This verse 14 may be an ancient extension of the Yast; it may of course be taken for granted that within a certain period at a very remote time, the Yast was altered and improved.

Verse 16 may have originally formed two sections; the formula 'we worship,' &c. having been omitted.

saves them, who with halberd raised on high guards all the corporeal world after setting of the sun, (17) who has never slept in quiet since the two Spirits made the worlds, [the bounteous and the evil one[1]], who guards the homes of Asha, who battles all (?) the days long and the nights with all the Daêvas [(Pâzand) the Mâzanian], (18) nor terror-stricken does he turn in affright before (their power); but before him all the Daêvas turn in affright against their will, and rush to darkness in their fear.

For his splendour and his glory, for his might . . . .

VIII.

19. We worship Sraosha (Obedience) the blessed, whom Haoma worshipped on the highest height of high Haraiti, he Haoma, the reviver[2], and the healer, the beautiful, the kingly[3], of the golden eye, (20) of the gracious words[4], of the warning and the guarding words, who intones our hymns on every side[5], who possesses understanding and of every brilliant form, which abounds in many an explanation[6] and revelation of the word, who has the first place in the Mãthra.

For his splendour and his glory, for his might . . . .

IX.

21. We worship Sraosha (Obedience) the blessed,

---

[1] This seems a gloss; its import is correct.

[2] The renovator, as completing the progress which makes things fresh, frashôkereti.

[3] Possibly compare soma rãgan; but see the following adjective, and read as alternative 'brilliant.'

[4] Possibly 'who excites to much speech.'

[5] Comp. pairî gaêthê, Y. XXXIV, 2.

[6] Having much Zand.

whose house stands with its thousand pillars, as victorious, on the highest height of high Haraiti, self-lighted from within, star-studded from without, (22) to whom the Ahuna-vairya has come, the axe of victory[1], and the Haptanghâiti, and the Fshûshô-mãthra which smites with victory, and all the Yasna sections.

For his splendour and his glory, for his might . . . .

X.

23. We worship Sraosha (Obedience) the blessed, by whose might and victorious power, and wise conduct, and (full) knowledge, the Bountiful Immortals[2] descend upon this earth of seven quarters.

24. Who as teacher of the law will stride forth upon this earth with its dwellers in the body, and ruling as he will.

And in this Religion, Ahura Mazda has been confessed[3] with faith, and the Good Mind likewise with Him, and Righteousness the Best, and Khshathra-vairya, and Piety the Bounteous, and the Universal Weal and Immortality; and the question to the Lord is asked, and Mazda's lore (is written).

25. O Sraosha (Obedience), thou blessed one, and stately! protect us for the lives; yea, for both, (for that) of this world which is corporeal, and for the world of mind, against unhappy[4] death, and the remorseless Wrath of rapine, against the hosts with ill-intent, who lift their bloody spears[5] against us;

[1] Comp. Vend. XIX, 10.

[2] They listen to Obedience, and so descend.

[3] The meaning 'doth confess,' if correct, would show a very great degeneration from the lore of the Gâthic period.

[4] Lit. 'evil.'

[5] Bannered spears; spears with streamers.

yea, against their assaults whom[1] the Wrath-demon will set on, and Vîdhâtu, demon-made. 26. Therefore may'st thou, O Sraosha, the blessed and the stately! grant swiftness to our teams, soundness to our bodies, and abundant observation[2] of our foes, and their smiting (as we mark them), and their sudden death.

For his splendour and his glory, for his might ....

XI.

27. We worship Sraosha (Obedience) the blessed, whom four racers draw in harness, white and shining, beautiful, and powerful[3], quick to learn, and fleet[4], obeying before speech, heeding orders from the mind, with their hoofs of horn gold-covered, (28) fleeter than (our) horses, swifter than the winds, more rapid than the rain(-drops as they fall); yea, fleeter than the clouds, or well-winged birds, or the well-shot arrow as it flies[5], (29) which overtake these swift ones all, as they fly after[6] them pursuing, but which are never overtaken when they flee, which plunge away from both the weapons (hurled on this side and on that) and draw Sraosha with them, the good Sraosha and the blessed; which from both the weapons (those on this side and on that) bear the good Obedience the blessed, plunging forward in their zeal, when he takes his course from India on the East, and when he lights down in the West.

For his splendour and his glory, for his might ....

---

[1] The hosts. [2] So the Pahlavi and Ner. See also Y. IX, 21.

[3] Spe*n*ta can hardly mean 'holy' here.

[4] Âsava for asaya(?); 'y' miswritten for 'v.' Comp. gâtava (form).

[5] Reading anghamanay*au* for a*x*hê manay*au*; otherwise, 'swifter than one's thought' (?).

[6] Lit. 'not those after overtake.' Possibly 'these who all overtake those who fly with turned backs, who are not overtaken from behind.'

XII.

30. We worship Obedience the blessed and the stately, who though lofty and so high, yea, even to the girdle, yet stoops to Mazda's creatures, (31) who thrice within the day, and three times of a night, will drive on to that Karshvar *Hv*aniratha, called the luminous, as he holds in both the hands[1] and poizes his knife-like battle-axe, which flies as of itself, and to cleave the Daêvas' skulls, (32) to hew down Angra Mainyu, the wicked, and to hew down Rapine of the bloody spear, to hew down the Daêvas of Mazendran[2], and every Demon-god.

For his splendour and his glory, for his might . . . .

XIII.

33. We worship Sraosha (Obedience) the blessed and the stately, him who smites with victory, both here and not here, and on this entire earth. And we worship all the (gifts) of Sraosha (Obedience) the blessed, the mighty, and the strong, whose body is the Mãthra.

Yea, we worship (all the martial gifts) of Sraosha (Obedience) the mighty, both armed with shielding armour, and a warrior strong of hand, skull-cleaver of the Daêvas, conquering the endowments[3] of the conqueror, the holy conqueror of the conqueror, and (his) victorious powers, and the Ascendency which it bestows, and we worship

[1] Snaithis must designate a two-handed weapon.

[2] Observe how far West the word Daêva is applied; also, if Hindvô is not in a gloss in verse 29, the fact proves that a vast geographical extent was familiar to the writers of the Avesta.

[3] Vanaitis, fem. as vîspau refers to attributes celebrated in the Yast.

this Ascendency of Sraosha's (the same which conquers theirs); and that of Arsti do we praise as well. 34. And every house by Sraosha guarded do we worship, wherein the blessed friendly Sraosha is befriended and made welcome, where the holy man is far advanced (?) in holy thoughts, and righteous words and deeds.

For his splendour and his glory, for his might, which smites with victory, I will worship him with the Yasna of the Yazads, with a Yasna loud-intoned, him Obedience the blessed, with the consecrated waters, and the good Blessedness, the lofty, and Nairyasangha, the stately, and may he come to us to aid us, he who smites with victory, Obedience the blessed!

YASNA LVIII (Sp. LVII).

The Fshûshô-Mãthra[1].

1. (Introduction.) (To the increase of our homage and praise of God) we offer this service[2] which, as our defence[3], may shield us, which is worship[4] with its beneficent results; and Blessedness is with it of a verity[5], and Piety as well. [(Pâzand) and of this worship the results here mentioned are the well-thought thought, the word well spoken, and the deed well done]; and let this our worship shelter us from the Daêva and from the evil-minded man. 2. And to this worship do we confide[6] our settle-

[1] This piece in the Gâthic dialect has claims to an antiquity as high as Y. XII. It recalls the Gâthas in many ways. The increaser of cattle is identical with the thrifty tiller, and is the typical saint.

[2] The Pahlavi has sûd a partial transcription, but the word is obscure.

[3] See nipâtû.

[4] Neme with K11.

[5] Hâ + get; comp. Indian sa + ghat; or possibly from hak.

[6] 'Make mention of.'

ments and persons for protection and care, for guarding, and for oversight; (3) and in this worship will we abide, O Ahura Mazda! and with joy.

In this worship do we exercise our choices; and to it will we approach, and to it will we belong; yea, to revering worship will we confide our settlements and persons for protection, and for care, for guarding, and for oversight, to such worship as is the praise of such as You[1].

Māthra.

4. The owner of herds is the righteous (one), and he is victorious when he strikes, and thus he is the best; [(Pâzand) we therefore offer (this) service (for herd-owners[2])] for the herd-owner is the father of the Kine by the help of him who follows the ritual order; and he is the father of the holy man as well, and of the sanctified creation[3]. He is in verity the bestower of blessings, and to him[4], O Ye Bountiful Immortals[5]! we render, (and his do we make) Your greatness, Your goodness, and Your (spiritual) beauty, and let this man, the cattle-owner, approach to guard over us; and may he be our watchman together with the Righteous Order, and with store for our nourishment and full generous liberality, together with sharing of the goods[6], with gentleness[7], and with Ahura Mazda's sacred Fire!

---

[1] Khshmâvatô is often Gâthic for 'You.'

[2] Pâzand, as fshûsh*e* is a plural, and not Gâthic. Or, 'we make men cattle-owners (we invite them to be such).'

[3] The creation is mentioned in connection with the Kine. The typical saint stands at the head of the clean creation.

[4] Whose?

[5] See below.

[6] Root vi + dâ (dhishâ); so also the Pahl. 'barâ dahi*s*nîh.'

[7] Akînîh va âtashi*k* î Aûharmazd-dâ*d*. The word is difficult.

5. O Ye Bountiful Immortals! as Ye have made us, so do Ye save us, holy men, and saintly women (as we are, and steadfast in the faith)[1]. Save us, O Ye Bountiful Immortals! Ye who rule aright, and who dispose (of all) aright, for none other do I know, save You; then with Your Righteousness[2] do Ye save us.

6. And we offer hereby our thoughts, and words, and actions, our herds, and men, to the Bountiful Spirit. And may the creative stars of Ahura Mazda, the Creator, shine down on us, and round about us[3] with full herds and healthy settlements, with healthy herds and healthy men, and with all in vigour, and endowed with the blessing of the Lord. 7. Praise to Thee, O Fire of Ahura Mazda! may'st thou come to (us in) the greatest one of the engrossing interests[4] for the help of the great (effort), for the joy-producing grace of the great (interest of our cause); grant us both Weal and Deathlessness!

8. We sacrifice to the entire collection of the Praises of the Yasna, with the careful structure of their language which has reached the most its object. And we offer (our homage) in our celebrations to Thy body, O Ahura Mazda! the most beautiful of forms, these stars, and to that one, the highest of the high [(Pâzand) such as the sun was called]. Yea, we worship the Praises of the Yasna which were the production of the world of old.

---

[1] Or, 'male and female holy ones, (the Amesha).'

[2] Y. XXXIV, 7.

[3] Lit. 'may we be closely beheld by the creative lights,' &c.

[4] Allusion to *maze-yaunghô*.

YASNA LIX (Sp. LVIII).

Mutual Blessings.

1–17. (See Y. XVII, 1–17.) 18–27. (See Y. XXVI, 1–10.) 28. We worship Verethraghna, the Ahura-made, the victorious blow; and we worship the Saoshyant, who smites with victory; and we sacrifice to this Baresman with its Zaothra and its girdle (which is its band) and which is spread with sanctity. And we sacrifice to (our) own soul(s), and to (our) own Fravashi(s). 29. (See Y. XVII, 19.) 30. (The Ratu speaks): O thou good (servant of the Lord)! may that be thine which is better than the good; may'st thou acquire that which is (thine) own[1] in the Zaothra; may'st thou attain to that reward which the Zaotar has been obtaining[2], who is far advanced in his good thoughts, and words, and deeds.

31. (The Zaotar speaks): May that happen to you (likewise) which is better than the good, and may that not happen which is worse than the evil, and may that likewise not be my lot. 32. As (our) Ahû (is) excellent, so (is our) Ratu (one who rules) from his Righteousness, a creator of mental goodness, and of life's actions done for Mazda, and the Kingdom (is) to Ahura which to the poor will offer a nurturer. A blessing is Asha called the Best, &c. We sacrifice to the Ahuna-vairya; we sacrifice to Asha Vahista[3] the most beautiful, the Bountiful

[1] Avŏ nafsman.

[2] Hanayamnô aungha, a periphrastic perfect.

[3] Asha Vahista occurs as immediately suggested by the Ashem

Immortal. And we sacrifice to the Fshûshô-mãthra, the by-spoken[1]. And we sacrifice to the entire collection of the Praises of the Yasna; (yea), to the Yasna Praises which were instituted in the world of yore.

YASNA LX (Sp. LIX).

Prayers for the Dwelling of the Sacrificer[2].

1. Thus that better than the good may he approach, who shows to us straight paths of profit appertaining to this bodily life and to the mental likewise, in the eternal (?) realms where dwells Ahura; yea, may he approach it, who is Thy worthy servant, and good citizen, O Great giver Lord[3]!

2. May these blessings approach this house, which are the wise perceptions of the saints, the sacred blessings bestowed through the ritual, their guileless characteristics, together with their recognition of what is due; and may the Righteous Order appear for this village, and the Divine Sovereign Power, together with the benefit and glorious welfare (which ensues),

3. And with these the long enduring prominence of this Religion of Ahura's, the Zarathustrian Faith. And may the Kine[4] be now with greatest speed within (the farm-yard of) this house, most speedily

Vohû formula, Asha Vahista seems therefore a proper name, both here and in the formula, if one place explains the other (?).

[1] The ever-spoken (?). The Yênhê and Ahuna follow.

[2] Said on the visitation of farm-houses by the travelling priest.

[3] See Y. XLIII, 3.

[4] Gaus seems feminine here, and used collectively, and haka has the Indian sense of saka.

may the rewarded sanctity and the strength of the holy man be here, most speedily as well Ahura's lore. 4. And may the good and heroic and bountiful Fravashis of the saints come here, and may they go hand in hand with us with the healing virtues of (their) blessed gifts as wide-spread as the earth, as far-spread as the rivers, as high-reaching[1] as the sun, for the furtherance[2] of the better men, for the hindrance of the hostile, and for the abundant growth of riches and of glory.

5. May Sraosha (Obedience) conquer disobedience[3] within this house, and may peace triumph over discord here, and generous giving over avarice, reverence[3] over contempt, speech with truthful words over lying utterance. May the Righteous Order gain the victory over the Demon of the Lie[4].

6. As in this (house) the Bountiful Immortals seek for good Yasnas and good praises from the blessed Sraosha (who governs here), and as they seek for (one) good sacrifice and act of homage (more especially their own) which is a good offering[5] (to them) for (our) salvation, and a good offering in praise, together with a long continued offering of the entire self[6], (7) let not then (their) brilliant glory[7] ever desert this house, nor the bright abundance, nor an illustrious[8] offspring legitimately[9] born, nor that long continued companionship which is the

---

[1] Earth-wide, stream-long, sun-high. [2] *Isti* seems a dative.

[3] The name Sraosha had not lost its original meaning; so of Âr(a)maiti.

[4] Asha-Drugem? [5] Possibly, 'good support.'

[6] Pahl. benafsman.

[7] *Hvâthravat hvarenô* determines the sense. [8] See '*hvâthravat*.'

[9] The Pahl. does not necessarily render 'heavenly;' the word elsewhere means 'original.'

furtherance of that good blessedness which teaches concerning glory[1]. 8–10 (= Y. VIII, 5–7).

11. In order that our minds may be[2] delighted, and our souls the best, let our bodies be glorified as well, and let them, O Mazda! go likewise openly (unto Heaven) as the best world[3] of the saints as devoted to Ahura, (12) and accompanied by Asha Vahista (who is Righteousness the Best), and the most beautiful! And may we see Thee, and may we, approaching, come around about Thee, and attain to entire companionship with Thee! And we sacrifice to the Righteous Order, the best, the most beautiful, the bounteous Immortal!

YASNA LXI (Sp. LX).

1. Let us peal[4] forth the Ahuna-vairya in our liturgy between the heaven and earth, and let us send forth the Asha Vahista in our prayer the same, and the Yênhê hâtãm. And let us send forth in our liturgies between the heaven and earth the pious and good prayer of the pious man for blessings, (2) for the encounter with, and for the displacement of Angra Mainyu with his creatures which are likewise evil as he is, for he is filled with death (for those whom he has made). Aye, let us send that petition forth for the encounter with, and for the dislodgment of the Ka*hv*aredhas and of the individual Ka*hv*aredha[5] the male, and the female

[1] Or, 'welfare.' [2] *A*unghãn.

[3] The nom. is difficult. The Ashem Vohû and Ahuna follow.

[4] De Harlez, 'faisons retentir.'

[5] The Pahlavi perhaps 'diminishers;' Darmesteter, 'causing to pine.'

(to the last individual of each), (3) and for the encounter with, and the dislodgment of the Kayadhas, and of the individual Kayadhians, male and female[1], and of the thieves and robbers, of the Zandas[2], and the sorcerers, of the covenant breakers, and of those who tamper with the covenants. 4. Yea, we send it forth for the encounter with, and for the overthrow of the murderers of the saints, and of those who hate and torment us for our Faith, and of those who persecute the ritual, and the tyrant full of death. Yea, let us peal them forth for the encounter with, and the overthrow of the wicked, O Zarathustra Spitama! whoever they may be, whose thoughts, and words, and works are not congenial to the holy ritual laws.

5. And how shall we drive the Demon of the Lie from hence from us[3]? Aye, how shall we, the prophets who are yet to serve and save (thy people), drive the Drug from hence, so that we, having power over her as being utterly without power, may drive her hence with blow from the seven Karshvars, for the encounter with, and for the dislodgment of the entire evil world[4]?

YASNA LXII (Sp. LXI).

To the Fire.

1. I offer my sacrifice and homage to thee, the Fire, as a good offering, and an offering with our hail

---

[1] 'Cannibals' has been suggested as the meaning here.

[2] The later Zendiks are of course not meant, unless we have an interpolation.

[3] Citation from the Gâthas, Y. XLV, 6.

[4] Citations follow.

of salvation, even as an offering of praise with benedictions, to thee, the Fire, O Ahura Mazda's son! Meet for sacrifice art thou, and worthy of (our) homage. And as meet for sacrifice, and thus worthy of our homage, may'st thou be in the houses of men (who worship Mazda). Salvation be to this man who worships thee in verity and truth, with wood in hand, and Baresman ready, with flesh in hand, and holding too the mortar. 2. And may'st thou be (ever) fed with wood as the prescription orders. Yea, may'st thou have thy perfume justly, and thy sacred butter without fail, and thine andirons regularly placed. Be of full-age as to thy nourishment, of the canon's age as to the measure of thy food, O Fire, Ahura Mazda's son! 3. Be now aflame[1] within this house; be ever without fail in flame; be all ashine within this house; be on thy growth[2] within this house; for long time be thou thus to the furtherance of the heroic (renovation), to the completion of (all) progress, yea, even till the good heroic (millennial) time when that renovation shall have become complete. 4. Give me, O Fire, Ahura Mazda's son! a speedy glory, speedy nourishment, and speedy booty, and abundant glory, abundant nourishment, abundant booty, an expanded mind, and nimbleness of tongue for soul and understanding, even an understanding continually growing in its largeness, and that never wanders[3], and long enduring virile power, (5) an offspring sure of foot, that never sleeps on watch [not for a third part of the day, or night], and that rises quick from bed[4], and

[1] Or, 'for giving light.'

[2] Or, 'to give light'? comp. ukhshânô and ukhshâ.

[3] Read apairyâthrem.

[4] Or, 'has the quickest place.'

likewise a wakeful offspring, helpful to nurture, or reclaim, legitimate, keeping order in men's meetings, (yea,) drawing men to assemblies through their influence and word, grown to power, skilful, redeeming others from oppression, served by many followers, which may advance my line (in prosperity and fame), and (my) Vîs, and my Za*n*tu, and (my) province, (yea, an offspring) which may deliver orders to the Province as (firm and righteous rulers). 6. And may'st thou grant me, O Fire, Ahura Mazda's Son! that whereby instructors may be (given) me, now and for evermore, (giving light to me of Heaven) the best life of the saints, brilliant, all glorious. And may I have experience [1] of the good reward, and the good renown, and of the long forecasting preparation of the soul. 7. The Fire of Ahura Mazda addresses this admonition to all for whom he cooks the night and morning (meal). From all these, O Spitama! he wishes [2] to secure good care, and healthful care (as guarding for salvation), the care of a true praiser. 8. At both the hands of all who come by me, I, the Fire, keenly look: What brings the mate to his mate (thus I say to him), the one who walks at large, to him who sits at home? [We worship the bounteous Fire, the swift-driving charioteer [3].]

9. And if this man who passes brings him wood brought (with good measure that is) with sacred care, or if he brings the Baresman spread with sanctity, or

---

[1] Bartholomae follows tradition boldly here, rendering 'aushalten, festhalten an; giriftar yehvûnâni(î).'

[2] Or, 'is worshipped for.'

[3] This curious gloss seems thrown in as a solace to the Fire for the expression preceding. It savours of the *Ri*k.

the Hadhânaêpata plant, then afterwards Ahura Mazda's Fire will bless him, contented, not offended, and in (its) satisfaction (saying thus). 10. May a herd of kine be with thee, and a multitude of men, may an active mind go with thee, and an active soul as well. As a blest soul may'st thou live through thy life, the nights which thou shall live. This is the blessing of the Fire for him who brings it wood (well) dried, sought out for flaming, purified with the earnest blessing of the sacred ritual truth[1]. 11. We strive after the flowing on of the good waters, and their ebb[2] as well, and the sounding of their waves, desiring their propitiation; I desire to approach them with my praise[3]. 12 = Y. III, 24, 25.

YASNA LXIII[4] (Sp. LXII).

(See Y. XV, 2; Y. LXVI, 2; Y. XXXVIII, 3.)

YASNA LXIV (Sp. LXIII).

(See Y. XLVI, 3; Y. L, 6–11.)

YASNA LXV (Sp. LXIV).

To Ardvi Sûra Anâhita, and the Waters.

1. I will praise the water Ardvi Sûra Anâhita, the wide-flowing (as it is) and healing in its influence,

---

[1] The Ashem Vohû occurs here. [2] Or, 'falling.'

[3] See as alternative Darmesteter's masterly rendering of the Âtas Nyâyis, 7–18.

[4] This chapter is composed of short passages from other portions of the Yasna collected together possibly for the purpose of filling out the number of sections to some figure no longer known.

efficacious against the Daêvas, devoted to Ahura's lore, and to be worshipped with sacrifice within the corporeal world, furthering all living things[1] (?) and holy, helping on the increase and improvement of our herds and settlements, holy, and increasing our wealth, holy, and helping on the progress of the Province, holy (as she is)? 2. (Ardvi Sûra Anâhita) who purifies the seed of all male beings, who sanctifies the wombs of all women to the birth, who makes all women fortunate in labour, who brings all women a regular and timely flow of milk, (3) (Ardvi Sûra Anâhita) with a volume sounding from afar[2], which is alone equal in its bulk to all the waters which flow forth upon earth, which flows down with mighty volume from high Hukairya to the sea Vouru-kasha. 4. And all the gulfs[3] in Vouru-kasha are stirred (when it falls down), all the middle doth well up when Ardvi Sûra Anâhita rushes in, when she plunges foaming into them, she, whose are a thousand tributaries, and a thousand outlets, and each as it flows in, or rushes out, is a forty days' ride in length to a rider mounted well.

5. And the (chief) outlet to this one water (Ardvi Sûra Anâhita) goes apart, dividing to all the seven Karshvars. And this outlet to my river, Ardvi Sûra Anâhita, bears off its waters always in summer and in winter. This my river purifies the seed of men, and wombs of women, and women's milk[4].

6. Let the saints' Fravashis now draw near, those of the saints who live, or have lived, of those born, or yet to be born; yea, let them come near which

[1] The Pahlavi has *gân*, or *gûy*, in which latter case the meaning 'springs' would be better.

[2] Or, 'famed from afar.'

[3] Lit. 'sides.'

[4] See Darmesteter's Âbân Yast, I–V.

have borne these waters up stream from the nearest ones (that lie below as the outlet pours away [1]).

7. Let not our waters be for the man of ill intent, of evil speech, or deeds, or conscience; let them not be for the offender of a friend, not for an insulter of a Magian [2], nor for one who harms the workmen, nor for one who hates his kindred. And let not our good waters (which are not only good, but) best, and Mazda-made, help on the man who strives to mar our settlements which are not to be corrupted, nor him who would mar our bodies, (our) uncorrupted (selves), (8) nor the thief, or bludgeon-bearing ruffian who would slaughter the disciples, nor a sorcerer, nor a burier of dead bodies, nor the jealous, nor the niggard, nor the godless heretic who slays disciples, nor the evil tyrant among men. Against these may our waters come as torments. As destructive may these come (?), may they come to him who has done those first (foul evils), as to him who does the last [3].

9. O waters! rest [4] still within your places while the invoking priest shall offer.

Shall not the invoker make offering to these good waters, and with the inculcated words? (And how shall this be done?) Shall he not be tongue-fettered, if he offers else than with the ritual? Shall (not) the words be so delivered as the Aêthrapaiti teaches? Where shall the blessings be (inserted)? Where the supplications with confessions? Where the gifts of those that offer? 10 [5]. (It shall be only thus) as Ahura Mazda showed before to Zarathustra, and as Zara-

[1] Or, 'drawn up in vapours for the supply of the waters by the rain.'

[2] So the indication of the Pahlavi.

[3] î-dî. [4] Or, 'rejoice ye.' [5] Response.

thustra taught the corporeal worlds (the men on earth)! Thou shalt pray the first petition to the waters, O Zarathustra, and after that thou shalt offer the Zaothras to the waters, sanctified, and sought out with pious care; and thou shalt pronounce these words (as follows, thus): (11) O ye waters, I beseech of you this favour; and grant ye me this great one in whose bestowal ye flow down to me for the bettering (of my state), with a never-failing truth. O ye waters, I beseech of you for wealth of many kinds (which gives) power (to its holder [1]), and for an offspring self-dependent whom multitudes will bless, and for whose wasting, or defeat, or death, or vengeful punishment, or overtaking, no one prays. 12. And this do I beseech of you, O waters, this, O ye lands, and this, ye plants! This wealth and offspring I beseech of You, O Ye Bountiful Immortals, who rule aright, who dispose (of all) aright, O Ye good beings, male and female [2], givers of good things; and this I beseech of you, O ye beneficent, mighty, and overwhelming Fravashis of the saints, and this (of thee), O Mithra of the wide pastures, and this of thee, O blest and stately Sraosha; and of thee, O Rashnu the most just, and of thee, O Fire, Ahura Mazda's son; and of thee, O lofty lord, the royal Apãm-napâ*t*, of the fleet horses; aye, of You all, ye Yazads, bestowers of the better gifts and holy. 13. And this do ye therefore grant me, O ye holy waters, and ye lands [3]!

14. And grant me likewise what is still greater than this all, and still better than this all, and more

[1] Powerful. [2] Some of the names are in the feminine.

[3] Here repeat as above from 'O ye plants' to 'givers of the better thing and holy.'

beautiful, and more exceeding precious (and that is, Immortality and Welfare [1]), O Ye Yazads, holy and ruling mightily, and powerful at once, and grant it speedily according to this Gâthic (?) word: (Yea), by veritable grace let that be done [2] (?) for us which is most promotive of our weal. 15. And according to this further word again: Grant me, Thou who art maker of the Kine, the plants, and the waters, Immortality and likewise Weal, O Ahura Mazda, Thou most bounteous Spirit. And grant me these two eternal gifts through Thy Good Mind in the doctrine [3].

16–18. (See Y. XV, 2; Y. LVI, 3–4 [4].)

YASNA LXVI (Sp. LXV).

To the Ahurian One [5].

1. I am now offering this Zaothra here with sanctity [6], together with the Haoma and the flesh, and the Hadhânaêpata lifted up with sacred regularity as to thee, O Ahurian One, for the propitiation of Ahura Mazda, of the Bountiful Immortals, of Sraosha (Obedience) the blessed, and of the Fire of Ahura Mazda, the ritual's lofty lord. 2. Y. VII, 5–19. 3. Y. XXII, XXVIII, 24–27.

YASNA LXVII (Sp. LXVI).

1–4. (See Y. XXIII, 1–4, replacing 'I desire to approach with sanctity' by 'I offer with sanctity;' see also Y. VII, 24.) 5–7. (See Y. XXXVIII, 3–5.)

---

[1] See below. [2] See Y. L, 11. [3] See Y. LI, 7.

[4] The Ahuna and Ashem Vohû follow.

[5] I should say Ardvi Sûra Anâhita; see Y. LXVIII, 10, where the good waters are addressed as Ahurian Ones of Ahura.

[6] Or, 'for a blessing.'

YASNA LXVIII (Sp. LXVII).

To the Ahurian One, and the Waters.

1. We offer this to thee, O Ahurian (daughter) of Ahura! as a help[1] (?) for life. If we have offended thee, let this Zaothra then attain to thee (for satisfaction), for it is thine with its Haoma, and its milk, and its Hadhânaêpata. 2. And may'st thou approach to me for milk and for libation, O Zaothra! as health, for healing, and for progress, for growth and in preparation for ceremonial merit, for good renown, for equanimity[2], and for that victory which makes the settlements advance.

3. Yea, we worship thee with sacrifice, O thou Ahurian (daughter) of Ahura with the Zaothras of the good thought; and we worship, O Ahura, one with the Zaothras of the good word and deed (4) for the enlightenment of the thoughts, and words, and actions, for preparation for the soul, for the settlement's advance, and to prepare the saints endowed with ritual merit.

5. And grant me, O thou Ahurian One! Heaven, and to have an offspring manly and legitimate, who may promote my house, my village, my tribe and province, and the authority thereof.

6. We sacrifice to thee, O thou Ahurian one! And we sacrifice to the sea Vouru-kasha, and to all waters upon earth, whether standing, or running, or waters of the well, or spring-waters which peren-

[1] The Pahlavi translator saw the root av in this sense here with K4, 11; P6, but the form is strange.

[2] So the Pahlavi indicates with no impossible suggestion.

nially flow, or the drippings of the rains, or the irrigations of canals. 7. With this hymn from the (spirit of) the Yasna do we worship thee, and with the homage which it offers as it is the most legitimate[1] Yasna, and homage of them (all) because of Righteousness the Best. We sacrifice to the good waters, and to the best, which Mazda created. 8. And we sacrifice to the two, to the milk and to the libation, which make the waters flow, and the plants sprout forth, opposing therein the Dragon Daêva-made, for the arrest of that cheat the Pairika, and to contradict the insulting malice of the Ashemaogha (the disturber and destroyer of our Faith), and of the unholy tyrant full of death, and of the human Daêva (worshipper) of hateful malice (and intent).

9. And may'st thou hear our sacrificial chants, O thou Ahurian (daughter) of Ahura! Yea, be propitiated by our Yasna, O Ahurian one! and so may'st thou be present[2] at our Yasna; may'st thou come to us to help, as we chant our full-offered Ya*s*t, with the full offering of Zaothras.

10. If any man shall sacrifice to you, O ye good waters, the Ahurian ones of Ahura! with the best and most fitting Zaothras offered piously, (11) to that man ye give both splendour and glory, with health and vigour of the body and prominence of form; yea, to him ye give possessions which entail abundant glory, and a legitimate scion, and a long enduring life, and (Heaven at the last), the best life of the saints, shining, all glorious. 12. And to me also do ye now give it, to me who am offering this Yasna as a priest[3].

[1] Or 'virtuous,' with Darmesteter. [2] May'st thou sit.
[3] Zôtô î ya*s*tar hômanam.

(Response[1].) And to us Mazdayasnians who are likewise offering sacrifice, do ye grant (both the desire and knowledge of the path that is correct[2]), to us colleagues, and disciples, Aêthrapaitis and Aêthryas, men and women as well as children, and maidens of the field, (13) who think good only, for the overwhelming of oppression and of malice in the raids of the invader, and in face of foes who hate. Grant to us both the desire[3] of, and the knowledge of that straightest path, the straightest because of Righteousness, and of (Heaven) the best life of the Saints, shining, all glorious. As the Ahû is excellent, so is the Ratu (one who rules) from the Righteous Order, a creator of mental goodness and of life's actions done for Mazda. And the kingdom (is) for Ahura, which to the poor may offer nurture. 14. (The Zaotar speaks): I beseech with my benediction for a safe abode, for a joyful and a long abode for the dwellers in this village from whence these Zaothras (which I offer come). And I pray in my benediction for a safe abode, and a quiet and a joyful one, and a long abiding to every Mazdayasnian village, and for a succour even with my wants, for a succour with salutations of salvation, and for one with praises, O Fire[4]! and for thee, O Ahurian one of Ahura! do I ask the fullest Yast.

15. And I pray for (?) Râman *Hv*âstra for this Province, and for healthfulness and healing. And I pray for it with my blessing for you pious men, for all. And I pray for him who is saintly with (true) goodness, whosoever he may be, between heaven

[1] Or, 'the priest continues speaking for the people.' [2] See below.
[3] Or, 'this desire, the knowledge.' [4] Or, 'of the Fire.'

and the earth, for a thousand healing remedies, and for ten thousand of the same.

16-19. (See Y. VIII, 5-8.) 20. Thus may it happen as I pray. 21. And by this may I gain[1] (that) blessing, the good Blessedness (our sanctity rewarded). And we address, and we invoke religious zeal and capability, and the waters with our Yasna[2] thus: O ye good waters! since (they are) yours, do ye, as you are asked, grant splendour and grant glory, ye who are well able so to give; and do ye, O ye waters! grant (once more) that helpful blessing which was gained from you of old!

22. Praise (be) to Ahura Mazda, and to the Bountiful Immortals. Praise (be) to Mithra of the wide pastures. Praise to the fleet-horsed sun. Praise to (the star which so we name, and with this sun) Ahura Mazda's eyes. Praise to the Kine[3] (the herds of blessed gift). Praise to Gaya (Maretan) and to the Fravashi of Zarathustra (first of) saints; yea, praise to the entire creation of the holy (and the clean), to those now living, and to those just passing into life, and to those of days to come. 23. And do Thou then Ahura, as in answer to these our prayers and songs of praise, cause us to prosper to salvation through Thy Good Mind, the Sovereign Power, and Thy Righteous Order (in Thy ritual and law[4])!

[1] Or, 'the good wisdom' from the second dâ (good adjustment).

[2] Passages follow from Y. XXXVIII, 2-5.

[3] The Gâthic Kine.

[4] See Y. XXXIII, 10. Citations follow from Y. XXXVI, 6; Y. XLIII, 6, also the Ashem and Y. III, 24, 25; then Y. XLVII, 1-7. Then the words 'we worship the chapter Spentâ-mainyu from the beginning,' then the Yênhê hâtãm.

YASNA LXIX (Sp. LXVIII).

This chapter is composed of fragments: see Y. XV, 2; and Y. LI, 1 and 22.

YASNA LXX (Sp. LXIX).

To the Bountiful Immortals, and the Institutions of Religion.

1. I would worship these (the Bountiful Immortals) with my sacrifice, those who rule aright, and who dispose (of all) aright, and this one (especially) I would approach with my praise, (Ahura Mazda). He is thus hymned (in our praise-songs). Yea, we worship in our sacrifice that deity and lord, who is Ahura Mazda, the Creator, the gracious helper, the maker[1] of all good things; and we worship in our sacrifice Zarathustra Spitâma, that chieftain (of the rite).

2. And we would declare those institutions established for us, exact (and undeviating as they are). And I would declare forth those of Ahura Mazda, those of the Good Mind, and of Asha Vahista (who is Righteousness the Best), and those of Khshatra-vairya (the Realm to be desired), and those of the Bountiful Âramaiti (the Piety within us), and those of Weal and Immortality, and those which appertain to the body[2] of the Kine, and to the Kine's soul, and those which appertain to Ahura Mazda's Fire, (3) and those of Sraosha (Obe-

[1] Reading tashvaunghem (?) (comp. dadhvaunghem), according to the indication of the Pahlavi.

[2] Tashan with change of accent. So the Pahlavi indicates.

dience) the blessed, and of Rashnu the most just, and those of Mithra of the wide pastures, and of (the good and) holy Wind, and of the good Mazdayasnian Religion, and of the good and pious Prayer for blessings, and those of the good and pious Prayer which frees one from belying, and the good and pious Prayer for blessing against unbelieving words [1]. 4. (And these we would declare) in order that we may attain unto that speech which is uttered with (true) religious zeal, or that we may be as prophets of the provinces, that we may succour him [2] who lifts his voice (for Mazda [3]), that we may be as prophets who smite with victory, the befriended of Ahura Mazda, and persons the most useful to Him [4], holy men (indeed) who think good thoughts, and speak good words, and do good deeds. 5. That he may approach us with the Good Mind [5], and that (our souls) may advance in good, let it thus come; yea, 'how may my soul advance in good? let it thus advance [6].'

---

6. We praise the flood and ebb of the good waters, and their roar, and that high Ahura, the royal Apãm-napâ*t*, the glittering one, of the fleet horses; and this for the sacrifice, and homage, and propitiation, and praise of the entire holy creation; and may Sraosha (Obedience) be here (to aid us). 7. (Yea), we sacrifice to Sraosha, Obedience the blessed [7].

---

[1] Read the gloss to the Pahlavi in Visp. IX, 3, anêranîhâ.
[2] Or, bare*n*tû, 'let them lift.'
[3] Y. XXXI, 12.
[4] See Y. XXXI, 22.
[5] Y. XLIV, 1.
[6] Y. XLIV, 8.
[7] The Yênhê hâtãm.

YASNA LXXI (Sp. LXX).

The Yasna Concluding.

1. Frashaostra, the holy, asked the saintly Zarathustra: Answer me, O thou most eminent Zarathustra, what is (in very truth) the memorised recital of the rites?

What is the completed delivery of the Gâthas[1]?
2. Upon this Zarathustra said: (It is as follows.) We worship Ahura Mazda with our sacrifice (as) the holy lord of the ritual order; and we sacrifice to Zarathustra likewise as to a holy lord of the ritual order; and we sacrifice also to the Fravashi of Zarathustra, the saint. And we sacrifice to the Bountiful Immortals, (the guardians[2]) of the saints. 3. And we sacrifice to (all) the good heroic and bounteous Fravashis of the saints, of the bodily (world on earth), and of the mental (those in Heaven). And we worship that one of ritual lords who attains the most his ends; and we sacrifice to that one of the Yazads, lords of the ritual order, who is the most strenuous, who gains the most, who reaches most to what he seeks, even that well-timed Prayer which is the prayer of that holy ritual lord, and which has approached the nearest (to us for our help).

4. We sacrifice to Ahura Mazda, the holy lord of

[1] This, while very ancient as regards us, is of course not genuine in its present shape. It was doubtless composed long after Frashaostra and Zarathustra had ceased to live. It may be, however, an expansion of an earlier document.

[2] 'The Amesha Spenta of the holy ones.'

the ritual order, and we worship His entire body[1], and we worship the Bountiful Immortals all; and we worship all the ritual lords. And we sacrifice to the entire Mazdayasnian Faith. And we worship all the sacred metres.

5. And we worship the entire bounteous Mãthra, even the entire system of the Faith set up against the Daêvas; and we worship its complete and long descent. And we sacrifice to all the holy Yazads, heavenly and earthly; and we worship all the good, heroic, and bountiful Fravashis of the saints. 6. And we worship all the holy creatures which Mazda created, and which possess the holy institutions[2], which were established holy in their nature[3], which possess the holy lore, and the holy sacrifice, which are holy, and for the holy, and to be worshipped by the holy. And we worship all the five[4] Gâthas, the holy ones, and the entire Yasna [its flow and its ebb[5], and the sounding (of its chants)]. 7. And we sacrifice to all the Praises of the Yasna, and to all the words which Mazda spake, which are the most fatal to evil thoughts, and words, and deeds; (8) and which designate[6] the evil thought, and word, and deed, and which then cut down and fell every evil thought, and word, and deed. [(Pâzand.) One would think of it as

[1] The heavenly bodies are thus termed elsewhere, and the sun is called his eye. (written for ı.

[2] Possibly, 'were created pure.'

[3] 'Shaped holy.'

[4] Or, 'are worshipped as holy,' vahmya*k*a, or yêsnyâ*k*a.

[5] This figure is too advanced to be probable. The text has been disturbed. The words describe the waters elsewhere.

[6] So with the Pahlavi, referring the word to the third kar, the root of khratu, passive (?) form, with active sense. It also, however, not impossibly might mean 'cut around,' preparatory to felling.

when the fire cuts, sucks out, and consumes the dry wood which has been sanctified and carefully selected (for its flame).] And we sacrifice to the strength, the victory, the glory, and the speed of all these words (as they go forth for their work). 9. And we sacrifice to all the springs of water, and to the water-streams as well, and to growing plants, and forest-trees [1], and to the entire land and heaven, and to all the stars, and to the moon and sun, even to all the lights without beginning (to their course) [2]. And we sacrifice to all cattle, and to the aquatic beasts, and to the beasts that live on land, and to all that strike the wing, and to the beasts that roam the plains, and to those of cloven hoof. 10. And to all Thy good and holy female (creatures) in the creation do we sacrifice, (O Thou who art) Ahura Mazda [3] the skilful maker! on account of which Thou hast made many things and good things (in Thy world). And we sacrifice to those male creatures in the creation which are Thine and which are meet for sacrifice because of Asha Vahista (of Righteousness the Best). And we sacrifice to all the mountains brilliant with holiness, and to all the lakes which Mazda created, and to all fires. And we sacrifice to all the truthful and correctly spoken words, (11) even those which have both rewards and Piety within them. Yea, we worship (you) for protection and shielding, for guarding and watching; and may ye be to me for preparation.

I call upon the Gâthas here, the bountiful holy ones,

[1] Elsewhere rendered 'stems.'

[2] Not determined like the course of a planet.

[3] We should expect the vocative after 'Thy.'

ruling in the ritual order; yea, we sacrifice to you, (O ye Gâthas!) for protection and shielding, for guarding and watching. Mine may ye be as a preparation. For me, for (mine) own soul I call on (you)[1], and we would worship (you) for protection and for shielding, for guarding and for watching. 12. And we sacrifice to Weal, the complete welfare, holy and ruling in its course in the ritual order; and we sacrifice to Deathlessness (the immortal being of the good), holy, and ruling in the ritual order. And we sacrifice to the question of the Lord, and to His lore, the holy chiefs, and to the heroic Haptanghâiti, the holy lord of the ritual order. 13. (Frasha.) Let the holy Zarathustra himself seek out a friend and a protector. And I say[2] to thee (O Zarathustra!) to make to thee a friend holy beyond the holy, and truer than the true, for that is the better thing; for he is evil who is the best to the evil, and he is holy to whom the holy is a friend[3], (14) for these are the best of words, those which Ahura Mazda spoke to Zarathustra.

And[4] do thou, O Zarathustra! pronounce these words at the last ending of (thy) life. 15. For if, O Zarathustra! thou shalt pronounce these words at the last ending of (thy) life I, Ahura Mazda, will keep your soul away from Hell. Yea, so far away shall I hold it as is the breadth and extension of the earth [(Pâzand) and the earth is as wide as it is long].

16. As thou dost desire, O holy (one)! so shalt thou be, holy shalt thou cause (thy) soul to pass over

---

[1] Or, 'I would invoke (mine) own soul;' see verse 18.

[2] Possibly the rejoinder of Frashaostra, or these are 'the best words' referred to in verse 14; but the section is a dialogue.

[3] Y. XLVI, 6.

[4] Ahura speaks.

the *K*inva*t* Bridge; holy shalt thou come into Heaven. Thou shalt intone the Gâtha U*s*tavaiti, reciting the salvation hail[1].

17. We sacrifice to the active man, and to the man of good intent, for the hindrance of darkness, of wasting of the strength and life, and of distraction. And we sacrifice to health and healing, to progress and to growth, for the hindrance of impurity, and of the diseases of the skin[2].

18. And we sacrifice to the (Yasna's) ending words, to those which end the Gâthas. And we sacrifice to the bounteous Hymns themselves which rule in the ritual course, the holy ones.

And we sacrifice to the Praise-songs of the Yasna which were the products of the world of yore; yea, we sacrifice to all the Staota-Yêsnya hymns. And we sacrifice to (our) own soul and to (our) Fravashi. 19–21. (See Y. VI, 14–16.) 22. I praise, invoke, and I weave my song to the good, heroic, bountiful Fravashis of the saints, to those of the house, and of the village, the district and the province, and to those of the Zarathu*s*trôtemas. 23. And we sacrifice to the Fire, Ahura Mazda's son, the holy ritual chief.

And we sacrifice to this Baresman having the Zaothra with it, and its girdle with it, and spread with sanctity, the holy ritual chief. And we sacrifice to Apãm-napâ*t*, and to Nairya-sangha, and to that Yazad, the wise man's swift Curse.

And we sacrifice to the souls of the dead, [which are the Fravashis of the saints]. 24. And we sacrifice to that lofty Lord who is Ahura Mazda Himself.

---

[1] Y. XLIII, 1 follows.

[2] Diseases arising from filth.

25. And we pray (again) for the Kine (once more) with these gifts and (ceremonial) actions which are the best[1]. 26–28. (See Y. VIII, 5–7.) 29–31. (See Y. LX, 11–13.)

YASNA LXXII. (See Y. LXI.)

[1] See Y. XXXV, 4; Y. XLVIII, 6.

VISPARAD.

VISPARAD I[1].

1. I announce[2], and (will) complete (my Yasna) to the lords[3] of the spiritual creatures, and to the lords of the earthly creatures, to the lords[3] of those which live under the waters, and to the lords of those which live upon land, to the lords of those which strike the wing, and to the lords of those which roam (wild) upon the plains, to the lords of those of (home-beasts) of the cloven hoof, holy lords of the ritual order.

2. I announce, and I (will) complete (my Yasna) to the Yearly festivals, the lords of the ritual order, to Maidhyô-zaremaya, the milk-giver, the holy lord of the ritual order, and to Maidhyô-shema, the pasture-giver, and to Paitishahya, the corn-giver, and to Ayâthrima, the furtherer or breeder, the spender of the seed of males, and to Maidhyâirya the cold[4], the holy lord of the ritual order, and to Hamaspath-maêdhaya, the especial time for ritual deeds[5], holy lords of the ritual order.

---

[1] This Visparad consists of additions to various portions of the Yasna; and its several chapters generally follow the corresponding portions of the Yasna in the Vendîdâd Sâdah. The word Visparad means 'all the chiefs,' referring to the 'lords of the ritual.' Chapter I should be read immediately after Yasna I, 9.

[2] Or, 'I invite.'

[3] Lords because ruling as chief objects of attention during their mention in the course of the sacrifice, also, as in this case, genii guarding over all of their class.

[4] So De Harlez, admirably following the Pahl. sardîk (sic).

[5] Pavan yazisn kardarîh.

3. I announce, and I (will) complete (my Yasna) to the settlements of the future one, when the future[1] shall produce them as it were anew, and I celebrate and will complete (my Yasna) to the Praises of the Yasna[2] collected, completed, and much-offered, and to the Myazdas of the saints of the ritual, male and female.

4. And I announce, and will complete (my Yasna) to the Seasons, the lords of the ritual order, and to the heard recital of the Ahuna-vairya, and to Righteousness the Best, to him who has (?) our praise, and to the Yênhê hâtãm, the frequent chant of sacrifice[3], the holy, and ruling in the ritual order.

5. And I announce and complete (my Yasna) to the Gâtha Ahunavaiti, the holy, ruling in the ritual order, and to those women who bring forth many sons of many talents, Mazda-given, and holy lords of the ritual order, and to that (chant) which has its Ahû and its Ratu[4] (before it in the Yasna).

And I celebrate, and will complete (my sacrifice) to the Yasna Haptanghâiti[5], holy, and ruling in the ritual order, [and to the water Ardvi Anâhita[6]].

6. And I announce, and I (will) complete (my Yasna) to the Gâtha Ustavaiti, the holy, ruling in the ritual order, and to the mountains which shine

[1] Aunghairyô, a collective, or zîzanen, a participle.

[2] Here is praise to a part of the Yasna itself, although not yet recited in the V. S.

[3] Its chief word is yazamaidê, it is 'the well-sacrificed,' the word often occurring.

[4] Or, 'to him who is devoted to the Ahuna, with its Ahû and Ratu (?).'

[5] Observe the priority of the Haptanghâiti; it should be read first.

[6] Interpolated.

with holiness, the abundantly brilliant[1] and Mazda-made, the holy lords of the ritual order.

And I announce, and (will) complete (my Yasna) to the Gâtha Spe*n*tâ-mainyu, the holy, ruling in the ritual order; and I celebrate and will complete (my Yasna) to Verethraghna (the blow of victory[2]) Ahura-given, the holy lord of the ritual order.

7. And I announce, and (will) complete (my Yasna) to the Gâtha Vohu-khshathra, holy, ruling in the ritual order, and to Mithra of the wide pastures, and to Râman *Hv*âstra, the holy lords of the ritual order. And I celebrate and will complete my Yasna to the Gâtha Vahi*s*tôi*s*ti, the holy, ruling in the ritual order. And I celebrate and will complete my Yasna to the good and pious Prayer for blessings, the benediction of the pious[3], and to that Yazad, the redoubted and swift Curse of the wise, the holy lord of the ritual order.

8. And I announce, and (will) complete (my Yasna) to the Airy*e*mâ-ishyô, the holy lord of the ritual order, and to the Fshûshô-mãthra, and to that lofty lord Hadhaokhdha[4], the holy lord of the ritual order.

9. And I announce, and (will) complete (my Yasna) to the questions asked of Ahura, and to the lore of Ahura, to the Ahurian Da*hv*yuma (Dahyuma), and to the Ahurian Zarathu*s*trôtema, holy lords of the ritual order, and to the farm-house with its pastures

---

[1] This sense is most obvious.

[2] The 'fiend-smiting' is the common meaning of *vri*trahã́; but verethra is clearly 'victory' in Zend; *vri*trá also equals defensive valour.

[3] Can dahmahê*k*a mean 'the departed saint' here?

[4] A lost part of the Avesta, two fragments of which only survive.

which give pasture to the Kine of blessed gift, and to the holy cattle-breeding man[1].

VISPARAD II[2].

1. In this Zaothra with this Baresman I desire to approach the lords of (the ritual) which are spiritual with my praise; and I desire to approach the earthly lords (as well). And I desire to approach the lords of the water with my praise, and the lords of the land; and I desire to approach with my praise those chiefs which strike the wing, and those which wander wild at large, and those of the cloven hoof, who are chiefs of the ritual (in their turn).

2. In this Zaothra with this Baresman I desire to approach the holy Yearly festivals with my praise, the lords of the ritual order, Maidhyô-zaremaya, the milk-giver, and Maidhyô-shema, the pasture-giver, and Paitishahya, the corn-giver, and Ayâthrima the breeder, the spender of the seed of males, Maidhyâirya, the cold, Hamaspathmaêdhaya, the especial time for ritual duties, the holy lords of the ritual order.

3. And in this Zaothra with this Baresman I desire to approach the future one of the settlements with my praise, the holy lord of the ritual order, when the future one shall produce (them as it were anew).

And in this Zaothra with this Baresman I desire to approach all these chieftains of the ritual with my praise whom Ahura Mazda mentioned to Zarathustra

[1] Comp. Y. XXIX, 2. Y. I, 10–23 follows.

[2] Visparad II should be read after Yasna II, 8, of which it is an extension.

for sacrifice and homage because of Asha Vahista (of Righteousness the Best).

4. And in this Zaothra with this Baresman I desire to approach Thee[1], the lord, with my praise, Thou who art Ahura Mazda, the spiritual lord and regulator[2] of the spiritual creatures [the lord and regulator of the spiritual creation].

And in this Zaothra with this Baresman I desire to approach thee, Zarathustra Spitâma, with my praise, the terrestrial (lord and regulator) of the terrestrial creation, [the lord and regulator of the terrestrial creation].

5. And in this Zaothra with this Baresman I desire to approach the man who recites the ritual rites with my praise, who is maintaining thus the thought well thought, and the word well spoken, and the deed well done, and Piety the bountiful, even him[3] who maintains the Mãthra of the Saoshyant, by whose actions the settlements are advanced in the righteous order.

6. And in this Zaothra with this Baresman I desire to approach the (yearly) Seasons with my praise, the holy lords of the ritual order, and the Ahuna-vairya as it is recited, and Asha Vahista when he is lauded[4], and the Yênhê hâtãm, the frequent chant of sacrifice.

7. And in this Zaothra with this Baresman I desire to approach the Gâtha Ahunavaiti with my praise.

---

[1] It is certainly not impossible that the idea of 'invoking the approach of Ahura' was meant, but 'approaching him' is more natural.

[2] Ahûmka ratûmka, applied to the same person, the usage arising from an erroneous rendering of the Ahuna-vairya; see Y. XIX, 12.

[3] Yô, with K7b, K11, daretem, passive form; or, 'who (has) the Mãthra held.' The text must, however, be in disorder.

[4] In the Ashem Vohû.

And in this Zaothra with this Baresman I desire to worship those women with my praise who are well-portioned[1], and of good parentage, and who are stately in their growth; yea, I desire to approach that chant in my praise which has the Ahû and the Ratu, [for He is verily the one who has the Ahû and the Ratu, that is, Ahura Mazda[2]].

And I desire to approach the heroic Yasna Haptanghâiti in my praise, the holy, and ruling in the ritual order; and Ardvi Sûra Anâhita, the holy, and ruling in the ritual order.

8. And in this Zaothra with this Baresman I desire to approach the Gâtha U*s*tavaiti with my praise, the holy, and ruling in the ritual order; and I desire to approach those mountains[3] with my praise which shine with holiness, abundantly glorious, Mazda-made, the holy lords of the ritual order, and the Gâtha Spe*n*tâ-mainyu, and Verethraghna, the blow of victory, Mazda-given, the holy lord of the ritual order, and the Victorious Ascendency (which it bestows).

9. And in this Zaothra with this Baresman I desire to approach the Gâtha Vohu-khshathra with my praise, the holy, and ruling in the ritual order, and Mithra of the wide pastures, and Râman *Hv*âstra, and the Gâtha Vahi*s*tôi*s*ti, and the pious and good prayer for blessings, and the pious and holy man, and that Yazad, the redoubted and swift curse of the wise.

10. And in this Zaothra with this Baresman I desire to approach the Airy*e*mâ-ishyô with my

---

[1] So the Pahlavi. [2] Erroneous Pâzand.

[3] This sentence affords support to my rendering of âyêsê, as expressing a desire to approach, rather than one for the approach of (the Genius of) the Mountain; at the same time the latter idea may very possibly be the correct one. (Expressions are curtailed.)

praise, and the Fshûshô-mãthra, and that lofty lord, the Hadhaokhdha, holy lord(s) of the ritual order.

11. And in this Zaothra with this Baresman I desire to approach the question asked of Ahura, and the lore of the Lord (which he reveals in answer), and the farm-house of the man possessed of pastures, and the pasture produced for the Kine of blessed gift, and the holy cattle-breeding man[1].

VISPARAD III.

Beginning of the Haoma Offering; Roll-call of the Priest[2].

1. (The Zaotar speaks.) (I call for) the Hâvanan[3], and would have him here.

(The Ratu answers.) I will come (and fulfil his duties).

(The Zaotar speaks.) I would have the Âtare-vakhsha[4] here.

(The Ratu answers.) I will come (and fulfil the services which fall to his charge).

(The Zaotar.) I would have the Frabaretar[5].

(The Ratu.) I will come (and fulfil the services which fall to his charge).

(The Zaotar.) I would have the Âbere*t*[6] present.

(The Ratu.) I will come (for him).

---

[1] Y. II, 10 follows Visparad II, 11.

[2] This chapter 1–5 follows Y. XI, 1–8 in the Vendîdâd Sâdah; so, appropriately.

[3] The Ratu answers for all according to the rubric printed by Westergaard, but of later origin than the text. It arose from the fact that the several offices were later united in that of the Ratu. Originally the corresponding official answered to his title. The Hâvanan was the Mobad who pounded the Haoma in the mortar.

[4] The Mobad who fed the Fire.

[5] The Mobad who aided the presentations. [6] The water carrier.

(The Zaotar.) I would have the Âsnatar[1].

(The Ratu.) I will come (and do the duties which he serves).

(The Zaotar.) I would have the Raêthwiskar[2] to be here.

(The Ratu.) I will come (for him).

(The Zaotar.) I would have the Sraoshâvareza[3] present, the wisest one, the most correct and veracious in his speech.

(The Ratu.) I will come. 2. (The Zaotar.) I would have the Fire-priest to be here, and the warrior, and the thrifty tiller[4] of the earth, and the house-lord, and the lords of the Vîs and the Zantu.

3. And I summon the youth of holy thoughts, words and works, and of good conscience; (yea), the youth of good speech, given (in marriage) to his kin[5]. And I summon the province-ranger, and the itinerant of many arts, and the house-mistress.

4. And I summon the woman advanced in her holy thoughts, and words, and deeds, and well subordinated, whose ruler is her lord[6], the holy one, who is (as) the bounteous Âramaiti; (yea), I summon even Thy wives, O Ahura! And I summon likewise the holy man advanced in his good thoughts, and words, and deeds, who is learned in pious lore, and innocent of the Kayadha, and by whose deeds the settlements are furthered in the righteous order.

---

[1] The washer.

[2] The mixer (?), or the Mobad who attended to disinfections.

[3] The Mobad who attended to penance.

[4] The typical layman.

[5] This important custom was fully treated in the lost Nask, No. 16 (or No. 18, by another reckoning).

[6] So the most, but ratukhshathra means elsewhere 'ruling in the ritual as supreme.'

5. Yea, we summon you, whoever you may be, if only chiefs of the Mazdayasnians; and we summon the Bounteous Immortals, and the pious Saoshya*n*ts (the prophets for our help), the most correct and truthful in their speech, the most zealous, the most glorious in their thoughts, the greatest ones, and the powerful; and we summon the Fire-priests, and the warriors, and the diligent husbandman of the Mazdayasnian Faith.

6[1]. (The Zaotar.) As an Ahû to be (revered and) chosen, the Âtarevakhsha (announcing) speaks forth[2] to me.

(The Ratu [?].) So let the Ratu from his righteousness, holy and learned, speak forth.

(The Ratu.) As an Ahû to be (revered and) chosen, the Zaotar (announcing) speaks forth[2] to me.

(The Zaotar.) So let the Ratu from (his) righteousness, holy and learned, speak forth.

(The Ratu.) Thou art the announcer for us, O Fire-priest! [(Pâzand.) It is the[3] Zaotar (who is meant).]

(The Zaotar.) I will come as this Zaotar, and recite the Staota Yêsnya with memorised intoning, chanting, and praise.

VISPARAD IV (Sp. V)[4].

1. (Yea,) we sacrifice to the thoughts of the mind, and to the good wisdom, and to the good and blessed

[1] This section follows Y. XI, 9–15 in the V. S., preceding a section described as Y. XI, 59, 60, in the B. V. S.

[2] Probably in an imperative sense, or, with some, an infinitive.

[3] Read Zaotasti which contains sandhi. It seems a gloss to explain the Âthraom (sic). It is zaotâ asti.

[4] This section, preceding Y. XI, closed in the B. V. S., seems to me

sanctity, and to the good religious knowledge, and to good health (of soul and body). [At their (several) seasons, and with the presence of seasonable circumstances, they are hymned[1].] 2. Confession is to be made for the Kine; we, Zarathustrian Mazdayasnians, celebrate at the sacrificial time for the Myazda-offering, at the time for the Ratufrîti, the prayer for blessings, for the sacrificial worship, homage, propitiation, and praise of the entire creation of the holy (and the clean).

VISPARAD V (Sp. VI)[2].

1. I come to You, O Ye Bountiful Immortals! as a praiser priest, and invoker, as a memoriser, reciting (Your ritual), and as a chanter for Your sacrifice and homage, Your propitiation, and Your praise; (yea, for Yours) the Bountiful Immortals, and for our preparation, (O ye holy Saoshyants!) and for your well-timed prayer for blessings, and your sanctification, and for our victorious smiting of our foes, beneficial (as it is) for our souls, for ours, the Saoshyants, (with you), and holy. 2. And I make my offering to You, O Ye Bountiful Immortals, who rule aright, and who dispose (of all) aright! (Yea), I offer You the flesh of my very body, and all the blessings of my life as well.

3. And I confess my belief in Thee, O Ahura

to belong properly after Yasna VIII, and the Myazda offering with the Ratufrîti.

[1] Pâzand.

[2] This piece should be read after Yasna XIV, with which it is nearly identical. The language of the translation is slightly varied to relieve the effect of sameness.

Mazda! and as a Mazdayasnian of the order of Zarathustra, and in accordance with his Faith.

VISPARAD VI (Sp. VII)[1].

In accordance with the precept, with praise, and with the joyful reception of grace, with Zaothras intelligently offered, with sacrificial words correctly spoken, I call the good Amesha Spenta by their names of beauty; yea, I worship the Bountiful Immortals by their beautiful names, with the blessing of the ritual Order, with the longing blessing of Righteousness the good.

VISPARAD VII (Sp. VIII)[2].

1. We worship the (sacrificial) words correctly uttered, and Sraosha (Obedience) the blessed, and the good Ashi, (the blest order of our rites), and Nairya-sangha. And we worship the victorious Peace as the unprostrated and unmoved. And we sacrifice to the Fravashis of the saints, and to the *K*inva*t* Bridge, and to the Garô Nmâna of Ahura, even Heaven, the best world of the saints, the shining and all glorious!

2. And we sacrifice to that better path[3] that leads to that Best World (as well). And we worship Arstâ*t* (Justice) the good, which helps the settlements to advance and flourish, benefiting them thereby, that Arstâ*t* which is the Mazdayasnian Faith; and (with her) we worship Rashnu the most just, and

[1] Nearly identical with Yasna XV.

[2] This chapter should be read after Yasna XVII, which it appropriately follows in the Vendîdâd Sâdah.

[3] Possibly 'the best (better) course of that best world.'

Mithra of the wide pastures. And we worship Pare*n*di the wealthy, wealthy with a wealth of thoughts, with a throng of words, and with a breadth of actions, [for she makes our persons agile (for good thoughts and words and actions)]. 3. And we worship that virile defensive[1] Heroism which possesses men who think beforehand, and heroic men, which is fleeter[2] than the fleet, stronger than the strong, which comes to him who is endowed by God, which, when especially made theirs by men, produces one who is a freer of the body. And we worship Sleep[3], the Mazda-made, the gladdener of the herd and men. 4. And we worship those things in the creation of the holy which are the ancient institutions, those formed before the sky, the water, the land, the plants, and the Kine of blessed gift. And we worship the sea Vouru-kasha, and the stormy wind which is made by Mazda, and the shining heaven, of old created, the first-made earthly object of (all) the earthly world.

5. And we worship thee, the Fire, O Ahura Mazda's son! the holy lord of the ritual order, and this Baresman, having the Zaothra with it, and the girdle with it, spread out with sanctity, the holy ritual chief, and we worship Apãm-napâ*t* (the son of waters).

---

[1] One might consider, 'virile power which has men and heroes in the mind beforehand;' but vareti = gûrdîh.

[2] Âsyay*a*u (sic) and takhmôtã*s*yay*a*u (sic) agree with feminines; possibly because of the male qualities referred to. They might be said to be in apposition rather than in agreement with the feminine.

[3] Sleep is elsewhere an evil; a Demon, Bûshyãsta, rules it; but this is untimely sleep; see, on the other hand, Y. XLIV, 5.

VISPARAD VIII (Sp. IX).

1. With this word be Thou approached[1], with the proper word be Thou present here, Thou who art Ahura Mazda, the holy, together with the good Yazads who are the Bountiful Immortals, who rule aright, and dispose (of all) aright, together with fifty, and a hundred, and a thousand, and ten thousand, and millions, and yet more.

2. And to Him who rules the best let the Kingdom be[2]!

VISPARAD IX (Sp. X)[3].

1. (I desire to offer my homage and my praise[4]) to the offered Haomas and Zaothras, and to those also which shall yet be offered, which smite victoriously, and are foes of hatred, and following in company (as they do) with the healing virtues of sanctity, following also in company with those of *K*isti (religious knowledge), and with the remedies of Mazda, and with those of Zarathustra and the Zarathu*s*trôtema, (2) and to the offered Haomas and Zaothras which accompany those remedies which belong to the holy disciple well versed in good devices[5], and accompanying those of the itinerant also versed in good devices[5], and accompanying those likewise of the good Mazdayasnian Faith, and those of the pious and beneficent Prayer for blessings, and of the pious and good veracity, and

---

[1] 'Mediated' (?), or 'known,' madhayangha (-uha).

[2] See Y. XXXV, 5.

[3] This section should be read before Y. XXII.

[4] Supplied necessarily from Visp. X, 2; see its genitive.

[5] Or, 'sciences' (in some cases medical).

of the pious word against unbelief, (3) for information and explanation, for preparation (?) and devotion, for the libation and complete offering, for the complete recital of the liturgy memorised as well; and to those Haomas which are pungent, bounteous, holy, and offered with sanctity (and for a blessing), to those which are yet to be offered with sanctity, and which are now being celebrated, and which are likewise in the future to be celebrated, to those which are being pressed with sanctity, and to those which are yet to be pressed, (to these I desire to approach, and to express my homage and my praise). 4. And I desire to express my homage and my praise to the strength of the strong, and to the victorious blow of the mighty, to the powerful Rectitude and Blessedness, to *K*isti and the Priority for the powerful Ascendency, and to these powerful Yazads which are the Bountiful Immortals, who rule aright, and dispose of all aright, ever-living, ever-helpful, who, male and female, dwell together with the Good Mind, (to these I desire in my homage and my praises to approach); (5) (yea, I desire to approach for homage and praises toward) our Universal Weal and Immortality, to the body of the Kine, and to the Kine's Soul. (And I desire to approach) the Fire of the spoken name [1], and toward that farm-house which is sanctified and which has fields and comfort [2], and mercy (for the poor); (6) as a praiser with praise for the sacrifice, homage, which is this praise of Ahura Mazda, of the Bountiful Immortals, and of the holy and lofty Lord, for the sacrifice, and homage of the Lord that most attains his ends, and which is this praise of that blessedness

[1] Having a Yast.

[2] Here is an instance where *hv*âthra may mean 'comfort.'

which has approached us, and of that well-timed prayer for blessings offered in the ritual, (7) which is likewise the praise of the Mãthra Spe*n*ta (the bounteous word of reason), and of the Mazdayasnian Religion, and the Praises of the Yasnas[1], which is also that of all the lords of the ritual, and of all the well-timed prayers for blessings, for the sacrifice, homage, propitiation, and glorification of the entire creation of the holy (and the clean).

VISPARAD X (Sp. XI)[2].

1. I desire to approach the Arezahis with my praise, and the Savahis, and Fradadhafshu, and Vîdadhafshu, and Vouru-bare*s*ti, and Vouru-*g*are*s*ti, and this Karshvar which is *Hv*aniratha. 2. And I desire to approach the stone mortar with my praise, and the iron mortar, and the cup that holds the Zaothra, and the hair (which stays the spilling[3]), and Thy Baresman spread with sanctity. And I desire to approach the Ahuna-vairya with my praise, and the ritual prayers beside Ahuna, and the standing offices of the Mazdayasnian Faith.

VISPARAD XI (Sp. XII).

1. To Ahura Mazda would we present[4] our offered Haomas and that which is lifted up, as the most

---

[1] Perhaps 'the Ya*s*ts in the Yasna,' otherwise the latter portion of the Yasna.

[2] This section follows Y. XXII.

[3] The varesa consists (as used at present) of three, five, or seven hairs from the tail of a white bull, which are tied to a gold, silver, copper, or brass ring. This can be used as long as the bull lives, but as often as it is used it must be reconsecrated. (Haug.)

[4] The wording is purposely varied in the renderings to avoid sameness.

beneficial to Verethraghna (the blow of victory) which furthers the settlements; and that which is offered to the good and holy king, and that which is offered to the holy ruler which rules according to, or in the ritual, and we make known our Haomas to the Bountiful Immortals, and to the good waters; and we present our Haomas each to (our) own soul[1]; and we announce our Haomas in our celebration to the entire creation of the holy (and the clean).

2. Yea, we present these Haomas and Haoma-implements, and these spread mats, and these Myazdas, these stones, the first in the creation, the stone mortar brought here with the yellow[2] Haoma in it, and the iron mortar brought here with the yellow Haoma in it, this Haoma-water, and this Baresman spread with sanctity, (3) these bodies, and (their) forces, these striving Zaothras (that seek to find Thy grace), this holy Haoma, and the flesh, and the holy man, and the saint's innate thoughts, even the Saoshya*n*ts' innate thoughts.

And we present this fresh milk as an offering, now lifted up with sanctity, and this Hadhânaêpata plant, lifted up with sanctity; (4) and we offer, and present these Zaothras with our celebration, having the Haoma with them, and the milk, and the Hadhânaêpata, to the good waters and offered up with piety. And we present the Haoma-water in our celebrations to the good waters, and both the stone and the iron mortar, (5) and this branch for the Baresman, and the prayer for blessings uttered at the fitting moment which has approached (for our help in its order with the prayers), and the recollec-

[1] To the soul of the person who may be reciting.

[2] Zâiri with K4.

tion and practice of the good Mazdayasnian law, and the heard recital of the Gâthas, the well-timed prayer for blessings as it comes uttered by the saint (and for our help), and ruling (while it is spoken) as a ritual lord, and these wood-billets, and the perfume even Thine, the Fire's, O Ahura Mazda's son! and all good objects (which are ours), and Mazda-made, and which have the seed of sanctity (or are that seed).

6. Yea, these we make known and we announce in this our celebration to Ahura Mazda (as our gift), and to Sraosha (Obedience) the blessed, and to Ashi (who is the recompense), and to Rashnu the most just, and to Mithra of the wide pastures, and to the Bountiful Immortals, and the Fravashis of the saints, and to their souls, and to the Fire of Ahura Mazda, the lord, and to the lofty lord (the Apãm-napâ*t*?), and to the Myazda, the lord, and to the well-timed prayer for blessings as it rules in the order of our prayers, for the sacrifice, homage, propitiation, and adoration of the entire creation of the holy (and the clean). 7. Yea, these we make known in this our celebration hereby for the Fravashi of Zarathu*s*tra Spitâma, the saint, for its sacrifice, homage, propitiation, and praise, and to the (Fravashi) of Anghuyu (?)[1] who hath loved righteousness, together with all the holy Fravashis of the saints, of those now dead, and of those of the living, and of those of men unborn, of the prophets that shall serve us, bringing on the renovation of the completed world. 8–11, see verses 2–5.

12. Yea, we would make these known hereby in our celebrations to the Bountiful Immortals, who rule

[1] Here, erroneously, a proper name as in Ya*s*t XIII. Possibly of that Zarathu*s*trian world (period) which loved righteousness; the word occurs after the name of Z. I think that '*y*' should be 'v.'

aright, and who dispose (of all) aright, the ever-living, ever-helpful, who are good (?), and bestowers of the good, who dwell with the Good Mind [(Pâzand) for they who are the Bountiful Immortals abide with the Good Mind, they who rule aright, and dispose (of all) aright, for thence they are regulated, and thence they arose, (namely,) from the Good Mind[1]]. 13. And we make known these our celebrations as the more promotive for this[2] house, for the furtherance of this house, and as benefits for this house, because of the increase of this household, as overcoming the restrictions which impede this household, and as overcoming the harmful malice which may mar this house, to bless its herds, and its retainers, born, and yet to be born, for the saints of the house as it was aforetime, of it as it[3] stands here now, and to which we likewise now belong as the Saoshya*n*ts of the provinces, (14) [which (is that we are Saoshya*n*ts) for the saints who do good deeds, and of the female saints who do good deeds, and of the saints who do the deeds conspicuously good, and of the females likewise thus, of the saints who do good deeds upon good deeds, and of the females thus the same]. 15. And we make these known in our celebrations to the good Fravashis of the saints which are formidable and overwhelming in their aid. 16. And we make these known in our celebrations hereby to Sraosha (Obedience) the blessed, and to the good

[1] Vohu Manah certainly appears the most prominent here. They arose from the 'good thought' of Ahura.

[2] This office was celebrated in private houses by itinerant priests.

[3] Yê*nh*ê aêm might be a citation from some lost prayer. The singular aêm may, however, be taken collectively, as families are spoken of.

Blessedness, and to Nairya-sangha, and to the victorious Peace, and to Ahura Mazda's Fire, and to the lofty lord, for sacrifice, homage, propitiation, and for praise, to the entire creation of the holy and the clean. 17, 18 = Visp. X, 1, 2.

19. (Sp. XIII.) Yea, we make that known which is lifted up in offering, and which is the Avesta[1] as the holy Ahura Mazda directed that it should be said, and as Zarathustra, the holy, directed, and as I, the priest, who am acquainted with their sacrifice and homage, am now letting it be known. I who understand the lawful and legitimate Avesta[2], and the ritual prescripts (20) for Your sacrifice, homage, and propitiation, O Ye who are the Bountiful Immortals, and for our preparation (?), and for the success of our well-uttered prayer for blessings, for victory, sanctification, and the well-being of our souls, (of ours), for (we are) the holy Saoshyants.

21. Yea, we make these known in our celebrations here, and we offer them to Him who is Ahura Mazda, of all the greatest, the master and the Lord.

VISPARAD XII (Sp. XIV)[3].

1. For the offered Haomas which have been offered in libation to that lofty Lord Ahura Mazda and to the holy Zarathustra Spitama (produce) abundance in cattle and in men; and this[4] abundance is (as) the good Sraosha, who accompanies (us) with the great

[1] Âvista probably = Avesta; compare Veda. The moral and ceremonial laws.

[2] Avestic. [3] Follows Y. XXVII.

[4] Hâ seems to have a certain conjunctive force like sa in composition, 'And thereto the good Sraosha;' or is it an interjection?

splendour of sanctity, and may he[1] be here with energetic effort (to aid us in our worship).

2. We offer the wise offerings of the Ahuna-vairya intoned with sanctity and yet to be intoned, possessing their many teachings of religious wisdom (as they do), and those of the two mortars which pour the Haomas out, and which are pushed forward with precision[2], and are now in the course of being thus advanced once more[3]. 3. (And so we teach as well the many teachings of the religious wisdom) contained in the words correctly spoken, in the Zarathustrian utterances[4], and in the ceremonies correctly practised, and the Baresmans spread exactly, and the Haomas pressed correctly, and the praise, Yasnas, and the doctrines of the Mazdayasnian Religion with their recitations, and their movements. 4. For thus they may become to us more full of devices and of wisdom, and so we offer these wise ritual deeds in the creation, so we impart them with their many points of meaning while we (ourselves) still ponder them as those which Ahura Mazda, the holy One, delivered, which have (as if) their nourishment from Vohu Manah[5] and their growth from the Righteous Order, which are the greatest of all beings, the best, and the most beautiful; for thus shall these be to us the more full of wisest meaning, and more full of incitation[6], and may we be among those (who are) of Spe*n*ta Mainyu's world in that we are imparting (to the chosen) these

[1] Recall he*k*â of Y. XLVI, 1.

[2] With punctilious sanctity.

[3] The Parsi priests at present make appropriate manipulations here.

[4] In the now ancient Gâthas, &c.

[5] Compare gaêth*a*u vîsp*a*u y*a*u vohû thraos*t*â mananghâ.

[6] Or, 'may we be more zealous than any who are in the creation of the bounteous spirit.'

precepts of the wisest meaning and these incitations which are contained therein. 5. And full of wisest meaning be ye two to us, O (thou) stone mortar, and (thou) the iron one, as ye are now turned, and as ye are now being advanced[1], ye two mortars of the house, [and of the village, of the tribe, and of the province, and ye who are in this house (itself), this village, tribe, and province]; yea, in those which are ours, Mazdayasnians, who are steadfast in our worship, who appear with our wood-billets and our perfumes, and with our supplicated blessings [(Pâzand) for so may they be to us, the more full of wisest teaching].

VISPARAD XIII (Sp. XV)[2].

1. According to the ritual we worship Ahura Mazda; according to the ritual we worship the Bountiful Immortals; and we sacrifice to the sacrificial word correctly spoken, and to every Mãthra (as to a sacred word of reason). And we sacrifice to Zarathustra, him who is especially the possessor of the Mãthra[3]; and we sacrifice to the 'blessings for the saints'[4]; and we worship the 'hail'[5] addressed to the Bountiful Immortals.

2. Also we worship the three principal (chapters) uttered (in the Yasna) without addition or omission[6];

---

[1] Referring to manipulations.

[2] This fragment follows Y. XXX in the Vendîdâd Sâdah, and was written in allusion to Y. XXVIII, Y. XXIX, and Y. XXX.

[3] Referring to mãthra srevaêmâ in Yasna XXVIII, 8.

[4] Referring to the words savakâ ashavabyô in Yasna XXX, 11.

[5] Referring to the word ustâ in Yasna XXX, 11.

[6] The three first chapters XXVIII–XXX; the text has bad grammar, or broken connection.

and we worship the three principal ones without addition or omission; we worship the three commencing ones entire without addition or omission[1]. And we worship the entirety[2] of the three principal ones without addition or omission; and their Hâs, their metrical lines, their words, and their word-structure [and their recital, memorising, chanting, and their steadfast offering].

VISPARAD XIV (Sp. XVI)[3].

1. (We worship Ahura Mazda, the holy Lord of the ritual order[4]; and we sacrifice to the Gâtha Ahunavaiti) with its measures, and word-structure, and its Zand, with its questions and counter-questions, with its words and its metric feet. And we sacrifice to these as well-recited, and now in the course of being recited, as well-worshipped, and now in the course of being used in worship[5]. 2. (Yea, we sacrifice to it) in

[1] It is difficult to see how anapishûtâ can mean 'without retrenchment,' but the context seems to require it, and the Pahlavi translation bears evidence to it. Perhaps read anapashûtâ.

[2] 'The whole three first.' Some suppose the three prayers to be intended (the Ahuna-vairya, the Ashem Vohû, and the Yênhê hâtãm). I think that the three chapters XXVIII-XXX are meant. As the piece follows those three chapters in the Vendîdâd Sâdah, so its expressions indicate a reference to them. This might tend to show that the Ahunavaiti was at one time, if not originally, divided at this place.

[3] This fragment was written in evident allusion to the entire Ahunavaiti, which it follows in the Vendîdâd Sâdah. It expresses the veneration acquired by the first Gâtha long after its composition.

[4] From the Vendîdâd Sâdah.

[5] Frâyazentãm may be a metaplasm; otherwise 'of the sacrificers.'

its own 'wisdom'[1], in its own 'clearness'[2], in its own 'loving intention'[2], in its sovereignty, and its own ritual order, and its 'acquired boon'[2], which is also that given by Ahura Mazda for the promotion of piety, for that thought which originates from the 'heart-devoted self'[2].

3. (Sp. Chapter XVII.) Also we worship the Ahuna-vairya, the holy lord of the ritual order, the holy lord with its Ahû and its Ratu [(Pâzand); for He is the one with the title Ahû and Ratu, who is Ahura Mazda[3]]. 4. And we sacrifice to the constituent parts of the Gâtha Ahunavaiti, to its chapters, and its metrical lines, its words, and word-structure, [and to its heard-recital, and memorised recital, its continuous and its steadfast offering].

VISPARAD XV (Sp. XVIII)[4].

1. Hold your feet in readiness, and your two hands, and your understandings[5], O ye Zarathustrian Mazdayasnians! for the well-doing of lawful deeds in accordance with the sacred Order, and for the avoidance of the unlawful and evil deeds which are contrary to the ritual. Let the good deeds for the furtherance of husbandry be done[6] here. Render ye the needy rich[7]. 2. Let Sraosha (Obedience) be present here for the worship of Ahura Mazda,

[1] Dãmi with K4. Possibly in their own house (dãmi=dani).

[2] These words probably allude severally, say, to dãm in Y. XXXI, 7, *k*ithrâ in Y. XXXI, 22, zaoshê in Y. XXXIII, 2, 10, âyaptâ in Y. XXVIII, 8, to zarzdau in Y. XXXI, 1.

[3] Erroneous.

[4] This piece is a later composed prelude to the Haptanghâiti, which it precedes in the Vendîdâd Sâdah.

[5] Sursum corda! [6] Comp. gavôi verezyâtãm, Y. XLVIII, 5.

[7] 'Place the needy with those without need.'

the most helpful, and the holy, who is so desired by us in the pronunciation, and for the service, and the pondering[1] of the Yasna Haptanghâiti, for the heart's devotion to it, for its memorisation, and its victorious and holy recital (or for the victorious saint), without addition or omission, (3) which has been intoned, and which shall yet be uttered as great, powerful, smiting with victory, separate from harmful malice, for the pronunciation of victorious words for Ahura Mazda's Fire. (4, 5 are identical with Visp. IX, 6, 7.)

VISPARAD XVI (Sp. XIX)[2].

1. And we worship the Fire here, Ahura Mazda's son, and the Yazads having the seed of fire in them, and the Rashnus having the seed of fire[3] in them; and we worship the Fravashis of the saints. And we worship Sraosha who smites with victory, and the holy man, and the entire creation of the holy (and the clean). 2. And we worship the Blessedness and the Fravashi of Zarathustra Spitâma, the saint. And we worship the saints and their blessed Fravashis (as of one). And we worship all their Fravashis (as considered each apart), and those of the saints within the Province, and those of the saints without the Province; yea, we worship the Fravashis of holy men and holy women (wherever they may be, those devoted to the Order of the Faith). And we sacrifice to those whose (service)

[1] Possibly mãzdâtaêka.

[2] This piece follows the Haptanghâiti in the Vendîdâd Sâdah; it was intended as a sequel to it.

[3] Having the power to propagate its worship, maintaining it unextinguished. De Harlez makes the admirable suggestion, 'bright as flame'; but the Pahlavi renders tokhmak.

for us in the Yasna Ahura Mazda, the holy, has known as the better [1], and of these Zarathustra is the living chief [2] and master. And we sacrifice to the fields and the waters, the lands and the plants, and to the constituent parts of the Yasna Haptanghâiti, its chapters, its metred lines, its words, and word-structure.

VISPARAD XVII (Sp. XX) [3].

And we strive after the good thoughts, words, and deeds inculcated in the Yasna Haptanghâiti. A blessing is the Right (called) the Best, (there is) weal; (there is) weal for this (man) when toward Righteousness Best (there is) right.

VISPARAD XVIII (Sp. XXI) [4].

1. We worship Ahura Mazda with the usta [5]. And we worship the Amesha Spenta with the usta, and the holy man, the saint. And we worship the prior world of the holy (and of the clean) with an usta, and the state of weal and salvation for the holy man (the saint). 2. And we worship that life-long state of blessedness (for the holy) which is the evil man's calamity [6]; yea, we worship his eternal [7] salvation, and with the salvation prayer. And we sacrifice to every saint who

---

[1] Comp. Y. LI, 22.

[2] Anghuska ratuska here referred to the same person; comp. ahû.

[3] An addition to chapter XVI.

[4] This piece having reference to various expressions in the Gâtha Ustavaiti, follows it in the Vendîdâd Sâdah.

[5] Referring to ustâ in Y. XLIII, 1.

[6] See Y. XLV, 7.

[7] Akaranem=the eternal thing; otherwise an adjective of two terminations; or, finally, read -ãm.

exists, who is now coming into existence, and who shall exist in future.

VISPARAD XIX (Sp. XXII)[1].

1. We worship Ahura Mazda the bountiful; and we worship the Bountiful Immortals (saying the Spenta). And we sacrifice to the bountiful saint, and to the bountiful anticipative understanding[2]. Also we sacrifice to the good and bountiful Âramaiti (the ready mind). And we worship her together with[3] the bountiful creatures in the creation of the pure. And we sacrifice to the holy creatures who have intelligence as their first[4], (to those foremost in their mind). And we worship the omniscient understanding, and Him who is Ahura Mazda (Himself). 2. And we sacrifice to the shining sun, which is the highest of the high; yea, we worship the sun together with the Bountiful Immortals, and the Mãthras with their good ceremonies[5]. Also we sacrifice to the glorious achievements, and to this glory (which we have gained). And we sacrifice to the herds which have the Fire and its blessings[6]. Also we worship the holy benefit which is so widely

---

[1] The word spenta throughout alludes to the Gâtha Spentâ-mainyu, but it is of course not without grammatical application.

[2] In the Bundahis especially referred to Ahura.

[3] Or, 'together with the bountiful creatures we worship the holy creatures.'

[4] This expression may have been accidentally determined by the position of the word manô in the Ahuna-vairya formula; see Y. XIX, 12.

[5] Or, 'the well-fulfilled.'

[6] 'Fire-made' is unintelligible; 'fire gifts-having' may refer to the flocks and herds, as expressing the source of that prosperity which is represented by the holy Fire.

diffused[1], and that wisdom which is the bounteous Âramaiti, whose are the laws[2] of the Righteous Order, and of those holy creatures who have Righteousness as their first.

VISPARAD XX (Sp. XXIII)[3].

1. (Homage to the Gâtha Vohu-khshathra[4]! We sacrifice to the Vohu-khshathra), (the good kingdom) even the Khshathra-vairya, the kingdom to be desired; and we sacrifice to the iron-founding[5], and to the (sacrificial) words[6] correctly spoken which smite (the foe) with victory, and which hold the Daêvas subject.

And we worship that reward and that health, that healing and that progress, that growth and that victorious smiting[7] (2) which are between the Vohu-khshathra and the Vahistôisti[8], (and which are acquired by us) by the memorised recital of the good thoughts, good words, and good deeds, for the withstanding of evil thoughts, and words, and deeds; yea, for the undoing of all treacherous thoughts (directed) against me, and of all false words, and unfair deeds. 3. [And we sacrifice to the later Yasna, the heroic Haptanghâiti[9], (and which as it recurs becomes) the holy ritual chief.]

---

[1] Pahl. fravaft sûd.   [2] Dâthra with K4.

[3] This piece from the later Avesta follows Y. LI, in the Vendîdâd Sâdah.

[4] From the Vendîdâd Sâdah.

[5] Associated with this Gâtha from Y. LI, 9.

[6] Compare Y. LI, 3.   [7] Y. LI, 9; also perhaps Y. LIII, 8, 9.

[8] Between; that is, described in the space between the Vohu-khshathra and the Vahistôisti, i.e. in Y. LII. See hamisteê in Y. LII, 4, and paitistâteê in Visp. XX, 2.

[9] This would seem misplaced; perhaps Y. XLII is meant, which follows the Haptanghâiti.

VISPARAD XXI (Sp. XXIV).

1. We strive earnestly, and we take up our Yasna and our homage to the good waters, and to the fertile fruit-trees (which bear as of themselves), and to the Fravashis of the saints; yea, we take up our Yasna, and our homage earnestly to those beings which are (so) good, the waters, and the trees, and the Fravashis of the saints, (2) and to the Kine, and to Gaya (Maretan), and to the Mãthra Spe*n*ta (the bounteous word-of-reason), the holy, which works (within and for us with effect), to these we take up our Yasnas and our homage with earnest zeal, and to Thee, O Ahura Mazda! and to thee, O Zarathu*s*tra, we do the same; and to thee, O lofty lord (the Apãm-napâ*t*), and to the Bountiful Immortals. 3. And we sacrifice to the listening (that hears our prayers) and to that mercy, and to the hearing of (our spoken) homage, and to that mercy which is (shown in response to our offered) praise. And we sacrifice to the frârâiti vîdushê, which is contained in the piece *hv*âdaênâi*s* ashaonîs; and we sacrifice to 'the good praise which is without hypocrisy, and which has no malice (as its end)'; and we sacrifice to the later Yasna and to its offering; and we sacrifice to the chapters of the later Yasna, and to its metrical lines, its words, and word-structure.

VISPARAD XXII (Sp. XXV).

With this chant (fully) chanted, and which is for the Bountiful Immortals and the holy Saoshya*n*ts (who are the prophets who shall serve us), and by means of these (ceremonial) actions, which are (of all) the best, we desire to utter our supplications for the Kine. It is that chant which the saint has recognised as good and fruitful of blessed gifts, and which the sinner does not know[1]. May we never reach that (ill-luck that the sinner) may outstrip us (in our chanting), not in the matter of a plan (thought out), or of words (delivered), or ceremonies (done[2]), nor yet in any offering whatever when he (?) approaches (us for harm).

VISPARAD XXIII (Sp. XXVI)[3].

1. We worship Ahura Mazda as the best[4] (worship to be offered in our gifts). We worship the Amesha Spe*n*ta (once more, and as) the best. We worship Asha Vahi*s*ta (who is Righteousness the Best). And we sacrifice to those (prayers) which are evident as the best; that is, the Praises of the Yasnas.

Also we sacrifice to that best wish, which is that of Asha Vahi*s*ta, and we worship Heaven, which is the best world of the saints, bright and all-glorious; and we sacrifice likewise to that best approach which leads to[5] it. 2. And we sacrifice to that reward,

[1] The parties are divided by knowledge and ignorance (compare the Gnosis). See Y. XXXI, 12

[2] Not in thought, word, or deed may we reach (his) priority in progress.

[3] This piece from the later Avesta follows Y. LIII, in the Vendîdâd Sâdah, and has reference to its expressions.

[4] It is an important suggestion which holds vahi*s*tem as equal to 'saying vahi*s*tem,' in allusion to the Vahi*s*tâ î*s*ti*s*; but as the word is inflected further on (see vahi*s*tahê), and as it moreover once applies to Asha, as Asha Vahi*s*ta, it is better to render it as having adjective application throughout, being none the less, of course, an intentional echo of the first word of Y. LIII, 1.

[5] Or, 'of it.'

health, healing, furtherance, and increase, and to that victory which is within[1] the two, the Ahuna-vairya and the Airy*e*mâ-ishyô, through the memorised recital of the good thoughts, words, and deeds (which they enjoin).

---

[1] Possibly 'between them,' meaning the Gâthas which are so placed.

ÂFRÎNAGÂN.

ÂFRÎNAGÂN.

As to the present use of these blessings, says Haug (ed. West): 'Âfrînagân are blessings which are to be recited over a meal consisting of wine, milk, and fruits, to which an angel, or the spirit of a deceased person, is invited, and in whose honour the meal is prepared. After the consecration (which only a priest can perform) is over, the meal is eaten by those who are present. The performance of these Âfrînagân is required of every Parsi at certain fixed seasons of the year. These are the six Gahanbârs, each lasting five days (at the six original seasons of the year) for which the Âfrînagân Gahanbâr is intended, the five Gâtha-days (the five last days of the year), during which the Âfrînagân Gâtha must be used; and, lastly, the third day (Ardibahist) of the first month (Fravardin) in the year, at which the performance of Âfrînagân Rapithwin, devoted to the spirit presiding over the southern quarter (who is the guardian of the way to paradise), is enjoined to every Parsi whose soul wants to pass the *K*invad after death.' (Essays, 2nd edition, page 224.)

I. ÂFRÎN[-AGÂN] GAHANBÂR[1].

1. I confess myself a Mazda-worshipper, and of Zarathustra's order, a foe of the Daêvas, devoted to the lore of the Lord, for the holy Hâvani[1], the regulator of the ritual order (and its lord in its turn), for its sacrifice, homage, propitiation, and praise; (and I confess myself) for Sâvanghi and for Vîsya, the holy lords of the ritual order, for their sacrifice, homage,

[1] The Âfrîn for the morning hours from 6 to 10.

propitiation, and praise, and for that of the Asnya, the day-lords of the days during daylight, and of the days in their length, for the Mâhya, month-lords, and the Yâirya, year-lords, and for those of the especial seasons, and for the worship, homage, propitiation, and praise of that lofty lord who is the Ritual Righteousness (itself); yea, for the worship, homage, propitiation, and praise of the lords of the days, months, years, and seasons—for those lords of the ritual order who are of all the greatest, who are the regulators of the ritual at the time of Hâvani.

2. To Maidhyô-zaremya [1], the lord [or to Maidhyô-shema [1], the lord, or to Paitishahya [1], the lord, or to Ayâthrima [1], Maidhyâirya [1], or Hamaspathmaêdhaya], be propitiation, homage, and praise.

3. O ye Mazdayasnians who are here present! offer ye [2] this ritual service, and present ye the Myazda which is that of the Maidhyô-zaremaya, taking a piece of sound flesh from a choice beast, with a full flow of milk.

4. If ye are able to do this, (well); if ye are unable to do it, ye may take then (a portion) of some liquor of equal value, it matters not which it is, and have it consumed as it is proper; and so be ye discreet from your obedience, most correctly faithful in your speech, most saintly from your sanctity, best ordered in your exercise of power, least straitened by oppressions, heart-easy with rejoicings, most merciful of givers, most helpful to the poor, fulfilling most the ritual, the blest and longed-for Asha, (coy ?) riches woman-minded (?) bringing (as reward). If ye can do this

[1] The name of the season at the time present, when the text is recited, is to be used.

[2] Bring ye, O these Mazdayasnians!

and with vigour, (well); (5) if not, bring wood to the Ratu's house. It matters not what kind, so it be well cut, and very dry, and in loads of fitting size. If that is possible, (well); if not, then let a man bring wood to the Ratu's dwelling, and heap it up as high as the ear, or to reach the fore-shoulder, or with the fore-arm measure, (or at least as high as the end of the hanging hand). If that is possible, (well); (6) but if it has not been possible, then let the worshipper (with the mind's offering) ascribe the power to him who rules the best, Ahura, (saying[1]): Wherefore for this cause verily we offer and ascribe the Sovereign Power to Ahura Mazda, who rules the best, and to Righteousness (the ritual and moral Order), and we complete our sacrifice to them. Thus is the Myazda offered with the well-timed prayer for blessings.

7. In case that a man does not give of the first Myazda which is that of the Maidhyô-zaremaya, O Spitama Zarathu*s*tra! the Ratu that has the right to that Myazda, and who has this person under his guidance, expels[2] that (false) disciple who has not his Myazda with him, as a man that does not worship, from the midst of the Mazda-worshippers. 8. In the case that a man does not give of the second Myazda, O Spitama Zarathu*s*tra! which is that of the Maidhyô-shema, then let[2] the Ratu to whom the Myazda should come, and who has the person under his guidance, expel that disciple, since he comes without his Myazda, as he would a man who refuses to recite his vows, from among the number of the Mazda-

[1] Or, 'because we offer.'

[2] Not 'renders him (detected) among the Mazdayasnians;' compare for form a*n*tarê-mrûyê; see also fra-dasti and fra-perenaoiti; also the present may be used for the imperative.

worshippers. 9. In the case that a man does not give of the third Myazda, O Spitama Zarathustra! which is that of Paitishahya, then let the Ratu who ought to receive that Myazda, and who has had the person under his guidance, expel that disciple which brings no Myazda, as a detected[1] reprobate, from among the number of the Mazdayasnians. 10. In case that a man does not offer of the fourth Myazda, O Spitama Zarathustra! which is that of the Ayâthrima, let the Ratu who ought to receive that Myazda, and who has the person under his guidance, expel that disciple, since he brings no Myazda, as a refuse[2] beast from among the number of the Mazdayasnians. 11. In the case that a man does not give of the fifth Myazda, which is that of the Maidhyâirya, then let the Ratu to whom that Myazda belongs as a perquisite, and who has that person under his guidance, expel him, since he brings no Myazda, as an alien[3], from among the number of the Mazdayasnians. 12. In case that a man does not give of the sixth Myazda, which is that of the Hamaspathmaêdhaya, O Spitama Zarathustra! let the Ratu to whom that Myazda belongs as a perquisite, and who has this person under his discipline to learn him the lore of Ahura, expel him, (as ignorant) since he brings no Myazda, from among the number of the Mazdayasnians. 13. And let him decry him afterwards without hesitation[4], and drive[5] him out; and let that Ratu lay upon him after-

[1] Possibly 'having a breast burnt by the ordeal,' and so 'detected;' or 'hot-breasted, vehement' (?); comp. úras.

[2] It may be '(his) excluded beast,' or 'his stray beast' (?).

[3] Or, possibly, 'he is rejected when offering himself as arrived from the settlements' (?).

[4] 'Without recoiling.'

[5] Syazdayôit.

wards the expiating deeds without reserve; and in accordance with these rules, let the disciple treat the Ratu. (Let him beware of failure to bring his Myazda, or if he fails let the disciple bear, as is befitting, what is due.) A blessing is Righteousness (called) the Best, it is weal, it is weal for this (man) when toward Righteousness Best there is right. 14. I bless with my prayer the royal Province-chiefs (who are faithful worshippers) of Ahura Mazda, the resplendent, the glorious, (beseeching) for superior strength for them, and for more important victory, and more influential rule, and desiring for them further authoritative power, and helpful support, and long duration to their reign, and the prolonged vitality of their frames, and health. 15. And I pray in my benediction for strength well-shaped and stately of growth, and which smites victoriously, Ahura-made, and crushing, and for an ascendency abundantly subduing all who are filled with furious hate, assaulting the evil-minded enemies, and destroying, as if at once, the deadly, godless[1] foes.

16. And I pray in my blessing that he (the province-governor) may conquer in victorious battles every malicious foe, and each malignant, profane in thoughts, and words, and actions, (17) that he may indeed be constantly victorious in his own religious thoughts, and words, and deeds, and unvarying in the smiting of every foe, and of every Daêva-worshipper, and that he may, as he proceeds[2], be well rewarded, and of good repute, possessing a far-foreseeing preparation of the soul. 18. And I pray with blessings thus: Live thou long and blessed be

[1] Unfriendly and untrue; '* avratyá.'

[2] Recall yôi zaze*n*tê vanghâu sravahî.

thou, 'hail' to thee; live for the aid of holy men, and for the crushing of the evil; and I pray for Heaven (for thee) the best world of the saints, shining, all glorious. And thus may it happen as I pray—[1]. 19. And I bless in my prayer the sacrifice, and homage, and the strength, and swiftness of the day-lords during daylight, and of the lords of the days in their length, of the month-lords, and the year-lords, and of the lords of the seasons[2] (in their course), and for the worship, homage, propitiation, and praise of the lofty lord who is the Righteous Ritual itself, and of those lords of the ritual who are of all the greatest, and who are the lords of the ritual at the time of Hâvani, for Maidhyô-zaremaya the lord, [(or) for Maidhyô-shema the lord, (or) for Paitishahya[2] the lord, or for Ayâthrima, Maidhyâirya, or Hamaspathmaêdhaya[2+3]].

II. ÂFRÎN[-AGÂN][4] GÂTHA[4].

1. As the Ahû is (revered and) to be chosen, so (is) the Ratu (one who rules) from the Righteous Order, a creator of mental goodness, and of life's actions done for Ahura, and the Kingdom (is) to Mazda, which to the poor may offer a nurturer.

I confess myself a Mazda-worshipper—for the praise of Ahura Mazda, the resplendent, the glorious, and of the Bountiful Immortals, for the bountiful and

---

[1] See Y. XXXV, 2. The Ahuna follows.

[2] The name varies with the season in which the sacrifice is made.

[3] As in 18.

[4] Recited during the days called after the Gâthas, the last five of the year. A long period of time must have elapsed since the Gâthas were composed, as they probably were not originally 'five.' and yet seem to have been only remembered as such.

holy Gâthas which rule in the ritual order. (Propitiation and praise be) to the Gâtha Ahunavaiti, and to the Gâtha Ustavaiti, to the Gâtha Spentâ-mainyu, and to the Gâtha Vohu-khshathra, and to the Gâtha Vahistôisti. 2. Propitiation to the Fravashis of the saints, the mighty, overwhelming, even to those of the saints of yore, who held the primeval faith (the Gâthic faith), and to those of the next of kin.

3. We sacrifice to Ahura Mazda, the resplendent, the glorious; and we sacrifice to the Amesha Spenta who rule aright, and who dispose (of all aright). And we sacrifice to the bounteous and holy Gâthas, which rule (as the first) in the ritual order.

We sacrifice to the Gâtha Ahunavaiti, the holy, as it rules in the ritual order; and we sacrifice to the Gâtha Ustavaiti, the holy, as it rules in the ritual order; and we sacrifice to the Gâtha Spentâ-mainyu, the holy, as it rules in the ritual order; and we sacrifice to the Gâtha Vohu-khshathra, the holy, as it rules in the ritual order; and we sacrifice to the Gâtha Vahistôisti, the holy, as it rules in the ritual order. 4 = Yt. XIII, 49–52[1].

III. ÂFRÎN[-AGÂN][2] RAPITHVIN[2].

1. I confess myself a Mazda-worshipper, of Zarathustra's order, a foe to the Daêvas, devoted to the lore of the Lord, for Rapithwina, the holy lord of the ritual order, for sacrifice, homage, propitiation, and praise, and for Frâdat-fshu[3] and Zantuma[4],

[1] Verses 5, 6 = Â. I, 14–18; for verse 6, see verses 1, 2; also see Â. I, 19.

[2] To be recited on the third day (Ardibahist) of the first month (Fravardin).

[3] A genius who furthered cattle.

[4] The genius of the Zantu, presiding over this Gâh Rapithvin.

the holy lord(s) of the ritual order. 2. And to Ahura Mazda, the resplendent, the glorious, and to the Bountiful Immortals, be propitiation, and to Asha Vahista (who is Righteousness the Best), and to the Fire, Ahura Mazda's son, and to all the holy Yazads, heavenly and earthly, and to the Fravashis of the saints, the mighty and overwhelming—.

3. For thus did Ahura Mazda speak to Spitama Zarathustra the word which was spoken for the ritual time of the Rapithwina, (saying): Ask us, O holy Zarathustra [1], what are Thy questions to be asked of us [2], for Thy question is as that mighty one when Thy ruler speaks his mighty wish [1]. 4. Then Zarathustra asked Ahura Mazda: O Ahura Mazda, most bountiful [3] creator of the material worlds and holy! what does that man acquire, what does he merit, what reward shall there be for that man (5) who shall recite the Rapithwina office with the Rapithwina prayer for blessing, and who shall sacrifice with [4] the Rapithwina office with hands (well) washed, and with (well) washed mortars, with the Baresman spread, and with Haoma high uplifted, and with fire brightly flaming, with Ahuna-vairya loud intoned, with Haoma-moistened tongue, and with a body Mãthra-bound? 6. And Ahura Mazda answered him: As the wind from the southern quarter, O Spitama! causes the entire material world to advance and to increase, and as it will bless it [5], rejoice it, and cause it to progress [6], such a like reward does such a man receive, (7) who

[1] Erroneous. [2] Ahmâi; see Y. XLIII, 10 with *e*hmâ.

[3] Insert 'spirit.' [4] Or, 'to.'

[5] Saoshyati*k*a; or can saoshya*n*ti be a locative absolute, preserving a fuller form?

[6] Or, 'causes it to enter into helpful joy' (?).

recites the Rapithwina-ratu with the Rapithwina blessing, and sacrifices with[1] it with (well) washed hands, and mortars, with Baresman spread, and Haoma lifted, with fire brightly flaming, and with Ahuna-vairya loud intoned, and with Haoma-moistened tongue, and a body Mãthra-bound! 8. Thus hath Ahura Mazda declared to Spitama Zarathustra the word which (should be) spoken at the Rapithwina time. 9, 10. (See Â. I, 14–19.)

[1] Or, 'to.'

THE GÂHS.

THE GÂHS.

THE Gâhs are the five divisions of the day. The Hâvani from 6 to 10 A.M., the Rapithwina from 10 A.M. to 3 P.M., the Uzayêirina from 3 to 6 P.M., the Aiwisrûthrima from 6 to 12 P.M., the Ushahina from 12 P.M. to 6 A.M. The Gâhs here following are prayers which must be recited at the Gâhs of the day; hence their name[1].

I. THE GÂH HÂVAN[2].

Unto Ahura Mazda be propitiation. A blessing is Righteousness (called) the Best—.

1. I confess myself a Mazda-worshipper, of Zarathustra's order, a foe to the Daêvas, devoted to the lore of the Lord, for the holy Hâvani, regulator of the ritual order, for its sacrifice, homage, propitiation, and praise, and for Sâvanghi and Vîsya, the righteous regulator(s) of the ritual order, for their homage, sacrifice, propitiation, and praise, and for those of the Asnya, the day-lords during daylight, and the Ayara, lords of the days in their length, and for the Mâhya, the month-lords, and the Yâirya, year-lords, and for those of the especial seasons.

2. And to Mithra of the wide pastures, of the thousand ears, of the myriad eyes, the Yazad of the spoken name[3], be sacrifice, homage, propitiation, and praise, and to Râman *Hv*âstra.

3, 4. And we sacrifice to Ahura Mazda the holy

---

[1] The term Gâh, itself, may have arisen from the practice of chanting the Gâthas at different fixed times in the day.

[2] To be recited every day at the time of Hâvani.

[3] Having a special Yast.

lord of the ritual Order, and to Zarathustra, and to the Fravashi of Zarathustra, the saint. And we sacrifice to the Bounteous Immortals, (the guardians) of the saints, and to the good, heroic, and bounteous Fravashis of the saints (of the living and of the dead), of the bodily, and of those in heaven. And we sacrifice to the highest of the lords, the one that most attains its ends; and we sacrifice to the most strenuous of the Yazads, the most satisfying of the lords of the ritual order, the one who reaches (what he seeks), the most infallibly of those who have as yet approached the nearest in the ritual, even to the timely prayer of the saint who rules in the ritual order. 5. And we sacrifice to the Hâvani, the holy lord of the ritual order, and to the Universal Weal, the holy, ruling in the ritual order, and to Deathlessness, the holy, ruling in the ritual order. And we sacrifice to the question and lore of the holy lord of the ritual. And we sacrifice to that heroic mighty Yasna, the Haptanghâiti, the lord of the ritual order. 6. And we sacrifice to Sâvanghi and Vîsya, the holy lord(s) of the ritual order; and we sacrifice to the Airyemâ-ishyô [1], the holy lord of the ritual order, the powerful, victoriously smiting, that which no hate can reach, which overwhelms all torments, and which passes over all torments with victory, which is the uppermost, and the middle, and the foremost, for the effective invocation of that surpassing Mãthra, the five Gâthas.

7, 8. And we sacrifice to Mithra of the wide pastures—, and to Râman *Hv*âstra, for the worship and exaltation of Vîsya, the chief. And we sacrifice to

[1] The personified prayer; see Y. LIV.

Vîsya, the holy lord of the ritual order, and to Mithra, and to Râman *Hv*âstra —.

9–11. And we sacrifice to thee, the Fire, O Ahura Mazda's son, the holy lord of the ritual order. And we sacrifice to this Baresman which has the Zaothra with it, and the girdle with it, and which is spread with exact sanctity, itself the holy lord. And we sacrifice to the Apãm-napâ*t*, and to Nairya-sangha, and to that Yazad, the swift curse of the wise. And we sacrifice to the souls of the dead, [which are the Fravashis of the saints]. And we worship that exalted Lord who is Ahura Mazda, the highest object of the ritual order, who is the one who has attained the most to homage in the ritual. And we sacrifice to all the words which Zarathu*s*tra spake, and to all the deeds well done, and to those which shall yet be done in days to come. (And) we sacrifice to that male one of beings whose (gift) in the offering Ahura doth know to be better, and of female saints, the same. As the Ahû is to be (revered and) chosen, so (is) the Ratu, one who rules from the Righteous Order, a creator of mental goodness, and of life's actions done for Mazda, and the Kingdom (is) to Ahura, which to the poor shall offer a nurturer—.

II. GÂH RAPITHVIN[1].

1. Propitiation to Ahura Mazda. A blessing is Asha Vahi*s*ta. I confess as a Mazda-worshipper, and of Zarathu*s*tra's order—for Rapithwina, the holy lord of the ritual order, for sacrifice, homage, propitiation, and for praise, and for Frâda*t*-fshu and Za*n*tuma, the holy lord(s) of the ritual order, for sacrifice, homage,

[1] Recited every day at the hour of Rapithwina.

propitiation, and for praise. 2. And propitiation be to Asha Vahista, and to Ahura Mazda's Fire, for sacrifice, homage, propitiation, and praise[1]. 3, 4. (See Y. LXXI, 2, 3.)

5. And we sacrifice to the Rapithwina, the holy lord of the ritual order, and to the Gâtha Ahunavaiti, the holy, and ruling in the ritual order; and to the Gâtha Ustavaiti, and to the Gâtha Spentâ-mainyu, and to the Gâtha Vohu-khshathra, and to the Gâtha Vahistôisti, holy, and ruling in the ritual order. 6. And we sacrifice to Frâdat-fshu, and to Zantuma, and to the Fshûshô-mãthra, even to the word correctly spoken, and we sacrifice to the (many) words correctly spoken, even to the victorious ones which slay the Demon-gods (the Daêvas[2]). And we sacrifice to the waters and the lands, and to the plants, and to the heavenly Yazads who are givers of the holy and the good. And we sacrifice to the Bountiful Immortals, (the guardians) of the saints.

7. And we sacrifice to the good, heroic, bountiful Fravashis of the saints, and to the heights of Asha (called) Vahista, and to the greatest Mãthras as moving us to action, the greatest as teaching faithfulness to holy vows, the greatest as referring to actions which are evidently just, and the greatest for the acquisition of the Mazdayasnian Faith. 8. And we sacrifice to that assembly and reunion which the Bountiful Immortals hold when they gather (?) on the heights of Heaven, for the sacrifice and homage of Zantuma, the lord.

And we (therefore) sacrifice to Zantuma (as) the holy lord of the ritual order. 9. And we sacrifice

---

[1] The Ahuna follows.

[2] Zarathustra conquered the Demon with the Ahuna-vairya.

to Asha Vahista (who is Righteousness the Best), and to the Fire, Ahura Mazda's son—. 10. Yea, we sacrifice to Thee, the Fire, Ahura Mazda's son, the holy ritual lord—.

I bless the sacrifice, homage, strength, and swiftness of Asha Vahista, and of the Fire, of Ahura Mazda—. And to this one be the glory!

III. GÂH UZIREN[1].

1. Propitiation to Ahura Mazda! A blessing is Asha Vahista—. I confess myself a Mazdayasnian of the order of Zarathustra, a foe to the Daêvas, devoted to the lore of the Lord, for the Uzayêirina, the holy lord of the ritual order, for sacrifice, homage, propitiation, and praise, and for Frâdat-vîra and Dahvyuma, the holy lord(s) of the ritual order, for their sacrifice, homage, propitiation, and praise. 2. And to that lofty Ahura, Apãm-napât, and to the waters which Mazda created be sacrifice, homage, propitiation, and praise[2]! 3, 4. (G. I, 3, 4.) 5. We sacrifice to the Uzayêirina, the holy lord of the ritual order. And we sacrifice to the Zaotar, the holy lord of the ritual order, and to the Hâvanan, and to the Âtarevakhsha, and to the Frabaretar, and to the Âberet, and to the Âsnatar, and the Raêthwiskar, and to the Sraoshâvareza, holy lords of the ritual order. 6. And we sacrifice to Frâdat-vîra and Dahvyuma, the holy lord of the ritual order. And we sacrifice to the stars, the moon, and the sun, and to the constellations (?), and we sacrifice to the stars without beginning (to their course ?), and to the glory of the doctrinal proclama-

[1] Recited every day at the hour of Uzayêirina.

[2] The Ahuna follows.

tions which are the evil man's distress[1]. 7. And we sacrifice to the manifest performer of the truth (the correct maintainer of the rites), the holy lord of the ritual order. And we sacrifice to the later lore; yea, we sacrifice to the manifest fulfiller of the truth, and to the (entire) creation of the holy (and the clean) by day and by night with Zaothras together with offered prayers, for the sacrifice and homage of Da*hv*yuma, the lord. And we sacrifice to Da*hv*yuma, the holy lord of the ritual order. 8. And we sacrifice to that lofty and royal lord, the brilliant Apãm-napâ*t* of the fleet horses; and we sacrifice to the water which is Mazda-made and holy. 9, 10. And we sacrifice to thee, the Fire, Ahura Mazda's son[2]. 11[3]. And I bless the sacrifice, homage, strength, and swiftness of that lofty Ahura Napâ*t*-apãm, and of the water which Mazda created[4].

IV. GÂH AIWISRÛTHRIMA[5].

1. Propitiation be to Ahura Mazda. A blessing is Asha Vahi*s*ta—. I confess myself a Mazdayasnian, and of Zarathu*s*tra's order, a foe to the Daêvas, devoted to the lore of the Lord, for Aiwisrûthrima, and Aibigaya[6], the holy lord(s) of the ritual order, for their sacrifice, homage, propitiation, and praise, and for Frâda*t*-vîspãm-hu*g*yâiti[7] and Zarathu*s*trôtema[8], the holy lord(s) of the ritual order, for their sacrifice, homage, propitiation, and praise. 2. And to the

---

[1] See Y. XLV, 7.
[2] The Yênhê hâtãm here follows.
[3] The Ahuna follows.
[4] The Ashem follows.
[5] Recited every day at the hour of Aiwisrûthrima.
[6] Or, 'that furthers life.'
[7] The genius presiding over all that furthers happiness.
[8] The genius presiding over the highest office in a province.

Fravashis of the saints, and to the women who have many sons, and to that prosperity of home which lasts without reverse throughout the year, and to Strength, well-shaped and stately, and to the victorious Blow Ahura-given, and for the crushing Ascendency which it bestows, (to all) be propitiation—. 3, 4. (See Gâh I, 3, 4.) 5. And we sacrifice to Aiwisrûthrima (and) Aibigaya, the holy lord(s) of the ritual order, and to thee, O Ahura Mazda's Fire! And we sacrifice to the stone-mortar, and to the iron-mortar, and to this Baresman spread with sanctity, with the Zaothra, and with its girdle, holy lords of the ritual order. Also we sacrifice to the sacred two, to the waters and the plants, and to the sacred vows for the soul, (as) holy lord(s) of the ritual order. 6. Also we sacrifice to Frâdat-vîspãm-hugyâiti (as) ruling in the ritual order; and we sacrifice to Zarathustra, the holy lord of the ritual; also we sacrifice to the Mãthra Spenta, (the bounteous word of reason[1]), and to the soul of the Kine, and to the Zarathustrôtema[2]. 7. Also we sacrifice to the Fire-priest, the holy lord of the ritual order, and to the charioteer (the warrior), the holy lord of the ritual order. Also we sacrifice to the thrifty tiller of the earth, the holy lord of the ritual order. And we sacrifice to the house-lord, and to the village-chief, and to the Zantu-chief, and to the province-chief of the province, the holy lord of the ritual order. 8. And we sacrifice to the youth of the good thoughts, good words, and good deeds, even to the youth of good conscience, the holy lord of the ritual order; yea, we

[1] The Gâthas and Vendîdâd; the first verse of the Gâthas mentions the Kine's soul.

[2] 'And to Zarathustra.'

sacrifice to the youth of the spoken word (who spoke the words which we hold so dear[1]), the holy lord of the ritual order. Yea, we sacrifice to the youth who is given to his kin (and married to his blood), the holy lord of the ritual order. And we sacrifice to him who ranges through the province[2], and to the itinerant with his many arts[3], the holy ritual lords. And we sacrifice to the house-mistress, holy, and ruling in the ritual order. 9. And we sacrifice to the holy woman forward[4] in good thoughts, and words, and deeds, receiving her instructions well, having her husband as her lord, the holy, and such as Âramaiti, the bounteous, is, and such as are thy wives, O Mazda, Lord!

And we sacrifice to the holy man most forward in good thoughts, and words, and works, wise as to piety, simple as to sin, by whose deeds the settlements advance in the holy order, for the worship and homage of the Zarathus*t*rôtema, the lord. And we sacrifice to the Zarathus*t*rôtema, the holy lord of the ritual order. 10. And we sacrifice to the good, heroic, bountiful Fravashis of the saints, and to the women who have many sons, and to that Prosperity which endures throughout the year, and to the well-shaped and stately Strength. And we sacrifice to the Blow of Victory, Ahura-given, and to the crushing Ascendency which it secures. 11, 12. (See Gâh I, 9, 10.) 13. (The Ahuna-vairya, &c.)

---

[1] See Yas*t* XXII.

[2] It is very probable that the Yasna was at that period celebrated from house to house.

[3] Medical?

[4] Is it possibly, 'favouring good thoughts,' &c.?

V. GÂH USHAHIN[1].

1. Propitiation to Ahura Mazda. I confess myself a Mazda-worshipper, of the order of Zarathustra, a foe to the Daêvas, devoted to the lore of the Lord, for the Ushahina, for sacrifice, homage, propitiation, and praise, and to Beregya and Nmânya, the holy lord(s) of the ritual order. 2. Propitiation be to Sraosha (Obedience) the blessed, endowed with recompense, smiting with the blow of victory, and causing the settlements to advance and to increase.

3, 4. (See Gâh I, 3, 4.) 5. We sacrifice to Ushahina, the holy lord of the ritual order; and we sacrifice to the beautiful Aurora, and to the dawn of morning; yea, we sacrifice to the morning, the shining[2], of the glittering horses, having the men of forethought (as its servants), yea, having men of forethought and heroes (awake and at their work), to the morning which gives light within the house[3]. And we sacrifice to the lights of dawn which are radiant with their light and fleetest horses which sweep over (?) the sevenfold earth. And we sacrifice to Ahura Mazda, the holy lord of the ritual order, and to the Good Mind, and to Asha Vahista (who is Righteousness the Best), and to Khshathra-vairya, and to Âramaiti, the bounteous and the good.

6. And we sacrifice to Beregya, even the holy lord of the ritual order, even to Nmânya with the longing desire for the good Asha, and with the longing desire for the good Mazdayasnian law, for the worship

[1] Recited every day at the hour of Ushahina.

[2] So, better than 'royal,' which is, however, possible.

[3] Or, 'while it abides.'

and homage of Nmânya, the lord. 7. And we sacrifice to Sraosha, and to Rashnu, the most just, and to Arstât, who causes the settlements to advance and to increase. 8, 9. (See Gâh I, 9, 10.) 10. And I bless the sacrifice, homage, strength, and swiftness of Sraosha (Obedience) the blessed, endowed with sanctity, smiting with the blow of victory, and who causes the settlements to advance; and I bless the sacrifice of Rashnu, the most just, and that of Arstât, who causes the settlements to advance and to increase[1].

[1] The Ashem and the Ahmâi raêska.

MISCELLANEOUS FRAGMENTS.

I.

1. (An incitation to the priest or worshipper.) As thou keepest company with the Good Mind, and with Righteousness the Best, and with Khshathra-vairya (the Kingdom to be desired), speak to the male and female disciples of Zarathustra Spitama the saint, (and declare) the praise which is to be spoken, that of the Yasna, even the words against which no anger[1] shall prevail.

2. And do thou, O Zarathustra[2]! declare our words for sacrifice and worship, ours, the Bountiful Immortals', that the waters may (thus) be sacrificed to by thee, and the plants, the Fravashis of the saints, and the created Yazads, heavenly and earthly, which are holy and beneficent.

II.

1. I confess myself a Mazda-worshipper—for the praise of Thraêtaona, the Âthwyan. Let them declare it—. Propitiation be to the Fravashi of Thraêtaona, the Âthwyan, the saint. 2. We sacrifice to Thraêtaona, the Âthwyan, the holy lord of the ritual order; and may we be free from the dog Kuro[3], and the Tarewani[3], and the Karpan, (we who are) of[4] those who sacrifice in order. 3. (The Ahuna

---

[1] Others 'the unrestricted words.'

[2] Perhaps 'Zarathustra' is here merely the equivalent of 'priest.'

[3] Obscure.

[4] Awkward formations.

follows.) Sacrifice, homage, strength, and swiftness be to the Fravashi of Thraêtaona, the saint. (The Ahem and Ahmâi raês*k*a follow.)

III.

1. All good thoughts, and all good words, and all good deeds are thought, and spoken, and done with intelligence; and all evil thoughts, and words, and deeds are thought, and spoken, and done with folly. 2. And let (the men who think, and speak, and do) all good thoughts, and words, and deeds inhabit[1] Heaven (as their home). And let those who think, and speak, and do evil thoughts, and words, and deeds abide in Hell. For to all who think good thoughts, speak good words, and do good deeds, Heaven, the best world, belongs. And this is evident, and as of course (?) (or, 'and therewith their seed').

IV.

1. I proclaim the Airy*e*mâ-ishyô as the greatest of all authoritative prayers, O Spitama! as the most influential and helpful for progress; and may the Saoshya*n*ts (who would further us) use it and revere it.

2. I am speaking in accordance with it, O Spitama! and therefore I shall rule as sovereign over creatures which are mine, I who am Ahura Mazda. Let no one rule as Angra Mainyu[2] over realms that are his own, O Zarathu*s*tra Spitama! 3. Let Angra Mainyu be hid beneath the earth[3]. Let the Daêvas likewise

[1] Ashaêta = â + shaêta used subjunctively.

[2] Insert 'of the evil faith.'

[3] In Y. IX, 14, 15, it is the Ahuna-vairya which drives the Daêvas beneath the earth.

disappear. Let the dead arise (unhindered by these foes), and let bodily life be sustained in these now lifeless bodies.

V.

1. To Ahura Mazda, the radiant, the glorious, to the Bountiful Immortals, to Force well-shaped and stately, to the Blow of Victory, Ahura-given, to the Victorious Ascendency (which it secures), to the path of pleasantness, to the good Zarenumant[1], to the 'Glowing' Mountain made by Mazda, and to all the Yazads! 2. We sacrifice to Ahura Mazda, the radiant, the glorious, and to the Bountiful Immortals who rule aright, who dispose (of all) aright, and to Force well-shaped and stately, and to the Blow of Victory, and to the Ascendency of Victory, and to the path of pleasantness, and to Zarenumant, the good, which Mazda created, and to the 'Glowing' Mount, and to every saint.

VI[2].

Propitiation be to the created body of the Kine of blessed endowment, and to the Kine's soul (so, if there is one cow presented[3]). Propitiation be to the body and soul of you two (so, if there are two[3]). —To your body and soul (if there are three, or the entire herd[3]). (The Ahuna follows.)

[1] According to the Bundahis, the name of a lake.

[2] This fragment was spoken when the milk was drawn from the cow, or cows, for the offering, and when the water was received with which the udder of the cow was to be washed. (Sp. transl. vol. iii, p. 254.)

[3] These words are in Persian introduced as rubric.

VII[1].

1. To the good waters, and to all the waters which Mazda created, and to that lofty lord, Apãm-napâ*t*, and to thee, O Ahurian One of Ahura, that water which Mazda created! be sacrifice, homage, propitiation, and praise. (The Ahuna follows.) 2. We utter our praises forth to thee, O Ahurian One of Ahura! and we complete good sacrifices, and deeds of adoration, with good gifts of offering, and gifts with praise, which are appropriate to thee among the holy Yazads. I will seek to render thee content. I will pour thee out. [Let them now recite the lofty Gâthas which belong to the ritual.]

VIII[2].

1. The moons* of the season will wane. Let the Mazdayasnian (pray) for a smiter who may destroy quickly (the demon who causes their decrease). And quickly indeed may the malignant one die off—. For no one of her adherents can maintain this Dru*g*(k) by prayers.

2. Smiting fiercely[3] with her weapon, she, the Dru*g*(k), goes on, and most mighty she has been. And she wanders on, O Zarathu*s*tra! as mindful of her might, and strong[4] in proportion as she advances

[1] This was to be spoken when the vessel containing the Zaothras was taken in hand (Sp.).

[2] This fragment is very much broken in its connections, and most corrupt in its grammatical forms. The translation is entirely conjectural. Section IX has also irregularities.

[3] Some form of dva may be conjectured.

[4] 'With her weapon.'

as the sinful Drug(k). But may Khshathra [1] be with me—, so that . . . . the deadly one may die away, for thereupon the blow of destruction shall come upon the Drug(k) [2].

IX.

1. The Ahuna-vairya is a prayer to be (revered and) chosen as the choice one of Mazda. The Khshathra-vairya is likewise such, and the Yâ daêna [3]. They (it) will gain the reward. Yathâ ahû vairyô. It is the word of Mazda. They are the words in season. It is the Mãthra-spenta word, the unsubdued, the undeceived, the victorious, the opponent of malice, the healing and victorious word of Mazda, which, as it is pronounced [4], gives most the victory to him who utters it. 2. I have declared the hymn which is most helpful and victorious against the words of Aêshma, which is health-giving and healing, and conducive to progress, the multiplier, and the furtherer of growth. And let the worshipper present it with a liberal offering . . . . with its pleasing words. Let that be done through veritable grace which helps us on the most [5]. The Kingdom (is) to Ahura, which to the poor may grant a nurturer [6].

---

[1] Khshathraka ? [2] See Y. XXX, 10.

[3] So I conjecture as the commencing words of some piece.

[4] 'For healing.' [5] Y. L, 11.

[6] Last line of the Ahuna.

INDEX.

In addition to the occurrences cited above, the words aêshma, aka manah, ameretatâ*t*, amesha spe*n*ta, asha, ashi vanguhi, asnya, âramaiti, âtharvan, drûg, frashakar*d*, ganrâk mînavad, haurvatâ*t*, î*s*ti, khshathra, *k*inva*t*, *k*isti, mazdayasnian, mâhya, mãthra, ratu, spe*n*ta mainyu, sraosha, vahi*s*ta manah, verethraghna, vîsya, vohu manah, zaotar occur as translated.

With regard to the subject indexed as the originality of the Gâthas, it is not intended to deny that the original migrations of the entire Aryan race may have been from the North-west.

On page 198 read Maidhyô-shema, Maidhyô-zaremaya; p. 204, -*g*yâiti; p. 209, -*g*yâitê.

Transliteration of Oriental Alphabets adopted for the Translations of the Sacred Books of the East.

CONSONANTS.	MISSIONARY ALPHABET. I Class.	II Class.	III Class.	Sanskrit.	Zend.	Pehlevi.	Persian.	Arabic.	Hebrew.	Chinese.
Gutturales.										
1 Tenuis	k	...	...	क	𐬐	[illegible]	ک	ك	כּ	k
2 ,, aspirata	kh	...	...	ख	𐬑	[illegible]	...	...	כ	kh
3 Media	g	...	...	ग	𐬔	[illegible]	گ	...	גּ	...
4 ,, aspirata	gh	...	...	घ	𐬖	[illegible]	...	...	ג	...
5 Gutturo-labialis	q	...	...	...	...	...	ق	ق	ק	...
6 Nasalis	ṅ (ng)	...	...	ङ	{ 𐬢 (ng) / 𐬣 (N) }	...	...	...	...	...
7 Spiritus asper	h	...	...	ह	𐬵 (𐬓 *hv*)	[illegible]	ه	ه	ה	h, hs
8 ,, lenis	'	...	...	...	...	...	ا	ا	א	...
9 ,, asper faucalis	‘h	...	...	...	...	...	ح	ح	ח	...
10 ,, lenis faucalis	’h	...	...	...	...	...	ع	ع	ע	...
11 ,, asper fricatus	...	‘*h*	...	...	...	...	خ	خ	ח	...
12 ,, lenis fricatus	...	’*h*	...	...	...	...	...	...	...	...
Gutturales modificatae (palatales, &c.)										
13 Tenuis	...	*k*	...	च	𐬗	[illegible]	چ	...	...	*k*
14 ,, aspirata	...	*kh*	...	छ	...	...	...	...	...	*kh*
15 Media	...	*g*	...	ज	𐬘	[illegible]	ج	ج	...	...
16 ,, aspirata	...	*gh*	...	झ	...	...	غ	غ	...	...
17 ,, Nasalis	ñ	...	...	ञ	...	...	...	...	...	...

CONSONANTS (*continued*).	MISSIONARY ALPHABET. I Class.	II Class.	III Class.	Sanskrit.	Zend.	Pehlevi.	Persian.	Arabic.	Hebrew.	Chinese.
18 Semivocalis	y	. . .	. . . .	य	[illegible] init. [illegible]	[illegible]	ي	ي	י	y
19 Spiritus asper	. . .	(y̆)	. . . .	. . .	. . . .	. . .	. . .	. . .	. . .	. . .
20 ,, lenis	. . .	(y̓)	. . . .	. . .	. . . .	. . .	. . .	. . .	. . .	. . .
21 ,, asper assibilatus . .	. . .	*s*	. . . .	श	[illegible]	[illegible]	ش	ش	. . .	. . .
22 ,, lenis assibilatus . .	. . .	*z*	. . . .	. . .	[illegible]	[illegible]	ژ	. . .	. . .	*z*
Dentales.										
23 Tenuis	t	. . .	. . . .	त	[illegible]	[illegible]	ت	ت	תּ	t
24 ,, aspirata	th	. . .	. . . .	थ	[illegible]	. . .	. . .	. . .	ת	th
25 ,, assibilata	. . .	. . .	TH	. . .	. . . .	. . .	ث	ث	. . .	. . .
26 Media	d	. . .	. . . .	द	[illegible]	[illegible]	د	د	דּ	. . .
27 ,, aspirata	dh	. . .	. . . .	ध	[illegible]	. . .	. . .	. . .	ד	. . .
28 ,, assibilata	. . .	. . .	DH	. . .	. . . .	. . .	ذ	ذ	. . .	. . .
29 Nasalis	n	. . .	. . . .	न	[illegible]	[illegible]	ن	ن	נ	n
30 Semivocalis	l	. . .	. . . .	ल	. . . .	[illegible]	ل	ل	ל	l
31 ,, mollis 1	. . .	*l*	. . . .	ळ	. . . .	. . .	. . .	. . .	. . .	. . .
32 ,, mollis 2	. . .	. . .	L	. . .	. . . .	. . .	. . .	. . .	. . .	. . .
33 Spiritus asper 1	s	. . .	. . . .	स	[illegible]	[illegible]	س (ث)	س	שׂ	s
34 ,, asper 2	. . .	. . .	s (ʃ)	. . .	. . . .	. . .	. . .	. . .	ס	. . .
35 ,, lenis	z	. . .	. . . .	. . .	[illegible]	[illegible]	ز (ذ)	ز	ז	z
36 ,, asperrimus 1	. . .	. . .	z (ʒ)	. . .	. . . .	. . .	ص	ص	צ	ʒ, ʒh
37 ,, asperrimus 2	. . .	. . .	ẓ (ʒ̣)	. . .	. . . .	. . .	ض	. . .	. . .	. . .

Dentales modificatae (linguales, &c.)										
38 Tenuis	...	*t*	....	ट	....	...	ط	ط	ט	...
39 „ aspirata	...	*th*	....	ठ	....	...	ظ	ظ	...	...
40 Media	...	*d*	....	ड	[illegible]	[illegible]	...	...	...	...
41 „ aspirata	...	*dh*	....	ढ	....	...	...	ض	...	...
42 Nasalis	...	*n*	....	ण	[illegible]	...	...	...	...	...
43 Semivocalis	r	...	....	र	[illegible]	[illegible]	ر	ر	ר	...
44 „ fricata	...	*r*	....	...	....	...	...	...	...	r
45 „ diacritica	...	...	R	...	....	...	...	...	...	...
46 Spiritus asper	sh	...	....	ष	[illegible]	[illegible]	...	...	...	sh
47 „ lenis	zh	...	....	...	....	...	...	...	...	...
Labiales.										
48 Tenuis	p	...	....	प	[illegible]	[illegible]	پ	...	פּ	p
49 „ aspirata	ph	...	....	फ	....	...	...	...	פ	ph
50 Media	b	...	....	ब	[illegible]	[illegible]	ب	ب	בּ	...
51 „ aspirata	bh	...	....	भ	....	...	...	...	ב	...
52 Tenuissima	...	*p*	....	...	....	...	...	...	...	...
53 Nasalis	m	...	....	म	[illegible]	[illegible]	م	م	מ	m
54 Semivocalis	w	...	....	...	[illegible]	...	...	...	...	w
55 „ aspirata	hw	...	....	...	....	...	...	...	...	...
56 Spiritus asper	f	...	....	...	[illegible]	[illegible]	ف	ف	...	f
57 „ lenis	v	...	....	व	»	[illegible]	و	و	ו	...
58 Anusvâra	...	*m*	....	ं	[illegible] ã	...	...	...	...	...
59 Visarga	...	*h*	....	ः	....	...	...	...	...	...

VOWELS.	MISSIONARY ALPHABET. I Class.	II Class.	III Class.	Sanskrit.	Zend.	Pehlevi.	Persian.	Arabic.	Hebrew.	Chinese.
1 Neutralis	0	...	....	...	....	...	...	...	◌ְ	ă
2 Laryngo-palatalis	ĕ	...	....	...	....	...	...	...	...	...
3 „ labialis	ŏ	...	....	...	....	𐭠 fin.	...	...	...	...
4 Gutturalis brevis	a	...	....	अ	𐬀	𐭠 init.	ـَ	ـَ	◌ַ	a
5 „ longa	â	(*a*)	....	आ	𐬁	𐭠	ـَا	ـَا	◌ָ	â
6 Palatalis brevis	i	...	....	इ	𐬌	...	ـِ	ـِ	◌ִ	i
7 „ longa	î	(*î*)	....	ई	𐬍	𐭉	ـِي	ـِي	◌ִי	î
8 Dentalis brevis	*li*	...	....	ऌ	....	...	...	...	...	...
9 „ longa	*lî*	...	....	ॡ	....	...	...	...	...	...
10 Lingualis brevis	*ri*	...	....	ऋ	....	...	...	...	...	...
11 „ longa	*rî*	...	....	ॠ	....	...	...	...	...	...
12 Labialis brevis	u	...	....	उ	𐬎	...	ـُ	ـُ	◌ֻ	u
13 „ longa	û	(*u*)	....	ऊ	𐬏	𐭅	ـُو	ـُو	וּ	û
14 Gutturo-palatalis brevis	e	...	....	...	𐬈(e) 𐬉(*e*)	...	...	...	◌ֶ	e
15 „ longa	ê (ai)	(*e*)	....	ए	𐬆, 𐬇	𐭉	...	...	◌ֵ	ê
16 Diphthongus gutturo-palatalis	âi	(*ai*)	....	ऐ	....	...	ـَيْ	ـَيْ	...	âi
17 „ „	ei (ĕi)	...	....	...	....	...	...	...	...	ei, êi
18 „ „	oi (ŏu)	...	....	...	....	...	...	...	...	...
19 Gutturo-labialis brevis	o	...	....	...	𐬊	...	...	...	◌ָ	o
20 „ longa	ô (au)	(*o*)	....	ओ	𐬋	𐭅	...	...	וֹ	...
21 Diphthongus gutturo-labialis	âu	(*au*)	....	औ	𐬈𐬎 (*au*)	...	ـَوْ	ـَوْ	...	âu
22 „ „	eu (ĕu)	...	....	...	....	...	...	...	...	...
23 „ „	ou (ŏu)	...	....	...	....	...	...	...	...	...
24 Gutturalis fracta	ä	...	....	...	....	...	...	...	...	...
25 Palatalis fracta	ï	...	....	...	....	...	...	...	...	...
26 Labialis fracta	ü	...	....	...	....	...	...	...	...	ü
27 Gutturo-labialis fracta	ö	...	....	...	....	...	...	...	...	...

Clarendon Press, Oxford

A SELECTION OF

BOOKS

PUBLISHED FOR THE UNIVERSITY BY

HENRY FROWDE,

AT THE OXFORD UNIVERSITY PRESS WAREHOUSE,

AMEN CORNER, LONDON.

ALSO TO BE HAD AT THE

CLARENDON PRESS DEPOSITORY, OXFORD.

[*Every book is bound in cloth, unless otherwise described.*]

LEXICONS, GRAMMARS, ORIENTAL WORKS, &c.

ANGLO-SAXON.—*An Anglo-Saxon Dictionary*, based on the MS. Collections of the late Joseph Bosworth, D.D., Professor of Anglo-Saxon, Oxford. Edited and enlarged by Prof. T. N. Toller, M.A. (To be completed in four parts.) Parts I and II. A—HWISTLIAN. 4to. 15*s*. each.

CHINESE.—*A Handbook of the Chinese Language*. By James Summers. 1863. 8vo. half bound, 1*l*. 8*s*.

—— *A Record of Buddhistic Kingdoms*, by the Chinese Monk FÂ-HIEN. Translated and annotated by James Legge, M.A., LL.D. Crown 4to. cloth back, 10*s*. 6*d*.

ENGLISH.—*A New English Dictionary, on Historical Principles:* founded mainly on the materials collected by the Philological Society. Edited by James A. H. Murray, LL.D., with the assistance of many Scholars and men of Science. Part I. A—ANT. Part II. ANT—BATTEN. Imperial 4to. 12*s*. 6*d*. each.

—— *An Etymological Dictionary of the English Language*. By W. W. Skeat, M.A. *Second Edition*. 1884. 4to. 2*l*. 4*s*.

——Supplement to the First Edition of the above. 4to. 2*s*. 6*d*.

—— *A Concise Etymological Dictionary of the English Language*. By W. W. Skeat, M.A. *Second Edition*. 1885. Crown 8vo. 5*s*. 6*d*.

GREEK.—*A Greek-English Lexicon*, by Henry George Liddell, D.D., and Robert Scott, D.D. Seventh Edition. Revised and Augmented throughout. 1883. 4to. 1*l*. 16*s*.

—— *A Greek-English Lexicon*, abridged from Liddell and Scott's 4to. edition, chiefly for the use of Schools. Twenty-first Edition. 1884. Square 12mo. 7*s*. 6*d*.

—— *A copious Greek-English Vocabulary*, compiled from the best authorities. 1850. 24mo. 3*s*.

—— *A Practical Introduction to Greek Accentuation*, by H. W. Chandler, M.A. Second Edition. 1881. 8vo. 10*s*. 6*d*.

HEBREW.—*The Book of Hebrew Roots*, by Abu 'l-Walîd Marwân ibn Janâh, otherwise called Rabbî Yônâh. Now first edited, with an Appendix, by Ad. Neubauer. 1875. 4to. 2*l*. 7*s*. 6*d*.

—— *A Treatise on the use of the Tenses in Hebrew*. By S. R. Driver, D.D. Second Edition. 1881. Extra fcap. 8vo. 7*s*. 6*d*.

—— *Hebrew Accentuation of Psalms, Proverbs, and Job*. By William Wickes, D.D. 1881. Demy 8vo. stiff covers, 5*s*.

ICELANDIC.—*An Icelandic-English Dictionary*, based on the MS. collections of the late Richard Cleasby. Enlarged and completed by G. Vigfússon, M.A. With an Introduction, and Life of Richard Cleasby, by G. Webbe Dasent, D.C.L. 1874. 4to. 3*l*. 7*s*.

—— *A List of English Words the Etymology of which is illustrated by comparison with Icelandic*. Prepared in the form of an APPENDIX to the above. By W. W. Skeat, M.A. 1876. stitched, 2*s*.

—— *An Icelandic Primer*, with Grammar, Notes, and Glossary. By Henry Sweet, M.A. Extra fcap. 8vo. 3*s*. 6*d*.

—— *An Icelandic Prose Reader*, with Notes, Grammar and Glossary, by Dr. Gudbrand Vigfússon and F. York Powell, M.A. 1879. Extra fcap. 8vo. 10*s*. 6*d*.

LATIN.—*A Latin Dictionary*, founded on Andrews' edition of Freund's Latin Dictionary, revised, enlarged, and in great part rewritten by Charlton T. Lewis, Ph.D., and Charles Short, LL.D. 1879. 4to. 1*l*. 5*s*.

MELANESIAN.—*The Melanesian Languages*. By R. H. Codrington, D.D., of the Melanesian Mission. 8vo. 18*s*.

SANSKRIT.—*A Practical Grammar of the Sanskrit Language*, arranged with reference to the Classical Languages of Europe, for the use of English Students, by Sir M. Monier-Williams, M.A. Fourth Edition. 8vo. 15*s*.

—— *A Sanskrit-English Dictionary*, Etymologically and Philologically arranged, with special reference to Greek, Latin, German, Anglo-Saxon, English, and other cognate Indo-European Languages. By Sir M. Monier-Williams, M.A. 1872. 4to. 4*l*. 14*s*. 6*d*.

SANSKRIT.—*Nalopákhyánam.* Story of Nala, an Episode of the Mahá-Bhárata: the Sanskrit text, with a copious Vocabulary, and an improved version of Dean Milman's Translation, by Sir M. Monier-Williams, M.A. Second Edition, Revised and Improved. 1879. 8vo. 15*s.*

—— *Sakuntalā.* A Sanskrit Drama, in Seven Acts. Edited by Sir M. Monier-Williams, M.A. Second Edition, 1876. 8vo. 21*s.*

SYRIAC.—*Thesaurus Syriacus:* collegerunt Quatremère, Bernstein, Lorsbach, Arnoldi, Agrell, Field, Roediger: edidit R. Payne Smith, S.T.P. Fasc. I-VI. 1868-83. sm. fol. each, 1*l.* 1*s.* Fasc. VII. 1*l.* 11*s.* 6*d.*

Vol. I, containing Fasc. I-V, sm. fol. 5*l.* 5*s.*

—— *The Book of Kalīlah and Dimnah.* Translated from Arabic into Syriac. Edited by W. Wright, LL.D. 1884. 8vo. 21*s.*

GREEK CLASSICS, &c.

Aristophanes: A Complete Concordance to the Comedies and Fragments. By Henry Dunbar, M.D. 4to. 1*l.* 1*s.*

Aristotle: The Politics, with Introduction, Notes, etc., by W. L. Newman, M.A., Fellow of Balliol College, Oxford. Vols. I. and II. *Nearly ready.*

Aristotle: The Politics, translated into English, with Introduction, Marginal Analysis, Notes, and Indices, by B. Jowett, M.A. Medium 8vo. 2 vols. 21*s.*

Catalogus Codicum Graecorum Sinaiticorum. Scripsit V. Gardthausen Lipsiensis. With six pages of Facsimiles. 8vo. *linen,* 25*s.*

Heracliti Ephesii Reliquiae. Recensuit I. Bywater, M.A. Appendicis loco additae sunt Diogenis Laertii Vita Heracliti, Particulae Hippocratei De Diaeta Libri Primi, Epistolae Heracliteae. 1877. 8vo. 6*s.*

Herculanensium Voluminum Partes II. 1824. 8vo. 10*s.*

Fragmenta Herculanensia. A Descriptive Catalogue of the Oxford copies of the Herculanean Rolls, together with the texts of several papyri, accompanied by facsimiles. Edited by Walter Scott, M.A., Fellow of Merton College, Oxford. Royal 8vo. *cloth,* 21*s.*

Homer: A Complete Concordance to the Odyssey and Hymns of Homer; to which is added a Concordance to the Parallel Passages in the Iliad, Odyssey, and Hymns. By Henry Dunbar, M.D. 1880. 4to. 1*l.* 1*s.*

—— *Scholia Graeca in Iliadem.* Edited by Professor W. Dindorf, after a new collation of the Venetian MSS. by D. B. Monro, M.A., Provost of Oriel College. 4 vols. 8vo. 2*l.* 10*s.* Vols. V and VI. *In the Press.*

—— *Scholia Graeca in Odysseam.* Edidit Guil. Dindorfius. Tomi II. 1855. 8vo. 15*s.* 6*d.*

Plato: Apology, with a revised Text and English Notes, and a Digest of Platonic Idioms, by James Riddell, M.A. 1878. 8vo. 8*s*. 6*d*.

—— *Philebus*, with a revised Text and English Notes, by Edward Poste, M.A. 1860. 8vo. 7*s*. 6*d*

—— *Sophistes and Politicus*, with a revised Text and English Notes, by L. Campbell, M.A. 1867. 8vo. 18*s*.

—— *Theaetetus*, with a revised Text and English Notes. by L. Campbell, M.A. Second Edition. 8vo. 10*s*. 6*d*.

—— *The Dialogues*, translated into English, with Analyses and Introductions, by B. Jowett, M.A. A new Edition in 5 volumes, medium 8vo. 1875. 3*l*. 10*s*.

—— *The Republic*, translated into English, with an Analysis and Introduction, by B. Jowett, M.A. Medium 8vo. 12*s*. 6*d*.

Thucydides: Translated into English, with Introduction, Marginal Analysis, Notes, and Indices. By B. Jowett, M.A. 2 vols. 1881. Medium 8vo. 1*l*. 12*s*.

THE HOLY SCRIPTURES, &c.

STUDIA BIBLICA.—Essays in Biblical Archæology and Criticism, and kindred subjects. By Members of the University of Oxford. 8vo. 10*s*. 6*d*.

ENGLISH.—*The Holy Bible in the earliest English Versions*, made from the Latin Vulgate by John Wycliffe and his followers: edited by the Rev. J. Forshall and Sir F. Madden. 4 vols. 1850. Royal 4to 3*l*. 3*s*.

[**Also reprinted from the above, with Introduction and Glossary by W. W. Skeat, M.A.**

—— *The Books of Job, Psalms, Proverbs, Ecclesiastes, and the Song of Solomon:* according to the Wycliffite Version made by Nicholas de Hereford, about A.D. 1381, and Revised by John Purvey, about A.D. 1388. Extra fcap. 8vo. 3*s*. 6*d*.

—— *The New Testament in English*, according to the Version by John Wycliffe, about A.D. 1380, and Revised by John Purvey, about A.D. 1388. Extra fcap. 8vo 6*s*.]

ENGLISH.—*The Holy Bible:* an exact reprint, page for page, of the Authorised Version published in the year 1611. Demy 4to. half bound, 1*l*. 1*s*.

—— *The Psalter, or Psalms of David, and certain Canticles,* with a Translation and Exposition in English, by Richard Rolle of Hampole. Edited by H. R. Bramley, M.A., Fellow of S. M. Magdalen College, Oxford. With an Introduction and Glossary. Demy 8vo. 1*l*. 1*s*.

—— *Lectures on Ecclesiastes.* Delivered in Westminster Abbey by the Very Rev. George Granville Bradley, D.D., Dean of Westminster. Crown 8vo. 4*s*. 6*d*.

GOTHIC.—*The Gospel of St. Mark in Gothic,* according to the translation made by Wulfila in the Fourth Century. Edited with a Grammatical Introduction and Glossarial Index by W. W. Skeat, M.A. Extra fcap. 8vo. 4*s*.

GREEK.—*Vetus Testamentum* ex Versione Septuaginta Interpretum secundum exemplar Vaticanum Romae editum. Accedit potior varietas Codicis Alexandrini. Tomi III. Editio Altera. 18mo. 18*s*.

—— *Origenis Hexaplorum* quae supersunt; sive, Veterum Interpretum Graecorum in totum Vetus Testamentum Fragmenta. Edidit Fridericus Field, A.M. 2 vols. 1875. 4to. 5*l*. 5*s*.

—— *The Book of Wisdom:* the Greek Text, the Latin Vulgate, and the Authorised English Version; with an Introduction, Critical Apparatus, and a Commentary. By William J. Deane. M.A. Small 4to. 12*s*. 6*d*.

—— *Novum Testamentum Graece.* Antiquissimorum Codicum Textus in ordine parallelo dispositi. Accedit collatio Codicis Sinaitici. Edidit E. H. Hansell, S.T.B. Tomi III. 1864. 8vo. half morocco. Price reduced to 24*s*.

—— *Novum Testamentum Graece.* Accedunt parallela S. Scripturae loca, etc. Edidit Carolus Lloyd, S.T.P.R. 18mo. 3*s*.

On writing paper, with wide margin, 10*s*.

—— *Novum Testamentum Graece* juxta Exemplar Millianum. 18mo. 2*s*. 6*d*. On writing paper, with wide margin, 9*s*.

—— *Evangelia Sacra Graece.* Fcap. 8vo. limp, 1*s*. 6*d*.

—— *The Greek Testament,* with the Readings adopted by the Revisers of the Authorised Version:—

(1) Pica type, with Marginal References. Demy 8vo. 10*s*. 6*d*.
(2) Long Primer type. Fcap. 8vo. 4*s*. 6*d*.
(3) The same, on writing paper, with wide margin, 15*s*.

—— *The Parallel New Testament,* Greek and English; being the Authorised Version, 1611; the Revised Version, 1881; and the Greek Text followed in the Revised Version. 8vo. 12*s*. 6*d*.

The Revised Version is the joint property of the Universities of Oxford and Cambridge.

GREEK.—*Canon Muratorianus:* the earliest Catalogue of the Books of the New Testament. Edited with Notes and a Facsimile of the MS. in the Ambrosian Library at Milan, by S. P. Tregelles, LL.D. 1867. 4to. 10*s*. 6*d*.

—— *Outlines of Textual Criticism applied to the New Testament.* By C. E. Hammond, M.A. Fourth Edition. Extra fcap. 8vo. 3*s*. 6*d*.

HEBREW, etc.—*The Psalms in Hebrew without points.* 1879. Crown 8vo. 3*s*. 6*d*.

—— *A Commentary on the Book of Proverbs.* Attributed to Abraham Ibn Ezra. Edited from a MS. in the Bodleian Library by S. R. Driver, M.A. Crown 8vo. paper covers, 3*s*. 6*d*.

—— *The Book of Tobit.* A Chaldee Text, from a unique MS. in the Bodleian Library; with other Rabbinical Texts, English Translations, and the Itala. Edited by Ad. Neubauer, M.A. 1878. Crown 8vo. 6*s*.

—— *Horae Hebraicae et Talmudicae*, a J. Lightfoot. A new Edition, by R. Gandell, M.A. 4 vols. 1859. 8vo. 1*l*. 1*s*.

LATIN.—*Libri Psalmorum* Versio antiqua Latina, cum Paraphrasi Anglo-Saxonica. Edidit B. Thorpe, F.A.S. 1835. 8vo. 10*s*. 6*d*.

—— *Old-Latin Biblical Texts: No. I.* The Gospel according to St. Matthew from the St. Germain MS. (g_1). Edited with Introduction and Appendices by John Wordsworth, D.D. Small 4to., stiff covers, 6*s*.

—— *Old-Latin Biblical Texts: No. II.* Portions of the Gospels according to St. Mark and St. Matthew, from the Bobbio MS. (k), &c. Edited by John Wordsworth, D.D., W. Sanday, M.A., D.D., and H. J. White, M.A. Small 4to., stiff covers, 21*s*.

OLD-FRENCH.—*Libri Psalmorum* Versio antiqua Gallica e Cod. MS. in Bibl. Bodleiana adservato, una cum Versione Metrica aliisque Monumentis pervetustis. Nunc primum descripsit et edidit Franciscus Michel, Phil. Doc. 1860. 8vo. 10*s*. 6*d*.

FATHERS OF THE CHURCH, &c.

St. Athanasius: Historical Writings, according to the Benedictine Text. With an Introduction by William Bright, D.D. 1881. Crown 8vo. 10*s*. 6*d*.

—— *Orations against the Arians.* With an Account of his Life by William Bright, D.D. 1873. Crown 8vo. 9*s*.

St. Augustine: Select Anti-Pelagian Treatises, and the Acts of the Second Council of Orange. With an Introduction by William Bright, D.D. Crown 8vo. 9*s*.

Canons of the First Four General Councils of Nicaea, Constantinople, Ephesus, and Chalcedon. 1877. Crown 8vo. 2*s*. 6*d*.

—— *Notes on the Canons of the First Four General Councils.* By William Bright, D.D. 1882. Crown 8vo. 5*s*. 6*d*.

Cyrilli Archiepiscopi Alexandrini in XII Prophetas. Edidit P. E. Pusey, A.M. Tomi II. 1868. 8vo. cloth, 2*l*. 2*s*.

—— *in D. Joannis Evangelium.* Accedunt Fragmenta varia necnon Tractatus ad Tiberium Diaconum duo. Edidit post Aubertum P. E. Pusey, A.M. Tomi III. 1872. 8vo. 2*l*. 5*s*.

—— *Commentarii in Lucae Evangelium* quae supersunt Syriace. E MSS. apud Mus. Britan. edidit R. Payne Smith, A.M. 1858. 4to. 1*l*. 2*s*.

—— Translated by R. Payne Smith, M.A. 2 vols. 1859. 8vo. 14*s*.

Ephraemi Syri, Rabulae Episcopi Edesseni, Balaei, aliorumque Opera Selecta. E Codd. Syriacis MSS. in Museo Britannico et Bibliotheca Bodleiana asservatis primus edidit J. J. Overbeck. 1865. 8vo. 1*l*. 1*s*.

Eusebius' Ecclesiastical History, according to the text of Burton, with an Introduction by William Bright, D.D. 1881. Crown 8vo. 8*s*. 6*d*.

Irenaeus: The Third Book of St. Irenaeus, Bishop of Lyons, against Heresies. With short Notes and a Glossary by H. Deane, B.D. 1874 Crown 8vo. 5*s*. 6*d*.

Patrum Apostolicorum, S. Clementis Romani, S. Ignatii, S. Polycarpi, quae supersunt. Edidit Guil. Jacobson, S.T.P.R. Tomi II. Fourth Edition, 1863. 8vo. 1*l*. 1*s*.

Socrates' Ecclesiastical History, according to the Text of Hussey, with an Introduction by William Bright, D.D. 1878. Crown 8vo. 7*s*. 6*d*

ECCLESIASTICAL HISTORY, BIOGRAPHY, &c.

Ancient Liturgy of the Church of England, according to the uses of Sarum, York, Hereford, and Bangor, and the Roman Liturgy arranged in parallel columns, with preface and notes. By William Maskell, M.A. Third Edition. 1882. 8vo. 15*s*.

Baedae Historia Ecclesiastica. Edited, with English Notes, by G. H. Moberly, M.A. 1881. Crown 8vo. 10*s*. 6*d*.

Bright (*W.*). *Chapters of Early English Church History.* 1878. 8vo. 12*s.*

Burnet's History of the Reformation of the Church of England. A new Edition. Carefully revised, and the Records collated with the originals, by N. Pocock, M.A. 7 vols. 1865. 8vo. *Price reduced to* 1*l.* 10*s.*

Councils and Ecclesiastical Documents relating to Great Britain and Ireland. Edited, after Spelman and Wilkins, by A. W. Haddan, B.D., and W. Stubbs, M.A. Vols. I. and III. 1869–71. Medium 8vo. each 1*l.* 1*s.*

Vol. II. Part I. 1873. Medium 8vo. 10*s.* 6*d.*

Vol. II. Part II. 1878. Church of Ireland; Memorials of St. Patrick. Stiff covers, 3*s.* 6*d.*

Hamilton (*John, Archbishop of St. Andrews*), *The Catechism of.* Edited, with Introduction and Glossary, by Thomas Graves Law. With a Preface by the Right Hon. W. E. Gladstone. 8vo. 12*s.* 6*d.*

Hammond (*C. E.*). *Liturgies, Eastern and Western.* Edited, with Introduction, Notes, and Liturgical Glossary. 1878. Crown 8vo. 10*s.* 6*d.*

An Appendix to the above. 1879. Crown 8vo. paper covers, 1*s.* 6*d.*

John, Bishop of Ephesus. The Third Part of his Ecclesiastical History. [In Syriac.] Now first edited by William Cureton, M.A. 1853. 4to. 1*l.* 12*s.*

—— Translated by R. Payne Smith, M.A. 1860. 8vo. 10*s.*

Leofric Missal, The, as used in the Cathedral of Exeter during the Episcopate of its first Bishop, A.D. 1050–1072; together with some Account of the Red Book of Derby, the Missal of Robert of Jumièges, and a few other early MS. Service Books of the English Church. Edited, with Introduction and Notes, by F. E. Warren, B.D. 4to. half morocco, 35*s.*

Monumenta Ritualia Ecclesiae Anglicanae. The occasional Offices of the Church of England according to the old use of Salisbury, the Prymer in English, and other prayers and forms, with dissertations and notes. By William Maskell, M.A. Second Edition. 1882. 3 vols. 8vo. 2*l.* 10*s.*

Records of the Reformation. The Divorce, 1527–1533. Mostly now for the first time printed from MSS. in the British Museum and other libraries. Collected and arranged by N. Pocock, M.A. 1870. 2 vols. 8vo. 1*l.* 16*s.*

Shirley (*W. W.*). *Some Account of the Church in the Apostolic Age.* Second Edition, 1874. Fcap. 8vo. 3*s.* 6*d.*

Stubbs (*W.*). *Registrum Sacrum Anglicanum.* An attempt to exhibit the course of Episcopal Succession in England. 1858. Small 4to. 8*s.* 6*d.*

Warren (*F. E.*). *Liturgy and Ritual of the Celtic Church.* 1881. 8vo. 14*s.*

ENGLISH THEOLOGY.

Bampton Lectures, 1886. *The Christian Platonists of Alexandria.* By Charles Bigg, D.D. 8vo. 10*s*. 6*d*.

Butler's Works, with an Index to the Analogy. 2 vols. 1874. 8vo. 11*s*.

Also separately,

Sermons, 5*s*. 6*d*. *Analogy of Religion*, 5*s*. 6*d*

Greswell's Harmonia Evangelica. Fifth Edition. 8vo. 1855. 9*s*. 6*d*.

Heurtley's Harmonia Symbolica: Creeds of the Western Church. 1858. 8vo. 6*s*. 6*d*.

Homilies appointed to be read in Churches. Edited by J. Griffiths, M.A. 1859. 8vo. 7*s*. 6*d*.

Hooker's Works, with his life by Walton, arranged by John Keble, M.A. Sixth Edition, 1874. 3 vols. 8vo. 1*l*. 11*s*. 6*d*.

—— the text as arranged by John Keble, M.A. 2 vols. 1875. 8vo. 11*s*.

Jewel's Works. Edited by R. W. Jelf, D.D. 8 vols. 1848. 8vo. 1*l*. 10*s*.

Pearson's Exposition of the Creed. Revised and corrected by E. Burton, D.D. Sixth Edition, 1877. 8vo. 10*s*. 6*d*.

Waterland's Review of the Doctrine of the Eucharist, with a Preface by the late Bishop of London. Crown 8vo. 6*s*. 6*d*.

—— *Works*, with Life, by Bp. Van Mildert. A new Edition, with copious Indexes. 6 vols. 1856. 8vo. 2*l*. 11*s*.

Wheatly's Illustration of the Book of Common Prayer. A new Edition, 1846. 8vo. 5*s*.

Wyclif. A Catalogue of the Original Works of John Wyclif, by W. W. Shirley, D.D. 1865. 8vo. 3*s*. 6*d*.

—— *Select English Works.* By T. Arnold, M.A. 3 vols. 1869–1871. 8vo. 1*l*. 1*s*.

—— *Trialogus.* With the Supplement now first edited. By Gotthard Lechler. 1869. 8vo. 7*s*.

HISTORICAL AND DOCUMENTARY WORKS.

British Barrows, a Record of the Examination of Sepulchral Mounds in various parts of England. By William Greenwell, M.A., F.S.A. Together with Description of Figures of Skulls, General Remarks on Prehistoric Crania, and an Appendix by George Rolleston, M.D., F.R.S. 1877. Medium 8vo. 25*s*.

Britton. A Treatise upon the Common Law of England, composed by order of King Edward I. The French Text carefully revised, with an English Translation, Introduction, and Notes, by F. M. Nichols, M.A. 2 vols. 1865. Royal 8vo. 1*l*. 16*s*.

Clarendon's History of the Rebellion and Civil Wars in England. 7 vols. 1839. 18mo. 1*l*. 1*s*.

Clarendon's History of the Rebellion and Civil Wars in England. Also his Life, written by himself, in which is included a Continuation of his History of the Grand Rebellion. With copious Indexes. In one volume, royal 8vo. 1842. 1*l*. 2*s*.

Clinton's Epitome of the Fasti Hellenici. 1851. 8vo. 6*s*. 6*d*.

—— *Epitome of the Fasti Romani*. 1854. 8vo. 7*s*.

Corpvs Poeticvm Boreale. The Poetry of the Old Northern Tongue, from the Earliest Times to the Thirteenth Century. Edited, classified, and translated, with Introduction, Excursus, and Notes, by Gudbrand Vigfússon, M.A., and F. York Powell, M.A. 2 vols. 1883. 8vo. 42*s*.

Freeman (E. A.). History of the Norman Conquest of England; its Causes and Results. In Six Volumes. 8vo. 5*l*. 9*s*. 6*d*.

—— *The Reign of William Rufus and the Accession of* Henry the First. 2 vols. 8vo. 1*l*. 16*s*.

Gascoigne's Theological Dictionary ("Liber Veritatum"): Selected Passages, illustrating the condition of Church and State, 1403–1458. With an Introduction by James E. Thorold Rogers, M.A. Small 4to. 10*s*. 6*d*.

Magna Carta, a careful Reprint. Edited by W. Stubbs, D.D. 1879. 4to. stitched, 1*s*.

Passio et Miracula Beati Olaui. Edited from a Twelfth-Century MS. in the Library of Corpus Christi College, Oxford, with an Introduction and Notes, by Frederick Metcalfe, M.A. Small 4to. stiff covers, 6*s*.

Protests of the Lords, including those which have been expunged, from 1624 to 1874; with Historical Introductions. Edited by James E. Thorold Rogers, M.A. 1875. 3 vols. 8vo. 2*l.* 2*s.*

Rogers (J. E. T.). History of Agriculture and Prices in England, A.D. 1259–1793.

Vols. I and II (1259–1400). 1866. 8vo. 2*l.* 2*s.*

Vols. III and IV (1401–1582). 1882. 8vo. 2*l.* 10*s.*

Saxon Chronicles (Two of the) parallel, with Supplementary Extracts from the Others. Edited, with Introduction, Notes, and a Glossarial Index, by J. Earle, M.A. 1865. 8vo. 16*s.*

Stubbs (W., D.D.). Seventeen Lectures on the Study of Medieval and Modern History, &c., delivered at Oxford 1867–1884. Demy 8vo. half-bound, 10*s.* 6*d.*

Sturlunga Saga, including the Islendinga Saga of Lawman Sturla Thordsson and other works. Edited by Dr. Gudbrand Vigfússon. In 2 vols. 1878. 8vo. 2*l.* 2*s.*

York Plays. The Plays performed by the Crafts or Mysteries of York on the day of Corpus Christi in the 14th, 15th, and 16th centuries. Now first printed from the unique MS. in the Library of Lord Ashburnham. Edited with Introduction and Glossary by Lucy Toulmin Smith. 8vo. 21*s.*

Statutes made for the University of Oxford, and for the Colleges and Halls therein, by the University of Oxford Commissioners. 1882. 8vo. 12*s.* 6*d.*

Statuta Universitatis Oxoniensis. 1886. 8vo. 5*s.*

The Examination Statutes for the Degrees of B.A., B. Mus., B.C.L., and B.M. Revised to Trinity Term, 1886. 8vo. sewed, 1*s.*

The Student's Handbook to the University and Colleges of Oxford. Extra fcap. 8vo. 2*s.* 6*d.*

The Oxford University Calendar for the year 1886. Crown 8vo. 4*s.* 6*d.*

The present Edition includes all Class Lists and other University distinctions for the five years ending with 1885.

Also, supplementary to the above, price 5s. (pp. 606),

The Honours Register of the University of Oxford. A complete Record of University Honours, Officers, Distinctions, and Class Lists; of the Heads of Colleges, &c., &c., from the Thirteenth Century to 1883.

MATHEMATICS, PHYSICAL SCIENCE, &c.

Acland (H. W., M.D., F.R.S.). Synopsis of the Pathological Series in the Oxford Museum. 1867. 8vo. 2*s*. 6*d*.

De Bary (Dr. A.). Comparative Anatomy of the Vegetative Organs of the Phanerogams and Ferns. Translated and Annotated by F. O. Bower, M.A., F.L.S., and D. H. Scott, M.A., Ph.D., F.L.S. With 241 woodcuts and an Index. Royal 8vo., half morocco, 1*l*. 2*s*. 6*d*.

Goebel (Dr. K.). Outlines of Classification and Special Morphology of Plants. A New Edition of Sachs' Text Book of Botany, Book II. English Translation by H. E. F. Garnsey, M.A. Revised by I. Bayley Balfour, M.A., M.D., F.R.S. With 407 Woodcuts. Royal 8vo. half Morocco, 21*s*.

Müller (J.). On certain Variations in the Vocal Organs of the Passeres that have hitherto escaped notice. Translated by F. J. Bell, B.A., and edited, with an Appendix, by A. H. Garrod, M.A., F.R.S. With Plates. 1878. 4to. paper covers, 7*s*. 6*d*.

Price (Bartholomew, M.A., F.R.S.). Treatise on Infinitesimal Calculus.

Vol. I. Differential Calculus. Second Edition. 8vo. 14*s*. 6*d*.

Vol. II. Integral Calculus, Calculus of Variations, and Differential Equations. Second Edition, 1865. 8vo. 18*s*.

Vol. III. Statics, including Attractions; Dynamics of a Material Particle. Second Edition, 1868. 8vo. 16*s*.

Vol. IV. Dynamics of Material Systems; together with a chapter on Theoretical Dynamics, by W. F. Donkin, M.A., F.R.S. 1862. 8vo. 16*s*.

Pritchard (C., D.D., F.R.S.). Uranometria Nova Oxoniensis. A Photometric determination of the magnitudes of all Stars visible to the naked eye, from the Pole to ten degrees south of the Equator. 1885. Royal 8vo. 8*s*. 6*d*.

—— *Astronomical Observations* made at the University Observatory, Oxford, under the direction of C. Pritchard, D.D. No. 1. 1878. Royal 8vo. paper covers, 3*s*. 6*d*.

Rigaud's Correspondence of Scientific Men of the 17th Century, with Table of Contents by A. de Morgan, and Index by the Rev. J. Rigaud, M.A. 2 vols. 1841–1862. 8vo. 18*s*. 6*d*.

Rolleston (George, M.D., F.R.S.). Scientific Papers and Addresses. Arranged and Edited by William Turner, M.B., F.R.S. With a Biographical Sketch by Edward Tylor, F.R.S. With Portrait, Plates, and Woodcuts. 2 vols. 8vo. 1*l*. 4*s*.

Westwood (J. O., M.A., F.R.S.). Thesaurus Entomologicus Hopeianus, or a Description of the rarest Insects in the Collection given to the University by the Rev. William Hope. With 40 Plates. 1874. Small folio, half morocco, 7*l*. 10*s*.

The Sacred Books of the East.

TRANSLATED BY VARIOUS ORIENTAL SCHOLARS, AND EDITED BY F. MAX MÜLLER.

[Demy 8vo. cloth.]

Vol. I. The Upanishads. Translated by F. Max Müller. Part I. The *Kh*ândogya-upanishad, The Talavakâra-upanishad, The Aitareya-âra*n*yaka, The Kaushîtaki-brâhma*n*a-upanishad, and The Vâ*g*asaneyi-sa*m*hitâ-upanishad. 10*s*. 6*d*.

Vol. II. The Sacred Laws of the Âryas, as taught in the Schools of Âpastamba, Gautama, Vâsish*th*a, and Baudhâyana. Translated by Prof. Georg Bühler. Part I. Âpastamba and Gautama. 10*s*. 6*d*.

Vol. III. The Sacred Books of China. The Texts of Confucianism. Translated by James Legge. Part I. The Shû King, The Religious portions of the Shih King, and The Hsiâo King. 12*s*. 6*d*.

Vol. IV. The Zend-Avesta. Translated by James Darmesteter. Part I. The Vendîdâd. 10*s*. 6*d*.

Vol. V. The Pahlavi Texts. Translated by E. W. West. Part I. The Bundahi*s*, Bahman Ya*s*t, and Shâyast lâ-shâyast. 12*s*. 6*d*.

Vols. VI and IX. The Qur'ân. Parts I and II. Translated by E. H. Palmer. 21*s*.

Vol. VII. The Institutes of Vish*n*u. Translated by Julius Jolly. 10*s*. 6*d*.

Vol. VIII. The Bhagavadgîtâ, with The Sanatsu*g*âtîya, and The Anugîtâ. Translated by Kâshinâth Trimbak Telang. 10*s*. 6*d*.

Vol. X. The Dhammapada, translated from Pâli by F. Max Müller; and The Sutta-Nipâta, translated from Pâli by V. Fausböll; being Canonical Books of the Buddhists. 10*s*. 6*d*.

Vol. XI. Buddhist Suttas. Translated from Pâli by T. W. Rhys Davids. 1. The Mahâparinibbâna Suttanta; 2. The Dhamma-*k*akka-ppavattana Sutta; 3. The Tevigga Suttanta; 4. The Akankheyya Sutta; 5. The *K*etokhila Sutta; 6. The Mahâ-sudassana Suttanta; 7. The Sabbâsava Sutta. 10*s*. 6*d*.

Vol. XII. The *S*atapatha-Brâhma*n*a, according to the Text of the Mâdhyandina School. Translated by Julius Eggeling. Part I. Books I and II. 12*s*. 6*d*.

Vol. XIII. Vinaya Texts. Translated from the Pâli by T. W. Rhys Davids and Hermann Oldenberg. Part I. The Pâtimokkha. The Mahâvagga, I-IV. 10*s*. 6*d*.

Vol. XIV. The Sacred Laws of the Âryas, as taught in the Schools of Apastamba, Gautama, Vâsish*th*a and Baudhâyana. Translated by Georg Bühler. Part II. Vâsish*th*a and Baudhâyana. 10*s*. 6*d*.

Vol. XV. The Upanishads. Translated by F. Max Müller. Part II. The Ka*th*a-upanishad, The Mu*nd*aka-upanishad, The Taittirîyaka-upanishad, The B*ri*hadâra*n*yaka-upanishad, The *S*veta*s*vatara-upanishad, The Pra*s*#*n*a-upanishad, and The Maitrâya*n*a-Brâhma*n*a-upanishad. 10*s*. 6*d*.

Vol. XVI. The Sacred Books of China. The Texts of Confucianism. Translated by James Legge. Part II. The Yî King. 10*s*. 6*d*.

Vol. XVII. Vinaya Texts. Translated from the Pâli by T. W. Rhys Davids and Hermann Oldenberg. Part II. The Mahâvagga, V-X. The *K*ullavagga, I-III. 10*s*. 6*d*.

Vol. XVIII. Pahlavi Texts. Translated by E. W. West. Part II. The Dâ*d*istân-î Dînîk and The Epistles of Mânû*s**k*îhar. 12*s*. 6*d*.

Vol. XIX. The Fo-sho-hing-tsan-king. A Life of Buddha by A*s*vaghosha Bodhisattva, translated from Sanskrit into Chinese by Dharmaraksha, A.D. 420, and from Chinese into English by Samuel Beal. 10*s*. 6*d*.

Vol. XX. Vinaya Texts. Translated from the Pâli by T. W. Rhys Davids and Hermann Oldenberg. Part III. The *K*ullavagga, IV-XII. 10*s*. 6*d*.

Vol. XXI. The Saddharma-pu*nd*arîka; or, the Lotus of the True Law. Translated by H. Kern. 12*s*. 6*d*.

Vol. XXII. *G*aina-Sûtras. Translated from Prâkrit by Hermann Jacobi. Part I. The Â*k*ârâṅga-Sûtra. The Kalpa-Sûtra. 10*s*. 6*d*.

Vol. XXIII. The Zend-Avesta. Translated by James Darmesteter. Part II. The Sîrôzahs, Ya*s*ts, and Nyâyi*s*. 10*s*. 6*d*.

Vol. XXIV. Pahlavi Texts. Translated by E. W. West. Part III. Dînâ-î Maînôg-î Khirad, *S*ikand-gûmânîk, and Sad-Dar. 10*s*. 6*d*.

Second Series.

Vol. XXV. Manu. Translated by Georg Bühler. 21*s.*

Vol. XXVI. The *S*atapatha-Brâhma*n*a. Translated by Julius Eggeling. Part II. 12*s.* 6*d.*

Vols. XXVII and XXVIII. The Sacred Books of China. The Texts of Confucianism. Translated by James Legge. Parts III and IV. The Lî *K*î, or Collection of Treatises on the Rules of Propriety, or Ceremonial Usages. 25*s.*

Vols. XXIX and XXX. The G*ri*hya-Sûtras, Rules of Vedic Domestic Ceremonies. Translated by Hermann Oldenberg.

Part I (Vol. XXIX), 12*s.* 6*d.* *Just Published.*
Part II (Vol. XXX). *In the Press.*

The following Volumes are in the Press:—

Vol. XXXI. The Zend-Avesta. Part III. The Yasna, Visparad, Âfrînagân, and Gâhs. Translated by the Rev. L. H. Mills.

Vol. XXXII. Vedic Hymns. Translated by F. Max Müller. Part I.

Vol. XXXIII. Nârada, and some Minor Law-books. Translated by Julius Jolly. [*Preparing.*]

Vol. XXXIV. The Vedânta-Sûtras, with *S*añkara's Commentary. Translated by G. Thibaut. [*Preparing.*]

*** *The Second Series will consist of Twenty-Four Volumes.*

Clarendon Press Series

I. ENGLISH, &c.

A First Reading Book. By Marie Eichens of Berlin; and edited by Anne J. Clough. Extra fcap. 8vo. stiff covers, 4*d.*

Oxford Reading Book, Part I. For Little Children. Extra fcap. 8vo. stiff covers, 6*d.*

Oxford Reading Book, Part II. For Junior Classes. Extra fcap. 8vo. stiff covers, 6*d.*

An Elementary English Grammar and Exercise Book. By O. W. Tancock, M.A. Second Edition. Extra fcap. 8vo. 1*s.* 6*d.*

An English Grammar and Reading Book, for Lower Forms in Classical Schools. By O. W. Tancock, M.A. Fourth Edition. Extra fcap. 8vo. 3*s.* 6*d.*

Typical Selections from the best English Writers, with Introductory Notices. Second Edition. In 2 vols. Extra fcap. 8vo. 3*s.* 6*d.* each.
Vol. I. Latimer to Berkeley. Vol. II. Pope to Macaulay.

Shairp (J. C., LL.D.). Aspects of Poetry; being Lectures delivered at Oxford. Crown 8vo. 10*s.* 6*d.*

A Book for the Beginner in Anglo-Saxon. By John Earle, M.A. Third Edition. Extra fcap. 8vo. 2*s.* 6*d.*

An Anglo-Saxon Reader. In Prose and Verse. With Grammatical Introduction, Notes, and Glossary. By Henry Sweet, M.A. Fourth Edition, Revised and Enlarged. Extra fcap. 8vo. 8*s.* 6*d.*

A Second Anglo-Saxon Reader. By the same Author. Extra fcap. 8vo. *Nearly ready.*

An Anglo-Saxon Primer, with Grammar, Notes, and Glossary. By the same Author. Second Edition. Extra fcap. 8vo. 2*s.* 6*d.*

Old English Reading Primers; edited by Henry Sweet, M.A.

I. Selected Homilies of Ælfric. Extra fcap. 8vo., stiff covers, 1*s.* 6*d.*

II. Extracts from Alfred's Orosius. Extra fcap. 8vo., stiff covers, 1*s.* 6*d.*

First Middle English Primer, with Grammar and Glossary. By the same Author. Extra fcap. 8vo. 2*s.*

Second Middle English Primer. Extracts from Chaucer, with Grammar and Glossary. By the same Author. Extra fcap. 8vo. 2*s.* *Just Published.*

Principles of English Etymology. First Series. By W. W. Skeat, Litt.D. Crown 8vo. *Nearly ready.*

The Philology of the English Tongue. By J. Earle, M.A. Third Edition. Extra fcap. 8vo. 7*s.* 6*d.*

An Icelandic Primer, with Grammar, Notes, and Glossary. By the same Author. Extra fcap. 8vo. 3*s.* 6*d.*

An Icelandic Prose Reader, with Notes, Grammar, and Glossary. By G. Vigfússon, M.A., and F. York Powell, M.A. Ext. fcap. 8vo. 10*s.* 6*d.*

A Handbook of Phonetics, including a Popular Exposition of the Principles of Spelling Reform. By H. Sweet, M.A. Extra fcap. 8vo. 4*s.* 6*d.*

Elementarbuch des Gesprochenen Englisch. Grammatik, Texte und Glossar. Von Henry Sweet. Extra fcap. 8vo., stiff covers, 2*s.* 6*d.*

The Ormulum; with the Notes and Glossary of Dr. R. M. White. Edited by R. Holt, M.A. 1878. 2 vols. Extra fcap. 8vo. 21*s.*

Specimens of Early English. A New and Revised Edition. With Introduction, Notes, and Glossarial Index. By R. Morris, LL.D., and W. W. Skeat, M.A.

Part I. From Old English Homilies to King Horn (A.D. 1150 to A.D. 1300). Second Edition. Extra fcap. 8vo. 9*s.*

Part II. From Robert of Gloucester to Gower (A.D. 1298 to A.D. 1393). Second Edition. Extra fcap. 8vo. 7*s.* 6*d.*

Specimens of English Literature, from the 'Ploughmans Crede' to the 'Shepheardes Calender' (A.D. 1394 to A.D. 1579). With Introduction, Notes, and Glossarial Index. By W. W. Skeat, M.A. Extra fcap. 8vo. 7*s.* 6*d.*

The Vision of William concerning Piers the Plowman, in three Parallel Texts; together with *Richard the Redeless.* By William Langland (about 1362–1399 A.D.). Edited from numerous Manuscripts, with Preface, Notes, and a Glossary, by W. W. Skeat, Litt.D. 2 vols. 8vo. 31*s.* 6*d.* *Just Published.*

The Vision of William concerning Piers the Plowman, by William Langland. Edited, with Notes, by W. W. Skeat, M.A. Third Edition. Extra fcap. 8vo. 4*s.* 6*d.*

Chaucer. I. *The Prologue to the Canterbury Tales;* the Knightes Tale; The Nonne Prestes Tale. Edited by R. Morris, Editor of Specimens of Early English, &c., &c. Extra fcap. 8vo. 2*s.* 6*d.*

—— II. *The Prioresses Tale; Sir Thopas;* The Monkes Tale; The Clerkes Tale; The Squieres Tale, &c. Edited by W. W. Skeat, M.A. Second Edition. Extra fcap. 8vo. 4*s.* 6*d.*

—— III. *The Tale of the Man of Lawe;* The Pardoneres Tale; The Second Nonnes Tale; The Chanouns Yemannes Tale. By the same Editor. Second Edition. Extra fcap. 8vo. 4*s.* 6*d.*

Gamelyn, The Tale of. Edited with Notes, Glossary, &c., by W. W. Skeat, M.A. Extra fcap. 8vo. Stiff covers, 1*s.* 6*d.*

Minot (Laurence). Poems. Edited, with Introduction and Notes, by Joseph Hall, M.A. Extra fcap. 8vo. *Nearly ready.*

Spenser's Faery Queene. Books I and II. Designed chiefly for the use of Schools. With Introduction, Notes, and Glossary. By G. W. Kitchin. D.D. Extra fcap. 8vo. 2*s.* 6*d.* each.

Hooker. Ecclesiastical Polity, Book I. Edited by R. W. Church, M.A. Second Edition. Extra fcap. 8vo. 2*s.*

OLD ENGLISH DRAMA.

The Pilgrimage to Parnassus with *The Two Parts of the Return from Parnassus.* Three Comedies performed in St. John's College, Cambridge, A.D. MDXCVII–MDCI. Edited from MSS. by the Rev. W. D. Macray, M.A., F.S.A. Medium 8vo. Bevelled Boards, Gilt top, 8*s.* 6*d.*

Marlowe and Greene. Marlowe's Tragical History of Dr. Faustus, and *Greene's Honourable History of Friar Bacon and Friar Bungay.* Edited by A. W. Ward, M.A. 1878. Extra fcap. 8vo. 5*s.* 6*d.* In white Parchment, 6*s.*

Marlowe. Edward II. With Introduction, Notes, &c. By O. W. Tancock, M.A. Extra fcap. 8vo. 3*s.*

SHAKESPEARE.

Shakespeare. Select Plays. Edited by W. G. Clark, M.A., and W. Aldis Wright, M.A. Extra fcap. 8vo. stiff covers.

The Merchant of Venice. 1*s.*
Richard the Second. 1*s.* 6*d.*
Macbeth. 1*s.* 6*d.*
Hamlet. 2*s.*

Edited by W. Aldis Wright, M.A.

The Tempest. 1*s.* 6*d.*
As You Like It. 1*s.* 6*d.*
Julius Cæsar. 2*s.*
Richard the Third. 2*s.* 6*d.*
King Lear. 1*s.* 6*d.*
Midsummer Night's Dream. 1*s.* 6*d.*
Coriolanus. 2*s.* 6*d.*
Henry the Fifth. 2*s.*
Twelfth Night. 1*s.* 6*d.*
King John. 1*s.* 6*d.*

Shakespeare as a Dramatic Artist; a popular Illustration of the Principles of Scientific Criticism. By R. G. Moulton, M.A. Crown 8vo. 5*s.*

Bacon. I. *Advancement of Learning.* Edited by W. Aldis Wright, M.A. Second Edition. Extra fcap. 8vo. 4*s.* 6*d.*

—— II. *The Essays.* With Introduction and Notes. By S. H. Reynolds, M.A., late Fellow of Brasenose College. *In Preparation.*

Milton. I. *Areopagitica.* With Introduction and Notes. By John W. Hales, M.A. Third Edition. Extra fcap. 8vo. 3*s.*

—— II. *Poems.* Edited by R. C. Browne, M.A. 2 vols. Fifth Edition. Extra fcap. 8vo. 6*s.* 6*d.* Sold separately, Vol. I. 4*s.*; Vol. II. 3*s.*

In paper covers:—

Lycidas, 3*d.* L'Allegro, 3*d.* Il Penseroso, 4*d.* Comus, 6*d.*
Samson Agonistes, 6*d.*

—— III. *Samson Agonistes.* Edited with Introduction and Notes by John Churton Collins. Extra fcap. 8vo. stiff covers, 1*s.*

Bunyan. I. *The Pilgrim's Progress, Grace Abounding, Relation of the Imprisonment of Mr. John Bunyan.* Edited, with Biographical Introduction and Notes, by E. Venables, M.A. 1879. Extra fcap. 8vo. 5*s.* In ornamental Parchment, 6*s.*

—— II. *Holy War, &c.* Edited by E. Venables, M.A. In the Press.

Clarendon. History of the Rebellion. Book VI. Edited by T. Arnold, M.A. Extra fcap. 8vo. 4*s.* 6*d.*

Dryden. Select Poems. Stanzas on the Death of Oliver Cromwell; Astræa Redux; Annus Mirabilis; Absalom and Achitophel; Religio Laici; The Hind and the Panther. Edited by W. D. Christie, M.A. Second Edition. Extra fcap. 8vo. 3*s.* 6*d.*

Locke's Conduct of the Understanding. Edited, with Introduction, Notes, &c., by T. Fowler, M.A. Second Edition. Extra fcap. 8vo. 2*s.*

Addison. Selections from Papers in the Spectator. With Notes. By T. Arnold, M.A. Extra fcap. 8vo. 4*s.* 6*d.* In ornamental Parchment, 6*s.*

Steele. Selections from the Tatler, Spectator, and Guardian. Edited by Austin Dobson. Extra fcap. 8vo. 4*s.* 6*d.* In white Parchment, 7*s.* 6*d.*

Pope. With Introduction and Notes. By Mark Pattison, B.D.

—— I. *Essay on Man.* Extra fcap. 8vo. 1*s.* 6*d.*

—— II. *Satires and Epistles.* Extra fcap. 8vo. 2*s.*

Parnell. The Hermit. Paper covers, 2*d.*

Gray. Selected Poems. Edited by Edmund Gosse. Extra fcap. 8vo. Stiff covers, 1*s.* 6*d.* In white Parchment, 3*s.*

—— *Elegy and Ode on Eton College.* Paper covers, 2*d.*

Goldsmith. The Deserted Village. Paper covers, 2*d.*

Johnson. I. *Rasselas; Lives of Dryden and Pope.* Edited by Alfred Milnes, M.A. (London). Extra fcap. 8vo. 4*s.* 6*d.*, or *Lives of Dryden and Pope* only, stiff covers, 2*s.* 6*d.*

—— II. *Vanity of Human Wishes.* With Notes, by E. J. Payne, M.A. Paper covers, 4*d.*

Boswell's Life of Johnson. With the Journal of a Tour to the Hebrides. Edited, with copious Notes, Appendices, and Index, by G. Birkbeck Hill, D.C.L., Pembroke College. With Portraits and Facsimiles. 6 vols. Medium 8vo. *Nearly ready.*

Cowper. Edited, with Life, Introductions, and Notes, by H. T. Griffith, B.A.

—— I. *The Didactic Poems of* 1782, with Selections from the Minor Pieces, A.D. 1779–1783. Extra fcap. 8vo. 3*s.*

—— II. *The Task, with Tirocinium,* and Selections from the Minor Poems, A.D. 1784–1799. Second Edition. Extra fcap. 8vo. 3*s.*

Burke. Select Works. Edited, with Introduction and Notes, by E. J. Payne, M.A.

—— I. *Thoughts on the Present Discontents; the two Speeches on America.* Second Edition. Extra fcap. 8vo. 4*s*. 6*d*.

—— II. *Reflections on the French Revolution.* Second Edition. Extra fcap. 8vo. 5*s*.

—— III. *Four Letters on the Proposals for Peace with the* Regicide Directory of France. Second Edition. Extra fcap. 8vo. 5*s*.

Keats. Hyperion, Book I. With Notes by W. T. Arnold, B.A. Paper covers, 4*d*.

Byron. Childe Harold. Edited, with Introduction and Notes, by H. F. Tozer, M.A. Extra fcap. 8vo. 3*s*. 6*d*. In white Parchment, 5*s*.

Scott. Lay of the Last Minstrel. Edited with Preface and Notes by W. Minto, M.A. With Map. Extra fcap. 8vo. Stiff covers, 2*s*. Ornamental Parchment, 3*s*. 6*d*.

—— *Lay of the Last Minstrel.* Introduction and Canto I., with Preface and Notes; by the same Editor. 6*d*.

II. LATIN.

Rudimenta Latina. Comprising Accidence, and Exercises of a very Elementary Character, for the use of Beginners. By John Barrow Allen, M.A. Extra fcap. 8vo. 2*s*.

An Elementary Latin Grammar. By the same Author. Forty-second Thousand. Extra fcap. 8vo. 2*s*. 6*d*.

A First Latin Exercise Book. By the same Author. Fourth Edition. Extra fcap. 8vo. 2*s*. 6*d*.

A Second Latin Exercise Book. By the same Author. Extra fcap. 8vo. 3*s*. 6*d*.

Reddenda Minora, or Easy Passages, Latin and Greek, for Unseen Translation. For the use of Lower Forms. Composed and selected by C. S. Jerram, M.A. Extra fcap. 8vo. 1*s*. 6*d*.

Anglice Reddenda, or Easy Extracts, Latin and Greek, for Unseen Translation. By C. S. Jerram, M.A. Third Edition, Revised and Enlarged. Extra fcap. 8vo. 2*s*. 6*d*.

Anglice Reddenda. Second Series. By the same Author. Extra fcap. 8vo. *Nearly ready.*

Passages for Translation into Latin. For the use of Passmen and others. Selected by J. Y. Sargent, M.A. Fifth Edition. Extra fcap. 8vo. 2*s*. 6*d*.

Exercises in Latin Prose Composition; with Introduction, Notes, and Passages of Graduated Difficulty for Translation into Latin. By G. G. Ramsay, M.A., LL.D. Second Edition. Extra fcap. 8vo. 4*s.* 6*d.*

Hints and Helps for Latin Elegiacs. By H. Lee-Warner, M.A. Extra fcap. 8vo. 3*s.* 6*d.*

First Latin Reader. By T. J. Nunns, M.A. Third Edition. Extra fcap. 8vo. 2*s.*

Caesar. The Commentaries (for Schools). With Notes and Maps. By Charles E. Moberly, M.A.

Part I. *The Gallic War.* Second Edition. Extra fcap. 8vo. 4*s.* 6*d.*
Part II. *The Civil War.* Extra fcap. 8vo. 3*s.* 6*d.*

The Civil War. Book I. Second Edition. Extra fcap. 8vo. 2*s.*

Cicero. Catilinarian Orations. By E. A. Upcott, M.A., Assistant Master in Marlborough College. *In the Press.*

Cicero. Selection of interesting and descriptive passages. With Notes. By Henry Walford, M.A. In three Parts. Extra fcap. 8vo. 4*s.* 6*d.*

Each Part separately, limp, 1*s.* 6*d.*

Part I. Anecdotes from Grecian and Roman History. Third Edition.
Part II. Omens and Dreams: Beauties of Nature. Third Edition.
Part III. Rome's Rule of her Provinces. Third Edition.

Cicero. De Senectute. Edited, with Introduction and Notes, by L. Huxley, M.A. Extra fcap. 8vo. 2*s.*

Or separately, Text and Introduction, 1*s.* Notes 1*s.*

Cicero. Selected Letters (for Schools). With Notes. By the late C. E. Prichard, M.A., and E. R. Bernard, M.A. Second Edition. Extra fcap. 8vo. 3*s.*

Cicero. Select Orations (for Schools). In Verrem I. De Imperio Gn. Pompeii. Pro Archia. Philippica IX. With Introduction and Notes by J. R. King, M.A. Second Edition. Extra fcap. 8vo. 2*s.* 6*d.*

Cornelius Nepos. With Notes. By Oscar Browning, M.A. Second Edition. Extra fcap. 8vo. 2*s.* 6*d.*

Horace. Selected Odes. With Notes for the use of a Fifth Form. By E. C. Wickham, M.A. In two Parts. Extra fcap. 8vo. *cloth,* 2*s.*

Or separately, Part I. Text, 1*s.* Part II. Notes, 1*s.*

Livy. Selections (for Schools). With Notes and Maps. By H. Lee-Warner, M.A. Extra fcap. 8vo. In Parts, limp, each 1*s.* 6*d.*

Part I. The Caudine Disaster. Part II. Hannibal's Campaign in Italy. Part III. The Macedonian War.

Livy. Books V–VII. With Introduction and Notes. By A. R. Cluer, B.A. Extra fcap. 8vo. 3*s.* 6*d.*

Livy. Books XXI, XXII, and XXIII. With Introduction and Notes. By M. T. Tatham, M.A. Extra fcap. 8vo. 4*s.* 6*d.*

Ovid. Selections for the use of Schools. With Introductions and Notes, and an Appendix on the Roman Calendar. By W. Ramsay, M.A. Edited by G. G. Ramsay, M.A. Third Edition. Extra fcap. 8vo. 5*s*. 6*d*.

Ovid. Tristia. Book I. The Text revised, with an Introduction and Notes. By S. G. Owen, B.A. Extra fcap. 8vo. 3*s*. 6*d*.

Plautus. Captivi. Edited by W. M. Lindsay, M.A. Extra fcap. 8vo. *In the Press.*

Plautus. The Trinummus. With Notes and Introductions. Intended for the Higher Forms of Public Schools. By C. E. Freeman, M.A., and A. Sloman, M.A. Extra fcap. 8vo. 3*s*.

Pliny. Selected Letters (for Schools). With Notes. By the late C. E. Prichard, M.A., and E. R. Bernard, M.A. Extra fcap. 8vo. 3*s*.

Sallust. With Introduction and Notes. By W. W. Capes, M.A. Extra fcap. 8vo. 4*s*. 6*d*.

Tacitus. The Annals. Books I–IV. Edited, with Introduction and Notes for the use of Schools and Junior Students, by H. Furneaux, M.A. Extra fcap. 8vo. 5*s*.

Terence. Andria. With Notes and Introductions. By C. E. Freeman, M.A., and A. Sloman, M.A. Extra fcap. 8vo. 3*s*.

—— *Adelphi.* With Notes and Introductions. Intended for the Higher Forms of Public Schools. By A. Sloman, M.A. Extra fcap. 8vo. 3*s*.

Tibullus and Propertius. Selections. Edited by G. G. Ramsay, M.A. In two Parts. Extra fcap. 8vo. (In one or two vols.) 6*s*. *Just Published.*

Virgil. With Introduction and Notes. By T. L. Papillon, M.A. Two vols. Crown 8vo. 10*s*. 6*d*. The Text separately, 4*s*. 6*d*.

Virgil. The Eclogues. Edited by C. S. Jerram, M.A. In two Parts. Crown 8vo. *Nearly ready.*

Catulli Veronensis Liber. Iterum recognovit, apparatum criticum prolegomena appendices addidit, Robinson Ellis, A.M. 1878. Demy 8vo. 16*s*.

—— *A Commentary on Catullus.* By Robinson Ellis, M.A. 1876. Demy 8vo. 16*s*.

Catulli Veronensis Carmina Selecta, secundum recognitionem Robinson Ellis, A.M. Extra fcap. 8vo. 3*s*. 6*d*.

Cicero de Oratore. With Introduction and Notes. By A. S. Wilkins, M.A.

Book I. 1879. 8vo. 6*s*. Book II. 1881. 8vo. 5*s*.

—— *Philippic Orations.* With Notes. By J. R. King, M.A. Second Edition. 1879. 8vo. 10*s*. 6*d*.

Cicero. Select Letters. With English Introductions, Notes, and Appendices. By Albert Watson, M.A. Third Edition. Demy 8vo. 18*s.*

—— *Select Letters.* Text. By the same Editor. Second Edition. Extra fcap. 8vo. 4*s.*

—— *pro Cluentio.* With Introduction and Notes. By W. Ramsay, M.A. Edited by G. G. Ramsay, M.A. 2nd Ed. Ext. fcap. 8vo. 3*s.* 6*d.*

Horace. With a Commentary. Volume I. The Odes, Carmen Seculare, and Epodes. By Edward C. Wickham, M.A. Second Edition. 1877. Demy 8vo. 12*s.*

—— A reprint of the above, in a size suitable for the use of Schools. Extra fcap. 8vo. 5*s.* 6*d.*

Livy, Book I. With Introduction, Historical Examination, and Notes. By J. R. Seeley, M.A. Second Edition. 1881. 8vo. 6*s.*

Ovid. P. Ovidii Nasonis Ibis. Ex Novis Codicibus edidit, Scholia Vetera Commentarium cum Prolegomenis Appendice Indice addidit, R. Ellis, A.M. 8vo. 10*s.* 6*d.*

Persius. The Satires. With a Translation and Commentary. By John Conington, M.A. Edited by Henry Nettleship, M.A. Second Edition. 1874. 8vo. 7*s.* 6*d.*

Juvenal. XIII Satires. Edited, with Introduction and Notes, by C. H. Pearson, M.A., and Herbert A. Strong, M.A., LL.D., Professor of Latin in Liverpool University College, Victoria University. In two Parts. Crown 8vo. Complete, 6*s.* *Just Published.*

Also separately, Part I. Introduction, Text, etc., 3*s.* Part II. Notes, 3*s.* 6*d.*

Tacitus. The Annals. Books I–VI. Edited, with Introduction and Notes, by H. Furneaux, M.A. 8vo. 18*s.*

Nettleship (H., M.A.). Lectures and Essays on Subjects connected with Latin Scholarship and Literature. Crown 8vo. 7*s.* 6*d.*

—— *The Roman Satura:* its original form in connection with its literary development. 8vo. sewed, 1*s.*

—— *Ancient Lives of Vergil.* With an Essay on the Poems of Vergil, in connection with his Life and Times. 8vo. sewed, 2*s.*

Papillon (T. L., M.A.). A Manual of Comparative Philology. Third Edition, Revised and Corrected. 1882. Crown 8vo. 6*s.*

Pinder (North, M.A.). Selections from the less known Latin Poets. 1869. 8vo. 15*s.*

Sellar (W. Y., M.A.). Roman Poets of the Augustan Age. VIRGIL. New Edition. 1883. Crown 8vo. 9*s.*

—— *Roman Poets of the Republic.* New Edition, Revised and Enlarged. 1881. 8vo. 14*s.*

Wordsworth (J., M.A.). Fragments and Specimens of Early Latin. With Introductions and Notes. 1874. 8vo. 18*s.*

III. GREEK.

A Greek Primer, for the use of beginners in that Language. By the Right Rev. Charles Wordsworth, D.C.L. Seventh Edition. Extra fcap. 8vo. 1*s*. 6*d*.

Easy Greek Reader. By Evelyn Abbott, M.A. In two Parts. Extra fcap. 8vo. 3*s*. *Just Published*.

The Text and Notes may be had separately, 1*s*. 6*d*. each.

Graecae Grammaticae Rudimenta in usum Scholarum. Auctore Carolo Wordsworth, D.C.L. Nineteenth Edition, 1882. 12mo. 4*s*.

A Greek-English Lexicon, abridged from Liddell and Scott's 4to. edition, chiefly for the use of Schools. Twenty-first Edition. 1884. Square 12mo. 7*s*. 6*d*.

Greek Verbs, Irregular and Defective; their forms, meaning, and quantity; embracing all the Tenses used by Greek writers, with references to the passages in which they are found. By W. Veitch. Fourth Edition. Crown 8vo. 10*s*. 6*d*.

The Elements of Greek Accentuation (for Schools): abridged from his larger work by H. W. Chandler, M.A. Extra fcap. 8vo. 2*s*. 6*d*.

A SERIES OF GRADUATED GREEK READERS:—

First Greek Reader. By W. G. Rushbrooke, M.L. Second Edition. Extra fcap. 8vo. 2*s*. 6*d*.

Second Greek Reader. By A. M. Bell, M.A. Extra fcap. 8vo. 3*s*. 6*d*.

Fourth Greek Reader; being Specimens of Greek Dialects. With Introductions, etc. By W. W. Merry, M.A. Extra fcap. 8vo. 4*s*. 6*d*.

Fifth Greek Reader. Selections from Greek Epic and Dramatic Poetry, with Introductions and Notes. By Evelyn Abbott, M.A. Extra fcap. 8vo. 4*s*. 6*d*.

The Golden Treasury of Ancient Greek Poetry: being a Collection of the finest passages in the Greek Classic Poets, with Introductory Notices and Notes. By R. S. Wright. M.A. Extra fcap. 8vo. 8*s*. 6*d*.

A Golden Treasury of Greek Prose, being a Collection of the finest passages in the principal Greek Prose Writers, with Introductory Notices and Notes. By R. S. Wright, M.A., and J. E. L. Shadwell, M.A. Extra fcap. 8vo. 4*s*. 6*d*.

Aeschylus. *Prometheus Bound* (for Schools). With Introduction and Notes, by A. O. Prickard, M.A. Second Edition. Extra fcap. 8vo. 2*s*.

—— *Agamemnon*. With Introduction and Notes, by Arthur Sidgwick, M.A. Second Edition. Extra fcap. 8vo. 3*s*.

—— *Choephoroi*. With Introduction and Notes by the same Editor. Extra fcap. 8vo. 3*s*.

Aristophanes. In Single Plays. Edited, with English Notes, Introductions, &c., by W. W. Merry, M.A. Extra fcap. 8vo.

I. The Clouds, Second Edition, 2*s.*

II. The Acharnians, 2*s.* III. The Frogs, 2*s.*

Cebes. Tabula. With Introduction and Notes. By C. S. Jerram, M.A. Extra fcap. 8vo. 2*s.* 6*d.*

Demosthenes. Olynthiacs and Philippics. Edited by Evelyn Abbott, M.A. Extra fcap. 8vo. In two Parts. *In the Press.*

Euripides. Alcestis (for Schools). By C. S. Jerram, M.A. Extra fcap. 8vo. 2*s.* 6*d.*

—— *Helena.* Edited, with Introduction, Notes, etc., for Upper and Middle Forms. By C. S. Jerram, M.A. Extra fcap. 8vo. 3*s.*

—— *Iphigenia in Tauris.* Edited, with Introduction, Notes, etc., for Upper and Middle Forms. By C. S. Jerram, M.A. Extra fcap. 8vo. cloth, 3*s.*

—— *Medea.* By C. B. Heberden, M.A. In two Parts. Extra fcap. 8vo. 2*s.*

Or separately, Part I. Introduction and Text, 1*s.*
Part II. Notes and Appendices, 1*s.*

Herodotus, Selections from. Edited, with Introduction, Notes, and a Map, by W. W. Merry, M.A. Extra fcap. 8vo. 2*s.* 6*d.*

Homer. Odyssey, Books I–XII (for Schools). By W. W. Merry, M.A. Twenty-seventh Thousand. Extra fcap. 8vo. 4*s.* 6*d.*

Book II, separately, 1*s.* 6*d.*

—— *Odyssey,* Books XIII–XXIV (for Schools). By the same Editor. Second Edition. Extra fcap. 8vo. 5*s.*

—— *Iliad,* Book I (for Schools). By D. B. Monro, M.A. Second Edition. Extra fcap. 8vo. 2*s.*

—— *Iliad,* Books I–XII (for Schools). With an Introduction, a brief Homeric Grammar, and Notes. By D. B. Monro, M.A. Second Edition. Extra fcap. 8vo. 6*s.*

—— *Iliad,* Books VI and XXI. With Introduction and Notes. By Herbert Hailstone, M.A. Extra fcap. 8vo. 1*s.* 6*d.* each.

Lucian. Vera Historia (for Schools). By C. S. Jerram, M.A. Second Edition. Extra fcap. 8vo. 1*s.* 6*d.*

Plato. Selections from the Dialogues [including the whole of the *Apology* and *Crito*]. With Introduction and Notes by John Purves, M.A., and a Preface by the Rev. B. Jowett, M.A. Extra fcap. 8vo. 6*s.* 6*d.*

Sophocles. For the use of Schools. Edited with Introductions and English Notes By Lewis Campbell, M.A., and Evelyn Abbott, M.A. *New and Revised Edition.* 2 Vols. Extra fcap. 8vo. 10*s.* 6*d.*

Sold separately, Vol. I, Text, 4*s.* 6*d.*; Vol. II, Explanatory Notes, 6*s.*

Sophocles. In Single Plays, with English Notes, &c. By Lewis Campbell, M.A., and Evelyn Abbott, M.A. Extra fcap. 8vo. limp.

Oedipus Tyrannus, Philoctetes. New and Revised Edition, 2*s.* each.
Oedipus Coloneus, Antigone, 1*s.* 9*d.* each.
Ajax, Electra, Trachiniae, 2*s.* each.

—— *Oedipus Rex:* Dindorf's Text, with Notes by the present Bishop of St. David's. Extra fcap. 8vo. limp, 1*s.* 6*d.*

Theocritus (for Schools). With Notes. By H. Kynaston, D.D. (late Snow). Third Edition. Extra fcap. 8vo. 4*s.* 6*d.*

Xenophon. Easy Selections (for Junior Classes). With a Vocabulary, Notes, and Map. By J. S. Phillpotts, B.C.L., and C. S. Jerram, M.A. Third Edition. Extra fcap. 8vo. 3*s.* 6*d.*

—— *Selections* (for Schools). With Notes and Maps. By J. S. Phillpotts. B.C.L. Fourth Edition. Extra fcap. 8vo. 3*s.* 6*d.*

—— *Anabasis*, Book I. Edited for the use of Junior Classes and Private Students. With Introduction, Notes, etc. By J. Marshall, M.A., Rector of the Royal High School, Edinburgh. Extra fcap. 8vo. 2*s.* 6*d.*

—— *Anabasis*, Book II. With Notes and Map. By C. S. Jerram, M.A. Extra fcap. 8vo. 2*s.*

—— *Cyropaedia*, Books IV and V. With Introduction and Notes by C. Bigg, D.D. Extra fcap. 8vo. 2*s.* 6*d.*

Aristotle's Politics. By W. L. Newman, M.A. [*In the Press.*]

Aristotelian Studies. I. On the Structure of the Seventh Book of the Nicomachean Ethics. By J. C. Wilson, M.A. 8vo. stiff, 5*s.*

Aristotelis Ethica Nicomachea, ex recensione Immanuelis Bekkeri. Crown 8vo. 5*s.*

Demosthenes and Aeschines. The Orations of Demosthenes and Æschines on the Crown. With Introductory Essays and Notes. By G. A. Simcox, M.A., and W. H. Simcox, M.A. 1872. 8vo. 12*s.*

Head (*Barclay V.*). *Historia Numorum: A Manual of Greek Numismatics.* Royal 8vo. half-bound. 2*l.* 2*s.* *Just Published.*

Hicks (*E. L., M.A.*). *A Manual of Greek Historical Inscriptions.* Demy 8vo. 10*s.* 6*d.*

Homer. Odyssey, Books I–XII. Edited with English Notes, Appendices, etc. By W. W. Merry, M.A., and the late James Riddell, M.A. 1886. Second Edition. Demy 8vo. 16*s.*

Homer. A Grammar of the Homeric Dialect. By D. B. Monro, M.A. Demy 8vo. 10*s.* 6*d.*

Sophocles. The Plays and Fragments. With English Notes and Introductions, by Lewis Campbell, M.A. 2 vols.

Vol. I. Oedipus Tyrannus. Oedipus Coloneus. Antigone. 8vo. 16*s.*

Vol. II. Ajax. Electra. Trachiniae. Philoctetes. Fragments. 8vo. 16*s.*

IV. FRENCH AND ITALIAN.

Brachet's Etymological Dictionary of the French Language, with a Preface on the Principles of French Etymology. Translated into English by G. W. Kitchin, D.D. Third Edition. Crown 8vo. 7*s.* 6*d.*

—— *Historical Grammar of the French Language.* Translated into English by G. W. Kitchin, D.D. Fourth Edition. Extra fcap. 8vo. 3*s.* 6*d.*

Works by GEORGE SAINTSBURY, M.A.

Primer of French Literature. Extra fcap. 8vo. 2*s.*

Short History of French Literature. Crown 8vo. 10*s.* 6*d.*

Specimens of French Literature, from Villon to Hugo. Crown 8vo. 9*s.*

MASTERPIECES OF THE FRENCH DRAMA.

Corneille's Horace. Edited, with Introduction and Notes, by George Saintsbury, M.A. Extra fcap. 8vo. 2*s.* 6*d.*

Molière's Les Précieuses Ridicules. Edited, with Introduction and Notes, by Andrew Lang, M.A. Extra fcap. 8vo. 1*s.* 6*d.*

Racine's Esther. Edited, with Introduction and Notes, by George Saintsbury, M.A. Extra fcap. 8vo. 2*s.*

Beaumarchais' Le Barbier de Séville. Edited, with Introduction and Notes, by Austin Dobson. Extra fcap. 8vo. 2*s.* 6*d.*

Voltaire's Mérope. Edited, with Introduction and Notes, by George Saintsbury. Extra fcap. 8vo. cloth, 2*s.*

Musset's On ne badine pas avec l'Amour, and *Fantasio.* Edited, with Prolegomena, Notes, etc., by Walter Herries Pollock. Extra fcap. 8vo. 2*s.*

The above six Plays may be had in ornamental case, and bound in Imitation Parchment, price 12*s.* 6*d.*

Sainte-Beuve. Selections from the Causeries du Lundi. Edited by George Saintsbury. Extra fcap. 8vo. 2*s.*

Quinet's Lettres à sa Mère. Selected and edited by George Saintsbury. Extra fcap. 8vo. 2*s.*

Gautier, Théophile. Scenes of Travel. Selected and Edited by George Saintsbury. Extra fcap. 8vo. 2*s.*

L'Éloquence de la Chaire et de la Tribune Françaises. Edited by Paul Blouët, B.A. (Univ. Gallic.). Vol. I. French Sacred Oratory. Extra fcap. 8vo. 2*s.* 6*d.*

Edited by GUSTAVE MASSON, B.A.

Corneille's Cinna. With Notes, Glossary, etc. Extra fcap. 8vo. *cloth*, 2*s.* Stiff covers, 1*s.* 6*d.*

Louis XIV and his Contemporaries; as described in Extracts from the best Memoirs of the Seventeenth Century. With English Notes, Genealogical Tables, &c. Extra fcap. 8vo. 2*s.* 6*d.*

Maistre, Xavier de. Voyage autour de ma Chambre. Ourika, by *Madame de Duras;* Le Vieux Tailleur, by *MM. Erckmann-Chatrian;* La Veillée de Vincennes, by *Alfred de Vigny;* Les Jumeaux de l'Hôtel Corneille. by *Edmond About;* Mésaventures d'un Écolier, by *Rodolphe Töpffer.* Third Edition, Revised and Corrected. Extra fcap. 8vo. 2*s.* 6*d.*

Molière's Les Fourberies de Scapin, and *Racine's Athalie.* With Voltaire's Life of Molière. Extra fcap. 8vo. 2*s.* 6*d.*

Molière's Les Fourberies de Scapin. With Voltaire's Life of Molière. Extra fcap. 8vo. stiff covers, 1*s.* 6*d.*

Molière's Les Femmes Savantes. With Notes, Glossary, etc. Extra fcap. 8vo. *cloth*, 2*s.* Stiff covers, 1*s.* 6*d.*

Racine's Andromaque, and *Corneille's Le Menteur.* With Louis Racine's Life of his Father. Extra fcap. 8vo. 2*s.* 6*d.*

Regnard's Le Joueur, and *Brueys and Palaprat's Le Grondeur.* Extra fcap. 8vo. 2*s.* 6*d.*

Sévigné, Madame de, and her chief Contemporaries, Selections from the Correspondence of. Intended more especially for Girls' Schools. Extra fcap. 8vo. 3*s.*

Dante. Selections from the Inferno. With Introduction and Notes. By H. B. Cotterill, B.A. Extra fcap. 8vo. 4*s.* 6*d.*

Tasso. La Gerusalemme Liberata. Cantos i, ii. With Introduction and Notes. By the same Editor. Extra fcap. 8vo. 2*s.* 6*d.*

V. GERMAN.

Scherer (W.). A History of German Literature. Translated from the Third German Edition by Mrs. F. Conybeare. Edited by F. Max Müller. 2 vols. 8vo. 21*s.*

Max Müller. The German Classics, from the Fourth to the Nineteenth Century. With Biographical Notices, Translations into Modern German, and Notes. By F. Max Müller, M.A. A New Edition, Revised, Enlarged, and Adapted to Wilhelm Scherer's 'History of German Literature,' by F. Lichtenstein. 2 vols. crown 8vo. 21*s.*

GERMAN COURSE. By HERMANN LANGE.

The Germans at Home; a Practical Introduction to German Conversation, with an Appendix containing the Essentials of German Grammar. Second Edition. 8vo. 2*s.* 6*d.*

The German Manual; a German Grammar, Reading Book, and a Handbook of German Conversation. 8vo. 7*s.* 6*d*

Grammar of the German Language. 8vo. 3*s.* 6*d.*

German Composition; A Theoretical and Practical Guide to the Art of Translating English Prose into German. 8vo. 4*s.* 6*d.*

Lessing's Laokoon. With Introduction, English Notes, etc. By A. Hamann, Phil. Doc., M.A. Extra fcap. 8vo. 4*s.* 6*d.*

Schiller's Wilhelm Tell. Translated into English Verse by E. Massie, M.A. Extra fcap. 8vo. 5*s.*

Also, Edited by C. A. BUCHHEIM, Phil. Doc.

Becker's Friedrich der Grosse. Extra fcap. 8vo. *In the Press.*

Goethe's Egmont. With a Life of Goethe, &c. Third Edition. Extra fcap. 8vo. 3*s.*

—— *Iphigenie auf Tauris.* A Drama. With a Critical Introduction and Notes. Second Edition. Extra fcap. 8vo. 3*s.*

Heine's Prosa, being Selections from his Prose Works. With English Notes, etc. Extra fcap. 8vo. 4*s.* 6*d.*

Heine's Harzreise. With Life of Heine, Descriptive Sketch of the Harz, and Index. Extra fcap. 8vo. paper covers, 1*s.* 6*d.*; cloth, 2*s.* 6*d.*

Lessing's Minna von Barnhelm. A Comedy. With a Life of Lessing, Critical Analysis, etc. Extra fcap. 8vo. 3*s.* 6*d.*

—— *Nathan der Weise.* With Introduction, Notes, etc. Extra fcap. 8vo. 4*s.* 6*d.*

Schiller's Historische Skizzen; Egmont's Leben und Tod, and *Belagerung von Antwerpen*. With a Map. Extra fcap. 8vo. 2*s*. 6*d*.

—— *Wilhelm Tell*. With a Life of Schiller; an historical and critical Introduction, Arguments, and a complete Commentary, and Map. Sixth Edition. Extra fcap. 8vo. 3*s*. 6*d*.

—— *Wilhelm Tell*. School Edition. With Map. 2*s*.

Modern German Reader. A Graduated Collection of Extracts in Prose and Poetry from Modern German writers:—

Part I. With English Notes, a Grammatical Appendix, and a complete Vocabulary. Fourth Edition. Extra fcap. 8vo. 2*s*. 6*d*.

Part II. With English Notes and an Index. Extra fcap. 8vo. 2*s*. 6*d*.

Niebuhr's Griechische Heroen-Geschichten. Tales of Greek Heroes. Edited with English Notes and a Vocabulary, by Emma S. Buchheim. School Edition. Extra fcap. 8vo., *cloth*, 2*s*. *Stiff covers*, 1*s*. 6*d*.

VI. MATHEMATICS, PHYSICAL SCIENCE, &c.

By LEWIS HENSLEY, M.A.

Figures made Easy: a first Arithmetic Book. Crown 8vo. 6*d*.

Answers to the Examples in Figures made Easy, together with two thousand additional Examples, with Answers. Crown 8vo. 1*s*.

The Scholar's Arithmetic: with Answers. Crown 8vo. 4*s*. 6*d*.

The Scholar's Algebra. Crown 8vo. 4*s*. 6*d*.

Aldis (W. S., M.A.). *A Text-Book of Algebra*. Crown 8vo. *Nearly ready*.

Baynes (R. E., M.A.). *Lessons on Thermodynamics*. 1878. Crown 8vo. 7*s*. 6*d*.

Chambers (G. F., F.R.A.S.). *A Handbook of Descriptive Astronomy*. Third Edition. 1877. Demy 8vo. 28*s*.

Clarke (Col. A. R., C.B., R.E.). *Geodesy*. 1880. 8vo. 12*s*. 6*d*.

Cremona (Luigi). *Elements of Projective Geometry*. Translated by C. Leudesdorf, M.A. 8vo. 12*s*. 6*d*.

Donkin. *Acoustics*. Second Edition. Crown 8vo. 7*s*. 6*d*.

Euclid Revised. Containing the Essentials of the Elements of Plane Geometry as given by Euclid in his first Six Books. Edited by R. C. J. Nixon, M.A. Crown 8vo. 7*s*. 6*d*.

Sold separately as follows,

Books I–IV. 3*s*. 6*d*. Books I, II. 1*s*. 6*d*.
Book I. 1*s*.

Galton (Douglas, C.B., F.R.S.). The Construction of Healthy Dwellings. Demy 8vo. 10*s*. 6*d*.

Hamilton (Sir R. G. C.), and J. Ball. Book-keeping. New and enlarged Edition. Extra fcap. 8vo. limp cloth, 2*s*.

Ruled Exercise books adapted to the above may be had, price 2*s*.

Harcourt (A. G. Vernon, M.A.), and *H. G. Madan, M.A. Exercises in Practical Chemistry.* Vol. I. Elementary Exercises. Third Edition. Crown 8vo. 9*s*.

Maclaren (Archibald). A System of Physical Education: Theoretical and Practical. Extra fcap. 8vo. 7*s*. 6*d*.

Madan (H. G., M.A.). Tables of Qualitative Analysis. Large 4to. paper, 4*s*. 6*d*.

Maxwell (J. Clerk, M.A., F.R.S.). A Treatise on Electricity and Magnetism. Second Edition. 2 vols. Demy 8vo. 1*l*. 11*s*. 6*d*.

—— *An Elementary Treatise on Electricity.* Edited by William Garnett, M.A. Demy 8vo. 7*s*. 6*d*.

Minchin (G. M., M.A.). A Treatise on Statics with Applications to Physics. Third Edition, Corrected and Enlarged. Vol. I. *Equilibrium of Coplanar Forces.* 8vo. 9*s*. Vol. II. *Statics.* 8vo. 16*s*.

—— *Uniplanar Kinematics of Solids and Fluids.* Crown 8vo. 7*s*. 6*d*.

Phillips (John, M.A., F.R.S.). Geology of Oxford and the Valley of the Thames. 1871. 8vo. 21*s*.

—— *Vesuvius.* 1869. Crown 8vo. 10*s*. 6*d*.

Prestwich (Joseph, M.A., F.R.S.). Geology, Chemical, Physical, and Stratigraphical. Vol. I. Chemical and Physical. Royal 8vo. 25*s*.

Roach (T., M.A.). Elementary Trigonometry. Crown 8vo. *Nearly ready.*

Rolleston's Forms of Animal Life. Illustrated by Descriptions and Drawings of Dissections. New Edition. (*Nearly ready.*)

Smyth. A Cycle of Celestial Objects. Observed, Reduced, and Discussed by Admiral W. H. Smyth, R.N. Revised, condensed, and greatly enlarged by G. F. Chambers, F.R.A.S. 1881. 8vo. *Price reduced to* 12*s*.

Stewart (Balfour, LL.D., F.R.S.). A Treatise on Heat, with numerous Woodcuts and Diagrams. Fourth Edition. Extra fcap. 8vo. 7*s*. 6*d*.

Vernon-Harcourt (*L. F., M.A.*). *A Treatise on Rivers and Canals*, relating to the Control and Improvement of Rivers, and the Design, Construction, and Development of Canals. 2 vols. (Vol. I, Text. Vol. II, Plates.) 8vo. 21*s.*

—— *Harbours and Docks;* their Physical Features, History, Construction, Equipment, and Maintenance; with Statistics as to their Commercial Development. 2 vols. 8vo. 25*s.*

Watson (*H. W., M.A.*). *A Treatise on the Kinetic Theory of Gases.* 1876. 8vo. 3*s.* 6*d.*

Watson (*H. W., D. Sc., F.R.S.*), *and S. H. Burbury, M.A.*

I. *A Treatise on the Application of Generalised Coordinates to the Kinetics of a Material System.* 1879. 8vo. 6*s.*

II. *The Mathematical Theory of Electricity and Magnetism.* Vol. I. Electrostatics. 8vo. 10*s.* 6*d.*

Williamson (*A. W., Phil. Doc., F.R.S.*). *Chemistry for Students.* A new Edition, with Solutions. 1873. Extra fcap. 8vo. 8*s.* 6*d.*

VII. HISTORY.

Bluntschli (*J. K.*). *The Theory of the State.* By J. K. Bluntschli, late Professor of Political Sciences in the University of Heidelberg. Authorised English Translation from the Sixth German Edition. Demy 8vo. half bound, 12*s.* 6*d.*

Finlay (*George, LL.D.*). *A History of Greece* from its Conquest by the Romans to the present time, B.C. 146 to A.D. 1864. A new Edition, revised throughout, and in part re-written, with considerable additions, by the Author, and edited by H. F. Tozer, M.A. 7 vols. 8vo. 3*l.* 10*s.*

Fortescue (*Sir John, Kt.*). *The Governance of England:* otherwise called The Difference between an Absolute and a Limited Monarchy. A Revised Text. Edited, with Introduction, Notes, and Appendices, by Charles Plummer, M.A. 8vo. half bound, 12*s.* 6*d.*

Freeman (*E.A., D.C.L.*). *A Short History of the Norman Conquest of England.* Second Edition. Extra fcap. 8vo. 2*s.* 6*d.*

George (*H. B., M.A.*). *Genealogical Tables illustrative of Modern History.* Third Edition, Revised and Enlarged. Small 4to. 12*s.*

Hodgkin (*T.*). *Italy and her Invaders.* Illustrated with Plates and Maps. Vols. I—IV., A.D. 376–553. 8vo. 3*l.* 8*s.*

Kitchin (*G. W., D.D.*). *A History of France.* With numerous Maps, Plans, and Tables. In Three Volumes. *Second Edition.* Crown 8vo. each 10*s.* 6*d.*

Vol. 1. Down to the Year 1453.

Vol. 2. From 1453–1624. Vol. 3. From 1624–1793.

Payne (*E. J., M.A.*). *A History of the United States of America.* In the Press.

Ranke (*L. von*). *A History of England*, principally in the Seventeenth Century. Translated by Resident Members of the University of Oxford, under the superintendence of G. W. Kitchin, D.D., and C. W. Boase, M.A. 1875. 6 vols. 8vo. 3*l*. 3*s*.

Rawlinson (*George, M.A.*). *A Manual of Ancient History.* Second Edition. Demy 8vo. 14*s*.

Select Charters and other Illustrations of English Constitutional History, from the Earliest Times to the Reign of Edward I. Arranged and edited by W. Stubbs, D.D. Fifth Edition. 1883. Crown 8vo. 8*s*. 6*d*.

Stubbs (*W., D.D.*). *The Constitutional History of England*, in its Origin and Development. Library Edition. 3 vols. demy 8vo. 2*l*. 8*s*.

Also in 3 vols. crown 8vo. price 12*s*. each.

—— *Seventeen Lectures on the Study of Medieval and Modern History*, &c., delivered at Oxford 1867–1884. Demy 8vo. half-bound, 10*s*. 6*d*.

Wellesley. A Selection from the Despatches, Treaties, and other Papers of the Marquess Wellesley, K.G., during his Government of India. Edited by S. J. Owen, M.A. 1877. 8vo. 1*l*. 4*s*.

Wellington. A Selection from the Despatches, Treaties, and other Papers relating to India of Field-Marshal the Duke of Wellington, K.G. Edited by S. J. Owen, M.A. 1880. 8vo. 24*s*.

A History of British India. By S. J. Owen, M.A., Reader in Indian History in the University of Oxford. In preparation.

VIII. LAW.

Alberici Gentilis, I.C.D., I.C., De Iure Belli Libri Tres. Edidit T. E. Holland, I.C.D. 1877. Small 4to. half morocco, 21*s*.

Anson (*Sir William R., Bart., D.C.L.*). *Principles of the English Law of Contract, and of Agency in its Relation to Contract.* Fourth Edition. Demy 8vo. 10*s*. 6*d*.

—— *Law and Custom of the Constitution.* Part I. Parliament. Demy 8vo. 10*s*. 6*d*.

Bentham (*Jeremy*). *An Introduction to the Principles of Morals and Legislation.* Crown 8vo. 6*s*. 6*d*.

Digby (*Kenelm E., M.A.*). *An Introduction to the History of the Law of Real Property.* Third Edition. Demy 8vo. 10*s*. 6*d*.

Gaii Institutionum Juris Civilis Commentarii Quattuor; or, Elements of Roman Law by Gaius. With a Translation and Commentary by Edward Poste, M.A. Second Edition. 1875. 8vo. 18*s*.

Hall (W. E., M.A.). International Law. Second Ed. 8vo. 21*s.*

Holland (T. E., D.C.L.). The Elements of Jurisprudence. Third Edition. Demy 8vo. 10*s.* 6*d.*

—— *The European Concert in the Eastern Question,* a Collection of Treaties and other Public Acts. Edited, with Introductions and Notes, by Thomas Erskine Holland, D.C.L. 8vo. 12*s.* 6*d.*

Imperatoris Iustiniani Institutionum Libri Quattuor; with Introductions, Commentary, Excursus and Translation. By J. B. Moyle, B.C.L., M.A. 2 vols. Demy 8vo. 21*s.*

Justinian, The Institutes of, edited as a recension of the Institutes of Gaius, by Thomas Erskine Holland, D.C.L. Second Edition, 1881. Extra fcap. 8vo. 5*s.*

Justinian, Select Titles from the Digest of. By T. E. Holland, D.C.L., and C. L. Shadwell, B.C.L. 8vo. 14*s.*

Also sold in Parts, in paper covers, as follows:—

Part I. Introductory Titles. 2*s.* 6*d.* Part II. Family Law. 1*s.*
Part III. Property Law. 2*s.* 6*d.* Part IV. Law of Obligations (No. 1). 3*s.* 6*d.*
Part IV. Law of Obligations (No. 2). 4*s.* 6*d.*

Lex Aquilia. The Roman Law of Damage to Property: being a Commentary on the Title of the Digest 'Ad Legem Aquiliam' (ix. 2). With an Introduction to the Study of the Corpus Iuris Civilis. By Erwin Grueber, Dr. Jur., M.A. Demy 8vo. 10*s.* 6*d.*

Markby (W., D.C.L.). Elements of Law considered with reference to Principles of General Jurisprudence. Third Edition. Demy 8vo. 12*s.* 6*d.*

Twiss (Sir Travers, D.C.L.). The Law of Nations considered as Independent Political Communities.

Part I. On the Rights and Duties of Nations in time of Peace. A new Edition, Revised and Enlarged. 1884. Demy 8vo. 15*s.*

Part II. On the Rights and Duties of Nations in Time of War. Second Edition Revised. 1875. Demy 8vo. 21*s.*

IX. MENTAL AND MORAL PHILOSOPHY, &c.

Bacon's Novum Organum. Edited, with English Notes, by G. W. Kitchin, D.D. 1855. 8vo. 9*s.* 6*d.*

—— Translated by G. W. Kitchin, D.D. 1855. 8vo. 9*s.* 6*d.*

Berkeley. The Works of George Berkeley, D.D., formerly Bishop of Cloyne; including many of his writings hitherto unpublished. With Prefaces, Annotations, and an Account of his Life and Philosophy, by Alexander Campbell Fraser, M.A. 4 vols. 1871. 8vo. 2*l.* 18*s.*

The Life, Letters, &c. 1 vol. 16*s.*

—— *Selections from.* With an Introduction and Notes. For the use of Students in the Universities. By Alexander Campbell Fraser, LL.D. Second Edition. Crown 8vo. 7*s.* 6*d.*

Fowler (*T.*, *D.D.*). *The Elements of Deductive Logic*, designed mainly for the use of Junior Students in the Universities. Eighth Edition, with a Collection of Examples. Extra fcap. 8vo. 3*s.* 6*d.*

—— *The Elements of Inductive Logic*, designed mainly for the use of Students in the Universities. Fourth Edition. Extra fcap. 8vo. 6*s.*

Edited by T. FOWLER, D.D.

Bacon. Novum Organum. With Introduction, Notes, &c. 1878. 8vo. 14*s.*

Locke's Conduct of the Understanding. Second Edition. Extra fcap. 8vo. 2*s.*

Danson (*J. T.*). *The Wealth of Households.* Crown 8vo. 5*s.*

Green (*T. H.*, *M.A.*). *Prolegomena to Ethics.* Edited by A. C. Bradley, M.A. Demy 8vo. 12*s.* 6*d.*

Hegel. The Logic of Hegel; translated from the Encyclopaedia of the Philosophical Sciences. With Prolegomena by William Wallace, M.A. 1874. 8vo. 14*s.*

Lotze's Logic, in Three Books; of Thought, of Investigation, and of Knowledge. English Translation; Edited by B. Bosanquet, M.A., Fellow of University College, Oxford. 8vo. *cloth*, 12*s.* 6*d.*

—— *Metaphysic*, in Three Books; Ontology, Cosmology, and Psychology. English Translation; Edited by B. Bosanquet, M.A. 8vo. *cloth*, 12*s.* 6*d.*

Martineau (*James*, *D.D.*). *Types of Ethical Theory.* Second Edition. 2 vols. Crown 8vo. 15*s.*

Rogers (*J. E. Thorold*, *M.A.*). *A Manual of Political Economy*, for the use of Schools. Third Edition. Extra fcap. 8vo. 4*s.* 6*d.*

Smith's Wealth of Nations. A new Edition, with Notes, by J. E. Thorold Rogers, M.A. 2 vols. 8vo. 1880. 21*s.*

Wilson (*J. M.*, *B.D.*), *and T. Fowler*, *D.D. The Principles of Morals* (Introductory Chapters). 8vo. *boards*, 3*s.* 6*d.*

X. ART, &c.

Hullah (*John*). *The Cultivation of the Speaking Voice.* Second Edition. Extra fcap. 8vo. 2*s.* 6*d.*

Ouseley (*Sir F. A. Gore*, *Bart.*). *A Treatise on Harmony.* Third Edition. 4to. 10*s.*

—— *A Treatise on Counterpoint, Canon, and Fugue*, based upon that of Cherubini. Second Edition. 4to. 16*s.*

—— *A Treatise on Musical Form and General Composition.* Second Edition. 4to. 10*s.*

Robinson (*J. C., F.S.A.*). *A Critical Account of the Drawings by Michel Angelo and Raffaello in the University Galleries, Oxford.* 1870. Crown 8vo. 4*s*.

Ruskin (*John, M.A.*). *A Course of Lectures on Art*, delivered before the University of Oxford in Hilary Term, 1870. 8vo. 6*s*.

Troutbeck (*J., M.A.*) *and R. F. Dale, M.A. A Music Primer* (for Schools). Second Edition. Crown 8vo. 1*s*. 6*d*.

Tyrwhitt (*R. St. J., M.A.*). *A Handbook of Pictorial Art.* With coloured Illustrations, Photographs, and a chapter on Perspective by A. Macdonald. Second Edition. 1875. 8vo. half morocco, 18*s*.

Upcott (*L. E., M.A.*). *An Introduction to Greek Sculpture.* Crown 8vo. 4*s*. 6*d*.

Vaux (*W. S. W., M.A.*). *Catalogue of the Castellani Collection of Antiquities in the University Galleries, Oxford.* Crown 8vo. 1*s*.

The Oxford Bible for Teachers, containing supplementary HELPS TO THE STUDY OF THE BIBLE, including Summaries of the several Books, with copious Explanatory Notes and Tables illustrative of Scripture History and the characteristics of Bible Lands; with a complete Index of Subjects, a Concordance, a Dictionary of Proper Names, and a series of Maps. Prices in various sizes and bindings from 3*s*. to 2*l*. 5*s*.

Helps to the Study of the Bible, taken from the OXFORD BIBLE FOR TEACHERS, comprising Summaries of the several Books, with copious Explanatory Notes and Tables illustrative of Scripture History and the Characteristics of Bible Lands; with a complete Index of Subjects, a Concordance, a Dictionary of Proper Names, and a series of Maps. Crown 8vo. *cloth*, 3*s*. 6*d*.; 16mo. *cloth*, 1*s*.

LONDON: HENRY FROWDE,
OXFORD UNIVERSITY PRESS WAREHOUSE, AMEN CORNER,

OXFORD: CLARENDON PRESS DEPOSITORY,
116 HIGH STREET.

☞ *The* DELEGATES OF THE PRESS *invite suggestions and advice from all persons interested in education; and will be thankful for hints, &c. addressed to the* SECRETARY TO THE DELEGATES, *Clarendon Press, Oxford.*